D1623757

Discover

Contents

Germany

Throughout this book, we use these icons to highlight special recommendations:

 The Best...
Lists for everything from bars to wildlife
– to make sure you don't miss out

 Don't Miss
A must-see – don't go home until you've been there

 Local experts reveal their
top picks and secret highlights

 Detour
Special places a little off the beaten track

 If you like...
Lesser-known alternatives to world-famous
attractions

These icons
help you
quickly identify
reviews in the
text and on
the map:

Sights

Eating

Drinking

Sleeping

Information

This edition written and researched by

Andrea Schulte-Peevers,

Kerry Christiani, Marc Di Duca, Anthony Haywood,

Hamburg & the North

p315

Berlin

p243

p285

Dresden & the East

Frankfurt & the Rhineland

p189

Bavaria

p93

Munich

p51

p153

Stuttgart & the Black Forest

Contents

Contents

On the Road

In Focus

Survival Guide

This Is Germany

Prepare for a roller coaster of feasts, treats and temptations as you take in Germany's soul-stirring scenery, spirit-lifting culture, beautiful cities, romantic palaces and walled medieval towns. As much fun as it may be to rev up the engine on the autobahn, do slow down to better appreciate the incredible historical and cultural kaleidoscope that is one of Europe's most fascinating countries.

There's something artistic in the way Germany's scenery unfolds from the corrugated coasts of the north to the moody forests, romantic river valleys and vast vineyards of central Germany. The icing on the cake is the off-the-charts splendour of the Alps, carved into rugged glory by the elements.

The story-book landscapes of Germany are equalled in grandeur only by the country's fascinating history. You'll see the past in towns whose streets were laid out long before Columbus set sail, and in sturdy castles looming above prim, half-timbered hamlets. You'll find vestiges of the Roman empire in Trier and Cologne and reminders of Hanseatic power in Hamburg and Lübeck. And then there's Berlin – exciting, forward-looking, yet still coming to terms with its unique past as a divided city.

Germany's great cities come in more flavours than a jar of jelly beans. Their cultural smorgasbord spans the spectrum from art museums and opera to cabaret and techno clubs. And wherever you go, you'll see Romanesque, Gothic and baroque classics rub rafters with the architectural creations of modern masters such as Daniel Libeskind and David Chipperfield.

German cuisine is so much more than sausages, pretzels, schnitzel and roast pork accompanied by mugs of foamy beer. Beyond the clichés awaits a cornucopia of regional and seasonal palate teasers. Be sure to sample the world-class wines, most notably riesling, the most famous and typical German varietal, while exploring wine estates and ancient cellars.

"
Prepare for a roller coaster of feasts, treats and temptations
"

Rothenburg ob der Tauber (p119)

25
Top Experiences

25 Germany's Top Experiences

Berlin Wall

Few events in history have the power to move the entire world. Like the Kennedy assassination, the moon landing and 9/11, the fall of the Berlin Wall in 1989 is one such event. If you were alive back then, you will probably remember the crowds of euphoric revellers cheering and dancing at the Brandenburg Gate. Although little is left of the physical barrier, its legacy lives on, both in the imagination and in places such as Checkpoint Charlie (p255), the Gedenkstätte Berliner Mauer (p258) and the East Side Gallery (p263) with its colourful murals. Berlin Wall artwork, East Side Gallery

Oktoberfest

Anyone with a taste for hop-scented froth knows that the daddy of all beer festivals, Oktobe fest (p84), takes place annually in Munich. The suds fest runs for 16 ethanol-fuelled days, with troops of crimson-faced oompah bands entertaining revellers, armies of traditionally garbed locals and foreigners guzzling their way through seven million litres of lager, and entire chicken farms hitting the grill. Find your favourite tent and raise your 1L stein.

Schloss Neuschwanstein

Commissioned by Bavaria's most celebrated (and loopiest) 19th-century monarch, King Ludwig II, Neuschwanstein Castle (p130) rises from alpine forests like a story-book illustration. Its chambers and halls reflect Ludwig's obsession with the mythical Teutonic past – and his love of Wagner – in a composition that puts even the flashiest oligarch's palazzo in the shade. This sugary folly is even said to have inspired Walt's castle at Disneyland.

The Best...
Castles & Palaces

SCHLOSS NEUSCHWANSTEIN
King Ludwig II was not quite of this world; neither is his most sugary palace. (p130)

WARTBURG
History pours from every nook and cranny of Eisenach's medieval beauty. (p312)

SCHLOSS SANSSOUCI
Fall under the spell of this frilly pleasure palace in Potsdam. (p281)

BURG ELTZ
Fancy yourself knight or damsel at this castle near the Moselle River. (p220)

The Best...
Views

EAGLE'S NEST
Be bedazzled by the Berchtesgadener Alps from this mountaintop roost with a sinister past. (p113)

FERNSEHTURM
Put Berlin at your feet from atop the TV Tower, the country's tallest building. (p260)

COLOGNE CATHEDRAL (KÖLNER DOM)
Clamber up Cologne's cathedral for gobsmacking panoramas of the city and the Rhine River. (p229)

ZUGSPITZE
Rack and pinion your way to the top of Germany's highest peak. (p108)

4 Black Forest

In mist, snow or sunshine, this slice of southwest Germany is beautiful. Every valley in the Black Forest (p173) reveals new surprises: half-timbered villages looking every inch the fairy-tale fantasy, thunderous waterfalls, cuckoo clocks the size of houses. Breathe in the cold air, drive roller coaster roads to middle-of-nowhere lakes, have your cake and then walk it off on trail after gorgeously wooded trail. Hear that? Silence. What a wonderful thing.

Schiltach (p176)

5 Romantic Rhine

The most scenic stretch of Rhine (p213) flows between Mainz and Koblenz. It's a veritable symphony of dramatic cliffs, near-vertical vineyards, hilltop castles, half-timbered hamlets and the mythical Loreley Rock. From every riverside village, trails meander through vineyards and forests, up to panoramic viewpoints and massive stone fortresses, and then back down to romantic evenings spent sampling the local rieslings.

Dresden

On a cold February night in 1945, hours of carpet bombing reduced Germany's 'Florence on the Elbe' to a smouldering pile. Dresden's comeback is nothing short of a miracle (p296). Reconstructed architectural jewels pair with stunning art collections that justify the city's place in the pantheon of European cultural capitals. Add to that an energetic pub quarter and you've got one enticing package.

Frauenkirche (p296)

Heidelberg

The 19th-century Romantics found sublime beauty and spiritual inspiration in Germany's oldest university town (p170). So did Mark Twain, who was beguiled by the ruins of the hillside castle. Generations of students have attended lectures, sung lustily with beer steins in hand, carved their names into tavern tables and, occasionally, been sent to the student jail. To this day, age-old traditions endure alongside world-class research, innovative cultural events and a lively nightlife.

Potsdam

You'll love Potsdam's marvellous palaces, idyllic parks, stunning views and inspired architecture (p279). Just across the Glienicke 'spy bridge' from Berlin, the state capital of Brandenburg was catapulted to prominence by King Frederick the Great. His rococo Sanssouci palace is the glorious crown of this Unesco-recognised city, and synthesises 18th-century artistic trends from around Europe into one stupendous masterpiece. Schloss Sanssouci (p281)

The Best...
Cities for Famous Germans

WEIMAR
Goethe and Gropius, Schiller and Nietzsche – a pantheon of German greats once resided in this provincial town. (p308)

LUTHERSTADT WITTENBERG
The place where Martin Luther kick-started the Reformation in 1517. (p305)

BONN
This former German capital was Beethoven's birthplace. (p236)

HAMBURG
To quote John Lennon, 'I was born in Liverpool, but I grew up in Hamburg'. (p328)

Nuremberg

Nuremberg (p131) may be synonymous with Nazi rallies and war trials, but there's so much more to this energetic city. Dürer hailed from the Altstadt (his house now a museum), Germany's first railway trundled from here to neighbouring Fürth, and being the country's toy capital there are lots of activities for kids to enjoy. When you're done with sightseeing the local beer makes a worthy companion to Nuremberg's delicious finger-sized sausages.

The Best...
Iconic Sites

BRANDENBURGER TOR
This Berlin city gate is the ultimate symbol of German reunification. (p254)

FRAUENKIRCHE
Reduced to rubble in WWII, this rebuilt landmark church restored Dresden's classic skyline. (p296)

HOLSTENTOR
A mighty twin-towered red-brick gate that was once part of Lübeck's fortifications. (p341)

ST MICHAELISKIRCHE
Feel your spirits soar when faced with Hamburg's hill-top church, better known as 'Michel'. (p329)

10 Cologne Cathedral

At unexpected moments you see it: Cologne's cathedral (Kölner Dom; p229), the twin-towered icon of the city towering over an urban vista, dominating the view up a road. Construction of this perfectly formed testament to faith and conviction began in 1248; the cathedral was consecrated a 'mere' six centuries later. You can feel echoes of the passage of time as you sit in its cavernous, stained-glass-lit interior. Climb a tower for spectacular views of the surrounding city.

Bamberg

Bamberg (p138) is full of Unesco-listed townhouses and was mercifully saved from destruction during WWII. Half of the Altstadt's beauty comes from its location, which straddles two waterways – the River Regnitz and the Rhine–Main–Danube Canal. After getting your fill of sightseeing, pop into one of Bamberg's numerous breweries, which produce the town's unique smoked beer – on tap at all of its characterful inns. There's beer drinking everywhere in Bamberg, especially in the Altstadt.

Klosterbräu brewery (p140)

CRAIG PERSHOUSE/GETTY IMAGES ©

12

Hamburg

Ancient, wealthy Hamburg (p328), on the Elbe River, traces it roots back to the Hanseatic League and beyond. By day you can tour its magnificent port, explore its history in restored quarters and discover shops selling strange and unusual goods you didn't think were sold. By night, some of Europe's best music clubs pull in the punters, and other diversions for virtually every taste are plentiful as well. And then, another Hamburg day begins. Elbe River and port

13 # Brandenburg Gate, Berlin

Who can forget the images beamed around the world in 1989, of happy throngs perched atop the Berlin Wall against the backdrop of the stately Brandenburger Tor (p254)? Overnight, the 18th-century royal city gate changed from a symbol of division and oppression to the symbol of a united Germany. The landmark is at its most atmospheric – and photogenic – at night, when light bathes its stately columns and proud Goddess of Victory sculpture in a golden glow.

Munich Residenz

This glorious royal compound (p75) is proof that Munich is more than the sum of its beer halls and Beemers. Bavaria's rulers made their homes and offices here for centuries, bequeathing to posterity a treasure chest of fine paintings, sculptures and all sorts of bling, including crowns and portable altars. Though restored following WWII damage, its interior is nothing short of stunning, especially the eye-popping Renaissance banquet hall and rococo court theatre.

The Best...
Gardens

ENGLISCHER GARTEN
Quaff a beer, watch the surfers or get naked at Munich's splendid green oasis. (p73)

HERRENHÄUSER GÄRTEN
Spend a relaxing afternoon in Hanover's mini-Versailles. (p347)

PARK SANSSOUCI
This popular Potsdam gem is big enough to enable you to escape the crowds. (p279)

TIERGARTEN
Berlin's perfect urban velocity antidote. (p263)

The Best...
Romantic Towns

ROTHENBURG OB DER TAUBER
Drain your camera batteries snapping this story-book medieval town. (p119)

HEIDELBERG
It's love at first sight for most, including Mark Twain. (p170)

BACHARACH
Hold hands while sauntering along the cobbled lanes of this romantic Rhine wine town. (p216)

SCHILTACH
Fall head over heels for this half-timbered Black Forest jewel. (p176)

Rothenburg ob der Tauber

With its jumble of neatly restored half-timbered houses enclosed by sturdy ramparts, Rothenburg ob der Tauber (p119) lays on the medieval cuteness with a trowel. One might even say it's too cute for its own good, if the day-tripper deluges are any indication. The trick is to experience this historic wonderland early or late in the day, when the last coaches have hit the road and you can soak up the romance all by yourself. Inset: Town walking tour sign

ABOVE: MARTIN MOOS/GETTY IMAGES © LEFT: WALTER BIBIKOW/GETTY IMAGES ©

Museumsinsel, Berlin

An imposing ensemble of five treasure houses, Museum Island (p259) is the highlight of Berlin's museum landscape. The Unesco World Heritage Site exhibits art and cultural history from the stone age to the 19th century. Feast your eyes on antiquities at the Pergamonmuseum (p262) and Altes Museum, report for an audience with Egyptian queen Nefertiti at the Neues Museum, take in 19th-century art at the Alte Nationalgalerie and marvel at medieval sculptures at the Bode-museum (pictured right).

Baden-Baden

Some 2000 years ago the Romans raved about *baden* (bathing) in Baden-Baden's thera-peutic waters, and the spring-fed town (p173) still hasn't lost its touch. Royalty and celebrities have put this classy Black Forest spa town on the global map, but its merits speak for themselves. Tucked at the foot of thickly wooded hills, this is a good-looking, good-living town of pristine belle époque villas, sculpture-strewn gardens, cupola-crowned spas, and ritzy boutiques and restaurants.

Stuttgart

From its humble beginnings as a 10th-century stud farm (hence the name), Stuttgart (p164) has grown into an economic powerhouse. The car industry has played a major role here ever since Gottfried Daimler first dabbled with internal combustion engines back in the 1880s. No surprise then, that the Mercedes-Benz and Porsche museums are top tourist draws. The city, surrounded by vine-covered hills and lavish parks, is also known for its nightlife and sophisticated cuisine scene.

The Best...
Museums

PERGAMONMUSEUM
This Berlin treasure trove opens a window onto antiquity. (p262)

DEUTSCHES MUSEUM
Munich's science museum takes you from the future back to the stone age. (p73)

KUNSTHALLE HAMBURG
Hit the artistic mother lode in this great northern city. (p329)

GRÜNES GEWÖLBE
Dresden's real-life equivalent of Aladdin's cave. (p301)

Berchtesgadener Land

19

In Germany's far south-eastern pocket, cradled by Austria, the Berchtesgadener Land (p112) is a sublime region, ringed by massive peaks, including the country's second highest. Mt Watzmann (2713m) looms above the Königssee (pictured right), which shimmers in shades of jade and emerald. Go underground into the historic salt mines, soar up to the Eagle's Nest – Hitler's mountain retreat – then read up on Berchtesgaden's role during the Third Reich at the Dokumentation Obersalzberg.

NORBERT ROSING/GETTY IMAGES ©

The Best...
Odes to the Auto

BMW MUSEUM
Munich's grand collection of Beemers is almost upstaged by the stunning building that houses them. (p79)

MERCEDES-BENZ MUSEUM
In a giant double-helix building in Stuttgart, this is a place of worship in a town where the car is god. (p165)

AUTOSTADT
Volkswagen offers up interactive fun even for those who can't tell a piston from a carburettor. (p350)

PORSCHE MUSEUM
This gleaming white jewel in Stuttgart is a temple of torque for the posh set. (p165)

㉠ Moselle River

A tributary of the Rhine, the Moselle (p220) zigzags lazily for 350km from Koblenz to northern France by way of Luxembourg. It's one of Europe's all-star waterways, hemmed in by ancient villages and miles of vineyards. Many of these cling courageously to vertiginous slopes from which a new generation of winemakers coaxes some of the most elegant, full-bodied rieslings you'll ever taste. It was the Romans that introduced grapes to this area; their legacy survives in Trier.

Beilstein (p220)

LOUISE HEUSINKVELD/GETTY IMAGES ©

German Food & Drink

If you crave traditional German comfort food, you'll certainly find plenty of places to indulge in a meat-and-potato-and-cabbage diet. These days, though, cities like Berlin (p269) and Hamburg (p334) brim with organic eateries, gourmet kitchens, vegan bistros and myriad ethnic restaurants. Talented chefs have been racking up Michelin stars, especially in the Black Forest. And then there's beer and bread – is there any other country that does either better? Gourmet wurst

Beer Halls & Gardens

Munich and Bavaria are synonymous with the beer hall, an institution of towering tankards, waitstaff in traditional regional outfits and resident oompah bands. The (grand)daddy of all is Munich's Hofbräuhaus (p83), but there are plenty of equally characterful spots throughout the south. Munich celebrated 200 years of beer gardens in 2012; there are at least another two centuries' worth of mug-hoisting to come. Munich's Hofbräuhaus

Frankfurt

Frankfurt (p200) is respected for its financial muscle and skyscraper banks, but the best way to discover its soul – and experience its surprisingly laid-back atmosphere – is to head away from the high-rises. It's easy to join frisbee-tossing locals in the grassy parkland along Main River, grab an espresso at an old-time cafe, and sip tart *Ebbelwei* (apple wine) while dining on hearty local fare in the wood-panelled wine taverns of Sachsenhausen. An der Hauptwache area

23

The Best...
WWII Sites

BERCHTESGADEN
Learn about Hitler's southern headquarters at the Dokumentation Obersalzberg, then exorcise Nazi ghosts at the Eagle's Nest. (p113) (p113)

CONCENTRATION CAMPS
The darkest side of WWII is commemorated in memorial exhibits at camps such as Dachau (p90), Buchenwald (p310) and Bergen-Belsen. (p349)

NUREMBERG
The Reichsparteitagsgelände hosted Nazi mass rallies; the courthouse held the Nuremberg Trials. (p134)

TOPOGRAPHIE DES TERRORS, BERLIN
The exhibition dissects the anatomy of the Nazi state on the site of one of its most feared institutions. (p261)

The Best...
Souvenirs

ROTHENBURG OB DER TAUBER
The Käthe Wohlfahrt Weihnachtsdorf sells Christmas angels, ornaments and nutcrackers year-round. (p122)

BERLIN
The Ampelmann, the little fellow on East Germany's pedestrian traffic lights, has evolved into its own brand. (p277)

LÜBECK
Some of the world's best marzipan hails from Niederegger in this northern German town. (p344)

OBERAMMERGAU
Carved wooden sculptures are a specialty throughout the Alps, especially in Oberammergau. (p109)

MEISSEN
Precious porcelain is the hallmark of this Elbe town, the cradle of European porcelain manufacturing. (p300)

Dessau-Rosslau

Chances are you have a little Bauhaus in your house – perhaps the chair you sit on or the table at which you eat your supper. 'Form follows function' was the credo of this influential 20th-century movement of architecture and design. Come to Dessau-Rosslau (p307) to see where Gropius, Klee, Kandinsky and other Bauhaus luminaries did their best work. The school building and some of the private homes of its teachers are included on Unesco's list of World Heritage Sites.

(25)

Trier

There was a time when Trier (p223) was the capital of Western Europe. OK, it was a couple of millennia ago when Roman emperor Constantine ruled his fading empire from the city, but the Roman legacy still survives in well-preserved amphitheatres, thermal baths and the famous Porta Nigra (p224). Of course, Unesco noticed... Today, Germany's oldest city is as unhurried as the Moselle River it sits on, within a grape toss of Germany's finest – and steepest – vineyards. Kaiserthermen (p224)

Germany's
Top Itineraries

Berlin & Beyond
Cool Meets Culture

5 DAYS

This whirlwind tour will definitely whet your appetite for more of Germany. Be swept away by the vibrancy of the eternally unfinished German capital, marvel at Dresden's rebirth and pay homage to a Prussian king more in love with fine arts than the battlefield.

POLAND

BERLIN ①

POTSDAM ②

GERMANY

DRESDEN ③

CZECH REPUBLIC

① Berlin (p243)

Start by ticking off the blockbuster sights in the historic centre, including the **Reichstag**, the **Brandenburg Gate**, the **Holocaust Memorial** and **Checkpoint Charlie**. The monumental antiquities of the **Pergamonmuseum** are a must-see, followed by a spin around the old Jewish quarter, the **Scheunenviertel**. Come to terms with what life was like in divided Berlin at the **Gedenkstätte Berliner Mauer** and the **East Side Gallery**. Berlin during the Third Reich gets full airplay at the **Topographie des Terrors**. If you have time and energy for another museum, head for the **Neues Museum** to flirt with an Egyptian queen.

BERLIN ➡ POTSDAM

🚗 1½ hours Via A115 & B1. 🚃 40 minutes S7.

② Potsdam (p279)

It's not only royal groupies who should make the easy side trip to Unesco-listed **Schloss & Park Sanssouci** in nearby Potsdam. The park and palace ensemble was Frederick the Great's favourite

summer retreat, a place where he could be '*sans souci*' (without cares). His grave is nearby. Tickets are timed, so get there early in the day and spend any wait time exploring the other park buildings and palaces, especially the enchanting **Chinesisches Haus**. If you're into WWII history, factor in a visit to **Schloss Cecilienhof**, the site of the 1945 Potsdam Conference.

BERLIN ➡ DRESDEN

🚗 2½ hours Via A103 & B1. 🚃 Two hours.

③ Dresden (p296)

Visit Dresden on a long day trip or stay overnight. Either way, concentrate your time in the rubble-resurrected historic centre; the **Frauenkirche** and the treasures of the **Grünes Gewölbe** in the former royal palace are unmissable. Be sure to admire the city's distinctive skyline on a boat ride or a stroll along the Elbe's north bank. For another culture fix, pick your favourite from among the many collections at the **Zwinger**: your options range from armour to paintings to porcelain.

Reichstag dome (p254), Berlin
USCHOOLS UNIVERSITY IMAGES/GETTY IMAGES ©

5 DAYS

Munich & the Bavarian Alps
Bavarian Blockbusters

When most travellers think of Germany, they think of beer gardens, fairy-tale castles, lederhosen, cute villages and the snow-covered Alps. Far from trying to dispel these clichés, this trip is a rewarding introduction to the best Germany's south has in store.

GERMANY

1 MUNICH

SCHLOSS NEUSCHWANSTEIN 2

3 GARMISCH-PARTENKIRCHEN

AUSTRIA

LIECHTENSTEIN

SWITZERLAND

ITALY

① Munich (p51)

With a couple of days in Munich, spend the first exploring the tangle of lanes in the historic centre, timing your stroll to catch the carillon at the **Neues Rathaus** and enjoy a lunchtime snack at the **Viktualienmarkt**. In the afternoon, get a sense of splendour that the Bavarian rulers surrounded themselves with by exploring the magnificent **Residenz**. If it's a sunny day, build in a stroll in the **Englischer Garten**, perhaps with a stop at the **Chinesischer Turm** beer garden. By all means, pop into the **Hofbräuhaus** to see what all the fuss is about, but also try a more local-flavoured beer hall for comparison. If art's your thing, head to the **Pinakothek** museums to admire the gamut of artistic endeavour from antique sculpture to avant-garde canvasses.

MUNICH ➌ FÜSSEN

🚗 **Two hours** Via A96 & B17. 🚄 **Two hours.**
🚌 **2½ hours.**

② Schloss Neuschwanstein (p130)

It's not Germany's oldest castle and certainly not its most historic, yet King Ludwig II's fairy-tale **Schloss Neuschwanstein** speaks to the imagination like no other.

The easiest way to get there from Munich is by guided coach tour, but going by car or train is also easily done. Whatever you do, get there early, and do make time for at least a short stroll through the surrounding woods to truly appreciate Neuschwanstein's magic. If you're driving, stop at the exuberant **Wieskirche**, a Unesco-listed rococo pilgrimage church. If you're heading straight on to Garmisch-Partenkirchen, make another stop in **Oberammergau** to admire its adorable painted houses and skilful woodcarvings.

FÜSSEN ➌ GARMISCH-PARTENKIRCHEN

🚗 **One hour** Via Austria. 🚌 **Two hours** RVO bus 9606.

③ Garmisch-Partenkirchen (p106)

Garmisch-Partenkirchen is the swishest of Germany's alpine resorts. The double-village itself is pretty enough, but you're here to embark on the spectacular cogwheel train-and-cable-car combo ride up the **Zugspitze**. On a good day, you can peer into four countries from this highest point in Germany. If it's winter, you might well be tempted to test your **skiing** mettle on slopes that regularly host international championships.

Chinesischer Turm (p83) in the Englischer Garten, Munich
HANS-PETER MERTEN/GETTY IMAGES ©

10
DAYS

Frankfurt to Freiburg
Romantic Ramblings

This trip delivers the mother lode of story-book scenery you've been dreaming about since childhood. Follow Germany's mightiest river, feel the gravitas of its oldest university, soak in soothing waters and explore landscapes that have spawned classic fairy tales.

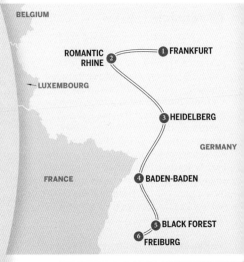

BELGIUM

ROMANTIC RHINE ② — ① FRANKFURT

— LUXEMBOURG

③ HEIDELBERG

GERMANY

FRANCE

④ BADEN-BADEN

⑤ BLACK FOREST
⑥ FREIBURG

❶ Frankfurt (p200)

The business of Frankfurt is business, but that's not all – as you'll discover taking in the impressive skyline mirrored in the Main River; poking around great art in the **Städel Museum**; quaffing *Ebbelwei* (apple wine) in a **Sachsenhausen** tavern and snooping around Goethe's family home, the **Goethe-Haus**.

FRANKFURT ❍ KOBLENZ VIA ROMANTIC RHINE

🚗 **Two hours** Via A66, A60 and B9.
🚆 **1¾ hours** Change in Mainz. ⛴ **Four hours** From Rüdesheim.

❷ Romantic Rhine (p213)

Like a fine wine, the show-stopping scenery along the Rhine River between **Koblenz** and **Rüdesheim** demands to be sipped, not gulped. Slow down to pay your respects to the mythical **Loreley**, sample fine rieslings in such higgledy-piggledy villages as **Bacharach** and shudder at the realities of medieval life at the **Marksburg** in Braubach. For added romance, spend a night in a castle hotel.

KOBLENZ ❍ HEIDELBERG

🚗 **1¾ hours** Via A61. 🚆 **1¾ hours**.

❸ Heidelberg (p170)

Mark Twain and William Turner were smitten by it, and so will you be. Take in the classic Heidelberg view – the proudly crumbling **Schloss**, the sprightly Neckar River and the **Alte Brücke** – while wandering along the **Philosophenweg**. Knock back a couple of beers in a cosy student tavern and don't leave without trying a *Studentenkuss* (student's kiss) confection.

HEIDELBERG ❍ BADEN-BADEN

🚗 **One hour** Via A5. 🚆 **1¼ hours** Change in Karlsruhe.

❹ Baden-Baden (p173)

Baden-Baden is the grande dame of German spa resorts, ageing but still elegant, with belle époque villas and tree-lined avenues. Royals, celebrities, politicians and mere mortals have for centuries soothed sore muscles in its luxurious **bathing temples**. Follow suit, then soak up the aristocratic air in the palatial **casino** where even Dostoevsky lost his shirt.

BADEN-BADEN ❍ TRIBERG

🚗 **Two hours** Via L96 & B500. 🚆 **1¼ hours**.

❺ Black Forest (p173)

Go cuckoo for the Black Forest, a storied pastiche of forest-cloaked hills, glacial lakes, snug valleys and half-timbered jewels like **Schiltach**. Learn about the region's age-old traditions in the Black Forest Open-Air Museum in **Gutach** and the cuckoo-clock wars of **Triberg**, then gobble up a slice of schnapps-drenched Black Forest cake.

TRIBERG ❍ FREIBURG

🚗 **One hour** Via L109 & B294. 🚆 **1¾ hours** Change in Offenbach.

❻ Freiburg (p177)

Take gorgeous scenery, mix in a medieval **Altstadt**, sprinkle with students and add a liberal dash of cool – eh voilà! – you have Freiburg. For a bird's-eye view, take the 3.6km cable car ride up the **Schauins-land** peak. Hitting the trail is great fun in the dramatic **Wutachschlucht** (Wutach Gorge), while wine lovers can indulge in fine vintages around nearby **Breisach**.

Schiltach (p176), Black Forest
HEINZ WOHNER/GETTY IMAGES ©

10 DAYS

Munich to Dresden
Historic Highlights

If you've got a soft spot for quaint medieval villages, dreamy palaces, boisterous beer halls, and proud cities that have forged history, this tour should more than satisfy you.

DRESDEN ⑥

⑤ WEIMAR

CZECH REPUBLIC

ROMANTIC ROAD ③ ④ NUREMBERG

GERMANY

① MUNICH

AUSTRIA

SWITZERLAND ② FÜSSEN

① Munich (p51)

It's impossible not to be charmed by the Bavarian capital. Spend a couple of days checking out such landmark sights as the **Residenz**, legendary beer halls such as the **Hofbräuhaus** and top-ranked art in the **Pinakothek** museums. After a metro-intense day, seek refuge in the vast **Englischer Garten**.

MUNICH ⟳ FÜSSEN

🚗 **Two hours** Via A96 & B17. 🚄 **Two hours.** 🚌 2½ **hours.**

② Ludwig II's Castles (p96)

South of Munich, approaching the mighty Alps, Bavaria's most-beloved king sought refuge from encroaching modernity in his fantasy palaces. The most famous, of course, is **Schloss Neuschwanstein**, a sugary confection above **Schloss Hohenschwangau**, the family's ancestral home. A short drive away, secluded **Schloss Linderhof** is, if anything, even more enchanting.

FÜSSEN ⟳ ROTHENBURG OB DER TAUBER

🚗 **Four hours** Via B17 & B25. 🚌 **Eight hours.**

③ Romantic Road (p116)

The Romantic Road stitches together some of Germany's prettiest medieval towns while traversing a landscape of pastoral beauty. Get your last city fix in Roman-founded **Augsburg**, then plunge on to **Nördlingen** and **Dinkelsbühl**, both cradled by massively thick town walls. **Rothenburg ob der Tauber** is a delightful pastiche of Hansel-and-Gretel houses, spidery cobbled lanes and hidden quiet corners.

ROTHENBURG OB DER TAUBER ⟳ NUREMBERG

🚗 **Four hours** Via B17, B25 & A6. 🚄 1½ **hours** With changes in Steinach and Ansbach.

④ Nuremberg (p131)

Home of emperors, birthplace of Albrecht Dürer and a Nazi mass rally site – Nuremberg has certainly had its moments in German history. Take the city's pulse around the **Hauptmarkt**, site of the famous Christkindlesmarkt, and gobble up the famous Nuremberg sausages.

NUREMBERG ⟳ WEIMAR

🚗 **Three hours** Via A73, A71 & B85. 🚄 3½ **hours** Change in Jena.

⑤ Weimar (p308)

This small Thuringian town was home to a pantheon of German intellectual giants in the 18th century. Compare Goethe's grand digs (today's **Goethe Nationalmuseum**) with Friedrich Schiller's relatively modest **Schiller Haus**. Sadly, Weimar's glorious legacy was tainted by the Nazi-built **Buchenwald Concentration Camp** nearby.

WEIMAR ⟳ DRESDEN

🚗 2½ **hours** Via A4. 🚄 2½ **hours** Change in Leipzig.

⑥ Dresden (p296)

There's little that can prepare you for the show-stopping silhouette of Dresden, sitting proud and pretty in its resurrected baroque splendour on the Elbe River. In the historic centre, the glorious dome of the rebuilt **Frauenkirche** is a shining beacon of the city's resilience. Sightseeing musts are the stunning treasures of the **Grünes Gewölbe** and the **Zwinger**, both housed in former royal palaces.

Schloss Linderhof (p109), Bavaria
ALFREDO DAGLI ORTI/THE ART ARCHIVE/CORBIS ©

2 WEEKS

Munich to Berlin
Top of the Pops

Germany is a rich quilt of exciting cities, soul-stirring scenery, historic landmarks and spirit-lifting culture – as you'll discover on this epic road trip that peels away the layers, exposing you to a banquet of treats, treasures and temptations.

① **Munich** (p51)

Begin your tour in Munich, home to some of the country's finest art museums, a huge city park, treasure-filled royal pads and, of course, the world's most famous beer hall, the **Hofbräuhaus**. Also earmark time for the charming town hall carillon, the bountiful traditional food market and the adrenaline-lure of the **BMW Museum**.

MUNICH ● GARMISCH-PARTENKIRCHEN
🚗 **1½ hours** Via A95 & B2. 🚃 **1½ hours**.

② **Garmisch-Partenkirchen** (p106)

Breathe the fresh mountain air in **Garmisch-Partenkirchen**, then have your breath taken away on an exhilarating trip up the **Zugspitze**, Germany's highest peak, aboard a train-and-cable-car combo that's a marvel of engineering. Come back down to earth huddled over a hearty roast pork dinner and foamy mugs of beer in a knick-knack-laden tavern.

FÜSSEN ● GARMISCH-PARTENKIRCHEN
🚗 **One hour** Via Austria. 🚃 **Two hours** RVO bus 9606.

③ **Romantic Road** (p116)

The name says it all and the reality is even better. Fall under the spell of this radiantly old-world ribbon of riches that kicks off with fabled **Schloss Neuschwanstein** and winds up 350km later in **Würzburg**, a city defined by wine, bishops and grand architecture. Along the way, you'll pass through lyrical landscapes, rampart-encircled medieval towns like **Dinkelsbühl** and **Rothenburg ob der Tauber**, lordly castles and other inspiring scenery.

FÜSSEN ● HEIDELBERG
🚗 **Eight hours** Via B25, A6 & A81. 🚃 **10½ hours** To Würzburg, then 🚃 **2½ hours** with change in Osterburken.

Speicherstadt (p329), Hamburg
GUY VANDERELST/GETTY IMAGES ©

MAINZ ➡ COLOGNE

🚗 3½ hours Via L419, B9 & A3. 🚃 2¾ hours Change in Koblenz. 🛥 11½ hours.

⑥ Cologne (p225)

Contagiously energetic, Cologne is embodied by its grand cathedral, the mighty **Kölner Dom**. Climb to the top for dazzling views, then dig for Roman roots at the **Römisch-Germanisches Museum** or flock to **Museum Ludwig** for killer canvasses. Wrap up in a beer hall with Rhenish fare paired with a crisp *Kölsch* beer.

COLOGNE ➡ HAMBURG

🚗 4½ hours Via A1. 🚃 Four hours.

④ Heidelberg (p170)

Germany's oldest university enchants with a fascinating mixture of history, vibrant modern life and nature. It's a magical place with a romantic, bustling and international ambience. Don't miss a tour of the majestic and impossibly romantic **castle**.

HEIDELBERG ➡ MAINZ

🚗 1¼ hour Via A67. 🚃 Two hours Change in Mannheim or Darmstadt.

⑤ Romantic Rhine (p213)

The Romantic Rhine is a scene-stealing combo of steeply terraced vineyards, craggy cliffs crowned by mighty medieval castles, and higgledy-piggledy villages. Start out in **Mainz** with its great cathedral and fabulous museum about moveable-type inventor – and local boy – Johannes Gutenberg. Take your sweet time drinking in the views along with the local wine as you follow the river north, perhaps stopping in postcard-pretty **Boppard** and fairy-tale-like **Bacharach**. And don't forget to say hello to the **Loreley**.

⑦ Hamburg (p328)

Make a study of cosmopolitan Hamburg for a day or two. It's a city that cradles an elegant centre, the edgy new waterfront **HafenCity** quarter, the red-brick **Speicherstadt** warehouse district and the **Reeperbahn**, a gloriously seedy red-light district, all under the same self-confident mantle.

HAMBURG ➡ BERLIN

🚗 3½ hours Via A24. 🚃 1¾ hours.

⑧ Berlin (p243)

Nearly a quarter century after its post-Wall rebirth, **Berlin** is an exciting combination of glamour and grit, teeming with top museums and galleries, elegant grand opera and hot-stepping dance clubs, gourmet temples and ethnic snack shacks. Whether your tastes run to posh or punk, you can sate them in the German capital.

Germany Month by Month

 ## January

Except in the ski resorts, the Germans have the country pretty much to themselves this month. Short, cold days make this a good time to explore museums and churches.

 ### Mountain Madness

Grab your skis or board and hit the slopes at resorts that range from glam (Garmisch-Partenkirchen) to family-friendly (Bavarian Forest). Whether you're a black diamond daredevil or Sesame Street novice, there's a piste with your name on it.

 ## February

It's not as sweltering as Rio, but the German Carnival is still a good excuse for a party. Ski resorts are busy thanks to school holidays so don't leave home without reservations.

Berlin Film Festival

Stars, starlets, directors and critics sashay down the red carpet for two weeks of screenings and glamourous parties at the Berlinale, one of Europe's most prestigious celluloid festivals.

Karneval/Fasching

The pre-Lenten season is celebrated with costumed street partying, parades and satirical shows. The biggest parties are along the Rhine in Düsseldorf, Cologne and Mainz, but the Black Forest and Munich also have their own traditions.

 ## March

Days start getting longer and the first inkling of spring is in the air. Fresh herring hits the menus, especially along the coastal regions, and dishes prepared with *Bärlauch* (wild garlic) are all the rage.

(left) June Kieler Woche
HOLGER LEUE/GETTY IMAGES ©

April

There's no escaping the Easter Bunny this month. And nothing heralds the arrival of spring like the first crop of white asparagus. Germans go nuts for it.

Walpurgisnacht

The pagan Witches' Sabbath festival on 30 April has Harz villages roaring to life, as young and old dress up as witches and warlocks, singing and dancing through the streets.

Maifest

Villagers celebrate the end of winter on 30 April by chopping down a tree for a *Maibaum* (Maypole); painting, carving and decorating it; and staging a merry revelry with traditional costumes, singing and dancing.

May

One of the loveliest months, often surprisingly warm and sunny, and perfect for ringing in beer-garden season. Plenty of public holidays, which Germans turn into extended weekends, resulting in busy roads and lodging shortages.

Karneval der Kulturen

Hundreds of thousands of revellers celebrate Berlin's multicultural tapestry with parties, exotic nosh and a fun parade of flamboyantly dressed dancers, DJs, artists and musicians.

Labour Day

The first of May is a public holiday in Germany, with some cities hosting political demonstrations for workers' rights.

Wave-Gotik-Treffen

Thousands of Goths paint the town black as they descend upon Leipzig during the long Whitsuntide/Pentecost weekend, for one of the world's largest Goth gatherings.

June

Germany's festival pace quickens and gourmets can rejoice in the bounty of fresh, local produce in the markets. Life moves outdoors, as summer means the sun doesn't set until around 9.30pm.

Vatertag

Father's Day, now also known as *Männertag* (Men's Day), is an excuse for men to get liquored up with the blessing of the missus. It's always on Ascension Day.

Kieler Woche

More than three million salty types flock to the Baltic Sea each year where Kiel hosts the world's biggest boat party, with hundreds of regattas, ship parades, historic vessels and nonstop partying.

Christopher Street Day

No matter what your sexual persuasion, come out and paint the town pink at major gay-pride celebrations in Berlin, Cologne and Hamburg.

July

School's out for the summer and peak travelling season starts. Definitely pre-book, regardless of whether you're heading to the mountains or the coast.

Samba Festival

This festival of song and dance brings around 100 bands and 3000 performers from a dozen nations, as well as up to 200,000 visitors, to Coburg.

Schleswig-Holstein Music Festival

Leading international musicians and promising new artists perform during this festival, held in castles, churches, warehouses and barns throughout Germany's northernmost state. Held from mid-July until August.

forming in historical re-enactments, along with a pageant and general merriment.

Wagner Festival

German high society descends upon Bayreuth to practise the art of listening to epic productions of Wagner operas staged in a custom-built festival hall (p141).

September

Often a great month weather-wise – not so hot, but plenty sunny. The main travel season is over but September is still busy thanks to lots of wine and autumn festivals. Trees may start turning into a riot of colour towards the end of the month.

Berlin Marathon

Sweat it out with the other 50,000 runners or just cheer 'em on during Germany's biggest street race, which has seen nine world records set since 1977.

Oktoberfest

Munich's legendary beer-swilling party (www.oktoberfest.de).

August

August tends to be the hottest month but days are often cooled down by afternoon thunderstorms. 'Tis the season for *Pfifferlinge* (chanterelle mushrooms) and fresh berries.

Shooting Festivals

More than a million Germans (mostly men) belong to shooting clubs and show off their skills at marksmen's festivals. The biggest one is in Hanover; the oldest in Düsseldorf.

Wine Festivals

With grapes ripening to a plump sweetness, the wine festival season starts, with tastings, folkloric parades, fireworks and the election of wine queens. The Dürkheimer Wurstmarkt is one of the biggest and most famous.

Kinderzeche

Dinkelsbühl on the Romantic Road hosts this 10-day festival, featuring children per-

October

Everybody's definitely back to school or business as days get shorter, colder and wetter. Trade-fair season kicks into high gear, affecting lodging prices and availability in Frankfurt, Berlin, Hamburg and other major cities. Tourist offices, museums and attractions keep shorter hours.

Frankfurt Book Fair

Bookworms invade Frankfurt for the world's largest book fair, with 7300 exhibitors from more than 100 countries.

November

Life moves pretty much indoors. On the plus side, queues at tourist sites are short, and theatre, concert, opera and other cultural events are plentiful. Bring warm clothes and rain gear.

 ## St Martinstag

This festival held on 10–11 November honours the 4th-century St Martin, known for his humility and generosity, with a lantern procession and a re-enactment of the famous scene where he cuts his coat in half to share with a beggar. This is followed by a big feast of stuffed, roasted goose.

 # December

Cold and sun-deprived days are brightened by Advent, the four weeks of festivities before Christmas celebrated with illuminated streets, markets, calendars, wreaths and home-baked cookies. Ski resorts usually get their first dusting of snow.

 ## Nikolaustag

On the eve of 5 December, German children put their shoes outside the door hoping that St Nick will fill them with sweets and small toys overnight. Ill-behaved children may find only a prickly rod left behind by St Nick's helper, Knecht Ruprecht.

 ## Christmas Markets

Mulled wine, spicy gingerbread cookies, shimmering ornaments – these and lots more are typical features of enchanting German Christmas markets, most held from late November until 24 December. Nuremberg's Christkindlesmarkt (p133) is especially famous.

 ## Silvester

New Year's Eve is called 'Silvester' in honour of the 4th-century pope under whom the Romans adopted Christianity as their official religion. The new year is greeted with fireworks launched by thousands of amateur pyromaniacs.

Far left: **September** Berlin Marathon
Left: **December** Christmas market stall, Nuremberg

What's New

For this new edition of Discover Germany, our authors have hunted down the fresh, the transformed, the hot and the happening. These are some of our favourites. For up-to-the-minute reviews and recommendations, see lonelyplanet.com/Germany.

1 **BERLIN BRANDENBURG AIRPORT**
With some well-publicised delays, we're not betting the farm, but we remain optimistic that planes will have started flying into Berlin's shiny new international airport before we update this book again. (BBI; www.berlin-airport.de)

2 **STÄDEL MUSEUM, FRANKFURT**
Until now, the Städel was most famous for its Old Masters collection, but that may change with the opening of the spectacular new underground wing showcasing post-WWII paintings and photographs. (p201)

3 **MILITÄRHISTORISCHES MUSEUM, DRESDEN**
Daniel Libeskind's poignant architecture creates a powerful setting for this revamped military history museum that's as much about peace as it is about war. (p297)

4 **MUSEUMSINSEL MASTERPLAN, BERLIN**
A long-term process will see all five museums restored and modernised by 2025. A central entrance and an Archaeological Promenade will link the buildings underground.

5 **MUSEUM BRANDHORST, MUNICH**
The biggest, brashest characters of pop art rule at the Brandhorst, an edgy addition to Munich's Kunstareal. Warhol, Hirst, Wombly, Flavin... the namedropping list is long. (p73)

6 **HUMBOLDT-BOX, BERLIN**
The biggest building project on the horizon is the reconstruction of the Prussian royal city palace in central Berlin. It will house museums, a library and spaces for public events. The Humboldt-Box provides a preview and a viewing platform of the construction site, which is set to go live in 2014. (p260)

7 **MUSEUM FOLKWANG, ESSEN**
Red-hot architect David Chipperfield provided the blueprint for these show-stopping new digs, housing a prized collection of 19th- and 20th-century masterpieces by such heavyweights as Gauguin and Van Gogh. (p210)

8 **MUSEUM DER BAYERISCHEN KÖNIGE, HOHENSCHWAN**
Hugging the picturesque little Alpsee, this former lakeside hotel near two of Germany's dreamiest castles – Neuschwanstein and Hohenschwangau – is full of Wittelsbach memorabilia, and provides a bit more background on the castles and the royal dynasty behind them. (p129)

9 **TRENDS IN EATING**
Top-flight chefs have rediscovered German country cooking and reinterpreted it in innovative and sophisticated ways. Long-ignored 'lowly' vegetables like turnips and parsnips have made a comeback and sidle up to organic meats, artisan cheeses and other ingredients sourced from sustainable farms.

Get Inspired

Books

- **Grimms Märchen** (Grimms Fairy Tales; 1812) Jacob and Wilhelm Grimm's fairy tales, passed down orally through generations.

- **Mr Norris Changes Trains** (1935) and **Goodbye to Berlin** (1939) Christopher Isherwood's chronicle of early-1930s Berlin was the basis of the movie *Cabaret*.

- **The Rise & Fall of the Third Reich** (1960) William Shirer's definitive tome about Nazi Germany remains powerful.

Films

- **Das Boot** (1981) Dives into the claustrophobic world of WWII U-boat warfare.

- **Good Bye, Lenin!** (2003) Drama-comedy about a young East Berliner protecting his ailing mother from the knowledge that the Wall has fallen.

- **Der Untergang** (Downfall; 2004) Chilling account of Hitler's last 12 days in his Berlin bunker.

- **Das Leben der Anderen** (The Lives of Others; 2006) Academy Award winner; unmasks the pervasiveness and destructiveness of East Germany's secret service, the Stasi.

Music

- **Ring of the Nibelungen** (1848–74) Richard Wagner's epic opera cycle.

- **The Threepenny Opera** (1928) Runaway hit musical by Brecht and Weill.

- **Atem** (1973) Groundbreaking album by electronic music pioneers Tangerine Dream.

- **Sehnsucht** (1994) Industrial metal band Rammstein's international breakthrough album.

Websites

- **Deutschland Online** (www.magazine-deutschland.de) Insightful features on culture, business and politics.

- **Facts about Germany** (www.tatsachen-ueber-deutschland.de) Reference tool on all aspects of German society.

- **German Films** (www.german-films.de) Anything you ever wanted to know about movies from Germany.

- **Deutsche Welle** (www.dw.de) Keep abreast of German affairs.

Short on time?

This list will give you an instant insight into the country.

Read *A Tramp Abroad* (1880), Mark Twain's timelessly witty observations, made while travelling around Germany in the 1970s.

Watch *Cabaret* (1972), the acclaimed film musical that captured the giddiness of the Weimar Republic amid the looming threat of Nazi Germany.

Listen to Beethoven pulling out all the stops in his nine symphonies (1800–24).

Log on to www.germany-tourism.de for information on sights, lodging, events and activities.

Richard Wagner (1813–83)

Need to Know

Currency
Euro (€)

Language
German

ATMs
Omnipresent in cities and towns, less so in villages.

Credit Cards
Visa and MasterCard increasingly accepted, but don't count on it.

Visas
Generally not required for tourist stays up to 90 days (or at all for EU nationals).

Mobile Phones
Mobile phones operate on GSM900/1800. German SIM cards can be used in dual- or tri-band phones.

Wi-Fi
Widely available in hotels, cafes and airports.

Internet Access
Internet cafes are common; €2 to €4 per hour.

Driving
Drive on the right; the steering wheel is on the left side of the car.

Tipping
Tip cabbies, servers and bartenders 5% to 10% for good service.

When to Go

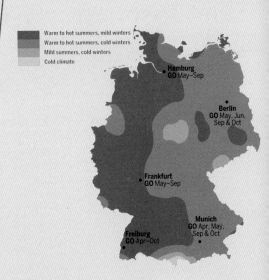

Warm to hot summers, mild winters
Warm to hot summers, cold winters
Mild summers, cold winters
Cold climate

Hamburg
GO May–Sep

Berlin
GO May, Jun, Sep & Oct

Frankfurt
GO May–Sep

Munich
GO Apr, May, Sep & Oct

Freiburg
GO Apr–Oct

High Season
(Jul & Aug)
- Busy roads and long lines at key sights
- Vacancies at a premium and peak prices in resorts
- Festivals celebrate everything from music to wine, sailing to samba

Shoulder
(Apr–Jun, Sep & Oct)
- Smaller crowds and lower prices, except public holidays
- Blooming flowers in spring; radiant foliage in autumn
- Sunny, temperate weather ideal for outdoor pursuits

Low Season
(Nov–Mar)
- No lines but shorter hours and seasonal closures at key sights
- Theatre, concert, opera season in full swing
- Ski resorts busiest in January and February

Advance Planning

- **Three months before** Shop around for flight deals; book accommodation if travelling in high season or during major festivals, trade shows or holidays; reserve tickets for major performances.

- **One month before** Make car-hire reservations, get rail passes, book tickets for Europabus; book a table at Michelin-starred restaurants.

- **Two weeks** Book online tickets for major sights (such as Schloss Neuschwanstein).

Your Daily Budget

Budget less than €100
- Hostel, camping or private room: €12–25
- Up to €8 per meal or self-cater
- Take advantage of happy hours and free or low-cost museums or entertainment

Midrange €100–200
- Private apartment or double room €60–100
- Cafe lunch, dinner at nice restaurant €30–40
- Couple of beers in a pub or beer garden €8

Top End over €200
- Loft apartment or double in top-end hotel €150
- Sit-down lunch, dinner at top-rated restaurant €100
- Concert or opera tickets €50

Exchange Rates

Australia	A$1	€0.80
Canada	C$1	€0.77
Japan	¥100	€0.98
NZ	NZ$1	€0.63
UK	UK£1	€1.24
US	US$1	€0.78

For current exchange rates see www.xe.com.

What to Bring

- **Foul-weather gear** For those days when the sun's a no-show.
- **Portable GPS with Germany maps** For headache-free navigating.
- **Loose pants** To accommodate a growing beer belly.
- **Smart clothes & shoes** For hitting fancy restaurants, the opera or big-city clubs.
- **Bathing suit & travel towel** For lolling in mineral springs or spontaneous lake jumps.
- **Earplugs** To counter noisy church bells and early-morning construction work.
- **Phrasebook** Most Germans speak some English but making the effort is hugely appreciated.

Arriving in Germany

Frankfurt Airport
Train S-Bahn train lines S8 and S9 link the airport with the city centre several times hourly (€4.10, 11 minutes)

Taxi Trips into town average €25

Munich Airport
Train S1 and S8 go to the city centre (€10.50, 45 minutes)

Bus The Lufthansa Bus connects to the city centre (€10.50, 45 minutes)

Taxi A taxi into town costs about €60

Getting Around

- **Air** Fly domestically only to cover major distances, such as Berlin–Munich or Hamburg–Munich.
- **Bicycle** Germany has some 200 signposted long-distance routes and bicycle lanes in cities.
- **Car** Ditch in cities, but handy for getting around the countryside.
- **Train** Deutsche Bahn (www.bahn.de) operates a comprehensive and comfortable rail network.

Accommodation

- **Gasthof or Gasthaus** Small countryside inn with simple rooms and attached restaurant.
- **Hostels** Both HI-affiliated and independents are ubiquitous; many offer private and family rooms.
- **Hotels** Available in all price ranges and comfort levels.
- **Pension** The German version of a B&B.
- **Privatzimmer** A guest room in a private home (popular in rural areas); booked through tourist offices.

Be Forewarned

- **Crowds** Expect heavy traffic and crowds at tourist sights around public holidays and in July and August.
- **Restaurants** Lunch is served between noon and 2.30pm, dinner between 6pm and 10pm; in cities restaurants are often open all day.
- **Shops** Closed on Sundays and public holidays (some exceptions in tourist towns) and daily at lunchtime in suburbs and rural areas.

Munich

Germany's second city is a flourishing success story that revels in its own contradictions. It's the natural habitat of well-heeled power dressers and lederhosen-clad thigh-slappers, Mediterranean-style street cafes and olde-worlde beer halls, high-brow art and high-tech industry, If you're looking for Alpine clichés, they're all here, but the Bavarian metropolis sure has many an unexpected card down its dirndl.

Statistics show Munich is enticing more visitors than ever, especially in summer and during Oktoberfest. Munich's walkable centre retains a small-town air but holds some world-class sights, especially its art galleries and museums. Throw in a king's ransom of royal Bavarian heritage, an entire suburb of Olympic legacy and a kitbag of dark tourism and you can see why it's such a favourite among those who seek out the past, but like to hit the town once they're done.

Views over Munich's rooftops

THOMAS WINZ/GETTY IMAGES ©

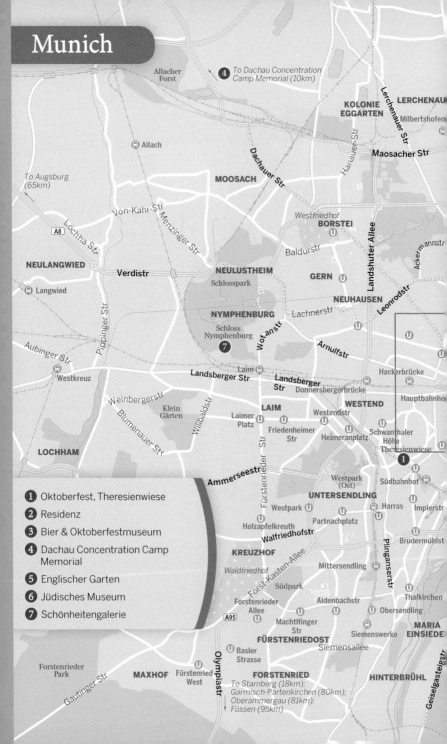

Munich

Allacher
Forst

4 To Dachau Concentration
Camp Memorial (10km)

**KOLONIE
EGGARTEN**

LERCHENAU

Milbertshofen

Lerchenauer Str

Hanauer Str

Maosacher Str

Allach

MOOSACH

Dachauer Str

To Augsburg
(65km)

A8

Lochha Str

Von-Kahr-Str

Menzinger Str

Westfriedhof

BORSTEI

Baldurstr

Landshuter Allee

Ackermannstr

NEULANGWIED

Langwied

Verdistr

NEULUSTHEIM

Schlosspark

GERN U

NEUHAUSEN

Leonrodstr

Pippinger Str

NYMPHENBURG

Lachnerstr

Schloss
Nymphenburg

7

Wotanstr

U

Arnulfstr

U

Aubinger Str

Westkreuz

Weinbergerstr

Blumenauer Str

Willibaldstr

Laim

Landsberger Str

**Landsberger
Str**

Donnersbergerbrücke

Hackerbrücke

Hauptbahnho

Klein
Gärten

LAIM

Laimer
Platz

Friedenheimer
Str

Westendstr

Heimeranplatz

WESTEND

Schwanthaler
Höhe

U

U

LOCHHAM

Fürstenrieder Str

Ammerseestr.

Theresienwiese

1

U

U

Westpark
(Ost)

Südbahnhof

U

U

1 Oktoberfest, Theresienwiese

2 Residenz

3 Bier & Oktoberfestmuseum

4 Dachau Concentration Camp
Memorial

5 Englischer Garten

6 Jüdisches Museum

7 Schönheitengalerie

UNTERSENDLING

Westpark U

U

U

Harras U

Implerstr

U

Holzapfelkreuth

Partnachplatz

Walfriedhofstr

Bruedermühlst

Plinganserstr

KREUZHOF

Forst-Kasten-Allee

Mittersendling

U

Waldfriedhof

Südpark

Aidenbachstr

U

Obersendling

Thalkirchen

Forstenrieder
Allee

A95

Machtlfinger
Str

U

U

Siemenswerke

**MARIA
EINSIEDE**

FÜRSTENRIEDOST

Siemensallee

Forstenrieder
Park

Gautinger Str

MAXHOF

Fürstenried
West

Olympiastr

U Basler
Strasse

FORSTENRIED

To Starnberg (18km);
Garmisch-Partenkirchen (80km);
Oberammergau (81km);
Füssen (95km)

HINTERBRÜHL

Geiselgasteigstr

Munich's Highlights

① Oktoberfest

Oktoberfest (p84) is the highlight of the year for residents, and visitors get a full dose of Bavarian culture. You rejoice with millions of fellow beer drinkers, sample dozens of different types of beer in a variety of beer tents and watch costume-clad parades celebrating German traditions.

Above: Inside a Beirzelt (beer tent) at Oktoberfest; Top Right: Serving steins of beer; Bottom Right: Parade participants in traditional Bavarian costume

Need to Know
TOP TIP Visit during the week. **OPENING HOURS** Beer tents are open 10am to 11.30pm weekdays (from 9am weekends). **For further coverage, see p84**

Oktoberfest Don't Miss List

HANS SPINDLER, OKTOBERFEST
ORGANISER & PROUD BAVARIAN

1 COSTUME & RIFLEMAN'S PARADE

Try to catch the Costume & Rifleman's Parade on the first Sunday of the Oktoberfest. This procession starts at 10am at Max-Joseph-Platz and marches for 7km through the city centre to the fairgrounds. The parade – an impressive insight into the customs rooted in Bavaria and other German states – includes regional costume groups leading oxen, 'troops' in historical uniforms, marching bands, riflemen, trumpeters on horseback, flag-throwers and decorated drays from Munich breweries.

2 BIERZELTE (BEER TENTS)

The atmosphere inside the beer tents is unforgettable – around 5000 guests all packed in, sitting at long tables, watching costume-clad waiters marching through the crowds with four, five or more litre-sized mugs in each fist! Each tent is hosted by a different brewery and serves quality mugs of foamy goodness. But if you want to hang out with lots of Müncheners (Munich residents), head to the Augustiner tent – it's the local favourite.

3 REVELLING AT LONG TABLES

One of most enjoyable parts of the festival is sitting at the long tables with strangers and friends and spontaneously breaking into song and rocking side to side as a group. Suddenly you've got a table of smiling new friends eager to exclaim *Prost!* (Cheers!) with you.

4 LOOPING AROUND FIVE TIMES

Aside from the beer drinking, the Oktoberfest is one big amusement park. One of my favourites is the modern Olympialooping, a gigantic roller coaster which makes no less than five dizzying loops. For a more traditional way to lurch your stomach to your knees, hop on the *Teufelsrad* (Devil's Wheel); it's been spinning folk around since 1910 (the aim is to stay standing as long as possible). This ride is as much fun to watch as it is to ride!

Residenz

Generations of Bavarian rulers expanded a medieval fortress into this vast and splendid compound (p75) that served as their primary residence and seat of government 1508 –1918. Today it's an Aladdin's cave of fanciful rooms and collections from all major periods – the Renaissance to baroque, rococo to neoclassicism. Below: Antiquarium; Top Right: Tapestry detail, Residenzmuseum; Bottom Right: Cuvilliés-Theatre

Need to Know

BUDGET At least two hours for a visit. **USE** the free audioguide for a more in-depth experience. **EXPLORE** The Renaissance-era palace gardens. **For further details, see p75**

Residenz Don't Miss List

DR CHRISTIAN QUAEITZSCH,
MUSEUM CURATOR AT BAVARIAN
DEPARTMENT OF STATE-OWNED PALACES,
GARDENS & LAKES

1 ANTIQUARIUM

This stunning banqueting hall is the most important secular Renaissance room north of the Alps. Take time to study the elaborate paintings that cover its walls and the barrel-vaulted ceiling. In the centre of the vault you see allegorical representation of the Virtues, while the paintings above the windows depict towns and palaces from the Duchy of Bavaria in the late 16th century.

2 REICHE ZIMMER (ORNATE ROOMS)

This series of rooms is the most lavish in the Residenz. It was designed in the 1730s by François Cuvilliés, one of the 'godfathers' of southern German rococo. Each room is more elaborate than the next. Note the harmonious interplay of furniture, carved wall panelling, rich textiles, paintings and art objects, especially in the state bedroom.

3 CUVILLIÉS-THEATRE

This court theatre is Cuvilliés' masterpiece, designed when rococo had reached its most mature phase. It's truly a magnificent space – its red, white and gold colour scheme creates a unique flair that is both intimate and festive. The carved decorations in the auditorium are all original.

4 SCHATZKAMMER DER RESIDENZ (TREASURY)

This is a priceless collection of jewels, ivories, and objects made of gold, enamel and crystal that's been amassed by Bavaria's rulers since the 16th century. One of the oldest objects is a portable altar from 890; one of the rarest is the 13th-century Crown of an English Queen. Other highlights: the Statuette of St George and the Crown of the Bavarian Kings.

5 GROTTENHOF (GROTTO COURT)

The architecture of the Residenz is defined by its 11 courts of which the Grotto Court is the loveliest. The name was inspired by the whimsical grotto attached to the outside of the Antiquarium that's decorated with shells, a fountain and mythological wall paintings.

The Alternative Oktoberfest

OK, there's no replacing the real thing. Sorry. But if you can't visit during the festival, you can do the next best thing – start with a visit to the Bier & Oktoberfestmuseum (p68) to learn about the history of German beer and its most famous beer event. Then kick back a litre-sized mug in one of Munich's best beer halls, like the Hofbräuhaus (p83) or the (less touristy) Augustiner Bräustuben (p83). Hofbräuhaus

3

4

Dachau Concentration Camp Memorial

This inscription greets you at the Nazis' first concentration camp (p90): 'The Way to freedom is to follow one's orders, exhibit honesty, orderliness, cleanliness, sobriety, truthfulness, the ability to sacrifice and love of the fatherland'. A tour takes you past photos of officers and inmates, descriptions of scientific experiments and a bunker where inmates were tortured.

CLARA MONITTO ©

Lolling in the Englischer Garten 5

LAURIE NOBLE/GETTY IMAGES ©

Munich's massive city park, the Englischer Garten (p73; English Garden), is a mix of contradictions: the Chinesischer Turm (Chinese Tower) is a beer garden, there are no English flower beds and in summer you'll see hundreds of naked sunbathers with their jackets, ties and dresses stacked neatly beside them.

CARO/ALAMY ©

6 Jüdisches Museum

The Jüdisches Museum (Jewish Museum; p68) displays sensitive exhibits that attempt to come to grips with the history of Judaism in Germany. A selection of objects gives you insight into the Jewish history of Munich as well as the variety of Jewish identities in the cultural history of the country.

7 Schönheitengalerie (Gallery of Beauties)

All the rooms are sumptuous at Schloss Nymphenburg (p80), but most majestic is the Schönheitengalerie, home to 38 portraits of women chosen by an admiring King Ludwig I. The most famous is of Helene Sedlmayr, a shoemaker's daughter wearing a lavish frock that the king gave her for the sitting.

Munich's Best…

Things for Free

○ **Glockenspiel** (p64) Crane your neck to historical scenes reenacted by the Rathaus carillon several times daily

○ **Viktualienmarkt** (p65) Enjoy the sights and smells of Munich's lively gourmet market

○ **Michaelskirche** (p65) Pay your respects to King Ludwig II who's buried in the crypt of this pretty church

○ **Asamkirche** (p68) This pint-sized baroque church is proof that great things come in small packages

Beer Halls & Gardens

○ **Hofbräuhaus** (p83) It's touristy and crowded yet an essential Munich experience

○ **Augustiner Bräustuben** (p83) An old-school, traditional spot to kick one back (or two, or three…)

○ **Chinesischer Turm** (p83) Imbibing with an exotic touch beneath a pagoda in the Englischer Garten

○ **Hirschau** (p84) Live jazz and a playground with minigolf course give this beer garden an edge

Places to Chill

○ **Schloss Nymphenburg** (p80) Relax in the elaborate surrounding gardens

○ **Englischer Garten** (p73) Munich's colossal city park is the best antidote after an evening sampling Munich's outstanding beer

○ **Japanisches Teehaus** (p73; Japanese Teahouse) Traditional tea ceremonies are held in summer

○ **Grottenhof** (p75; Grotto Court) The most enchanting courtyard in the Residenz has whimsical decorations and restful ambience

Cheap Eats

○ **Königsquelle** (p80)
A crowd-pleasing mix of German and pan-European fare

○ **Cafe Frischhut** (p82)
Come to this local institution for delectable pastries – freshly made and gut-filling

○ **Bergwolf** (p82) Had one too many beers? Restore balance to the brain with a spicy *Currywurst* at this beloved hang-out

○ **Bratwurstherzl** (p80)
Gobble up organic beechwood-grilled sausages served on heart-shaped plates

ADVANCE PLANNING

○ **One year before**
Book Oktoberfest accommodation, just like six million other beer lovers

○ **One to two months before** Reserve tickets for the opera or the Philharmonie

○ **A few days before**
Book a table for weekend dinner at upscale and trendy restaurants

RESOURCES

○ **Tourismus Urlaub Reise München** (www.muenchen-tourist.de) Munich's official tourism website

○ **Museen in Muenchen** (www.museen-in-muenchen.de) Excellent museum portal with exhaustive listings

○ **Munich Found** (www.munichfound.de) Munich's expat magazine

○ **Toy Town Germany** (www.toytowngermany.com) English-language community website with specialised Munich pages

○ **Oktoberbest** (www.oktoberfest.de) Definitive Oktoberfest website

GETTING AROUND

○ **Car** Avoid!

○ **Public transport** Inexpensive and efficient

○ **Taxi** Handy at night and for groups

○ **Walk** Central Munich is compact enough to explore on foot.

BE FOREWARNED

○ **Drunk people** During Oktoberfest, crime and staggering drunks are major problems, especially at the southern end of the Hauptbahnhof late in the evening – there are dozens of assaults every year. Leave early or stay *very* cautious.

○ **Bicycles** Make sure you don't wander onto bike lanes, especially when waiting to cross the road and when alighting from buses and trams.

○ **Static crazy** The Föhn (pronounced foon) is a weather-related annoyance peculiar to southern Germany. Static-charged wind brings dense pressure that sits on the city, causing headaches and general crankiness.

○ **Museums** Most are closed Monday or Tuesday.

Left: Selection of cheeses, Viktualienmarkt;
Above: Schloss Nymphenburg
(LEFT) CLARA MONITTO ©; (ABOVE) H & D ZIELSKE/GETTY IMAGES ©

Munich Walking Tour

If you have limited time or just want to get a quick overview of what Munich has to offer, follow this easy tour, which checks off major landmarks while criss-crossing the historic city centre.

WALK FACTS

- **Start**
  Marienplatz
- **Finish**
  Theatinerkirche
- **Distance** 5km
- **Duration** Two hours

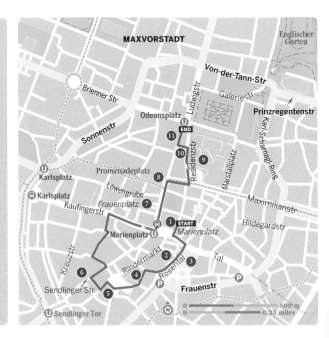

1 Marienplatz

Kick off at central Marienplatz, punctuated by the Mariensäule (St Mary's Column). Two or three times daily, the glockenspiel chimes from the Neues Rathaus, the impressive neo-Gothic town hall, the entrance of which is fronted by the blue-bottomed Fischbrunnen (Fish Fountain).

2 St Peterskirche

The steeple of the St Peterskirche affords great views of the old town, including the Altes Rathaus, now home to a toy museum.

3 Viktualienmarkt

One of central Europe's finest gourmet markets, Viktualienmarkt moved to this square in 1807 when it outgrew Marienplatz. Many of the stalls have been run by generations of the same family. Head for the market's beer garden for an alfresco lunch with a brew.

4 Münchner Stadtmuseum

This fine museum chronicles Munich's history with interesting exhibits set up in chronological order.

5 Jüdisches Museum

The museum is part of the new Jewish complex on St-Jakobs-Platz that also includes a community centre with a restaurant and a bunkerish synagogue (rarely open to the public).

6 Asamkirche

This jewel-like late-baroque church is a masterpiece by the Asam brothers Cosmas Damian and Egid Quirin who lived next door. This was originally their private chapel.

7 Frauenkirche

Munich's landmark church was reconstructed after wartime bombing, but today is a fairly spartan affair. Note the bronze plaques of Pope Benedict XVI and his predecessor John Paul II affixed to nearby pillars.

8 Fünf Höfe

The modernist design of this cosmopolitan shopping arcade is as interesting as the fancy flagship and concept stores lining its passageways. It also an art space with high-calibre changing installations.

9 Residenz

Vast, sprawling and impressive, the Residenz was the seat of government and residence of the Wittelsbach rulers for several centuries. Badly bombed in WWII, it was meticulously restored and is again a sparkling repository of fine art, furniture and architectural detail.

10 Feldherrnhalle

This bombastic structure honours the Bavarian army and positively drips with testosterone. The statues represent Thirty Years' War general Johann Tilly and Karl Phillip von Wrede, an ally-turned-foe of Napoléon.

11 Theatinerkirche

Also known as St Kajetan's, the grandiose Theatinerkirche is easily recognised by its mustard-yellow facade and massive twin towers. It's the final six-feet-under destination of several Wittelsbach rulers.

Munich in...

ONE DAY

Kick off with the recommended walking tour, taking in the main historic sights – from the bustling **Marienplatz** to the tranquil **Hofgarten**. Feel free to drop into the **Hofbräuhaus** for a break or to build a spot of shopping along pedestrianised Kaufingerstrasse and Neuhauser Strasse into the route. In the afternoon, get your art and culture fix in one or two of the **Pinakothek** museums, then cap off the day with a classic Bavarian meal, for instance in the **Augustiner Bräustuben**.

TWO DAYS

Tour the royal splendour of the **Residenz**, then relax in the **Englischer Garten**, perhaps swinging by the Eisbach to watch the daredevil **surfers** and ending up at the **Chinesischer Turm** beer garden for pretzel and beer. Alternatively, if you're a car-ficionado, worship at the altar of the auto by visiting the **BMW Museum**. In the evening, treat your ears either to a concert at the **Kulturzentrum Gasteig** or **Jazzclub Unterfahrt** and finish the night with cocktails at **Schumann's Bar**.

Frauenkirche (p65)

Discover Munich

Glockenspiel, Neues Rathaus
KEREN SU/GETTY IMAGES ©

MUNICH

089 / POP 1.38 MILLION

◉ Sights

Marienplatz & Around

The heart and soul of the Altstadt, Marienplatz (Mary's Sq) is a popular gathering spot and packs a lot of personality into its relatively small frame. It's anchored by the **Mariensäule** (Mary's Column; Map p70), built in 1638 to celebrate victory over Swedish forces during the Thirty Years' War; it's topped by a golden statue of the Virgin Mary balancing on a crescent moon.

NEUES RATHAUS   Historic Building
(New Town Hall; Map p70; Marienplatz; ⓈMarienplatz, ⓇMarienplatz) The coal-blackened facade of the neo-Gothic Neues Rathaus is festooned with gargoyles, statues and a dragon scaling the turrets; the tourist office is on the ground floor.

The **Glockenspiel** (Map p70) has 43 bells and 32 figures that perform two actual historic events. The top half tells the story of a knight's tournament held in 1568 to celebrate the marriage of Duke Wilhelm V to Renata of Lothringen, while the bottom half portrays the Schäfflertanz.

ALTES RATHAUS   Historic Building
(Old Town Hall; Map p70; Marienplatz; ⓈMarienplatz, ⓇMarienplatz) The eastern side of Marienplatz is dominated by the Altes Rathaus. On 9 November 1938 Joseph Goebbels gave a hate-filled speech here that launched the nationwide Kristallnacht pogroms. Today it houses the adorable **Spielzeugmuseum** (Toy Museum; Map p70; www.toymuseum.de; Marienplatz 15; adult/child €4/1; ⏱10am-5.30pm) with its

huge collection of rare and precious toys from Europe and the US.

ST PETERSKIRCHE
Church

(Church of St Peter; Map p70; Rindermarkt 1; church admission free, tower adult/child €1.50/1; ⊙tower 9am-5.30pm Mon-Fri, from 10am Sat & Sun; Ⓢ Marienplatz, Ⓡ Marienplatz) Some 306 steps stand between you and the best view of central Munich, from the 92m-tall tower of the St Peterskirche, Munich's oldest church (built in 1150). Also known as Alter Peter (Old Peter), it's a virtual textbook of art through the centuries, with its Gothic St-Martin-Altar, Johann Baptist Zimmermann baroque ceiling fresco and Ignaz Günther rococo sculptures.

FREE HOFBRÄUHAUS
Beer Hall

(Map p70; www.hofbraeuhaus.de; Am Platzl 9; Ⓢ Marienplatz, Ⓡ Marienplatz) Even teetotal-ling ubercool kitsch-haters will at some point gravitate, out of simple curiosity, to the Hofbräuhaus, the world's most celebrated beer hall. The writhing hordes of tourists tend to overshadow the sterling interior, where dainty twirled flowers and Bavarian flags adorn the medieval vaults.

Beer guzzling and pretzel snapping has been going on here since 1644 and the ballroom upstairs was the site of the first large meeting of the National Socialist Party on 20 February 1920.

FRAUENKIRCHE
Church

(Church of Our Lady; Map p70; Frauenplatz 1; admission €2; ⊙7am-7pm Sat-Wed, to 8.30pm Thu, to 6pm Fri) The landmark Frauenkirche, built 1468–88, is Munich's spiritual heart and the Mt Everest among its churches. No other building in the central city may stand taller than its onion-domed twin towers, which reach a sky-scraping 99m. From April to October, you can enjoy panoramic city views from the south tower.

Of note is the epic cenotaph (empty tomb) of Ludwig the Bavarian just past the entrance and the bronze plaques of Pope Benedict XVI and his predecessor John Paul II affixed to nearby pillars.

MICHAELSKIRCHE
Church

(Church of St Michael; Map p70; Kaufingerstrasse 52; crypt admission €2; ⊙crypt 9.30am-4.30pm Mon-Fri, to 2.30pm Sat & Sun; Ⓢ Karlsplatz,

Ⓡ Karlsplatz, Ⓡ Karlsplatz) Completed in 1597, St Michael's was the largest Renaissance church north of the Alps when it was built. Its dank crypt is the final resting place of the Mad King, whose humble tomb is usually drowned in flowers. It boasts an impressive unsupported barrel-vaulted ceiling and the massive bronze statue between the two entrances shows the archangel finishing off a dragonlike creature, a classic Counter Reformation–era symbol of Catholicism triumphing over Protestantism. The building has been, and is set to be, under heavy renovation for years but you can still go inside.

Viktualienmarkt & Around

The bustling **Viktualienmarkt** (Map p70; ⊙Mon-Fri & Sat morning; Ⓢ Marienplatz, Ⓡ Marienplatz) is one of Europe's great food markets. In summer the entire place is transformed into one of the finest and most expensive beer gardens around, while in winter people huddle for warmth and schnapps in the small pubs around the square. The enormous **maypole** bears artisans' symbols and the traditional blue-and-white Bavarian stripes.

MÜNCHNER STADTMUSEUM
Museum

(City Museum; Map p70; ✆2332 2370; www .stadtmuseum-online.de; St-Jakobs-Platz 1; adult/concession/child €6/3/free, audioguide €3; ⊙10am-6pm Tue-Sun; Ⓢ Marienplatz, Ⓡ Marienplatz) Installed for the city's 850th birthday in 2008, the **Typisch München** (Typical Munich) exhibition at this unmissable museum tells Munich's story in an imaginative, uncluttered and engaging way. Taking up the whole of a rambling building, exhibits in each section represent something quintessential about the city; a booklet/audioguide relates the tale behind them, thus condensing a long and tangled history into easily digestible themes.

What could not be boiled down for this exhibition is the city's role in the rise of the Nazis, and this notorious chapter has been rightly left as a powerful separate exhibition called **Nationalsozialismus in München**. This occupies an eerily windowless annex of the main building.

Central Munich

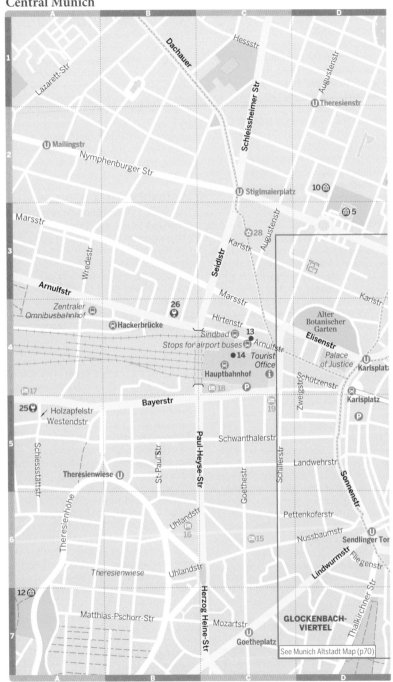

See Munich Altstadt Map (p70)

MUNICH MUNICH

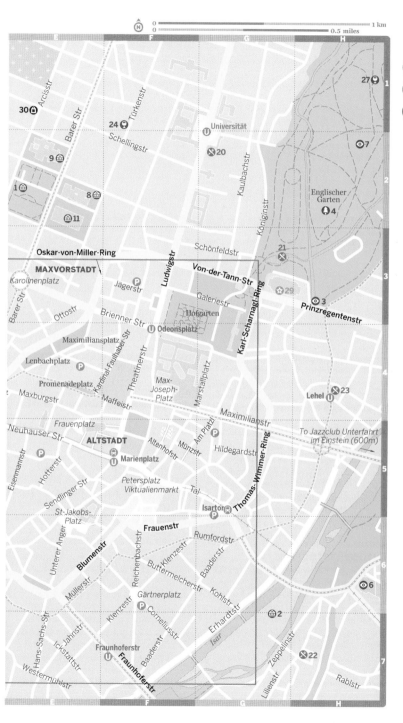

0 — 1 km
0 — 0.5 miles
Ⓝ

Arcisstr

30🔒

Barer Str

Türkenstr

24☕

Schellingstr

Ⓤ Universität

30🔒

9🏛

8🏛

1🏛

🏛11

Kaulbachstr

Königinstr

⊙7

Englischer
Garten

♨4

Oskar-von-Miller-Ring

Schönfeldstr

MAXVORSTADT

Karolinenplatz

Ludwigstr

Von-der-Tann-Str

21
✕

☆29

⊙3

Barer Str

Jägerstr

Ottostr

Brienner Str

Galeriestr

Hofgarten

Prinzregenstr

Maximiliansplatz

Kardinal-Faulhaber-Str

Theatinerstr

Ⓤ Odeonsplatz

Karl-Scharnagl-Ring

Lenbachplatz

Promenadeplatz

Maffeistr

Max-
Joseph-
Platz

Marstallplatz

Lehel Ⓤ ✕23

Maxburgstr

Frauenplatz

Neuhauser Str

ALTSTADT

Altenhofstr

Maximilianstr

Eisenmannstr

Hotterstr

Ⓤ Marienplatz

Am Platzl

Münzstr

Hildegardstr

To Jazzclub Unterfahrt
im Einstein (600m)

Sendlinger Str

Petersplatz
Viktualienmarkt

Tal

Thomas-Wimmer-Ring

St-Jakobs-
Platz

Isartor 🚇

Frauenstr

Rumfordstr

Unterer Anger

Blumenstr

Reichenbachstr

Buttermelcherstr

Klenzestr

Baaderstr

Kohlstr

⊙6

Müllerstr

Gärtnerplatz

🏛2

Hans-Sachs-Str

Jahnstr

Klenzestr

Cornellusstr

Erhardtstr

Zeppelinstr

✕22

Ickstattstr

Fraunhoferstr
Ⓤ

Baaderstr

Isar

Fraunhoferstr

Westermühlstr

Lilienstr

Rablstr

Central Munich

JÜDISCHES MUSEUM   Museum

(Jewish Museum; Map p70; www.juedisches-museum-muenchen.de; St-Jakobs-Platz 16; adult/child €6/3; ◔10am-6pm Tue-Sun; ⓢ Sendlinger Tor, Ⓜ Sendlinger Tor) Coming to terms with its Nazi past has not historically been a priority in Munich, which is why the opening of the Jewish Museum in 2007 was hailed as a milestone. The permanent exhibit offers an insight into Jewish history, life and culture in Munich, creatively presented over three floors. The Holocaust is dealt with, but the accent is clearly on contemporary Jewish culture.

BIER &
OKTOBERFESTMUSEUM   Museum

(Beer & Oktoberfest Museum; Map p70; www.bier-und-oktoberfestmuseum.de; Sterneckerstrasse 2; adult/concession €4/2.50; ◔1-5pm Tue-Sat; Ⓜ Isartor, Ⓜ Isartor) Head to this popular museum to learn all about Bavarian suds and the world's most famous booze-up. The four floors heave with old brewing vats, historic photos and some of the earliest Oktoberfest regalia. The 14th-century building has some fine medieval features, including painted ceilings and a kitchen with an open fire. There's an earthy pub downstairs (evenings only).

ASAMKIRCHE   Church

(Map p70; Sendlinger Strasse 34; ⓢ Sendlinger Tor, Ⓜ Sendlinger Tor) Though pocket-sized, the late-baroque Asamkirche, built in 1746, is as rich and epic as a giant's treasure chest. Its creators, the brothers Cosmas Damian Asam and Egid Quirin Asam, dipped deeply into their considerable talent box to swathe every inch of wall space with paintings, *putti* (cherubs), gold leaf and stucco flourishes.

Residenz & Around

The Residenz (p75) is a suitably grand palace that reflects the splendour and power of the Wittelsbach clan, the Bavarian rulers who lived here from 1385 to 1918.

Four giant bronze **lion statues** (Map p70) guard the entrance to the palace on Residenzstrasse, supported by pedestals festooned with a half-human, half-animal face. Note the creatures' remarkably shiny noses. If you wait a moment, you'll see the reason for the sheen: scores of people walk by and casually rub one or all four noses. It's supposed to bring wealth and good luck.

SCHATZKAMMER DER RESIDENZ
Museum

(Residence Treasury; Map p70; adult/concession/under 18yr with parents €7/6/free; ⊙9am-6pm Apr–mid-Oct, 10am-5pm mid-Oct–Mar) The Residenzmuseum entrance also leads to the Schatzkammer der Residenz, a veritable banker's bonus worth of jewel-encrusted bling of yesteryear, from golden toothpicks to finely crafted swords, miniatures in ivory to gold entombed cosmetics trunks.

CUVILLIÉS-THEATER
Theatre

(Map p70; adult/child €3.50/free; ⊙2-6pm Mon-Sat, from 9am Sun Apr-Jul & mid-Sep–mid-Oct, 9am-6pm daily Aug–mid-Sep, shorter hours mid-Oct–Mar) Commissioned by Maximilian III in the mid-18th century, François Cuvilliés fashioned one of Europe's finest rococo theatres. Famous for hosting the premiere of Mozart's opera *Idomeneo*, the theatre had restoration work done in the mid noughties that revived its former glory and its stage once again hosts high-brow musical and operatic performances.

FELDHERRNHALLE
Historic Building

(Field Marshalls Hall; Map p70; Residenzstrasse 1; [S] Odeonsplatz) Corking up Odeonsplatz's south side is Friedrich von Gärnter's Feldherrnhalle, modelled on the Loggia dei Lanzi in Florence.

It was here on 9 November 1923 that police stopped the so-called Beer Hall Putsch, Hitler's attempt to bring down the Weimar Republic. A fierce skirmish left 20 people, including 16 Nazis, dead. A plaque in the pavement of the square's eastern side commemorates the police officers who perished in the incident.

THEATINERKIRCHE
Church

(Map p70; Theatinerstrasse 22; [S] Odeonsplatz) Also known at St Kajetan's, the mustard-yellow Theatinerkirche, built to commemorate the 1662 birth of Prince Max Emanuel, was dreamed up by Swiss architect Enrico Zuccalli. It's a voluptuous design with two massive twin towers flanking a giant cupola (dome). Inside, an intensely ornate dome lords over the *Fürstengruft* (royal crypt), the final destination of several Wittelsbach rulers, including King Maximilian II (1811–64).

Maxvorstadt & the Englischer Garten

ALTE PINAKOTHEK
Art Museum

(Map p66; www.pinakothek.de; Barer Strasse 27; adult/child €7/5, Sun €1, audio guide €4.50; ⊙10am-8pm Tue, to 6pm Wed-Sun; 🚉 Pinakotheken, 🚌 Pinakotheken) Munich's main repository of Old European Masters is crammed with all the major players that decorated canvases between the 14th and 18th centuries. This neoclassical temple was masterminded by Leo von Klenze and is a delicacy even if you can't tell your Rembrandt from your Rubens.

The collection is world famous for its exceptional quality and depth, especially when it comes to German masters. The oldest works are altar paintings, of which the *Four Church Fathers* (1483) by Michael Pacher, and Lucas Cranach the Elder's *Crucifixion* (1503), an emotional rendition of the suffering Jesus, stand out.

NEUE PINAKOTHEK
Art Museum

(Map p66; www.pinakothek.de; Barer Strasse 29; adult/child €7/5, Sun €1; ⊙10am-6pm Thu-Mon, to 8pm Wed; 🚉 Pinakotheken, 🚌 Pinakotheken) Picking up where the Alte Pinakothek leaves off, the Neue Pinakothek harbours a well-respected collection of 19th- and early-20th-century paintings and sculpture, from rococo to Jugendstil (art nouveau).

All the world-famous household names get wall space here, including crowd-pleasing French impressionists such as Monet, Cézanne and Degas as well as Van Gogh, whose bold pigmented *Sunflowers* (1888) radiates cheer.

PINAKOTHEK DER MODERNE
Art Museum

(Map p66; www.pinakothek.de; Barer Strasse 40; adult/child €10/7, Sun €1; ⊙10am-6pm Tue, Wed & Fri-Sun, 10am-8pm Thu; 🚉 Pinakotheken, 🚌 Pinakotheken) Germany's largest modern art museum opened in 2002 in a blockbusting building by Stephan Braunfels that sets the perfect stage for

Munich Altstadt

MUNICH MUNICH

0.25 miles
500 m

MAXVORSTADT

Königinstr

Von-der-Tann-Str

Karl-Scharnagl-Ring

Galeriestr

Hofgarten

Ludwigstr

46

Brienner Str

Odeonsplatz U

18

Jägerstr

Oskar-von-Miller-Ring

33

Maximiliansplatz

Ottostr

Lenbachplatz

Maxburgstr

Barer Str

Karolinenplatz

Karlstr

Elisenstr

Alter Botanischer Garten

Palace of Justice

Karlsplatz

Karlsplatz

Schützenstr

To Hauptbahnhof (100m)

20

Neuhauser Str

Herzogspitalstr

Zweigstr

Adolf-Kolping-Str

49

29

23

21

Altheimer Eck

13

Frauenplatz

Kaufingerstr

Marienplatz U

7

Schäfflerstr

Löwengrube

Promenadeplatz

22

Kardinal-Faulhaber-Str

Salvatorstr

Maffeistr

Theatinerstr

54

Residenzstr

6

11
2

8

10

15

5

Residenzmuseum

16

Max-Joseph-Platz

51
48

Marstallstr

Maximilianstr

Am Platzl

Hofbräuhaus

44

28

Hildegardstr

Neuturmstr

Münzstr

Pfisterstr

Sparkassenstr

Altenhofstr

Hofgraben

Schrammerstr

14
Tourist
Office
12

Ledererstr

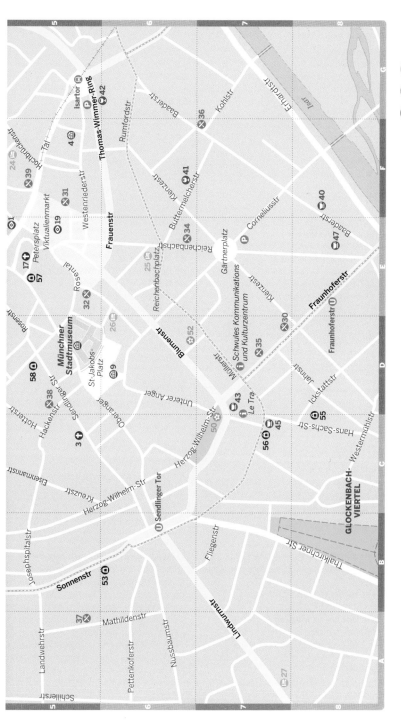

Munich Altstadt

◎ Top Sights

◎ Sights

◎ Activities, Courses & Tours

◎ Sleeping

◎ Eating

◎ Drinking

◎ Entertainment

◎ Shopping

artists and designers who have dominated their respective fields throughout the last century.

The museum unites four significant collections under a single roof. The **State Gallery of Modern Art** has some exemplary modern classics by Picasso, Klee, Dalí and Kandinsky, and many lesser-known works that will be new to many visitors.

In a world obsessed by retro style, the **New Collection** is the busiest section of

the museum. Housed in the basement it focuses on applied design from the industrial revolution via art nouveau and Bauhaus to today. VW Beetles, Eames chairs and early Apple Macs stand alongside more obscure interwar items that wouldn't be out of place in a Kraftwerk video.

The **State Graphics Collection** boasts 400,000 pieces of art on paper, including drawings, prints and engravings by such craftsmen as Leonardo da Vinci and Paul Cézanne.

Finally, there's the **Architecture Museum**, with entire studios of drawings, blueprints, photographs and models by such top practitioners as baroque architect Balthasar Neumann, Bauhaus maven Le Corbusier and 1920s expressionist Erich Mendelsohn.

MUSEUM BRANDHORST Gallery
(Map p66; www.museum-brandhorst.de; Theresienstrasse 35a; adult/child €7/5, Sun €1; ⏱10am-8pm Tue, to 6pm Wed-Sun; 🚊Maxvorstadt/Sammlung Brandhorst, 🚊Pinakotheken) A big, bold and aptly abstract building, clad entirely in vividly multihued ceramic tubes, the Brandhorst jostled its way into the Munich Kunstareal in a punk blaze of colour mid-2009. Its walls, floor and occasionally ceiling provide space for some of the most challenging works of art in the city, some of them instantly recognisable 20th-century images by Andy Warhol, who dominates the collection.

GLYPTOTHEK Art Museum
(Map p66; www.antike-am-koenigsplatz.mwn.de; Königsplatz 3; adult/concession €3.50/2.50, Sun €1; ⏱10am-5pm, to 8pm Thu, closed Mon; 🚊Königsplatz, Ⓢ Königsplatz) If you're a fan of classical art or simply enjoy the sight of naked guys without noses (or other pertinent body parts), make a beeline to the Glyptothek. One of Munich's oldest museums, it's a feast of art and sculpture from ancient Greece and Rome.

An undisputed highlight is the marble *Barberini Faun* (220 BC), a sleeping satyr rendered in meticulous anatomical detail and striking a pose usually assumed by racy centrefolds.

ENGLISCHER GARTEN Park
(Map p66; Ⓢ Universität) The sprawling English Garden is among Europe's biggest city parks – bigger than even London's Hyde Park and New York's Central Park and a favourite playground for locals and visitors alike.

Several historic follies lend the park a playful charm. The wholly unexpected Chinesischer Turm (p83; Chinese Tower), now at the heart of Munich's oldest beer garden, was built in the 18th century during a pan-European craze for all things oriental. Further south, at the top of a gentle hill, stands the heavily photographed 1838 **Monopteros** (Map p66), a small Greek temple. Its ledges are often knee-to-knee with dangling legs belonging to people admiring the view of the Munich skyline.

Another hint of Asia awaits further south at the **Japanisches Teehaus** (Japanese Teahouse; Map p66; ☎224 319; ⏱3pm, 4pm, 5pm Sat & Sun Apr-Oct), built for the 1972 Olympics beside an idyllic duck pond.

South of the Altstadt
DEUTSCHES MUSEUM Museum
(Map p66; ☎21 791; www.deutsches-museum.de; Museumsinsel 1; adult/child €8.50/3; ⏱9am-5pm; 🚊Deutsches Museum) If you're one of those people for whom science is an

Chinesischer Turm (p83)
HANS-PETER MERTEN/GETTY IMAGES ©

No Wave Goodbye

Possibly the last sport you might expect to see being practised in Munich is surfing, but go to the southern tip of the English Garden at Prinzregentenstrasse and you'll see scores of people leaning over a bridge to cheer on wetsuit-clad daredevils as they hang on an artificially created wave in the **Eisbach** (Map p66). It's only a single wave, but it's a damn fine one.

unfathomable turn-off, a visit to the Deutsches Museum might just show you that physics and engineering are more fun than you thought. Spending a few hours in this temple to technology is an eye-opening journey of discovery and the exhibitions and demonstrations will certainly be a hit with young, spongelike minds.

There are tons of interactive displays (including glass blowing and paper making), live demonstrations and experiments, model coal and salt mines, and engaging sections on cave paintings, geodesy, microelectronics and astronomy. In fact, it can be pretty overwhelming after a while, so it's best to prioritise what you want to see. The place to entertain little ones is the fabulous **KinderReich** (Childrens Kingdom; ⊘9am-4.30pm) where 1000 activities, from a kid-size mouse wheel to a fully explorable fire engine and heaps of colourful blocks, await.

The Deutsches Museum's collection is so huge that some sections have been moved to separate locations. Vehicles are now in the **Verkehrszentrum** (Transport & Mobility Centre; Map p66; ☑089 500 806 762; www.deutsches-museum.de/verkehrszentrum; Theresienhöhe 14a; adult/child €6/3; ⊘9am-5pm; [S]Theresienwiese), while aircraft are at the **Flugwerft Schleissheim** (☑315 7140; www.deutsches-museum.de/flugwerft; Effnerstrasse 18; adult/child €6/3; ⊘9am-5pm).

Combination tickets to all three museums cost €15 and may be used on separate days.

 ## Tours

RADIUS TOURS
Guided Tours

(Map p66; ☑543 487 7720; www.radiustours .com; opposite track 32, Hauptbahnhof; ⊘8.30am-6pm Apr-Oct, to 2pm Nov-Mar) Entertaining and informative English-language tours include the two-hour **Priceless Munich** (⊘10am daily) walk where you pay the guide as much as you think the tour was worth; the fascinating 2.½-hour **Hitler and The Third Reich** (adult/student €12/10; ⊘3pm Apr–mid-Oct, 11.30am Fri-Tue mid-Oct–Mar) tour; and the three-hour **Prost! Beer and Food** (☑5502 9374; www.radiusmunich.com; adult/student €22/€20; ⊘6pm selected days) tour. The company also runs popular excursions to Neuschwanstein, Salzburg and Dachau as well as a range of other themed tours.

MIKE'S BIKE TOURS
Bike Tours

(Map p70; ☑2554 3987; www.mikesbiketours .com; departs Altes Rathaus, Marienplatz; tours from €24) This outfit runs guided bike tours of the city from the Altes Rathaus on Marienplatz. The standard tour is around four hours long (with a one-hour beer garden break; lunch not included); the extended tour runs for seven hours and covers 15km.

MUNICH WALK TOURS
Walking Tours

(Map p66; ☑2423 1767; www.munichwalktours .de; Arnulfstrasse 2; tours from €12) In addition to running an almost identical roster to Munich's other tour companies and acting as an agent for them (see website for times and prices), this place also hires out bicycles (€15 per 24 hours) and offers internet access (€1 per 45 minutes).

GRAYLINE HOP-ON-HOP-OFF TOURS
Bus Tours

(www.grayline.com/Munich; adult/child from €13/7; ⊘every 20min) This tour-bus company offers a choice of three tours from one-hour highlights to 2½-hour grand

PNC/GETTY IMAGES ©

Don't Miss **Residenzmuseum**

Home to the Bavaria's Wittelsbach rulers from 1508 until WWI, the **Residenz** is Munich's number one attraction. The amazing treasures, as well as all the trappings of their lifestyles over the centuries, are on display at the Residenzmuseum, which takes up around half of the palace. Allow at least two hours to see everything at a gallop.

The tours kick off at the **Grottenhof**, home of the wonderful *Perseusbrunnen* (Perseus Fountain), with its namesake holding the dripping head of Medusa. Next door is the famous **Antiquarium**, a barrel-vaulted hall smothered in frescoes and built to house the Wittelsbach's enormous antique collection. It's widely regarded as the finest Renaissance interior north of the Alps. Further along the tour route, the neo-Byzantine **Hofkirche** was built for Ludwig I in 1826. After WWII only the red-brick walls were left. It reopened as an atmospheric concert venue in 2003.

Upstairs are the **Kurfürstenzimmer** (Elector's Rooms), with some stunning Italian portraits and a passage lined with two dozen views of Italy, painted by local romantic artist Carl Rottmann. Also up here are François Cuvilliés' **Reiche Zimmer** (Rich Rooms), a six-room extravaganza of exuberant rococo carried out by the top stucco and fresco artists of the day; they're a definite highlight. More rococo magic awaits in the **Ahnengallery** (pictured above), with 121 portraits of the rulers of Bavaria in chronological order.

The **Hofkapelle**, reserved for the ruler and his family, fades quickly in the memory when you see the exquisite **Reichekapelle** with its blue and gilt ceiling, inlaid marble and 16th-century organ. Considered the finest rococo interior in southern Germany, the **Steinzimmer** (Stone Room) is another spot to linger longer. It was the emperor's quarters and is awash with intricately patterned and coloured marble.

NEED TO KNOW

Map p70; ☏ 290 671; www.residenz-muenchen.de; adult/child €7/free, combination ticket for the museum, Schatzkammer and Cuvilliés-Theater €13/free; ⏱ 9am-6pm Apr–mid-Oct, 10am-5pm mid-Oct–Mar

Munich for Kids

There are plenty of parks for romping around, swimming pools and lakes for cooling off and family-friendly beer gardens with children's playgrounds for making new friends. Many museums have special kid-oriented programs, but the highly interactive Deutches Museum (p73) specifically lures the single-digit set.

Kids love animals, of course, making the zoo **Tierpark Hellabrunn** (Hellabrunn Zoo; 625 080; www.tierpark-hellabrunn.de; Tierparkstrasse 30; adult/child €11/4.50; 9am-6pm Apr-Sep, to 5pm Oct-Mar; 52 from Marienplatz) a sure bet. Petting baby goats, feeding pelicans, watching falcons and hawks perform, or even riding a camel should make for some unforgettable memories. For a fishy immersion head to the new **SeaLife München** (Willi-Daume-Platz 1; adult/child 3-14yr €15.95/10.50; 10am-7pm; S Olympiazentrum) in the Olympic Park. Dino fans gravitate to **Paläontologisches Museum** (Palaeontological Museum; Map p66; 2180 6630; www.palmuc.de; Richard-Wagner-Strasse 10; admission free; 8am-4pm Mon-Thu, to 2pm Fri; Königsplatz, S Königsplatz), while budding scientists will find plenty to marvel at in the **Museum Mensch und Natur** (Museum of Humankind & Nature; 179 5890; www.musmn.de; Schloss Nymphenburg; adult/child €3/2, Sun €1; 9am-5pm Tue, Wed & Fri, to 8pm Thu, 10am-6pm Sat & Sun; Schloss Nymphenburg) in Schloss Nymphenburg.

The adorable singing and dancing marionettes performing at the **Münchner Marionettentheater** (Map p70; 265 712; www.muenchner-marionettentheater.de; Blumenstrasse 32; tickets €8-18; 3pm Wed-Sun, 8pm Sat) have enthralled generations of wee ones. At the **Münchner Theater für Kinder** (Map p66; 594 545; www.muenchner-theater-fuer-kinder.de; Dachauer Strasse 46; tickets €8-11) budding thespians can enjoy fairy tales and children's classics à la *Max & Moritz* and *Pinocchio*.

tour, as well as excursions to Ludwig II's castles, the Romantic Road, Dachau, Berchtesgaden, Zugspitze and Salzburg. All tours can be booked online and buses are of a recent vintage. The main **departure point** (Map p70) is outside the Karstadt department store opposite the Hauptbahnhof.

NEW MUNICH   Walking Tours
(www.newmunich.com; walking tour 10.45am & 1pm) Departing from Marienplatz, these English-language walking tou rs tick off all Munich's central landmarks in three hours. Guides are well informed and fun, though they are under pressure to get as much as they can in tips at the end of the tour. The company runs a number of other tours to Dachau (€21) and Neuschwanstein (€35) as well as a four-hour pub crawl (€14) from the Hauptbahnhof.

Sleeping

Altstadt & Around

BAYERISCHER HOF   Hotel €€€
(Map p70; 212 00; www.bayerischerhof.de; Promenadeplatz 2-6; r €250-450; Theatinerstrasse) One of the grande dames of the Munich hotel trade, rooms at the Hof come in a number of styles, from busy Laura Ashley to minimalist cosmopolitan. The super central location, pool and on-site cinema come in addition to impeccably behaved staff. Marble, antiques and oil paintings abound, and with ample cash you can dine till you burst at any one of the five fabulous restaurants.

CORTIINA   Hotel €€€
(Map p70; 242 2490; www.cortiina.com; Ledererstrasse 8; s €165-270, d €225-345; P S Marienplatz, Marienplatz) Tiptoeing between hip and haute, this hotel scores

best with trendy, design-minded travellers. The street-level lounge usually buzzes with cocktail-swigging belles and beaus, but all traces of hustle evaporate the moment you step into your minimalist, feng shui–inspired room.

HOTEL BLAUER BOCK
Hotel €€

(Map p70; ☎ 231 780; www.hotelblauerbock.de; Sebastiansplatz 9; s €55-99, d €90-153; 🛜; Ⓢ Marienplatz, Ⓡ Marienplatz) A stuffed olive's throw away from the Viktualienmarkt, this simple hotel has successfully slipped through the net of gentrification to become the Altstadt's best deal. The cheapest, unmodernised rooms have shared facilities, the updated en suite chambers are of a 21st-century vintage, and all are quiet, despite the location. Superb restaurant.

HOTEL MANDARIN ORIENTAL MUNICH
Hotel €€€

(Map p70; ☎ 290 980; www.mandarinoriental .com; Neuturmstrasse 1; d €525-645; Ⓟ ❄ @ 🛜 ✈; Ⓢ Marienplatz, Ⓡ Marienplatz) These magnificent neo-Renaissance digs lure the world's glamourous, rich, powerful and famous with opulently understated rooms and top-notch service. Paul McCartney,

Bill Clinton and Prince Charles have crumpled the sheets here. Service is polite almost to a fault, but incredibly breakfast and internet access are extra.

HOTEL AM VIKTUALIENMARKT
Hotel €€

(Map p70; ☎ 231 1090; www.hotel-am -viktualienmarkt.de; Utzschneider-strasse 14; d €50-120; 🛜; Ⓢ Marienplatz, Ⓡ Marienplatz) Owners Elke and her daughter Stephanie run this good-value property with panache and a sunny attitude. The best of the up-to-date 26 rooms have wooden floors and framed poster art. All this, plus the city-centre location, makes it a superb deal.

Around the Hauptbahnhof

ANNA HOTEL
Design Hotel €€€

(Map p70; ☎ 599 940; www.geisel-privathotels .de; Schützenstrasse 1; s €160-215, d €175-235; ❄ @; Ⓢ Karlsplatz, Ⓡ Karlsplatz, Ⓡ Karlsplatz) Urban sophisticates love this designer den where you can retire to rooms dressed in sensuous Donghia furniture and regal colours, or others with a minimalist feel tempered by teakwood, marble and mosaics. The swanky restaurant-bar here is a 24/7 beehive of activity.

Deutches Museum (p73)

HOTEL COCOON
Design Hotel €€

(Map p70; ☎5999 3907; www.hotel-cocoon.de; Lindwurmstrasse 35; s/d €79/99; Ⓢ Sendlinger Tor, Ⓜ Sendlinger Tor) If retro design is your thing, you just struck gold. Things kick off in the reception with faux '70s veneer and suspended '60s ball chairs, and continue in the rooms, which are all identical in cool oranges and greens. Every room has LCD TV, iPod dock, 'laptop cabin' and the hotel name above every bed in 1980s-style robotic lettering.

The glass showers actually stand in the sleeping area, with only a kitschy Alpine meadow scene veiling life's vitals. Another branch, **Cocoon Stachus** (Map p70; Adolf-Kolping-Strasse 11), opened in 2012.

SCHILLER 5
Hotel €€

(Map p70; ☎515 040; www.schiller5.com; Schillerstrasse 5; s/d from €102/144; Ⓟ ❄ ⓦ; Ⓢ Hauptbahnhof, Ⓜ Hauptbahnhof, Ⓡ Hauptbahnhof) Not only are the pads at this semi-apartment hotel smartly trimmed, you also get a lot for your euro here in the shape of a well-equipped kitchenette, sound system, coffee machine and extra large bed in every room. Some guests complain of street noise so try to bag a room away from the hustle below.

SOFITEL MUNICH BAYERPOST
Hotel €€€

(Map p66; ☎599 480; www.sofitel.com; Bayerstrasse 12; s/d from €140/160; Ⓟ ❄ @ ⓦ; Ⓢ Hauptbahnhof, Ⓜ Hauptbahnhof Süd, Ⓡ Hauptbahnhof) The restored Renaissance facade of a former post office hides this high-concept jewel, which wraps all that's great about Munich – history, innovation, elegance, the art of living – into one neat and appealing package. Be sure to make time for the luxurious spa; its grotto-like pool juts into the atrium lobby lidded by a tinted glass roof.

WOMBAT'S HOSTEL
Hostel €

(Map p66; ☎5998 9180; www.wombats-hostels .com; Senefelderstrasse 1; dm €12-24, d from €70; @ ⓦ; Ⓢ Hauptbahnhof, Ⓜ Hauptbahnhof, Ⓡ Hauptbahnhof) Munich's top hostel is a professionally run affair with a whopping 300 dorm beds plus private rooms. Dorms are basic with no frill or theme, but with en suite facilities, sturdy lockers and comfy pine bunks in a central location near the train station, who needs gimmicks? A free welcome drink awaits in the bar, but breakfast is €3.80 extra.

HOTEL UHLAND
Hotel €€

(Map p66; ☎543 350; www.hotel -uhland.de; Uhlandstrasse 1; s/d from €69/87; Ⓟ ⓦ; Ⓢ Theresienwiese) The Uhland is an enduring favourite with regulars who expect their hotel to feel like a home away from home. Three generations of family members are constantly finding ways to improve their guests' experience, be it with wi-fi, bathroom phones, ice cubes, bike hire or mix-your-own organic breakfast muesli.

BMW-Welt

HOTEL MARIANDL

Hotel €€

(Map p66; ☎552 9100; www.mariandl.com; Goethestrasse 51; s €65-115, d €70-165; Ⓢ Sendlinger Tor, Ⓜ Sendlinger Tor) If you like your history laced with quirkiness, you'll find both aplenty in this rambling neo-Gothic mansion. It's an utterly charming place where rooms convincingly capture the Jugendstil period with hand-selected antiques and ornamented ceilings. Breakfast is served until 4pm in the Vienna-style downstairs cafe, which also has live jazz or classical music nightly.

MEININGER'S

Hostel, Hotel €

(Map p66; ☎5499 8023; www.meininger-hostels .de; Landsbergerstrasse 20; dm/s/d without breakfast from €15/45/80; @ 🛜; Ⓜ Holzapfelstrasse.) About 800m west of the Hauptbahnhof, this energetic hostel-hotel has basic, clean and bright rooms with big dorms divided into two for a bit of privacy. Room rates vary wildly depending on date, events taking place in Munich and occupancy. Breakfast is an extra €4, bike hire €12 per day.

Englischer Garten & Around

LA MAISON

Design Hotel €€

(☎3303 5550; www.hotel-la-maison.com; Occamstrasse 24; s/d from €109/119; P ❄ @; Ⓢ Münchner Freiheit) Discerningly retro and immaculate in shades of imperial purple and uber-cool grey, this sassy number wows with its rooms flaunting heated oak floors, jet-black washbasins and starkly contrasting design throughout, though the operators still can't resist the coy pack of gummi bears on the expertly ruffed pillows! Cool bar on ground level.

GÄSTEHAUS ENGLISCHER GARTEN

Guesthouse €€

(☎383 9410; www.hotelenglischergarten.de; Liebergesellstrasse 8; s €68-177, d €79-177; P @ 🛜; Ⓢ Münchner Freiheit) Cosily inserted into a 200-year-old ivy-clad mill, this small guesthouse on the edge of the English Garden offers a Bavarian version of the British B&B experience. Not all rooms are en suite, but the breakfast is generous and there's cycle hire (€12 per day).

Detour: BMW-Welt & Museum

The glass and steel double-cone tornado spiralling down from a dark cloud the size of an aircraft carrier next to the Olympiapark is the Wagnerian chunk of 21st-century architecture that holds **BMW-Welt** (BMW World; ☎0180-2118 822; www.bmw -welt.de; admission free, tours adult/child €7/5; ☉9am-6pm; Ⓢ Olympiazentrum). This is truly a petrol head's wet dream.

Straddle a powerful motorbike, marvel at technology-packed saloons and estates (no tyre kicking please), browse the 'lifestyle' shop or take the 80-minute guided tour.

BMW Welt is linked via a bridge to BMW Headquarters – another stunning building of four gleaming cylinders – and to the silver bowl-shaped **BMW Museum** (www.bmw -welt.de; adult/child €12/6; ☉10am-6pm Tue-Sun). The seven themed 'houses' examine the development of BMW's product line and include sections on motorcycles and motor racing. However, the interior design of this truly unique building, with its curvy retro feel, futuristic bridges, squares and huge backlit wall screens, almost upstages the exhibits.

PENSION AM KAISERPLATZ

Guesthouse €

(☎395 231, 349 190; www.amkaiserplatz.de; Kaiserplatz 12; s €35-49, d €53-67; 🛜; Ⓜ Kurfürstenplatz) One of the best value places to stay in the city centre, this family-run B&B in a grand Jugendstil building has generously cut, high-ceilinged rooms furnished with four decades worth of furniture. Continental breakfast is served in your room by the always-around-to-help owners.

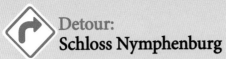

Detour:
Schloss Nymphenburg

This commanding **palace** (www.schloss-nymphenburg.de; adult/child €6/5; ⏲9am-6pm Apr–mid-Oct, 10am-4pm mid-Oct–Mar; 🚇Schloss Nymphenburg) and its lavish gardens sprawl around 5km northwest of the Altstadt. Begun in 1664 as a villa for Electress Adelaide of Savoy, the stately pile was extended over the next century to create the royal family's summer residence. The main palace building consists of a large villa and two wings of creaking parquet floors and sumptuous period rooms. Right at the beginning of the self-guided tour comes the high point of the entire Schloss, the **Schönheitengalerie** (Gallery of Beauties; 📞179 080; Schloss Nymphenburg; ⏲9am-6pm Apr–mid-Oct, 10am-4pm mid-Oct–Mar), housed in the former apartments of Queen Caroline. Some 38 portraits of attractive females chosen by an admiring King Ludwig I peer prettily from the walls. Further along the tour route comes the **Queen's Bedroom**, which still contains the sleigh bed on which Ludwig II was born, and the **King's Chamber**, resplendent with three-dimentional ceiling frescoes. Also in the main building is the **Marstall-museum** (adult/concession €4.50/3.50; ⏲9am-6pm Apr–mid-Oct, 10am-4pm mid-Oct–Mar), displaying royal coaches and riding gear. This includes Ludwig II's fairy-tale-like rococo sleigh, ingeniously fitted with oil lamps for his crazed nocturnal outings. The sprawling park behind Schloss Nymphenburg is a favourite spot with Münchners and visitors for strolling, jogging or whiling away a lazy afternoon.

Toilets are shared but there are in-room showers (literally). Cash only.

Eating

Munich's food was once described by Viennese actor Helmut Qualtinger as 'garnish for the beer', and while that may still ring true in traditional beer halls and restaurants, where the menu rarely ventures beyond the roast pork and sausage routine, elsewhere Munich can claim to have southern Germany's most exciting cuisine scene. There's lots of exciting innovation going on in Munich's kitchens, where the best dishes make use of fresh regional, seasonal and organic ingredients. The Bavarian capital is also the best place between Vienna and Paris for a spot of internationally flavoured dining, especially when it comes to Italian and Afghan food, and even vegetarians can look forward to something other than noodles and salads.

FRAUNHOFER Bavarian €€
(Map p70; Fraunhoferstrasse 9; mains €7-17.50; ⏲4pm-1am; 🔀; 🚇Müllerstrasse) With its screechy parquet floors, stuccoed ceilings, wood panelling and virtually no trace that the last century even happened, this wonderfully characterful brewpub is one of the city centre's best places to explore the region with a fork. The menu is a checklist of southern German favourites, but also features at least a dozen vegetarian dishes as well as Starnberg fish.

TANTRIS Fine Dining €€€
(📞361 9590; www.tantris.de; Johann-Fichte-Strasse 7; menu from €75; ⏲lunch & dinner Tue-Sat; Ⓢ Dietlindenstrasse) Tantris means 'the search for perfection' and here, at one of Germany's most famous restaurants, they're not far off it. The interior design is full-bodied '70s - all postbox reds, truffle blacks and illuminated yellows - the food gourmet sublimity and the service sometimes as unintrusive as it is efficient. The wine cellar is probably Germany's best. Reservations and a fat wallet essential.

BRATWURSTHERZL
Franconian €

(Map p70; ☎295 113; Dreifaltigkeitsplatz 1; mains €6-10; ☺10am-11pm Mon-Sat; Ⓢ Marienplatz, Ⓡ Marienplatz) Cosy panelling and an ancient vaulted brick ceiling set the tone of this Old Munich chow house with a Franconian focus. Homemade organic sausages are grilled to perfection on an open beechwood fire and served on heart-shaped pewter plates. They're best enjoyed with a cold beer straight from the wooden keg.

KÖNIGSQUELLE
Alpine €€

(Map p70; ☎220 071; Baaderplatz 2; mains €9-18; ☺dinner; Ⓡ Isartor, Ⓡ Isartor) This Munich institution is well loved for its attentive service, expertly prepared food and dark, well-stocked hardwood bar containing what must be the Bavarian capital's best selection of malt whiskys. The hardly decipherable, handwritten menu hovers somewhere mid-Alps with anything from schnitzel to linguine and goat's cheese or cannelloni to choose from.

WEISSES BRAUHAUS
Bavarian €€

(Map p70; Tal 7; mains €8-15; Ⓢ Marienplatz, Ⓡ Marienplatz) The *Weisswurst* (veal sausage) sets the standard for the rest to aspire to; sluice down a pair with the unsurpassed Schneider *Weissbier*. Of an evening the dining halls are charged with red-faced, ale-infused hilarity, with Alpine whoops accompanying the rabble-rousing oompah band.

WIRTSHAUS IN DER AU
Bavarian €€

(Map p66; ☎448 1400; Lilienstrasse 51; mains €8-19; ☺5pm-midnight Mon-Fri, from 10am Sat & Sun; Ⓡ Deutsches Museum) Though this traditional Bavarian restaurant has a solid 21st-century vibe, it's that time-honoured staple the dumpling that's been declared speciality here (it even runs a dumpling-making course in English). Once a brewery, the space-rich indoor dining area has chunky tiled floors, a lofty ceiling and a crackling fireplace in winter. When spring springs, the beer garden fills.

PRINZ MYSHKIN
Vegetarian €€

(Map p70; ☎265 596; www.prinzmyshkin.com; Hackenstrasse 2; mains €10-17; ☺11am-12.30am; ☑; Ⓢ Marienplatz, Ⓡ Marienplatz) This place is proof, if any were needed, that the vegetarian experience has left the sandals, beards and lentils era. Munich's premier meat-free dining spot fills out an open-plan, but strangely intimate vaulted dining space, a former brewery, with health-conscious eaters, who come to savour

Schloss Nymphenburg

imaginative dishes such as curry-orange-carrot soup, tofu stroganoff, 'Save the Tuna' pizza and unexpectedly good curries.

LA VECCHIA MASSERIA · Italian €€

(Map p70; Mathildenstrasse 3; mains €6-15; ⏱11.30am-12.30am; S Sendlinger Tor, 🚇Sendlinger Tor) One of Munich's more typically Italian *osteria*, this loud but unquestionably romantic place has earthy wooden tables, antique tin buckets, baskets and clothing irons conjuring up the ambience of an Apennine farmhouse. If you're (un)lucky the chef might come out to greet you in his trademark straw hat.

POTTING SHED · Burgers €€

(Occamstrasse 11; tapas €2.50-10.50, burgers €11.50-13.90; ⏱from 6pm; S Münchner Freiheit) This relaxed hang-out serves tapas, gourmet burgers and cocktails to an easy-going evening crowd. The burger menu whisks you round the globe, but it's the house speciality, the 'Potting Shed Special' involving an organic beef burger flambéed in whisky, that catches the eye on the simple but well-concocted menu.

CAFE LUITPOLD · Cafe €€

(Map p70; www.cafe-luitpold.de; Briennerstrasse 11; mains €10-18; ⏱8am-7pm Mon, to 11pm Tue-Sat, 9am-7pm Sun; S Odeonsplatz) A cluster of postbox-red streetside tables and chairs announces you've arrived at this stylish but not uber-cool retreat. It offers a choice of three spaces – a lively bar, a less-boisterous columned cafe and a cool palm-leaved atrium. Good for a daytime coffee and cake halt or a full evening blow-out with all the trimmings.

CAFÉ AN DER UNI · Cafe €

(Map p66; Ludwigstrasse 24; snacks & mains €5-9; ⏱8am-1am Mon-Fri, from 9am Sat & Sun; 📶🖊; S Universität) Anytime is a good time to be at charismatic CADU. Enjoy breakfast (served until a hangover-friendly 11.30pm), a cuppa java or a Helles (light beer) in the lovely garden hidden by a wall from busy Ludwigstrasse.

XII APOSTEL · Italian €€

(Map p66; Thierschplatz 6; mains €6-17; ⏱11am-1am Mon-Fri & Sun, noon-2am Sat; 🚇Lehel) Despite the expensive, exclusive feel of the dramatic dining space at this new, somewhat overstyled Italian job, resplendent in high ceiling frescoes, wood panelling and Chester-field-style seating, the pizza-pasta menu here will not overwhelm your wallet. The triangular upstairs bar is a cool night spot in its own right. Staff speak little English.

BERGWOLF · Fast Food €

(Map p70; Fraunhoferstrasse 17; ⏱noon-2am Mon-Thu, to 4am Fri & Sat, to 10pm Sun, closed 3-6pm Sun-Fri; S Fraunhoferstrasse) At this favourite pit stop for night owls, the poison of choice is *Currywurst*, a sliced spicy sausage provocatively dressed in a curried ketchup and best paired with a pile of crisp fries.

CAFE FRISCHHUT · Cafe €

(Map p70; Prälat-Zistl-Strasse 8; pastries €1.70; ⏱7am-6pm Mon-Sat; S Marienplatz, 🚇Marienplatz) This incredibly

Patrons at Augustiner Bräustuben

Out & About in Munich

Munich's gay and lesbian scene is the liveliest in Bavaria but it's tame if compared to Berlin, Cologne or Amsterdam. The rainbow flag flies especially proudly along Müllerstrasse and the adjoining Glockenbachviertel and Gärtnerplatzviertel. To plug into the scene, keep an eye out for the freebie mags *Our Munich* and *Sergej,* which contain up-to-date listings and news about the community and gay-friendly establishments around town. Another source is www.gaymunich.de, which has a small section in English. For help with lodging, check out www.gaytouristoffice.com.

Max & Milian (Map p70; Ickstattstrasse 2) is Munich's bastion for queer lit, nonfiction and mags. **Sub** ('the Sub' or 'Schwules Kommunikations und Kulturzentrum'; 🖉 260 3056; www.subonline.org; Müllerstrasse 14; ☺ 7-11pm Sun-Thu, to midnight Fri & Sat) is a one-stop service and information agency; lesbians can also turn to **Le Tra** (🖉 725 4272; www.letra.de; Angertorstrasse 3; ☺ 2.30-5pm Mon & Wed, 10.30am-1pm Tue).

Favourite hang-outs include the cafe-bar **Nil** (Map p70; www.cafenil.com; Hans-Sachs-Strasse 2; meals €3.50-8; ☺ 3pm-3am), the gastropub **Deutsche Eiche** (Map p70; 🖉 231 1660; www.deutsche-eiche.com; Reichenbachstrasse 13), the **Prosecco** (Map p70; 🖉 2303 2329; www.prosecco-munich.de; Theklatstrasse 1) bar/club and **Bei Carla** (Map p70; 🖉 4187 4168; Buttermelcherstrasse 9) for lesbians.

popular institution serves just four traditional pastries, one of which – the *Schmalznudel* (an oily type of doughnut) – gives the place its local nickname. Every baked goodie you munch here is crisp and fragrant as they're always fresh off the hotplate out front.

 ## Drinking

Bavaria's brews are best sampled in a venerable old *Bierkeller* (beer hall) or *Biergarten* (beer garden). People come here primarily to drink, and although food may be served, it is generally an after-thought. In beer gardens you are usually allowed to bring your own picnic as long as you sit at tables without tablecloths and order something to drink. Sometimes there's a resident brass band pumping oompah music.

AUGUSTINER BRÄUSTUBEN   Beer Hall
(Map p66; Landsberger Strasse 19; ☺ 10am-midnight; 🚋 Holzapfelstrasse) Depending on the wind, an aroma of hops envelops you as you approach this ultra-authentic beer hall inside the actual Augustiner brewery,

popular with the brewmeisters themselves (there's an entire table reserved just for them). The Bavarian grub here is superb, especially the *Schweinshaxe* (pork knuckle).

HOFBRÄUHAUS   Beer Hall
(Map p70; Am Platzl 9; ☺ 9am-11.30pm; ⓢ Marienplatz, 🚋 Kammerspiele, Ⓤ Marienplatz) The mothership of all beer halls. Every visitor to Munich should, at some point, make a pilgrimage to this temple of ale, if only once. The swigging hordes of tourists, swaying to the inevitable oompah band, is like something from a film set.

CHINESISCHER TURM   Beer Garden
(Chinese Tower; Map p66; 🖉 383 8730; Englischer Garten 3; ☺ 10am-11pm; 🚋 Chinesischer Turm, 🚋 Tivolistrasse) This one's hard to ignore because of its English Garden location and pedigree as Munich's oldest beer garden (open since 1791). Camera-toting tourists and laid-back locals, picnicking families and businessmen sneaking a sly brew clomp around the wooden pagoda, showered by the strained sounds of an oompah band.

Oktoberfest

It all started as an elaborate wedding toast – and turned into the world's biggest collective booze-up. In October 1810 the future king, Bavarian Crown Prince Ludwig I, married Princess Therese and the newlyweds threw an enormous party at the city gates, complete with a horse race. The next year Ludwig's fun-loving subjects came back for more. The festival was extended and, to fend off autumn, was moved forward to September. As the years rolled on, the racehorses were dropped and sometimes the party had to be cancelled, but the institution called Oktoberfest was here to stay.

Nearly two centuries later, this 16-day extravaganza draws more than six million visitors a year to celebrate a marriage of good cheer and outright debauchery. A special beer is brewed for the occasion (Wies'nbier), which is dark and strong. Müncheners spend the day at the office in lederhosen and dirndl in order to hit the festival right after work.

On the meadow called Theresienwiese (Wies'n for short), a temporary city is erected, consisting of beer tents, amusements and rides – just what drinkers need after several frothy ones! The action kicks off with the Brewer's Parade at 11am on the first day of the festival. The parade begins at Sonnenstrasse and winds its way to the fairgrounds via Schwanthalerstrasse. At noon, the lord mayor stands before the thirsty crowds at Theresienwiese and, with due pomp, slams a wooden tap into a cask of beer. As the beer gushes out, the mayor exclaims, *O'zapft ist's!* (it's tapped!).

AUGUSTINER KELLER Beer Garden
(Map p66; ☎594 393; Arnulfstrasse 52; ☺10am-1am Apr-Oct; ⚌; ⌂Hopfenstrasse) Every year this leafy 5000-seat beer garden, about 500m west of the Hauptbahnhof, buzzes with fairy-lit thirst-quenching activity from the first sign that spring may have *gesprungen*. The ancient chestnuts are thick enough to seek refuge under when it rains, or else lug your mug to the actual beer cellar. Small playground.

HIRSCHAU Beer Garden
(☎322 1080; Gysslingstrasse 15; Ⓢ Dietlindenstrasse) This monster beer garden accommodates 1700 drinkers and puts on live jazz almost daily in summer. Dispatch the kids to the playground and adjacent minigolf course while you indulge in some tankard caressing.

ALTER SIMPL Pub
(Map p66; Türkenstrasse 57; ☺11am-3am Mon-Fri, to 4am Sat & Sun; ⌂Schellingstrasse) Thomas Mann and Hermann Hesse used to knock 'em back at this well-scuffed and wood-panelled thirst parlour. A bookishly intellectual ambience still pervades and this is an apt spot to curl up with a weighty tome over a few Irish ales. The curious name, by the way, is an abbreviation of the satirical magazine *Simplicissimus*.

BAADER CAFÉ Cafe
(Map p70; Baaderstrasse 47; ☺9.30am-1am; ⌂Fraunhoferstrasse) Around for over a quarter of a century, this literary think-and-drink place lures all sorts, from short skirts to tweed jackets, who linger over daytime coffees and night-hour cocktails. It's normally packed, even on winter Wednesday mornings, and is popular for Sunday brunch.

TRACHTENVOGL Cafe, Lounge
(Map p70; Reichenbachstrasse 47; ☺10am-1am Sun-Thu, to 2am Fri & Sat; ⌂Fraunhoferstrasse) At night you'll have to shoehorn your way into this buzzy lair favoured by a chatty, boozy crowd of scenesters, artists and

students. Daytimes are mellower, all the better to slurp its hot-chocolate menu and check out the cuckoo clocks and antlers, left over from the days when this was a folkoric garment shop.

SCHUMANN'S BAR
Bar

(Map p70; ☏ 229 060; Odeonsplatz 6-7; ⏱8am-3am Mon-Fri, 6pm-3am Sat & Sun; Ⓢ Odeonsplatz) Urbane and sophisticated, Schumann's has been shaking up Munich's nightlife with libational flights of fancy in an impressive range of more than 220 concoctions. It's also good for weekday breakfasts.

BRAUNAUER HOF
Beer Garden

(Map p70; ☏ 223 613; Frauenstrasse 42; ⏱11.30am-11pm Mon-Sat; 🚆 Isartor, 🚆 Isartor) Near the Isartor, this pleasingly twisted beer garden is centred on a snug courtyard. There's a hedge maze, a fresco with a bizarre bunch of historical figures and a golden bull that's illuminated at night.

CAFÉ AM HOCHHAUS
Cafe

(Map p70; www.cafeamhochhaus.de; Blumenstrasse 29; ⏱8pm-3am; 🚆 Müllerstrasse) Nightly DJs keep this tiny, grungey joint happy till the wee hours with standing room only and pavement spillout. Decor? Think chipped school chairs, black paint and funky photo wallpaper.

⭐ Entertainment

MÜNCHNER PHILHARMONIKER
Classical Music

(Map p66; ☏ 480 980; www .mphil.de; Rosenheimer Strasse 5; 🚆 Am Gasteig) Munich's premier orchestra regularly performs at the **Kulturzentrum Gasteig** (Gasteig Culture Centre; Map p66; ☏ 480 980; www .gasteig.de; Rosenheimer Strasse 5; 🚆 Am Gasteig). Book tickets early as performances usually sell out.

KULTFABRIK
Club Complex

(www.kultfabrik.de; Grafingerstrasse 6; 🚆 Ostbahnhof) If you've been to Munich before, you may remember this one-stop nightlife shop near the Ostbahnhof as Kunstpark Ost. Now the former dumpling factory has a different name but it still has more than a dozen, mostly mainstream, venues as well as numerous fast-food eateries, making it the best place in Munich to *carpe noctem*.

Electro and house beats charge up the crowd at the loungy 11er, while hard-rock hounds mash it up at Titty Twister and metal freaks bang on at Refugium. Nostalgic types can become dancing queens at such '70s and '80s emporia as Noa, Rafael and Q Club while central European rockabillies jive till the wee hours at Eddy's. For the latest line-ups, happy hours and other useful information, check the website or look around for KuFa's own listings mag, the free *Das K-Magazin*.

MUNICH ENTERTAINMENT

Kultfabrik
IMAGEBROKER / ALAMY ©

Below: Bavarian traditional costumes, Loden-Frey;
Right: Amusement ride, Oktoberfest
(BELOW) BONGARTS/GETTY IMAGES ©; (RIGHT) GETTY IMAGES ©

BAYERISCHE STAATSOPER Opera
(Bavarian State Opera; Map p70; ☎218 501; www
.bayerische.staatsoper.de; Max-Joseph-Platz 2)
Considered one of the best opera companies in the world, the Bavarian State Opera
puts the emphasis on Mozart, Strauss and
Wagner but doesn't shy away from early
baroque pieces by Monteverdi and others
of the period. In summer it hosts the
prestigious **Opernfestspiele** (Opera Festival;
www.muenchner-opern-festspiele.de). Performances are at the **Nationaltheater** (Map p70;
☎box office 089 218 501; www.staatstheater.
bayern.de; Max-Joseph-Platz 2; Marienplatz)
in the Residenz and often sell out. The
opera's house band is the Bayerisches
Staatsorchester, in business since 1523
and thus Munich's oldest orchestra.

JAZZCLUB UNTERFAHRT
IM EINSTEIN Blues, Jazz
(☎448 2794; www.unterfahrt.de; Einstein-
strasse 42; Ⓢ Max-Weber-Platz) Join a diverse
crowd at this long-established, intimate
club for a mixed bag of
acts ranging from old bebop
to edgy experimental. The Sunday
open-jam session is legendary.

FC BAYERN MÜNCHEN Soccer
(☎6993 1333; www.fcbayern.de; Ⓢ Fröttmaning) Like it or not, the Germans can play
football and none do it better in the
Bundesrepublik than Bayern Munich,
Germany's most successful team both
nationally and on a European level. Home
games are played at the impressive,
chameleon-like **Allianz Arena** (☎tour
01805-555 101; www.allianz-arena.de; Werner-
Heisenberg-Allee 25, Fröttmaning; tour adult/
child €10/6.50; ☺tours 1pm, in English; Ⓢ Fröttmaning), built for the 2006 World Cup.

HARRY KLEIN Nightclub
(Map p70; www.harrykleinclub.de; Sonnenstrasse
8; ☺from 11pm; Ⓢ Karlsplatz, 🚊 Karlsplatz,
🚊 Karlsplatz) Since its move out of the Op-
timolwerke to the city centre, Harry Klein
has come to be regarded as one of the
best elektroclubs in the world. Nights here
are an amazing alchemy of electro sound

and visuals, with live video art projected onto the walls Kraftwerk style, blending to awe-inspiring effect with the music.

P1 Nightclub

(Map p66; www.p1-club.de; Prinzregentenstrasse 1; Nationalmuseum/Haus der Kunst) If you make it past the notorious face control at Munich's premier late spot, you'll encounter a crowd of Bundesliga reserve players, Q-list celebs, the odd lost piece of central European aristocracy and quite a few Russian speakers too busy seeing and being seen to actually have a good time. But it's all part of the fun, and the decor and summer terrace have their appeal.

CAFÉ AM BEETHOVENPLATZ Jazz

(Map p66; 552 9100; Goethestrasse 51; S Sendlinger Tor) Downstairs at the Hotel Mariandl (p78), this is Munich's oldest music cafe. It has an eclectic menu of sounds ranging from bossa nova to piano to Italian *canzoni* (songs). Reservations advised.

 **Shopping**

HOLAREIDULIJÖ Clothing

(Map p66; Schellingstrasse 81; noon-6.30pm Tue-Fri, 10am-1pm Sat; Schellingstrasse) Munich's only secondhand traditional clothing store is worth a look even if you don't intend to buy anything. The shop's name is a phonetic yodel, and apparently, wearing hand-me-down lederhosen greatly reduces the risk of chaffing.

PORZELLAN MANUFAKTUR NYMPHENBURG Ceramics

(179 1970; Nördliches Schlossrondell 8; 10am-5pm Mon-Fri; Schloss Nymphenburg) Features traditional and contemporary porcelain masterpieces by the royal manufacturer. Also in the Altstadt at Odeonsplatz 1.

SEBASTIAN WESELY Souvenirs

(Map p70; Rindermarkt 1; 9am-6.30pm Mon-Fri, to 6pm Sat; S Marienplatz, R Marienplatz) If you're in the market for traditional souvenirs, this little shop (in business

87

since 1557) has floor-to-ceiling shelves of carved angels, pewter tankards, beer steins, carved figurines and handmade candles. The salespeople are quick with a smile and happy to help.

SPORT SCHECK
Outdoor Equipment, Sports

(Map p70; Sendlinger Strasse 6; ⏱10am-8pm Mon-Sat; Ⓢ Marienplatz, Ⓡ Marienplatz) First-rate outdoor and sports gear for flits into Bavarian backcountry.

LODEN-FREY
Traditional Clothing

(Map p70; Maffeistrasse 5-7; ⏱10am-8pm Mon-Sat; Ⓡ Theatinerstrasse) Stocks a wide range of Bavarian wear. Expect to pay at least €300 for a good leather jacket, pair of lederhosen or dirndl.

RARITÄTEN & SAMMLUNGSOBJEKTE
Collectables

(Map p70; Müllerstrasse 33; ⏱10am-2pm Mon-Sat; Ⓡ Müllerstrasse) Rummage through heaps of glass-eyed dolls, old beer steins, 1980s toy cars and even the odd traditional glass painting at this cosy

emporium, well stocked with quirky collectibles gathered from Bavaria's forgotten drawers and dustiest attics. Great for sourcing unique souvenirs.

FOTO-VIDEO-MEDIA SAUTER
Photography

(Map p70; Sonnenstrasse 26; ⏱9.30am-8pm Mon-Fri, to 7pm Sat; Ⓢ Sendlinger Tor) The largest camera and video shop in town.

ℹ️ Information

Tourist office (☎2339 6500; www.muenchen.de) **Hauptbahnhof** (Bahnhofplatz 2; ⏱9am-8pm Mon-Sat, 10am-6pm Sun); Marienplatz (Marienplatz 8, Neues Rathaus; ⏱10am-7pm Mon-Fri, to 5pm Sat, to 2pm Sun)

ℹ️ Getting There & Away

Air

Munich Airport (MUC; www.munich-airport.de), aka Flughafen Franz-Josef Strauss, is second in importance only to Frankfurt for international and domestic connections. The main carrier is Lufthansa (Terminal 2), but around 70 other companies operate from the airport's two runways, from major carriers such as British Airways and Emirates to minor operations such as Luxair and Carpatair.

Only one major airline from the UK doesn't use Munich's main airport – Ryanair flies into Memmingen's **Allgäu Airport** (www.allgaeu-airport.de), 125km to the west. It is served by bus up to seven times a day; the journey takes one hour and 40 minutes, and the fare is €13 (return €19.50).

Bus

Europabus links Munich to the Romantic Road. For times and fares for this service and all other national and international coaches contact **Sindbad** (☎5454 8989; Arnulfstrasse 20) near the Hauptbahnhof.

Monopteros (p73), Englischer Garten
KONRAD WOTHE/GETTY IMAGES ©

BEX BerlinLinienBus (www.berlinlinienbus.de) runs daily between Berlin and Munich ZOB (one way/return €43/86, 8½ hours) via Ingolstadt, Nuremberg, Bayreuth and Leipzig.

Car & Motorcycle

Munich has autobahns radiating in all directions. Take the A9 to Nuremberg, the A8 to Salzburg, the A95 to Garmisch-Partenkirchen and the A8 to Ulm or Stuttgart.

Train

Train connections from Munich to destinations in Bavaria are excellent and there are also numerous services to more distant cities within Germany and around Europe. All services leave from the Hauptbahnhof (Central Station), which is set to undergo major modernisation in coming years.

Staffed by native English speakers, Euraide (www.euraide.de; Desk 1, Reisezentrum, Hauptbahnhof; ⊙9.30-8pm Mon-Fri May-Jul, 10am-7pm Mon-Fri Aug-Apr) is a friendly agency based at the Hauptbahnhof that sells all Deutche Bahn (DB) products, makes reservations and can create personalised rail tours of Germany and beyond. EurAide's free newsletter, the *Inside Track*, is packed with practical information about the city and surroundings.

Train connections from Munich:

Frankfurt €95, 3¼ hours hourly

Nuremberg €52, 1¼ hours twice hourly

Regensburg €25.20, 1½ hours hourly

Würzburg €67, two hours twice hourly

ⓘ Getting Around

Central Munich is compact enough to explore on foot. To get to the outlying suburbs, make use of the public-transport network, which is extensive and efficient, if showing its age slightly.

To/From the Airport

Munich's airport is about 30km northeast of the city and linked by S-Bahn (S1 and S8) to the Hauptbahnhof. The trip costs €10, takes about 40 minutes and runs every 20 minutes almost 24 hours a day.

The Lufthansa Airport Bus shuttles at 20-minute intervals between the airport and Arnulfstrasse at the Hauptbahnhof between 5am

City Tour Card

The Munich **City Tour Card** (www.citytourcard-muenchen.com; 1/3 days €9.90/19.90) includes all public transport in the *Innenraum* (Munich city – zones 1 to 4; marked white on transport maps) and discounts of between 10% and 50% for over 50 attractions, tours, eateries and theatres. These include the Residenz, the BMW Museum and the Bier & Oktoberfestmuseum. It's available at some hotels, tourist offices, Munich public transport authority (MVV) offices and U-Bahn, S-Bahn and Deutche Bahn (DB) vending machines.

and 8pm. The trip takes about 45 minutes and costs €10.50 (return €17).

If you have booked a flight from Munich's 'other' airport at Memmingen (around 125km to the west), there's a special bus from the same place near the Hauptbahnhof that makes the trip up to seven times a day.

A taxi from Munich Airport to the Altstadt costs in the region of €50 to €70.

Car & Motorcycle

Driving in central Munich can be a nightmare; many streets are one way or pedestrian only, ticket enforcement is Orwellian and parking is a nightmare. Car parks (indicated on the tourist-office map) charge about €1.50 to €2 per hour.

Public Transport

Munich's efficient public-transport system is composed of buses, trams, the U-Bahn and the S-Bahn. It's operated by MVV (www.mvv-muenchen.de), which maintains offices in the U-Bahn stations at Marienplatz, Hauptbahnhof, Sendlinger Tor, Ostbahnhof and Poccistrasse. Staff hand out free network maps and timetables, sell tickets and answer questions. Automated trip planning in English is best done online. The U-Bahn and S-Bahn run almost 24 hours a day, with perhaps a short gap between 2am and 4am. Night buses and trams operate in the city centre. The City of Munich region is divided into four zones with most places of visitor interest (except Dachau and the airport) conveniently clustering within the white *Innenraum* (inner zone).

Short rides (*Kurzstrecke*; four bus or tram stops; or two U-Bahn or S-Bahn stops) cost €1.20, longer trips cost €2.50. Children aged between six and 14 pay a flat €1.20 regardless of the length of the trip. Day passes are €5.60 for individuals and €10.20 for up to five people travelling together. Three-day passes are €13.80/23.70 for one/five people. There's also a weekly pass called IsarCard, which costs €18.20 but is only valid from Monday to Sunday – if you buy it on Wednesday, it's still only good until Sunday. Bikes cost €2.50 to take aboard and may only be taken on U-Bahn and S-Bahn trains, but not during the 6am to 9am and 4pm to 6pm rush hours.

Bus drivers sell single tickets and day passes but tickets for the U-/S-Bahn and other passes must be purchased from vending machine at stations or MVV offices. Tram tickets are available from vending machines aboard. Most tickets must be stamped (validated) at station platform entrances and aboard buses and trams before use. The fine for getting caught without a valid ticket is €40.

AROUND MUNICH
Dachau

Dachau was the Nazis' first concentration camp, built by Heinrich Himmler in March 1933 to house political prisoners. All in all it 'processed' more than 200,000 inmates, killing between 30,000 and 43,000, and is now a haunting memorial that will stay long in the memory. Expect to spend two to three hours here to fully absorb the exhibits. Note that children under 12 may find the experience too disturbing.

Officially called the **KZ-Gedenkstätte Dachau** (Dachau Memorial Site; www.kz -gedenkstaette-dachau.de; Alte Römerstrasse 75; admission free; ⊙9am-5pm), the place to start is the new visitors centre, which houses a bookshop, cafe and tour-booking desk where you can pick up an audio-guide (€3.50). It's on your left as you enter the main gate. Two-and-a-half-hour-long tours (€3) also run from here from Tuesday to Sunday at 11am and 1pm.

You pass into the compound itself through the Jourhaus, originally the only entrance. Set in wrought iron, the chilling slogan *'Arbeit Macht Frei'* (Work Sets You Free) hits you at the gate.

View of interior, Dachau

The **museum** is at the southern end of the camp. Here, a 22-minute English-language documentary runs at 10am, 11.30am, 12.30pm, 2pm and 3pm and uses mostly post-liberation footage to outline what took place here. Either side of the small cinema extends an exhibition relating the camp's harrowing story, from a relatively orderly prison for religious inmates, leftists and criminals to an overcrowded concentration camp racked by typhus, and its eventual liberation by the US Army in April 1945.

Disturbing displays include photographs of the camp, its officers and prisoners (all male until 1944), and of horrifying 'scientific experiments' carried out by Nazi doctors. There's also a lot of information on the rise of the Nazis and other concentration camps around Europe, a scale model of the camp at it's greatest extent and numerous uniforms and everyday objects belonging to inmates and guards alike.

Dachau is about 16km northwest of central Munich. The S2 makes the trip from Munich Hauptbahnhof to the station in Dachau in 21 minutes. You'll need a two-zone ticket (€5). Here change to bus 726 (direction Saubachsiedlung) to get to the camp. Show your stamped ticket to the driver. By car, follow Dachauer Strasse straight out to Dachau and follow the KZ-Gedenkstätte signs.

Starnberg

Around 25km southwest of Munich, glittering Lake Starnberg (Starnberger See) was once the haunt of Bavaria's royal family, but now provides a bit of easily accessible R&R for anyone looking to escape the hustle of the Bavarian capital.

At the northern end of the lake, the affluent, century-old town of Starnberg is the heart of the Fünf-Seen-Land (Five-Lakes-Area). Besides Lake Starnberg the area comprises the Ammersee and the much smaller Pilensee, Wörthsee and Wesslinger See. Naturally the region attracts water-sports enthusiasts, but also has enough history to keep fans of the past happy.

King Ludwig II famously (and mysteriously) drowned along with his doctor in Lake Starnberg. The spot where his body was found, in the village of Berg on the eastern shore, is marked with a large cross backed by a *Votivkapelle* (Memorial Chapel). Berg is 5km from Starnberg and can be reached on foot in around an hour.

From early May to mid-October **Bayerische-Seen-Schifffahrt** (08151-8061; www.seenschifffahrt.de) runs boat services from Starnberg to other lakeside towns as well as offering longer cruises. Boats dock behind the S-Bahn station in Starnberg.

If you'd rather get around the lake under your own steam, **Bike It** (08151-746 430; Bahnhofstrasse 1) hires out two-wheelers. **Paul Dechant** (08151-121 06; Hauptstrasse 20) near the S-Bahn station hires out rowing, pedal and electric-powered boats from €11 per hour.

Starnberg is a half-hour ride on S6 train from Munich Hauptbahnhof (€5).

Bavaria

From the cloud-shredding Alps to the fertile Danube plain, Bavaria keeps its clichéd promises. Story-book castles bequeathed by an oddball king poke through dark forest, cowbells tinkle in flower-filled meadows, the thwack of palm on lederhosen accompanies the clump of frothy stein on timber bench, and medieval walled towns go about their time-warped business.

Discover Bavaria's Nazi past in Nuremberg and Berchtesgaden, sip world-class wines in Würzburg, get on the Wagner trail in Bayreuth or seek out countless kiddy attractions across the state. On top of it all, the Alps extend for 250km of show-stopping scenery that has hikers and skiers on cloud nine.

And, whatever you do in Germany's southeast, every occasion is infused with that untranslatable feel-good air of *Gemütlichkeit* (cosiness) that makes exploring the region such an engaging experience.

Schloss Linderhof (p109)

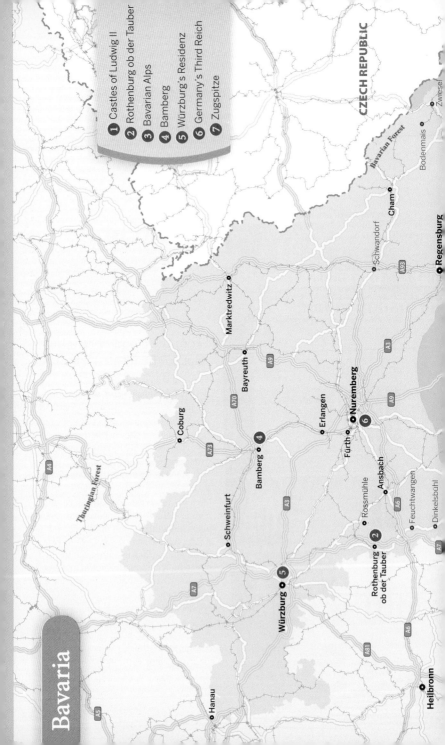

Bavaria

1. Castles of Ludwig II
2. Rothenburg ob der Tauber
3. Bavarian Alps
4. Bamberg
5. Würzburg's Residenz
6. Germany's Third Reich
7. Zugspitze

CZECH REPUBLIC

Bavarian Forest

Zwiesel
Bodenmais
Cham
Schwandorf
Regensburg
Marktredwitz
Bayreuth
Nuremberg
Erlangen
Fürth
Coburg
Bamberg
Schweinfurt
Rossmühle
Ansbach
Feuchtwangen
Dinkelsbühl
Würzburg
Rothenburg ob der Tauber
Thuringian Forest
Hanau
Heilbronn

Bavaria Highlights

1

Castles of Ludwig II

Gazing upon Schloss Neuschwanstein from the Marienbrücke (Mary's Bridge), it's easy to understand the genius of King Ludwig II. It's rare to find a structure that blends so perfectly with nature as Schloss Neuschwanstein does with the gorgeous scenery around Schwangau. Above: Schloss Neuschwanstein; Top Right: Memorial to Ludwig II, Lake Starnberg; Bottom Right: inside Schloss Herrenchiemsee

Need to Know

HEAR Classical music at the Herrenchiemsee Festival (www.herrenchiem see-festspiele.de). **EAT** Traditional dishes. **For further coverage, see p130**

The Magic of Ludwig II Don't Miss List

BY CORNELIA ZIEGLER, AUTHOR OF A DEFINITIVE GUIDEBOOK ON LUDWIG II

1 SCHLOSS NEUSCHWANSTEIN

Ludwig dreamed of flying. In fact, it was one of the reasons he was declared mad. But then, a mere five years after his death, Otto Lilienthal started his first flying experiments... I often remember this strange irony when riding the cable car to the top of Tegelberg mountain and looking down at the castle (p130).

2 SCHLOSS LINDERHOF

When visiting Ludwig's enchanting residential palace (p109), don't skip the park with its exotic buildings. Travel to the Orient in the Moorish Kiosk, channel ancient Germanic tribes in the Hundinghütte (a romantic building within the park) or delve into a Wagner-inspired dream world in the famous Venus Grotto where the king enjoyed floating in a shell-shaped boat.

3 SCHLOSS HERRENCHIEMSEE

Before or after visiting Schloss Herrenchiemsee (p114), pop by the local history museum *(Heimatmuseum)* in Prien. The original 19th-century farmhouse contains a cosy parlour decorated with a portrait of the king, as was typical back then in rural Bavaria.

4 LAKE STARNBERG

Annually on the Sunday following the anniversary (13 June) of Ludwig's death, a memorial service is held in a chapel on Lake Starnberg, 30km south of Munich. Afterwards, a wreath is sunk at the spot where the king drowned in 1886. There's truly no better place to get a sense of the intense fascination this mysterious monarch still exudes to this day.

5 MUNICH

Ludwig was born in Schloss Nymphenburg (p80) in Munich, one of the loveliest park-and-palace ensembles in all of Europe. The rooms where he was born and the collection of magnificent royal coaches in the Marstall museum are major highlights. In the town centre, don't miss the Cuvilliés Theatre (at the Residenz, p69), a rococo jewel, where the king attended many private performances.

Rothenburg ob der Tauber

Medieval Rothenburg ob der Tauber (p119) is a jumble of neatly restored half-timbered houses enclosed by sturdy ramparts. It's an essential stop along the Romantic Road but, alas, overcrowding can detract from its charm. We show you how to experience this historic wonderland sans crowds. Below: The town's rooftops; Top Right: View of the old city behind the fortifications; Bottom Right: Section of the *Stadtmauer* (town wall)

Need to Know

VIEWS Are best from the top of the Rathaus (p121; town hall). **STAY** Overnight to experience Rothenburg at its magical best. **TRY** A *Schneeballen* confection. For further details, see p119

Rothenburg ob der Tauber Don't Miss List

BY LOTHAR SCHMIDT, CERTIFIED NATURE & HISTORY GUIDE

1 TAUBERMÜHLENWEG
Leave the madding crowds behind on a walk through this idyllic valley carved by the Tauber River, which courses past dozens of medieval mills. Start in town at the Rossmühle and follow the flat and easy trail, perhaps stopping at the family-friendly Unter den Linden beer garden.

2 ST WOLFGANGSKIRCHE
This was the pilgrimage **church** (Klingentor; adult/child €1.50/0.50; ☺ 11am-1pm & 2-5pm Wed-Mon Apr-Sep, 11am-4pm daily Oct) of the shepherds and actually part of Rothenburg's defensive system. You can still see the embrasures on the northern wall and go underneath the church to the gun emplacements and dungeons. Inside are three beautiful altars decorated with saints worshipped by the shepherds, like St Wolfgang and St Wendelin.

3 REICHSSTADTMUSEUM
This wonderful museum (p120) inside a late 13th-century Dominican convent has interesting town history exhibits, but the medieval rooms are actually a highlight by themselves, especially the convent kitchen. Don't miss the weapons collection, which includes a hunting rifle that belonged to French queen Marie Antoinette.

4 FRANZISKANERKIRCHE
The Jakobskirche (p119) with Tilman Riemen-schneider's famous Sacred Blood Altar is a definite must, but to see an early work by this master artist head to Franziskanerkirche, one of Rothenburg's oldest churches. You'll have plenty of quiet to contemplate the altar and the original rood screen that once separated clergy and people.

5 STADTMAUER (TOWN WALL)
Another must-do is a walk atop the town wall (p120) from around 1400 and still in its original condition. A 2.5km-long stretch of it is accessible. Follow in the footsteps of the sentries as you walk 5m to 7m above the ground and enjoy tremendous views over Rothenburg's red roofs.

Grapple with Alpine Grandeur

In the Bavarian Alps nature has been as prolific and creative as Picasso in his prime. A gorgeous patchwork of mountains, lakes, forests and meadows, it should convert even the most dedicated lummox to the great outdoors. Garmisch-Partenkirchen (p106), Oberstdorf (p110) and Berchtesgaden (p112) make excellent bases, no matter what season you're visiting. Garmisch-Partenkirchen area

3

4 ## Bamberg: Bishops & Beer

One of Germany's loveliest cities, Bamberg (p138) is bisected by rivers and canals and beautifully sited on seven hills. Take time to explore its atmospheric jumble of crooked lanes, medieval buildings and proud churches with steeples that puncture the skyline. A contagious energy bubbles away in its many brewpubs where you must try the unique local *Rauchbier*, a smoky beer with a century-old tradition.

MICHAEL SNELL/ALAMY ©

Marvel at Würzburg's Residenz 5

The Unesco-listed Residenz (p117)
was made possible by the deep
pockets of local bishops and the
genius of two of the finest creative
minds of the period, Balthasar Neumann and Giovanni Tiepolo. As one
of Germany's key baroque palaces
and such a successful alchemy of
art and architecture, it will leave you
stunned and inspired.

Confront Germany's Third Reich Legacy

The dark legacy of the Third Reich is never
far in many German cities, especially in
places that played key roles in Nazi Germany. Visit two of them – Berchtesgaden
(p112) and Nuremberg (p131) – to
experience how the towns and its people
are dealing with the darkest moment
in their country's history in an honest,
responsible and comprehensive fashion.
Dokumentation Obersalzberg (p113), Berchtesgaden

Soar to the top of the Zugspitze

The 'roof of Germany', the Zugspitze (p108)
is the country's highest mountain, soaring 2964m above the chic ski resort of
Garmisch-Partenkirchen. Only seasoned
mountaineers should make the 'breathtaking' ascent to the top, but fortunately the
rest of us can make the dramatic trip aboard
a comfortable cogwheel train and cable car.

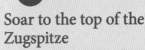

Bavaria's Best...

Christmas Markets

- **Augsburg** (p126) Angel musicians and a magical town hall

- **Nuremberg** (p133) Germany's most famous market

- **Regensburg** (p145) Three markets, including a torch-lit one at the palace

- **Rothenburg ob der Tauber** (p119) Stalls sparkling in an idyllic maze of medieval lanes

Beer Halls & Gardens

- **Klosterschenke Weltenburg** (p122) Monastic brew in an idyllic setting; near Regensburg

- **Kneitinger** (p148) Quintessential Bavarian brewpub; Regensburg

- **Weib's Brauhaus** (p124) Delicious suds from a woman brewmaster; Dinkelsbühl

- **Schlenkerla** (p140) Try its famous *Rauchbier*; Bamberg

Inspiring Hikes

- **Eiskapelle** (p112) A 200m-high ice cavern near Königssee

- **Jagdschloss Schachen** (p107) King Ludwig II's exotic mountain retreat

- **Partnachklamm** (p107) Narrow 700m-long gorge, in winter with icicles and frozen waterfalls

- **Zugspitze** (p108) For experienced hikers only

Need to Know

Curiosities

◦ **Echo Wall** (p112) Echoes bounce off the rocky walls; Berchtesgaden

◦ **Felsengänge** (p136) Underground medieval passages; Nuremberg

◦ **Käthe Wohlfahrt Weihnachtsdorf** (p122) It's Christmas – year-round; Rothenburg ob der Tauber

◦ **Walhalla** (p148) Marble temple to giants of thought and deed; near Regensburg

ADVANCE PLANNING

◦ **As early as possible** Book accommodation, especially in summer, around Oktoberfest and December during the Christmas-market season (especially in Nuremberg).

◦ **One week before** Buy online tickets for Schloss Neuschwanstein and Hohenschwangau.

◦ **One day before** Make wine-tasting reservations, eg in Würzburg.

RESOURCES

◦ **Bavarian Tourism Association** (www.bayern.by)

◦ **Castles in Bavaria** (www.schloesser.bayern.de)

◦ **State of Bavaria** (www.bayern.de)

◦ **Train and bus timetables** (www.bahn.de)

GETTING AROUND

◦ **Air** Frankfurt and Munich are the main gateways to Bavaria.

◦ **Bus** Check out the **Europabus** (p116) for travelling along the Romantic Road.

◦ **Car** Having a car is perfect for tooling around the region and pretty much essential in rural areas.

◦ **Train** For small groups, the **Bayern-Ticket** (www.bahn.de; €22, plus per additional passenger €4) gives up to five adults unlimited 2nd-class regional train travel for one weekday, or from midnight to 3am on weekends.

BE FOREWARNED

◦ **Minimum stay** Some lodging providers require you to stay for two or three days in peak season, or pay a surcharge.

◦ **Private rooms** Tourist offices can help you find inexpensive *Privatzimmer* (homestays).

◦ **Regional buses** Public bus services often stop early in the evening and is suspended on weekends.

Left: Christmas market (p133), Nuremberg;
Above: Walhalla monument, near Regensburg

(LEFT) HEINZ WOHNER/GETTY IMAGES ©;
(ABOVE) QUADRIGA IMAGES/GETTY IMAGES ©

Bavarian Itineraries

Bavaria presents the mother lode of historic cities, soul-stirring scenery and spirit-lifting culture, as these two tours reveal. Slow down to connect with this enchanting land and its treats and treasures.

3 DAYS

GARMISCH-PARTENKIRCHEN TO BERCHTESGADEN

Alpine Adventure

This driving tour twists through the foothills of the Bavarian Alps. Kick off in **(1) Garmisch-Partenkirchen**, Germany's posh winter resort where a train-and-cable-car combo whisks you up the Zugspitze, Germany's highest mountain. First up the next day is **(2) Oberammergau**, an impossibly cute village famous for its Passion Play (performed every 10 years), 500-year-old carving tradition and frescoed facades. Build in a stop at the breathtaking **(3) Wieskirche**, near Steingaden. Rising from an Alpine meadow, it is the pinnacle of rococo exuberance. Afterwards, drop by **(4) Schloss Linderhof**, King Ludwig II's most romantic castle surrounded by whimsical French gardens. For even more of the 'mad' king, swing by the Chiemsee lake. One of its islands is home to the grandest of Ludwig's palace, **(5) Schloss Herrenchiemsee**, a tribute to French King Louis XIV. Spend day three immersing yourself in the scenery of **(6) Berchtesgaden**; must-dos include a boat trip on the emerald Königssee, the jaw-dropping ride up to the Eagle's Nest and a stop at the Dokumentation Obersalzberg.

Above: Viewing platform near Garmisch-Partenkirchen (p106);
Right: Facade of the Altes Rathaus (p139), Bamberg

5 DAYS

BAMBERG TO REGENSBURG

Biggest Hits

This grand sweep of Bavaria's blockbusters travels through centuries of German history, ticking off bustling cities, Unesco-listed World Heritage Sites and romantic towns along the way. The first stop is **(1) Bamberg**, which wows with atmosphere-steeped backstreets and a stunning collage of stately medieval buildings. Don't leave without trying its unusual *Rauchbier* (smoked beer). Hook west to **(2) Würzburg**, a lively city shaped by wine, bishops and great architecture. Its *pièce de résistance* is the baroque former bishop's residence with the stunning staircase by Balthasar Neumann. Head south to **(3) Rothenburg ob der Tauber**, whose fairy-tale looks and charming lanes make for an irresistible sightseeing cocktail, even if it's often deluged by tourists. See p99 for tips on how to escape the crowds. Cut across to **(4) Nuremberg**, which gave birth both to Renaissance master Albrecht Dürer and Nazi mass rallies. The city's finger-sized sausages are among Germany's 'top dogs'. Wrap up in **(5) Regensburg**, sitting pretty on the Danube with a vibrant blend of medieval architecture and 21st-century verve.

Discover Bavaria

Viewing platform near Garmisch-Partenkirchen
GETTY IMAGES ©

BAVARIAN ALPS

Stretching west from Germany's remote southeastern corner to the Allgäu region near Lake Constance, the Bavarian Alps (Bayerische Alpen) form a stunningly beautiful natural divide along the Austrian border.

The region is pocked with quaint frescoed villages, spas and health retreats, and possibilities for skiing, snowboarding, hiking, canoeing and paragliding – much of it year-round. The ski season lasts from about late December until April, while summer activities stretch from late May to November.

ℹ Getting Around

There are few direct train routes between main centres, meaning buses are the most efficient method of public transport in the Alpine area. If you're driving, sometimes a short cut via Austria works out to be quicker (such as between Garmisch-Partenkirchen and Füssen or Oberstdorf).

Garmisch-Partenkirchen

☑ 08821 / POP 26,000

An incredibly popular hang-out for outdoorsy types and moneyed socialites, the double-barrelled resort of Garmisch-Partenkirchen is blessed with a fabled setting a snowball's throw from the Alps. To say you 'wintered in Garmisch' still has an aristocratic ring, and the area offers some of the best skiing in the land, including runs on Germany's highest peak, the Zugspitze (2964m).

Garmisch has a more cosmopolitan, 21st-century feel, while Partenkirchen has retained its old-world Alpine village vibe.

 Sights & Activities

PARTNACHKLAMM   Gorge
(www.partnachklamm.eu; adult/child €3/1.50;
⊙9am-5pm Oct-Easter, 8am-6pm Easter-Sep)
One of the area's main attractions is the
dramatically beautiful Partnachklamm, a
narrow 700m-long gorge with walls rising
up to 80m. A circular walk hewn from the
rock takes you through the gorge, which is
spectacular in winter when you can walk
beneath curtains of icicles and frozen
waterfalls.

JAGDSCHLOSS SCHACHEN   Castle
(920 30; adult/concession €4.50/3.50;
⊙Jun-Oct) A popular hiking route is to
King Ludwig II's hunting lodge, Jagdschloss Schachen, which can be reached
via the Partnachklamm in about a four-
hour hike. A plain wooden hut from the
outside, the interior is surprisingly magnificent; the **Moorish Room** is something
straight out of *Arabian Nights*.

Sleeping

The tourist office operates a 24-hour
outdoor room-reservation noticeboard.

HOTEL GARMISCHER HOF   Hotel €€
(9110; www.garmischer-hof.de; Chamonix-
strasse 10; s €59-94, d €94-136; ☎☀) Property of the Seiwald family since 1928, this
welcoming inn has had many a climber,
skier and Alpine adventurer crease the
sheets. Rooms are simply furnished but
cosy, breakfast is served in the vaulted
cafe-restaurant and there's a sauna providing après-ski relief.

REINDL'S
PARTENKIRCHNER HOF   Hotel €€€
(943 870; www.reindls.de; Bahnhofstrasse 15;
s/d from €80/176; P@☎) Though Reindl's
doesn't look worthy of its five stars from
the outside, this elegant, tri-winged
luxury hotel is stacked with perks, a wine
bar and a top-notch gourmet restaurant. Rooms are studies in folk-themed
elegance and some enjoy gobsmacking
mountain views.

GASTHOF ZUM RASSEN   Hotel €€
(2089; www.gasthof-rassen.de; Ludwigstrasse
45; s €32-53, d €52-90; P) This beautifully
frescoed 14th-century building is home to
a great budget option where the simply
furnished, contemporary rooms contrast
with the traditionally frilly styling of the
communal areas. The cavernous event
hall, formerly a brewery, houses Bavaria's
oldest folk theatre.

Eating

GASTHOF
FRAUNDORFER   Bavarian €€
(9270; Ludwigstrasse 24; mains €8-20,
breakfast €9.80; ⊙7am-1am Thu-Mon, from 5pm
Wed) If you came to the Alps to experience
yodelling, knee slapping and red-faced
locals in lederhosen, you just arrived at
the right address. Steins of frothing ale
fuel the increasingly raucous atmosphere
as the evening progresses, and monster
portions of plattered pig meat push belt
buckles to the limit.

ZUM WILDSCHÜTZ   Bavarian €€
(3290; Bankgasse 9; mains €6-17; ⊙11am-
10pm) The best place in town for fresh
venison, rabbit, wild boar and other
seasonal game dishes, this place is, not
surprisingly, popular with hunters.

ISI'S GOLDENER ENGEL   Bavarian €€
(948 757; Bankgasse 5; mains €8-15;
⊙11.30am-2.30pm & 5-10pm) The 'Golden
Angel' is a rococo riot, complete with
wacky frescoes and gold-leaf-sheathed
ceilings that wouldn't look out of place in
a church. It's family run, neighbourhood
adored and delivers classic Bavarian
cooking, including a mean pork knuckle
with the crust done just so.

BRÄUSTÜBERL   German €€
(2312; Fürstenstrasse 23; mains €6-17) A
short walk from the centre, this quintessentially Bavarian tavern is the place to
cosy up with some local nosh, served by
waiters in traditional garb, while the
enormous enamel coal-burning stove
revives chilled extremities.

GETTY IMAGES ©

Don't Miss **Zugspitze**

Views from Germany's rooftop are quite literally breathtaking and, on good days, extend into four countries. Skiing and hiking are the main activities here. The trip to the Zugspitze summit is as memorable as it is popular; beat the crowds by starting early in the day and, if possible, skip weekends altogether. In Garmisch, board the **Zahnradbahn** (cogwheel train) at its own station behind the Hauptbahnhof. Trains first chug along the mountain base to the Eibsee, a forest lake, then wind their way through a mountain tunnel up to the Schneeferner Glacier (2600m). Here, you'll switch to the **Gletscherbahn** cable car for the final ascent to the summit. When you're done soaking in the panorama, board the **Eibsee-Seilbahn**, a steep cable car, that sways and swings its way back down to the Eibsee in about 10 minutes. It's not for vertigo sufferers, but the views surely are tremendous.

Most people come up on the train and take the cable car back down, but it works just as well the other way around. Either way, the entire trip costs €39/21.50 per adult/child in winter and €49.50/28 in summer. Winter rates include a day ski pass.

NEED TO KNOW

www.zugspitze.de

ℹ **Information**

Tourist office (☏180 700; www.gapa.de; Richard-Strauss-Platz 2; ⏱8am-6pm Mon-Sat, 10am-noon Sun)

ℹ **Getting There & Around**

Garmisch-Partenkirchen has hourly connections from Munich (€19, 1½ hours), and special packages combine the return trip with a Zugspitze day ski pass (around €45). The A95 from Munich is the direct road route.

Wieskirche

Known as 'Wies' for short, the **Wieskirche** (☏08862-932 930; www.wieskirche.de; ⏱8am-5pm) is one of Bavaria's best-known baroque churches and a Unesco-listed World Heritage Site. About a million visitors a year flock to see this stuccoed wonder, the monumental work of the legendary artist brothers Dominikus and Johann Baptist Zimmermann.

In 1730 a farmer in Steingaden, about 30km northeast of Füssen, witnessed the miracle of his Christ statue shedding tears. Pilgrims poured into the town in such numbers over the next decade that the local abbot commissioned a new church to house the weepy work. Inside the almost circular structure, eight snow-white pillars are topped by gold capital stones and swirling decorations. The unsupported dome must have seemed like God's work in the mid-17th century, its surface adorned with a pastel ceiling fresco celebrating Christ's resurrection.

From Füssen, regional **RVO bus 73** (www.rvo-bus.de) makes the journey up to six times daily. The Europabus also stops here long enough in both directions to have a brief look round then get back on. By car, take the B17 northeast and turn right (east) at Steingaden.

Schloss Linderhof

A pocket-sized trove of weird treasures, **Schloss Linderhof** (☑ 08822-920 30; adult/concession €8.50/7.50; ☉ 9am-6pm Apr–mid-Oct, 10am-4pm mid-Oct–Mar) was Ludwig II's smallest but most sumptuous palace, and the only one he lived to see fully completed. Finished in 1878, the palace hugs a steep hillside in a fantasy landscape of French gardens, fountains and follies. The reclusive king used the palace as a retreat and hardly ever received visitors here.

Linderhof's myth-laden, jewel-encrusted rooms are a monument to the king's excesses that so unsettled the governors in Munich. The **private bedroom** is the largest, heavily ornamented and anchored by an enormous 108-candle crystal chandelier weighing 500kg. An artificial waterfall, built to cool the room in summer, cascades just outside the window. The **dining room** reflects the king's fetish for privacy and inventions. The king ate from a mechanised dining board, whimsically labelled 'Table, Lay Yourself', that sank through the floor so that his servants could replenish it without being seen.

Created by the famous court gardener Carl von Effner, the gardens and outbuildings, open April to October, are as fascinating as the castle itself. The highlight is the oriental-style **Moorish Kiosk**, where Ludwig, dressed in oriental garb, would preside over nightly entertainment from a peacock throne. Underwater light dances on the stalactites in the **Venus Grotto**, an artificial cave inspired by a stage set for Wagner's *Tannhäuser*.

Linderhof is about 13km west of Oberammergau and 26km northwest of Garmisch-Partenkirchen. Bus 9622 travels to Linderhof from Oberammergau 10 times a day. If coming from Garmisch-Partenkirchen, change in Ettal or Oberammergau.

Oberammergau
☑ 08822 / POP 5230

Quietly quaint Oberammergau occupies a wide valley surrounded by the dark forests and snow-dusted peaks of the Ammergauer Alps. The centre is packed with traditional painted houses, woodcarving shops and awestruck tourists who come here to learn about the town's world-famous Passion Play. It's also a great budget base for hikes and cross-country skiing trips into easily accessible Alpine backcountry.

A blend of opera, ritual and Hollywood epic, the **Passion Play** (www.passionplay-oberammergau.com) has been performed every year ending in a zero (plus some extra years for a variety of reasons) since the late 17th century as a collective thank-you from the villagers for being spared the plague. Half the village takes part, sewing amazing costumes and growing hair and beards for their roles (no wigs or false hair allowed). The next performances will take place between May and October 2020, but tours of the **Passionstheater** (☑ 945 8833; Passionswiese 1; theatre tour & Oberammergau Museum admission adult/child/concession €8/3/6; ☉ tours 9.30am-5pm Apr-Oct) enable you to take a peek at the costumes and sets anytime.

The town's other claim to fame is **Lüftmalerei**, the eye-popping house facades painted in an illusionist style. The pick of the crop is the amazing **Pilatushaus** (Ludwig-Thoma-Strasse 10; ☉ 3-5pm Tue-Sat

May-Oct), with painted columns that snap into 3-D as you approach.

Oberammergau is also celebrated for its intricate **woodcarvings**. Workshops abound around town, where skilled craftspeople can produce anything from an entire nativity scene in single walnut shell to a life-size Virgin Mary. Speciality shops and the **Oberammergau Museum** (☑ 941 36; www.oberammergaumuseum.de; Dorfstrasse 8; ☺ 10am-5pm Tue-Sun Apr-Oct) display fine examples of the art.

The **tourist office** (☑ 922 740; www .ammergauer-alpen.de; Eugen-Papst-Strasse 9a; ☺ 9am-6pm Mon-Fri, to 1pm Sat) can help find accommodation. Hourly trains connect Munich with Oberammergau (change at Murnau; €18.10, 1¾ hours). Hourly **RVO bus 9606** (www.rvo-bus.de) goes direct to Garmisch-Partenkirchen via Ettal; change at Echelsbacher Brücke for Füssen.

Ettal

Ettal would be just another bend in the road were it not for its famous monastery, **Kloster Ettal** (www.kloster-ettal.de; Kaiser-Ludwig-Platz 1).The highlight here is the sugary rococo basilica housing the monks' prized possession, a marble madonna brought from Rome by Ludwig der Bayer in 1330. However, some might argue that the real high point is sampling the monastically distilled Ettaler Kloster-likör, an equally sugary herbal *digestif*.

Ettal is 5km south of Oberammergau, an easy hike along the Ammer River. Otherwise take bus 9606 from Garmisch-Partenkirchen or Oberammergau.

Oberstdorf

☑ 08322 / POP 9900

Spectacularly situated in the western Alps, the Allgäu region feels a long, long way from the rest of Bavaria, both in its cuisine (more *Spätzle* than dumplings) and the dialect, which is closer to the Swabian of Baden-Württemberg. The Allgäu's chief draw is the car-free resort of Oberstdorf, a major skiing centre a short hop from Austria.

Left: Wood carvings, Oberammergau; **Below:** Ski lifts near Oberstdorf
(LEFT) GETTY IMAGES ©; (BELOW) AFP/GETTY IMAGES ©

Activities

Oberstdorf is almost ringed by towering peaks and offers some top-drawer hiking. In-the-know skiers value the resort for its friendliness, lower prices and less-crowded pistes. The village is surrounded by 70km of well-maintained cross-country trails and three ski fields: the **Nebelhorn** (half-day/day passes €32/37.50), **Fellhorn/Kanzelwand** (half-day/day passes €33.50/39) and **Söllereck** (half-day/day passes €21.50/26).

GAISALPSEEN   Hiking
For an exhilarating day walk, ride the Nebelhorn cable car to the upper station, then hike down via the Gaisalpseen, two lovely alpine lakes (six hours).

Sleeping

WEINKLAUSE   Guesthouse €€
(☏969 30; www.weinklause.de; Prinzenstrasse 10; s €67, d €106-126; P) Willing to take one nighters at the drop of a felt hat, this superb lodge offers all kinds of rooms and apartments, some with kitchenette, others with jaw-dropping, spectacular alpine views. A generous breakfast is served in the restaurant, which comes to life most nights with local live music.

Eating & Drinking

NORDI STÜBLE   Swabian €€
(☏7641; cnr Walserstrasse & Luitpoldstrasse; mains €8.50-21.50; ⊙4pm-late Tue-Sat, from noon Sun) Family owned and run, this intimate neighbourhood eatery, a small wood-panelled dining room bedecked in rural junk of yesteryear, is the place to enjoy local takes on schnitzel and *Maultaschen* (pork and spinach ravioli).

**OBERSTDORFER
DAMPFBIERBRAUEREI**   Brewery
(Bahnhofsplatz 8; ⊙11am-1am) Knock back a few 'steamy ales' at Germany's southernmost brewery, right next to the train station.

111

Information

The main **tourist office** (☏7000; www.oberstdorf .de; Prinzregenten-Platz 1; ◷9am-5pm Mon-Fri, 9.30am-noon Sat) and its **branch office** (Bahnhofplatz; ◷10am-5pm daily) at the train station run a room-finding service.

Getting There & Away

There are at least five direct trains daily from Munich (€30, 2½ hours), otherwise change in Buchloe.

Berchtesgaden & Berchtesgadener Land

☏ 08652 / POP 7600

Wedged into Austria and framed by six formidable mountain ranges, the Berchtesgadener Land is a drop-dead-gorgeous corner of Bavaria steeped in myths and legends. Much of the area is protected by law within the Berchtesgaden National Park, which was declared a 'biosphere reserve' by Unesco in 1990. The village of Berchtesgaden is the obvious base for hiking circuits into the park.

Away from the trails, the main draws are the mountaintop Eagle's Nest, a lodge built for Hitler and now a major dark-tourism destination, and Dokumentation Obersalzberg, a museum that chronicles the region's sinister Nazi past.

◉ Sights

KÖNIGSSEE   Lake

Crossing the serenely picturesque, emerald-green Königssee makes for some unforgettable memories and once-in-a-lifetime photo opportunities. Contained by steep mountain walls some 5km south of Berchtesgaden, it's Germany's highest lake (603m), with drinkably pure waters shimmering into fjordlike depths.

Escape the hubbub of the bustling lakeside tourist village by taking an electric **boat tour** (www.seenschifffahrt.de; return adult/child €13.30/6.70) to St Bartholomä, a quaint onion-domed chapel on the western shore. At some point, the boat will stop while the captain plays a horn towards the **Echo Wall** – the sound will bounce seven times. Pure magic! The effect only fails during heavy fog. From the dock at St Bartholomä, an easy trail leads to the wondrous **Eiskapelle** in about one hour.

Königssee

UIG/GETTY IMAGES ©

Detour:
Eagle's Nest

Berchtesgaden's most sinister draw is Mt Kehlstein, a sheer-sided peak at Obersalzberg where Martin Bormann, a key henchman of Hitler's, engaged 3000 workers to build a diplomatic meeting house for the Führer's 50th birthday. Perched at 1834m, the innocent-looking **lodge** (☑ 2969; www.kehlsteinhaus.de; ☺ mid-May–Oct), called Kehlsteinhaus in German occupies one of the world's most breathtaking spots. Ironically, Hitler is said to have suffered from vertigo and rarely enjoyed the spectacular views himself. The Allies never regarded the site worth bombing and it survived WWII untouched. Today the Eagle's Nest houses a restaurant that donates profits to charity.

To get there, drive or take half-hourly bus 838 from the Hauptbahnhof to the Hotel Intercontinental then walk to the Kehlstein bus departure area. From here the road is closed to private traffic and you must take a special bus up the mountain (35 minutes). The final 124m stretch to the summit is in a luxurious, brass-clad elevator. See p114 for guided tours.

You can also skip the crowds by meandering along the lake shore. It's a nice and easy 3.5km return walk to the secluded **Malerwinkel** (Painter's Corner), a lookout famed for its picturesque vantage point.

DOKUMENTATION OBERSALZBERG   Museum

(www.obersalzberg.de; Salzbergstrasse 41, Obersalzberg; adult/conc €3/free; ☺ 9am-5pm daily Apr-Oct, 10am-3pm Tue-Sun Nov-Mar) In 1933 the quiet mountain retreat of Obersalzberg (3km from Berchtesgaden) became the southern headquarters of Hitler's government, a dark period that's given the full historical treatment at the Dokumentation Obersalzberg. You'll learn about the forced takeover of the area, the construction of the compound and the daily life of the Nazi elite. All facets of Nazi terror are dealt with, including Hitler's near-mythical appeal, his racial politics, the resistance movement, foreign policy and the death camps. A section of the underground bunker network is open for perusal.

SALZBERGWERK   Historic Site

(www.salzzeitreise.de; Bergwerkstrasse 83; adult/child €15.50/9.50; ☺ 9am-5pm May-Oct, 11am-3pm Nov-Apr) Once a major producer of 'white gold', Berchtesgaden has

thrown open its salt mines for fun-filled 90-minute tours. Kids especially love donning miners' garb and whooshing down a wooden slide into the depths of the mine. Down below, highlights include mysteriously glowing salt grottoes and crossing a 100m-long subterranean salt lake on a wooden raft.

Activities

BERCHTESGADEN NATIONAL PARK   Hiking

(www.nationalpark-berchtesgaden.de) The wilds of the 210-sq-km Berchtesgaden National Park offer some of the best hiking in Germany. A good introduction is a 2km trail up from St Bartholomä beside the Königssee to the notorious Watzmann-Ostwand, where scores of mountaineers have met their deaths. Another popular hike goes from the southern end of the Königssee to the Obersee. For details of routes visit the **national park office** (☑ 643 43; Franziskanerplatz 7; ☺ 9am-5pm), or buy a copy of the *Berchtesgadener Land* (sheet 794) map in the Kompass series.

JENNER-KÖNIGSSEE AREA   Skiing

(☑ 958 10; www.jennerbahn.de; daily pass adult/child €29.20/15.50) The Jenner-Königssee area at Königssee is the biggest and most

113

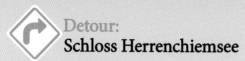

Detour:
Schloss Herrenchiemsee

Most foreign visitors arrive at the shores of the Bavarian Sea – as Chiemsee is affectionately known – in search of King Ludwig II's **Schloss Herrenchiemsee** (688 70; www.herren-chiemsee.de; adult/child/concession €8/free/7; tours 9am-6pm Apr-Oct, 9.40am-4.15pm Nov-Mar), pictured right.

An island just 1.5km across the Chiemsee from Prien, Herreninsel is home to Ludwig II's Versailles-inspired Schloss Herrenchiemsee. Begun in 1878, it was never intended as a residence, but as a homage to absolutist monarchy, as epitomised by Ludwig's hero, the French Sun King, Louis XIV. Ludwig spent only 10 days here and even then was rarely seen, preferring to read at night and sleep all day.

The rooms that were completed outdo each other in opulence. The vast Gesandtentreppe (Ambassador Staircase), a double staircase leading to a frescoed gallery and topped by a glass roof, is the first visual knockout on the guided tour, but that fades in comparison to the stunning Grosse Spiegelgalerie (Great Hall of Mirrors). This tunnel of light runs the length of the garden (98m, or 10m longer than that in Versailles). It sports 52 candelabra and 33 great glass chandeliers with 7000 candles, which took 70 servants half an hour to light.

The Paradeschlafzimmer (State Bedroom) features a canopied bed perching altarlike on a pedestal behind a golden balustrade. But it's the king's bedroom, the Kleines Blaues Schlafzimmer (Little Blue Bedroom), that really takes the cake. The decoration is sickly sweet, encrusted with gilded stucco and wildly extravagant carvings. The room is bathed in a soft blue light emanating from a glass globe at the foot of the bed.

Trains run hourly from Munich to Prien (€16.40, one hour). To reach the palace, take the hourly or half-hourly ferry from Prien-Stock (€7.10 return, 15 to 20 minutes) or from Bernau-Felden (€8.30, 25 minutes, May to October). From the boat landing on Herreninsel, it's about a 20-minute walk through pretty gardens to the palace. Palace tours, offered in German or English, last 30 minutes.

varied of five local ski fields. For equipment hire and courses, try **Skischule Treff-Aktiv** (979 707; www.treffaktiv.de; Jennerbahnstrasse 19).

WATZMANN THERME   Spa
(946 40; www.watzmann-therme.de; Bergwerkstrasse 54; 2hr/4hr/day €9.70/12.20/13.90; 10am-10pm) The Watzman Therme is Berchtesgaden's thermal wellness complex, with several indoor and outdoor pools and various hydrotherapeutic treatment stations, a sauna and inspiring Alpine views.

 Tours

EAGLE'S NEST TOURS   Tour
(649 71; www.eagles-nest-tours.com; Königsseer Strasse 2; adult/child €50/35; 1.15pm mid-May–Oct) Experience the sinister legacy of the Obersalzberg area, including the Eagle's Nest and the underground bunker system, on a four-hour guided tour with Eagle's Nest Tours. Buses depart from the tourist office and reservations are advised.

Sleeping

HOTEL KRONE Hotel €€
(📞946 00; www.hotel-krone-berchtesgaden.de; Am Rad 5; s €44-54, d €82-108) Ambling distance from the town centre, this family-run gem provides almost unrivalled views of the valley and the Alps beyond. The wood-rich cabin-style rooms are generously cut affairs, with carved ceilings, niches and bedsteads all in fragrant pine.

HOTEL BAVARIA Hotel €€
(📞660 11; www.hotelbavaria.net; Sunklergässchen 11; r €50-130; P) In the same family for over a century, this well-run hotel offers a romantic vision of Alpine life with rooms bedecked in frilly curtains, canopied beds, heart-shaped mirrors and knotty wood galore. Five of the pricier rooms have their own whirlpools. Breakfast is a gourmet affair, with sparkling wine and both hot and cold delectables.

Eating

LE CIEL International €€€
(📞975 50; www.restaurant-leciel.de; Hintereck 1; mains €30-40; ⏰6.30-10.30pm Tue-Sat) Don't let the Hotel InterConti location turn you off: Le Ciel really is as heavenly as its French name suggests and it has the Michelin star to prove it. Testers were especially impressed by Ulrich Heimann's knack for spinning regional ingredients into such inspired gourmet compositions. Service is smooth and the circular dining room is magical. Only 32 seats, so book ahead if you can.

GASTSTÄTTE ST BARTHOLOMÄ
Bavarian €€
(📞964 937; St Bartholomä; mains €7-16) Perched on the shore of the Königssee, and reached by boat, this is a tourist haunt that actually serves delicious food made with ingredients picked, plucked and hunted from the surrounding forests and the lake. Savour generous platters of venison in mushroom sauce with dumplings and red sauerkraut in the large beer garden or indoors.

HOLZKÄFER Cafe, Bar €
(📞600 90; Buchenhöhe 40; dishes €4-9; ⏰11am-1am Wed-Mon) This funky log cabin in the Obersalzberg hills is a great spot for a night out with fun-loving locals. Cluttered with antlers, carvings and backwoods oddities, it's known for its tender pork roasts, dark beer and Franconian wines.

Information

Tourist office (www.berchtesgaden.de; Königsseer Strasse 2; ⏰8.30am-6pm Mon-Fri, to 5pm Sat, 9am-3pm Sun Apr–mid-Oct, reduced hours mid-Oct–Mar)

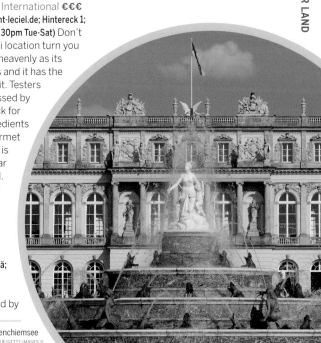

Schloss Herrenchiemsee
OTTO STADLER/GETTY IMAGES ©

Hitler's Mountain Retreat

Of all the German towns tainted by the Third Reich, Berchtesgaden has a burden heavier than most. Hitler fell in love with nearby Obersalzberg in the 1920s and bought a small country home, later enlarged into the imposing Berghof.

After seizing power in 1933, Hitler established a part-time headquarters here and brought much of the party brass with him. They bought, or often confiscated, large tracts of land and tore down farmhouses to erect a 7ft-high barbed-wire fence. Obersalzberg was sealed off as the fortified southern headquarters of the NSDAP (National Socialist German Workers' Party).

In the final days of WWII, the Royal Air Force levelled much of Obersalzberg, though the Eagle's Nest, Hitler's mountaintop eyrie, was left strangely unscathed.

ⓘ Getting There & Away

Travelling from Munich by train involves a change at Freilassing (€30.90, three hours, five connections daily). Berchtesgaden is south of the Munich–Salzburg A8 autobahn.

THE ROMANTIC ROAD

From the vineyards of Würzburg to the foot of the Alps, the almost 400km-long Romantic Road (Romantische Strasse) draws two million visitors every year, making it by far the most popular of Germany's holiday routes. It passes through more than two dozen cities and towns, including Rothenburg ob der Tauber, Dinkelsbühl and Augsburg. Expect lots of Japanese signs and menus, tourist coaches and kitsch galore, but also a fair wedge of Gemütlichkeit and geniune hospitality from those who earn their living on this most romantic of routes.

ⓘ Getting There & Around

Though Frankfurt is the most popular gateway for the Romantic Road, Munich is a good choice as well, especially if you decide to take the bus. Direct trains run from Munich to Füssen (€24, two hours) at the southern end of the Romantic Road every two hours, more often if you change in Buchloe. It is possible to do this route using train connections and local buses, but the going is complicated, tedious and slow, especially at weekends. The ideal way to travel is by car, though many foreign travellers prefer to take Deutsche

Touring's Europabus (☎069-790 3230; www .romanticroadcoach.de), which can get incredibly crowded in summer. From April to October the special coach runs daily in each direction between Frankfurt and Füssen (for Neuschwanstein); the entire journey takes around 12 hours. There's no charge for breaking the journey and continuing the next day.

Tickets are available for short segments of the trip, and reservations are only necessary during peak-season weekends. Reservations can be made through travel agents, Deutsche Touring, EurAide in Munich, and Deutsche Bahn's Reisezentrum offices in the train stations.

Würzburg

☎ 0931 / POP 133,500

This scenic town straddles the Main River and is renowned for its art, architecture and delicate wines.

For centuries the resident prince-bishops wielded enormous power and wealth, and the city grew in opulence under their rule. Their crowning glory is the Residenz, one of the finest baroque structures in Germany and a Unesco World Heritage Site.

◎ Sights

FESTUNG MARIENBERG Fortress

Panoramic views over the city's red rooftops and vine-covered hills extend from Festung Marienberg (Marienberg Fortress), which has presided over Würzburg since the city's prince-bishops

DE AGOSTINI/GETTY IMAGES ©

Don't Miss **Residenz**

The Unesco-listed Residenz is one of Germany's most important and beautiful baroque palaces and is a great way to kick off or end a journey along the Romantic Road.

Johann Philipp Franz von Schönborn, unhappy with his old-fashioned digs up in Marienberg Fortress, hired young architect Balthasar Neumann to build a new palace in town. Construction started in 1720. Today the 350 rooms are home to government institutions, flats, faculties of the university and a museum, but the grandest spaces have been restored for visitors to admire. Visits are by guided tour only. German-language groups leave every half an hour; English tours leave at 11pm and 3pm year-round and, additionally, at 4.30pm April to October.

In 1750 the ceiling above Neumann's brilliant **Grand Staircase**, a single central set of steps that splits and zigzags up to the 1st floor, was topped by what still is the world's largest fresco (667 sq metres), by Tiepolo. It allegorically depicts the four then-known continents (Europe, Africa, America and Asia).

Take in the ice-white stucco of the **Weisser Saal** (White Hall), a soothing interlude in mind-boggling stucco and papier mâché, before entering the **Kaisersaal** (Imperial Hall), canopied by yet another impressive Tiepolo fresco. Other meticulously restored staterooms include the gilded stucco **Spiegelkabinett** (Mirror Hall), covered with a unique mirrorlike glass painted with figural, floral and animal motifs that make you feel as if you're standing inside a Fabergé egg.

In the residence's south wing, the **Hofkirche** (Court Church) is another Neumann and Tiepolo co-production. Its marble columns, gold leaf and profusion of angels match the Residenz in splendour and proportions.

Behind the Residenz, the **Hofgarten** has whimsical sculptures of children, mostly by court sculptor Peter Wagner.

NEED TO KNOW

www.residenz-wuerzburg.de; Balthasar-Neumann-Promenade; adult/child €7.50/6.50;
⏱9am-6pm Apr-Oct, 10am-4.30pm Nov-Mar

JAM WORLD IMAGES/ALAMY ©

commenced its construction in 1201; they governed from here until 1719.

The prince-bishops' pompous lifestyle is on show in the residential wing at the **Fürstenbaumuseum** (adult/child €4.50/3.50; ⏱9am-6pm Tue-Sun mid-Mar–Oct), the highlight of which is a huge tapestry showing the entire family of Julius Echter von Mespelbrunn.

A striking collection of Tilman Riemenschneider sculptures take pride of place in the **Mainfränkisches Museum** (www.mainfraenkisches-museum .de; adult/child €4/2; ⏱10am-5pm Tue-Sun). The fortress is a 30-minute walk up the hill from the Alte Mainbrücke via the **Tellsteige trail**, which is part of the 4km-long **Weinwanderweg** (wine hiking trail) through the vineyards around Marienberg.

DOM ST KILIAN Church
(www.dom-wuerzburg.de) Würzburg's Romanesque Dom St Kilian was built between 1040 and 1237, although numerous alterations have added Gothic, Renaissance and baroque elements. The whole ecclesiatical caboodle was under heavy renovation at the time of writing, but was set to reopen in early 2013.

Sleeping

HOTEL REBSTOCK Hotel €€
(☎309 30; www.rebstock.com; Neubaustrasse 7; s/d from €101/120; ❄ @ 🛜) Don't be misled by the Best Western sign out front: Würzburg's top digs, in a squarely renovated rococo town house, has 70 unique, stylishly finished rooms, impeccable service and an Altstadt location. The list of illustrious former guests includes Franz Beckenbauer and Cliff Richard. Bike hire available.

HOTEL ZUM WINZERMÄNNLE Guesthouse €€
(☎541 56; www.winzermaennle.de; Domstrasse 32; s €56-70, d €86-100; P @) After the war this former winery in the city's pedestrianised heart was rebuilt in its original style as a guesthouse by the same charming family. Well-furnished rooms and communal areas are bright and often seasonally decorated. Breakfast and parking are an extra €5 and €8 respectively.

BABELFISH Hostel €
(☎304 0430; www.babelfish-hostel.de; Haugerring 2; dm €17-23, s/d €45/70) This uncluttered and spotlessly clean hostel has 74 beds spread over two floors, a sunny rooftop

terrace, 24-hour reception (2nd floor), wheelchair-friendly facilities and little extras like card keys and a laundry room.

 Eating

BÜRGERSPITAL
WEINSTUBE Wine Restaurant €€

(🕿352 880; Theaterstrasse 19; mains €7-23; ⏱lunch & dinner) The cosy nooks of this labyrinthine medieval place are among Würzburg's most popular eating and drinking spots. Choose from a broad selection of Franconian wines (declared Germany's best in 2011) and wonderful regional dishes, including *Mostsuppe,* a tasty wine soup.

ALTE MAINMÜHLE Franconian €€

(🕿167 77; Mainkai 1; mains €7-21; ⏱10am-midnight) Accessed straight from the old bridge, the double-decker terrace suspended above the Main River gets crammed with tourists and locals alike savouring modern twists on old Franconian favourites. Summer alfresco dining is accompanied by pretty views of the Festung Marienberg.

JULIUSSPITAL Wine Restaurant €€

(🕿540 80; Juliuspromenade 19; mains €8-21; ⏱10am-midnight) This attractive *Weinstube* (traditional wine tavern) features fabulous Franconian fish and even better wines. Ambient lighting, scurrying waiters and walls occupied by oil paintings make this the place to head for a special do.

🛈 **Information**

Tourist office (🕿372 398; www.wuerzburg.de; Marktplatz; ⏱10am-6pm Mon-Fri, 10am-2pm Sat Apr-Dec, plus 10am-2pm Sun May-Oct, reduced hours Jan-Mar)

🛈 **Getting There & Away**

BUS The Romantic Road Europabus stops at the main bus station next to the Hauptbahnhof, and at the Residenzplatz.

TRAIN Train connections from Würzburg:

Bamberg €19, one hour, twice hourly

Frankfurt €33, one hour, hourly

Nuremberg €19.20 to €27, one hour, twice hourly

Rothenburg ob der Tauber Change in Steinach; €12.20, one hour, hourly

Rothenburg ob der Tauber
🕿 09861 / POP 11,000

A well-polished gem from the Middle Ages, Rothenburg ob der Tauber (meaning 'above the Tauber River') is the main tourist stop along the Romantic Road. With its web of cobbled lanes, higgledy-piggledy houses and towered walls, the town is impossibly charming. Preservation orders here are the strictest in Germany – and at times it feels like a medieval theme park – but all's forgiven in the evenings, when the yellow lamplight casts its spell long after the last tour buses have left.

 Sights

JAKOBSKIRCHE Church

(Klingengasse 1; adult/child €2/0.50; ⏱9am-5pm) One of the few places of worship in Bavaria to charge cheeky admission, Rothenburg's Lutheran parish church was begun in the 14th century and finished in the 15th. The building sports some wonderfully aged stained-glass windows, but its real pièce de résistance is Tilman Riemenschneider's carved **Heilig Blut Altar** (Sacred Blood Altar). The gilded cross above the main scene depicting the Last Supper incorporates Rothenburg's treasured reliquary: a capsule made of rock crystal said to contain three drops of Christ's blood.

MITTELALTERLICHES
KRIMINALMUSEUM Museum

(🕿5359; www.kriminalmuseum.rothenburg.de; Burggasse 3-5; adult/child €4.20/2.60; ⏱10am-6pm May-Oct, shorter hours Nov-Apr) Brutal implements of torture and punishment from medieval times are on show at this gruesomely fascinating museum. Exhibits include chastity belts, masks of disgrace for gossips, a cage for cheating bakers, a neck brace for quarrelsome women and a beer-barrel pen for drunks, and there are also displays on local witch trials. Visitors can have their photo taken in the stocks outside.

119

Rothenburg ob der Tauber

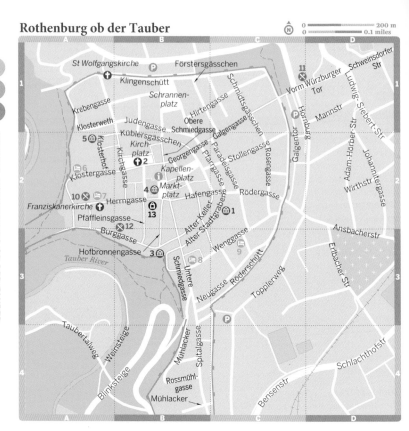

DEUTSCHES WEIHNACHTSMUSEUM
Museum

(409 365; www.weihnachtsmuseum.de; Herrngasse 1; adult/child/family €4/2/7; 10am-5.30pm daily Easter-Christmas, 11am-4pm Sat & Sun mid-Jan–Easter) If you're glad Christmas comes but once every 365 days, then stay well clear of the Käthe Wohlfahrt Weihnachtsdorf (p122), a Yuletide superstore that also houses the Christmas Museum. This repository of all things 'Ho! Ho! Ho!' traces the development of various Christmas customs and decorations, and includes a display of 150 Santa figures, plus lots of retro baubles and tinsel – particularly surreal in mid-July when the mercury outside is pushing 30°C. Not as big a hit with kids as you might predict, as they can't get their hands on anything.

TOWN WALLS
Historic Site

With time and fresh legs, a 2.5km circular walk around the unbroken ring of the town walls gives a sense of the importance medieval man put on defending his settlements. For the most impressive views head to the west side of town, where a sweeping view of the Tauber Valley includes the **Doppelbrücke**, a double-decker bridge.

REICHSSTADTMUSEUM
Museum

(www.reichsstadtmuseum.rothenburg.de; Klosterhof 5; adult/concession €4/3.50; 10am-5pm Apr-Oct, 1-4pm Nov-Mar) Highlights of the Reichsstadtmuseum, housed in a former Dominican convent, include the *Rothenburger Passion* (1494), a cycle of 12 panels by Martinus Schwarz, and the oldest convent kitchen in Germany, as well as weapons and armour.

Rothenburg ob der Tauber

RATHAUS   Historic Building
(Marktplatz; Rathausturm adult/concession €2/0.50; ⓧRathausturm 9.30am-12.30pm & 1-5pm daily Apr-Oct, noon-3pm daily Dec, shorter hours Sat & Sun Nov & Jan-Mar) The Rathaus on Marktplatz was begun in Gothic style in the 14th century, and was completed during the Renaissance. Climb the 220 steps to the viewing platform of the **Rathausturm** to be rewarded with wide-screen views of the Tauber.

ALT-ROTHENBURGER HANDWERKERHAUS   Historic Building
(⌨5810; Alter Stadtgraben 26; adult/child €2.50/1; ⓧ11am-5pm Mon-Fri, from 10am Sat & Sun Easter-Oct, 2-4pm daily Dec) Hidden down a little alley is the Alt-Rothenburger Handwerkerhaus, where numerous artisans – including coopers, weavers, cobblers and potters – have their workshops today, and have had their workshops for the house's more than 700-year existence.

Tours

The tourist office (p122) runs 90-minute walking tours (€7; in English) at 11am and 2pm from April to October.

Sleeping

HOTEL HERRNSCHLÖSSCHEN   Hotel €€€
(⌨873 890; www.herrnschloesschen.de; Herrngasse 20; r from €195) The whole place is a blend of ancient and new, with Gothic arches leaping over faux-retro furniture and ageing oak preventing ceilings from crashing down onto chic 21st-century beds. The hotel's restaurant has established itself as one of the town's most innovative dining spots.

HOTEL RAIDEL   Hotel €
(⌨3115; www.gaestehaus-raidel.de; Wenggasse 3; s/d €45/69; 🛜) With 500-year-old exposed beams studded with wooden nails, antiques throughout and a welcoming owner, as well as musical instruments for the guests to play, this is the place to check in if you're craving some genuine romance on the Romantic Road.

BURG-HOTEL   Hotel €€
(⌨948 90; www.burghotel.eu; Klostergasse 1-3; s €100-135, d €100-170; P 🛜) Each of the 15 elegantly furnished guest rooms at this boutique hotel built into the town walls has its own private sitting area. The lower floors shelter a decadent spa with tanning beds, saunas and rainforest showers, and a cellar with a Steinway piano; while phenomenal valley views unfurl from the breakfast room and stone terrace.

KREUZERHOF HOTEL GARNI   Guesthouse €
(⌨3424; www.kreuzerhof-rothenburg.de; Millergasse 2-6; s €45, d €59-72) Away from the tourist swarms, this quiet family-run B&B has charming, randomly furnished rooms with antique touches in a medieval town house and annexe. There's free tea and coffee and the generous breakfast is an energy-boosting set-up for the day.

If You Like...
Rococo Churches

If the Residenz in Würzburg or the Wieskirche gave you a taste for rococo churches, the following masterpieces will likely make you swoon as well.

1 BASILIKA VIERZEHNHEILIGEN
(☏09571-950 80; admission free; ☉6.30am-7pm Apr-Oct, 7.30am-dusk Nov-Mar) In Bad Staffelstein, about 30km north of Bamberg via the A73, Basilika Vierzehnheiligen is a sumptuous pilgrimage church dreamed up by Balthasar Neumann. The intersecting oval rotundas, play of light and trompe l'oeil ceiling make the interior appear much larger than it is.

2 KLOSTERSCHENKE WELTENBURG
(☏09441-675 70; www.klosterschenke -weltenburg.de; Asamstrasse 32; ☉8am-7pm Apr-Nov, closed Mon-Wed Mar) In a scenic spot on the Danube Gorge, some 30km southwest of Regensburg, sits Kloster Weltenburg (Weltenburg Abbey), home not only to a famous brewery but also to a fabulous church designed by Cosmas Damian and Egid Quirin Asam. Its eye-popping high altar shows St George triumphant on horseback, with the skewered dragon and rescued princess at his feet. Drive there via the B16 or take a boat from Kelheim.

3 KLOSTER ANDECHS
(Andechs Monastery; ☏08152-3760; www .andechs.de; Bergstrasse 2; admission free) About 45km southwest of Munich, this 10th-century hilltop monastery in Andechs has a fabulous church endowed with rococo riches of Johann Baptist Zimmermann. It's one of Bavaria's most important pilgrimage churches. It owns two relics of enormous importance: branches that are thought to come from Christ's crown of thorns, and a victory cross of Charlemagne, whose army overran much of Western Europe in the 9th century.

 Eating

VILLA MITTERMEIER   Franconian €€€
(☏945 40; www.villamittermeier.de; Vorm Würzburger Tor 9; mains €18-26; ☉dinner Tue-Sat, lunch Sat) The kitchen ninjas at this classy establishment serve top-notch Michelin-starred cuisine in five settings, including a black-and-white tiled 'temple', an alfresco terrace and a barrel-shaped wine cellar. The artistic chefs rely on locally harvested produce, and the wine list (400-plus varieties) is probably Franconia's best.

BÜRGERKELLER   Franconian €
(☏2126; Herrngasse 24; mains €6.80-12.80; ☉dinner) Down a short flight of steps in a frescoed 16th-century cellar, this hidden spot serves local, seasonal produce, such as autumn mushrooms and spring asparagus, as part of classic Franconian mains.

ZUR HÖLL   German €€
(☏4229; Burggasse 8; dishes €6.50-18; ☉dinner) This medieval wine tavern, with an appreciation for slow food, is in the town's oldest original building, dating back to the year 900. The menu of regional specialities is limited but refined, though it's the wine, some from nearby Würzburg, that people really come for.

 Shopping

KÄTHE WOHLFAHRT WEIHNACHTSDORF
          Christmas Decorations
(☏4090; www.wohlfahrt.com; Herrngasse 1) With its mind-boggling assortment of Yuletide decorations and ornaments, this huge shop lets you celebrate Christmas every day of the year (to go with the local snowballs). Many of the items are handcrafted with amazing skill and imagination; prices are accordingly high.

ⓘ Information

Tourist office (☏404 800; www.rothenburg.de; Marktplatz 2; ☉9am-6pm Mon-Fri, 10am-5pm Sat & Sun Apr-Oct, 9am-5pm Mon-Fri, 10am-1pm Sat Nov-Mar) Offers free internet access.

WIDMANN WIDMANN/GETTY IMAGES ©

Getting There & Away

BUS The Europabus (p116) stops in the main bus park at the Hauptbahnhof and on the more central Schrannenplatz.

CAR The A7 autobahn runs right past town.

TRAIN You can go anywhere by train from Rothenburg, as long as it's Steinach. Change there for services to Würzburg (€12.20, one hour and 10 minutes). Travel to and from Munich (from €37.30, three hours) can involve up to three different trains.

Getting Around

The city has five car parks right outside the walls. The town centre is closed to nonresident vehicles from 11am to 4pm and 7pm to 5am weekdays, and all day at weekends; hotel guests are exempt.

Dinkelsbühl

09851 / POP 11,500

Some 40km south of Rothenburg, immaculately preserved Dinkelsbühl proudly traces its roots to a royal residence founded by Carolingian kings in the 8th century. Saved from destruction in the Thirty Years' War and ignored by WWII bombers, this is arguably the Romantic Road's quaintest and most authentically medieval halt. For a good overall impression of the town, walk along the fortified walls with their 18 towers and four gates.

Sights

HAUS DER GESCHICHTE Museum
(☏902 440; Altrathausplatz 14; adult/child €4/2; ◷9am-6pm Mon-Fri, 10am-5pm Sat & Sun May-Oct, 10am-5pm daily Nov-Apr) Near the Wörnitzer Tor, Dinkelsbühl's history comes under the microscope at the Haus der Geschichte, which occupies the old town hall. There's an interesting section on the Thirty Years' War and a gallery with paintings depicting Dinkelsbühl at the turn of the century.

MÜNSTER ST GEORG Church
(Marktplatz 1) Standing sentry over the heart of Dinkelsbühl is one of southern Germany's purest late-Gothic hall churches. Rather austere from the outside, the interior stuns with an incredible fan-vaulted ceiling. A curiosity is the **Pretzl Window** donated by the bakers' guild; it's located in the upper section of the last window in the right aisle.

123

MUSEUM OF THE 3RD DIMENSION — Museum

(📞6336; www.3d-museum.de; Nördlinger Tor; adult/concession/under 12yr €10/8/6; ⏰10am-6pm daily Jul & Aug, 11am-5pm daily Apr-Jun, Sep & Oct, 11am-5pm Sat & Sun Nov-Mar) Located just outside the easternmost town gate, this is probably the first museum dedicated entirely to simulating acid trips. Inside there are three floors of holographic images, stereoscopes and attention-grabbing 3-D imagery (especially in the nude section on the 3rd floor).

🛏 Sleeping & Eating

DINKELSBÜHLER KUNST-STUBEN — Guesthouse €€

(📞6750; www.kunst-stuben.de; Segringer Strasse 52; s €60, d €80-85, ste €90; @) Personal attention and charm by the bucketload make this guesthouse, situated near the westernmost gate (Segringer Tor), one of the best on the entire Romantic Road. Furniture (including the four-posters) is all handmade by Voglauer, the cosy library is perfect for curling up in with a good read, and the new suite is a matchless deal for travelling families.

DEUTSCHES HAUS — Hotel €€

(📞6058; www.deutsches-haus-dkb.de; Weinmarkt 3; s €79-90, d €129; 📶) Concealed behind the town's most ornate and out-of-kilter facade, the 19 elegant rooms at this central inn opposite the Münster St Georg flaunt antique touches and big 21st-century bathrooms. Downstairs Dinkelsbühl's hautiest restaurant serves game and fish prepared according to age-old recipes.

HAUS APPELBERG — Bavarian €

(📞582 838; www.haus-appelberg.de; Nördlinger Strasse 40; dishes €5.20-10.50; ⏰6pm-midnight Mon-Sat) At Dinkelsbühl's best-kept dining secret, owners double up as cooks to keep tables supplied with traditional dishes such as local fish, Franconian sausages and *Maultaschen*. There are well-appointed rooms upstairs for sleeping off any overindulgences.

WEIB'S BRAUHAUS — Pub €

(📞579 490; Untere Schmiedgasse 13; mains €5-13.50; ⏰11am-1am Thu-Mon, 6pm-1am Wed; 🍴) A female brewmaster presides over the copper vats at this sage-green half-timbered pub-restaurant, which has a good-time vibe thanks to its friendly crowd of regulars. Many dishes are made with the house brew, including the popular *Weib's Töpfle* ('woman's pot') – pork in beer sauce with croquettes.

ℹ Information

Tourist office (📞902 440; www.dinkelsbuehl.de; Altrathausplatz 14; ⏰9am-6pm Mon-Fri, 10am-5pm Sat & Sun May-Oct, 10am-5pm daily Nov-Apr)

Museum of the 3rd Dimension, Dinkelsbühl

REALIMAGE/ALAMY ©

Getting There & Away

The Europabus stops right in the Altstadt at Schweinemarkt.

Nördlingen

📝 09081 / POP 19,000

Charmingly medieval, Nördlingen sees fewer tourists than its better known neighbours and manages to retain an air of authenticity, which is a relief after some of the Romantic Road's kitschy extremes. The town lies within the Ries Basin, a massive impact crater gouged out by a meteorite more than 15 million years ago. The crater – some 25km in diameter – is one of the best preserved on earth, and has been declared a special 'geopark'. Nördlingen's 14th-century walls, all original, mimic the crater's rim and are almost perfectly circular.

Sights

You can circumnavigate the entire town in around an hour by taking the sentry walk (free) on top of the walls all the way.

ST GEORGSKIRCHE Church
(tower adult/child €2.50/1.70; ⊙tower 9am-6pm Apr-Jun, Sep & Oct, to 7pm Jul & Aug, to 5pm Nov-Mar) Dominating the heart of town, the immense late-Gothic St Georgskirche got its baroque mantle in the 18th century. To truly appreciate Nördlingen's circular shape and the dished-out crater in which it lies, scramble up the 350 steps of the church's 90m-tall **Daniel Tower**.

RIESKRATER MUSEUM Museum
(📝847 10; www.rieskrater-museum.de; Eugene-Shoemaker-Platz 1; adult/child €4/1.50; ⊙10am-4.30pm Tue-Sun May-Oct, to noon Nov-Apr) Situated in an ancient barn, this unique museum explores the formation of meteorite craters and the consequences of such violent collisions with Earth. Rocks, including a genuine moon rock (on permanent loan from NASA), fossils and other geological displays shed light on the mystery of meteors.

STADTMAUERMUSEUM Museum
(Löpsinger Torturm; adult/concession €2/1; ⊙10am-4.30pm Apr-Oct) A fascinating exhibition on the history of the town's defences is on show at this tower-based museum, the best place to kick off a circuit of the walls.

BAYERISCHES EISENBAHNMUSEUM Museum
(www.bayerisches-eisenbahnmuseum.de; Am Hohen Weg 6a; adult/child €6/3; ⊙noon-4pm Tue-Sat, 10am-5pm Sun May-Sep, noon-4pm Sat, 10am-5pm Sun Oct-Mar) Half museum, half junkyard retirement home for locos that have puffed their last, this trainspotter's paradise occupies a disued engine depot across the tracks from the train station (no access from the platforms).

Sleeping & Eating

KAISERHOF HOTEL SONNE Hotel €€
(📝5067; www.kaiserhof-hotel-sonne.de; Marktplatz 3; s €55-65, d €75-120; Ⓟ) Right on the main square, Nördlingen's top digs once hosted crowned heads and their entourages, but have quietly gone to seed in recent years. However, rooms are still packed with character, mixing modern comforts with traditional charm, and the atmospheric regional restaurant downstairs is still worth a shot.

SIXENBRÄU STÜBLE Bavarian €€
(Bergerstrasse 17; mains €5-17; ⊙10am-2pm Tue & Wed, 10am-2pm & 5pm-midnight Thu-Sat, 10am-10pm Sun) An attractive gabled town house near the Berger Tor houses this local institution, which has been plonking wet ones on the bar since 1545. The pan-Bavarian menu has heavy carnivorous leanings, and there's a beer garden where, in the words of the menu, you can take on some *Bayerische Grundnahrungsmittel* (Bavarian nutritional staple).

Information

Geopark Ries Information Centre (www .geopark-ries.de; Eugene-Shoemaker-Platz; ⊙10am-4.30pm Tue-Sun) Free exhibition on the crater.

Tourist Office (☎ 841 16; www.noerdlingen.de; Marktplatz 2; ⏰ 9.30am-6pm Mon-Thu, to 4.30pm Fri, 10am-2pm Sat Easter-Oct, plus 10am-2pm Sun Jul & Aug, Mon-Fri only mid-Nov–Easter)

ⓘ Getting There & Away

BUS The Europabus stops at the Rathaus.

TRAIN Journeys to and from Munich (€24.50, two hours) and Augsburg (€14.40, 1¼ hours) require a change in Donauwörth.

Augsburg

☎ 0821 / POP 264,700

The largest city on the Romantic Road (and Bavaria's third largest), Augsburg is also one of Germany's oldest, founded by the stepchildren of Roman emperor Augustus over 2000 years ago. As an independent city state from the 13th century, it was also one of its wealthiest, free to raise its own taxes, with public coffers bulging on the proceeds of the textile trade. Banking families such as the Fuggers and the Welsers even bankrolled entire countries and helped out the odd skint monarch. However, from the 16th century, religious strife and economic decline plagued the city. Augsburg finally joined the Kingdom of Bavaria in 1806.

 Sights

RATHAUSPLATZ   Square

The heart of Augsburg's Altstadt, this large, pedestrianised square is anchored by the **Augustusbrunnen**, a fountain honouring the Roman emperor; its four figures represent the Lech River and the Wertach, Singold and Brunnenbach Brooks.

Rising above the square are the twin onion-domed spires of the Renaissance **Rathaus**, built by Elias Holl from 1615 to 1620 and crowned by a 4m-tall pine cone, the city's emblem (also an ancient fertility symbol). Upstairs is the **Goldener Saal** (Rathausplatz; adult/concession €3/2; ⏰ 10am-6pm), a huge banquet hall with an amazing gilded and frescoed coffered ceiling.

For panoramic views over Rathausplatz and the city, climb to the top of the **Perlachturm** (Rathausplatz; adult/child

€1.50/1; ⏰ 10am-6pm daily Apr-Nov), a former guard tower, and also an Elias Holl creation.

ST ANNA KIRCHE   Church

(Im Annahof 2, off Annastrasse; ⏰ 10am-12.30pm & 3-6pm Tue-Sat, 10am-12.30pm & 3-4pm Sun) Often regarded as the first Renaissance church in Germany, the rather plain-looking (and well-hidden) **St Anna Kirche** contains a bevy of treasures, as well as the sumptuous **Fuggerkapelle**, where Jacob Fugger and his brothers lie buried, and the lavishly frescoed **Goldschmiedekapelle** (Goldsmiths' Chapel; 1420). The church played an important role during the Reformation. In 1518 Martin Luther, in town to defend his beliefs before the papal legate, stayed at what was then a Carmelite monastery. His rooms have been turned into the **Lutherstiege**, a small museum about the Reformation, under renovation at the time of writing.

DOM MARIÄ HEIMSUCHUNG   Church

(Hoher Weg; ⏰ 7am-6pm) Augsburg's cathedral, the Dom Mariä Heimsuchung, has its origins in the 10th century but was Gothicised and enlarged in the 14th and 15th centuries. The star treasures here are the so-called 'Prophets' Windows'. Depicting David, Daniel, Jonah, Hosea and Moses, they are among the oldest figurative stained-glass windows in Germany, dating from the 12th century. Look out for four paintings by Hans Holbein the Elder, including one of Jesus' circumcision.

FUGGEREI   Historic Site

(www.fugger.de; Jakober Strasse; adult/concession €4/3; ⏰ 8am-8pm Apr-Sep, 9am-6pm Oct-Mar) The legacy of Jakob Fugger 'The Rich' lives on at Augsburg's Catholic welfare settlement, the Fuggerei, which is the oldest of its kind in existence.

Around 200 people live here today and their rent remains frozen at 1 Rhenish guilder (now €0.88) *per year,* plus utilities and three daily prayers. Residents wave to you as you wander through the car-free lanes of this gated community flanked by its 52 pin-neat houses (containing 140 apartments) and little gardens.

Augsburg's Rathaus

WESTEND61/GETTY IMAGES ©

To see how residents lived before running water and central heating, one of the apartments now houses the **Fuggereimuseum**, while there's a modern apartment open for public viewing at Ochsengasse 51.

 Sleeping

DOM HOTEL Hotel €€

(☎ 343 930; www.domhotel-augsburg.de; Frauentorstrasse 8; s €70-135, d €90-155; **P** **@** **☎** **≋**) Augsburg's top choice packs a 500-year-old former bishop's guesthouse (Martin Luther and Kaiser Maxmilian I stayed here) with 57 rooms, all different but sharing an understated air and pristine upkeep; some have cathedral views.

HOTEL AM RATHAUS Hotel €€

(☎ 346 490; www.hotel-am-rathaus-augsburg.de; Am Hinteren Perlachberg 1; s €79-98 d €98-125; **☎**) Just steps from Rathausplatz and Maximilianstrasse, this central boutique hotel hires out 31 rooms with freshly neutral decor and a sunny little breakfast room. Attracts a business-oriented clientel, so watch out for special weekend deals.

STEIGENBERGER DREI MOHREN HOTEL Hotel €€€

(☎ 503 60; www.augsburg.steigenberger.de; Maximilianstrasse 40; r €125-280; **P** **✳** **@** **☎**) A proud Leopold Mozart stayed here with his prodigious kids in 1766 and it remains Augsburg's oldest and grandest hotel. Recently renovated, the fully refreshed rooms are the last word in soothing design in these parts and come with marble bathrooms and original art. Dine in house at the gastronomic extravaganza which is Maximilians, a great place to swing by for Sunday brunch.

 Eating

In the evening, Maximilianstrasse is the place to tarry, with cafes tumbling out onto the pavements and Augsburg's young and beautiful watching the world go by.

BAYERISCHES HAUS AM DOM Bavarian €€

(☎ 349 7990; Johannisgasse 4; mains €7-16) Enjoy an elbow massage from the locals at chunky timber benches, while refuelling on Bavarian and Swabian dishes, cheap lunch options (€6) or a sandwich served by waitstaff clad in traditional fashion.

BAVARIA AUGSBURG

127

BAUERNTANZ
German €€

(Bauerntanzgässchen 1; mains €7-16; ⏱11am-11.30pm) Belly-satisfying helpings of creative Swabian and Bavarian food (*Spätzle*, veal medallions, and more *Spätzle*) are plated up by friendly staff at this prim Alpine tavern with lace curtains, hefty timber interior and chequered fabrics.

FUGGEREISTUBE
Bavarian €€

(☎308 70; Jakoberstrasse 26; mains €10-19; ⏱lunch & dinner Tue-Sat, lunch Sun) Old-fashioned fine dining involving expertly crafted Bavarian and Swabian dishes in an understated dining space with arching ceilings and terracotta-tiled floors. The reassuringly short and seasonal menu reboots on a daily basis.

ℹ Information

Tourist office (☎502 070; www.augsburg-tourismus.de; Rathausplatz; ⏱9am-6pm Mon-Fri, 10am-5pm Sat, 10am-3pm Sun)

ℹ Getting There & Away

The Romantic Road Europabus stops at the Hauptbahnhof and the Rathaus. Augsburg is just off the A8 northwest of Munich.

Augsburg train connections:
Füssen €19.20, two hours, every two hours
Munich €12.20 to €20, 30 to 45 minutes, three hourly

Füssen

☎08362 / POP 14,200

Nestled at the foot of the Alps, tourist-busy Füssen is the southern climax of the Romantic Road, with the nearby castles of Neuschwanstein and Hohenschwangau the highlight of many a southern Germany trip. The town of Füssen is worth half a day's exploration and, from here, you can easily escape from the crowds into a landscape of gentle hiking trails and Alpine vistas.

Sights

SCHLOSS HOHENSCHWANGAU
Castle

(☎930 830; www.hohenschwangau.de; adult/concession €12/11, with Neuschwanstein €23/21; ⏱8am-5.30pm Apr-Sep, 9am-3.30pm Oct-Mar) Ludwig spent his formative years at the sun-yellow Schloss Hohenschwangau. His father, Maximilian II, rebuilt this palace in a neo-Gothic style from 12th-century ruins left by Schwangau knights.

Far less showy than Neuschwanstein, Hohenschwangau has a distinctly lived-in feel and every piece of furniture is a used original. Some rooms have frescoes from German history and legend (including the story of the Swan Knight, *Lohengrin*). The swan theme runs throughout. Here Ludwig first met Wagner, and the **Hohenstaufensaal** features a square piano where the hard-up composer would entertain Ludwig with excerpts from his latest oeuvre. Some rooms have frescoes from German history and legend. If visiting both Hohenschwangau and Neuschwanstein in the same day, timed tickets are always issued so that Hohenschwangau is first on your itinerary.

Schloss Hohenschwangau
MEDIOIMAGES/PHOTODISC/GETTY IMAGES ©

Ludwig II, the Fairy-Tale King

Every year on 13 June, a stirring ceremony takes place in Berg, on the eastern shore of Lake Starnberg. A small boat quietly glides towards a cross just offshore and a plain wreath is fastened to its front. The sound of a single trumpet cuts the silence as the boat returns from this solemn ritual in honour of the most beloved king ever to rule Bavaria: Ludwig II.

The cross marks the spot where Ludwig died under mysterious circumstances in 1886. His early death capped the life of a man at odds with the harsh realities of a modern world no longer in need of a romantic and idealistic monarch. Ludwig was an enthusiastic leader initially, but Bavaria's days as a sovereign state were numbered, and he became a puppet king after the creation of the German Reich in 1871 (which had its advantages, as Bismarck gave Ludwig a hefty allowance). Ludwig withdrew completely to drink, draw up castle plans and view concerts and operas in private. His obsession with French culture and the Sun King, Louis XIV, inspired the fantastical palaces of Neuschwanstein (p130), Linderhof (p109) and Herrenchiemsee (p114) – lavish projects that spelt his undoing.

In January 1886, several ministers and relatives arranged a hasty psychiatric test that diagnosed Ludwig as mentally unfit to rule. That June, he was removed to Schloss Berg on Lake Starnberg. A few days later the dejected bachelor and his doctor took a Sunday-evening lakeside walk and were found several hours later, drowned in just a few feet of water.

No one knows with certainty what happened that night. Conspiracy theories abound. That summer the authorities opened Neuschwanstein to the public to help pay off Ludwig's huge debts. King Ludwig II was dead, but the myth, and a tourist industry, were just being born.

HOHES SCHLOSS   Castle, Gallery
(Magnusplatz 10; adult/concession €6/4; ☉galleries 11am-5pm Tue-Sun Apr-Oct, 1-4pm Fri-Sun Nov-Mar) Füssen's compact historical centre is a tangle of lanes lorded over by the **Hohes Schloss**, a late-Gothic confection and one-time retreat of the bishops of Augsburg. The inner courtyard is a masterpiece of illusionary architecture dating back to 1499; you'll do a double take before realising that the gables, oriels and windows are not quite as they seem. The north wing of the palace contains the **Staatsgalerie**, with regional paintings and sculpture from the 15th and 16th centuries. The **Städtische Gemäldegalerie** (City Paintings Gallery) below is a showcase of 19th-century artists.

**MUSEUM DER
BAYERISCHEN KÖNIGE**   Museum
(Museum of the Bavarian Kings; www.museum derbayerischenkoenige.de; Alpseestrasse 27; adult/concession €8.50/7; ☉8am-7pm Apr-Sep,

10am-6pm Oct-Mar) Palace-fatigued visitors often head straight for the bus stop, coach park or nearest beer after a tour of the Königsschlösser, most overlooking the area's third attraction, the worthwhile Museum der Bayerischen Könige, installed in a former lakeside hotel 400m from the castle ticket office (heading towards Alpsee Lake). The big-window views across the lake to the Alps are almost as stunning as the Wittelsbach bling on show, including Ludwig II's famous blue and gold robe. The architecturally stunning museum is packed with historical background on Bavaria's first family and well worth the extra legwork.

 Sleeping

**ALTSTADT HOTEL
ZUM HECHTEN**   Hotel €€
(☏916 00; www.hotel-hechten.com; Ritterstrasse 6; s €59-65 d €90-99; ☎) The Altstadt Hotel Zum Hechten is is one of

CLARA MONITTO ©

Don't Miss **Schloss Neuschwanstein**

Appearing through the mountaintops like a misty mirage is the world's most famous castle, and the model for Disney's citadel, fairy-tale Schloss Neuschwanstein.

King Ludwig II planned this castle himself, with the help of a stage designer rather than an architect, and it provides a fascinating glimpse into the king's state of mind. Built as a romantic medieval castle, work started in 1869 and, like so many of Ludwig's grand schemes, was never finished. For all the coffer-emptying sums spent on it, the king spent just over 170 days in residence.

Ludwig foresaw his showpiece palace as a giant stage on which to re-create the world of Germanic mythology in the operatic works of Richard Wagner. Its epicentre is the lavish **Sängersaal** (Minstrels' Hall), created to feed the king's obsession with Wagner and medieval knights.

Other completed sections include Ludwig's *Tristan and Isolde*–themed **bedroom**, dominated by a huge Gothic-style bed crowned with intricately carved cathedral-like spires; a gaudy artificial grotto (another allusion to *Tannhäuser*); and the Byzantine **Thronsaal** (Throne Room) with an incredible mosaic floor containing over two million stones.

For the postcard view of Neuschwanstein and the plains beyond, walk 10 minutes up to **Marienbrücke** (Mary's Bridge), which spans the spectacular Pöllat Gorge over a waterfall just above the castle. It's said Ludwig liked to come here after dark to watch the candlelight radiating from the Sängersaal.

NEED TO KNOW

📞 930 830; www.hohenschwangau.de; adult/concession €12/11, with Hohenschwangau €23/21;
🕐 8am-5pm Apr-Sep, 9am-3pm Oct-Mar

Füssen's oldest hotels and a barrel of fun. Public areas are traditional in style but the bedrooms are mostly airy, light and brightly renovated. Children are welcome and one of Füssen's better eateries awaits downstairs.

HOTEL SONNE   Hotel €€

(✆9080; www.hotel-sonne.de; Prinzregenten-
platz 1; s/d from €79/109; Ⓟ 🛜) Although
traditional looking from outside, this
Altstadt favourite offers an unexpected
design-hotel experience within. Themed
rooms feature everything from swooping
bed canopies to heavy velvet drapes and
antique-style furniture, all intended to
make you feel as though you've bagged a
royal residence for the night.

 Eating

BEIM OLIVENBAUER   Alpine €€

(Ottostrasse 7; mains €6-16; ⏲11.30am-
11.30pm) Northern Italy meets Tyrol
meets the Allgäu at this fun eatery,
its interior a jumble of Doric columns,
mismatched tables and chairs, multihued
paint and assorted rural knick-knackery.
Treat yourself to a wheel of pizza and a
glass of Austrian wine, or go local with
a plate of *Maultaschen* and a mug of
Paulaner. There's a kids corner in the
main dining room and a sunny beer
garden out front. Takeaway pizza
service available.

ZUM HECHTEN   Bavarian €€

(Ritterstrasse 6; mains €7-16; ⏲10am-10pm)
Füssen's best hotel-restaurant keeps
things regional with a menu of Allgäu
staples like schnitzel and noodles,
Bavarian pork-themed favourites, and
local specialities such as venison goulash
from the Ammertal. Postmeal, relax in
the wood-panelled dining room caressing
a König Ludwig Dunkel, one of Germany's
best dark beers brewed by the current
head of the Wittelsbach family.

**FRANZISKANER
STÜBERL**   Bavarian €€

(✆371 24; Kemptener Strasse 1; mains €5.50-15;
⏲lunch & dinner) This quaint restaurant
specialises in *Schweinshaxe* (pork
knuckle) and schnitzel, prepared in more
varieties than you can shake a haunch
at. Noncarnivores go for the scrumptious
Käsespätzle (rolled cheese noodles) and
the huge salads.

Castle Tickets & Tours

Both Hohenschwangau and
Neuschwantstein must be seen on
guided tours (in German or English),
which last about 35 minutes each
(Hohenschwangau is first). Timed
tickets are only available from
the **Ticket Centre** (✆930 40; www
.hohenschwangau.de; Alpenseestrasse 12;
⏲tickets 8am-5pm Apr-Sep, 9am-3pm
Oct-Mar) at the foot of the castles. In
summer come as early as 8am to
ensure you get in that day. When
visiting both castles, enough time
is left between tours for the steep
30- to 40-minute walk between the
castles. Or you can shell out €5 for
a horse-drawn carriage ride, which
is only marginally quicker.

ℹ **Information**

Füssen tourist office (✆938 50; www.fuessen
.de; Kaiser-Maximilian-Platz 1; ⏲9am-6.30pm
Mon-Fri, 10am-2pm Sat, 10am-noon Sun May-Oct,
9am-5pm Mon-Fri, 10am-2pm Sat Nov-Apr)

ℹ **Getting There & Away**

BUS The Europabus (p116) leaves from stop 3
outside Füssen train station at 8am. It arrives in
Füssen after 8pm.

TRAIN If you want to do the castles in a single
day from Munich, you'll need to start early. The
first train leaves Munich at 4.48am (€24, change
in Kaufbeuren), reaching Füssen at 7.26am.
Otherwise, direct trains leave Munich once every
two hours throughout the day. RVO buses 78
and 73 serve the castles from Füssen Bahnhof (€4
return). Taxis to the castles are about €10 each way.

NUREMBERG & THE DANUBE
Nuremberg
✆0911 / POP 503,000

Nuremberg (Nürnberg), Bavaria's
second-largest city and the unofficial

BAVARIA NUREMBERG

Map labels:

Bucher Str
Vestnertorgraben
Söldnersgasse
12
7
Obere
Schildgasse
Johannisstr
Neutorgraben
Tiergärtnerplatz
Am Ölberg
Bergstr
Egidien-platz
Tetzelgasse
Neutor
Neutormauer
A-Dürer-Str
1
21
A-Dürerplatz
Burgstr
Lammsgasse
Agnesgasse
4
Theresienstr
Füll
20
Bindergasse
Weinmarkt
15
Hallertor
Weissgerbergasse
Rathaus
18
platz
2
Maxplatz
9
Karlstr
Tourist Office
10
Tucherstr
Pegnitz River
Kettensteg
Augustinerstr
Hauptmarkt
5
Neue Gasse
Kontumazgarten
Westtormauer
Max-brücke
Henker-steg
Karls-brücke
8
Hauptmarkt
Spitalgasse
Westtorgraben
Westtor
Unschlitt-platz
19
22
Fleisch-brücke
Museums-brücke
Spital-brücke
Spittlertorgraben
Spittlertormauer
K-Grillenberger-Str
Mühlgasse
Hintere Ledergasse
Kaiserstr
Adlerstr
23
Findelgasse
Bankgasse
Pfarrgasse
Peter-vischer-Str
Spittlertorgasse
Schloßfegergasse
Weisser Turm
Ludwig-platz
Hefners-platz
Karolinenstr
Brunnengasse
Breite Gasse
Lorenzkirche
Lorenzkirche
Ludwigstr
Dr-Kurt-Schumacher-Str
Frauengasse
Königstr
Spittlertor
Ottostr
Jakobstr
Färberstr
Kornmarkt
Klaragasse
Peuntgasse
13
14
6
Gräsergasse
Luitpoldstr
17
Tourist Office
Künstlerhaus
Frauentormauer
Kartäusergasse
Kolpinggasse
Lord Sterngasse
Frauentorgraben
Färbertor
16
Karthäusertor
Sternstr
Frauentormauer
To Memorium Nuremberg Trials (1km)
Sandstr
Steinbühler Str
Zeltnerstr
Essenweinstr
Opernhaus
Lessingstr
Richard Wagner Platz
Tafelhofstr
Hauptbahnhof
3
Eilgutstr

---

capital of Franconia, is an energetic place where the nightlife is intense and the beer is as dark as coffee. As one of Bavaria's biggest draws it is alive with visitors year-round, but especially during the spectacular Christmas market.

For centuries, Nuremberg was the undeclared capital of the Holy Roman Empire and the preferred residence of most German kings, who kept their crown jewels here. Rich and stuffed with architectural wonders, it was also

Nuremberg

The Nazis saw a perfect stage for their activities in working-class Nuremberg. It was here that the fanatical party rallies were held, the boycott of Jewish businesses began and the infamous Nuremberg Laws outlawing Jewish citizenship for people were enacted.

After WWII the city was chosen as the site of the War Crimes Tribunal, now known as the Nuremberg Trials.

 Sights

HAUPTMARKT　　　　　　　　　Square
This bustling square in the heart of the Altstadt is the site of daily markets as well as the famous Christkindlesmarkt. At the eastern end is the ornate Gothic

a magnet for famous artists, though the most famous of all, Albrecht Dürer, was actually born here. By the 19th century, the city had become a powerhouse in Germany's industrial revolution.

133

(1350–1358) **Pfarrkirche Unsere Liebe Frau** (Hauptmarkt 14), also known simply as the Frauenkirche. The work of Prague cathedral builder Peter Parler, it's the oldest Gothic hall church in Bavaria and stands on the ground of Nuremberg's first synagogue. It was built as a repository for the crown jewels of Charles IV, who, fearing theft, sent them instead to Prague for safe keeping. The western facade is beautifully ornamented and is where, every day at noon, crowds crane their necks to witness a spectacle called *Männleinlaufen*. It features seven figures, representing electoral princes, parading clockwise three times around Emperor Karl IV to chimed accompaniment.

Rising from the square like a Gothic spire, the gargoyle-adorned, 19m-tall **Schöner Brunnen** (Beautiful Fountain) is a gilded replica of the 14th-century original, though it no longer spouts water. Look for the seamless golden ring in the ornate wrought-iron gate on the southwestern side. Local superstition has it that if you turn it three times, your wish will come true.

KAISERBURG
Castle

(www.schloesser.bayern.de; adult/child incl museum €7/6; ☉9am-6pm Apr-Sep, 10am-4pm Oct-Mar) Construction of Nuremberg's landmark, the immensely proportioned Kaiserburg, began during the reign of Hohenstaufen King Konrad III in the 12th century and dragged on for about 400 years. The complex, for centuries the receptacle of the Holy Roman Empire's treasures, consists of three parts: the Kaiserburg and Stadtburg (the Emperor's Palace and City Fortress), as well as the Burggrafenburg (Count's Residence), which was largely destroyed in 1420.

The **Kaiserburg Museum** chronicles the history of the castle and provides a survey of medieval defence techniques. Other Tardis-like sections open to visitors include the royal living quarters, the Imperial and Knights' Halls, and the **Romanesque Doppelkapelle** (Twin Chapel).

Enjoy panoramic city views from atop the **Sinwellturm** (Sinwell Tower; 113 steps) or peer into the amazing 48m-deep **Tiefer Brunnen** (Deep Well).

MEMORIUM NUREMBERG TRIALS
Historic Building

(☏3217 9372; www.memorium-nuremberg.de; Bärenschanzstrasse 72; adult/concession €5/3; ☉10am-6pm Wed-Mon) Nazis were tried in 1945 to 1946 for crimes against peace and humanity in Schwurgerichtssaal 600 (Court Room 600) of what is still Nuremberg's regional courthouse. These became known as the Nuremberg trials, held by the Allies in the city for obvious symbolic reasons. The initial and most famous trial, conducted by international prosecutors, saw 24 people accused, 19 of whom were convicted and sentenced. Hermann Göring, the Reich's field marshall, cheated the hangman by taking a

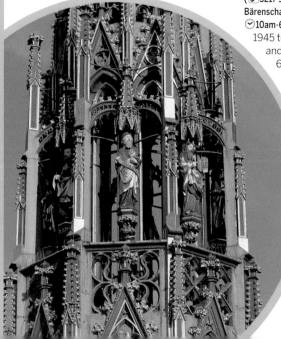

Schöner Brunnen (detail)
CHARLES BOWMAN/GETTY IMAGES ©

cyanide capsule in his cell hours before his scheduled execution.

In addition to viewing the courtroom (if not in use), a new exhibition provides comprehensive background to the trials and their significance to the world today.

To get here, take the U1 towards Bärenschanze (get off at Sielstrasse). It's about 2km from the centre of the Altstadt.

REICHSPARTEITAGSGELÄNDE
Historic Site

(Luitpoldhain) If you've ever wondered where the infamous black-and-white images of ecstatic Nazi supporters hailing their Führer were filmed, it was here in Nuremberg. This orchestrated propaganda began as early as 1927 but, after 1933, Hitler opted for a purpose-built venue, the **Reichsparteitagsgelände**. Much of the outsize grounds was destroyed during Allied bombing raids, but four square kilometres remain, enough to get a sense of the megalomania behind it.

At the northwestern edge was the **Luitpoldarena**, designed for mass SS and SA parades. The area is now a park. South of here, the half-built **Kongresshalle** (Congress Hall) was meant to outdo Rome's Colosseum in both scale and style.

A visit to the **Dokumentationszentrum** (📞231 7538; Bayernstrasse 110; adult/concession €5/3; ⏱9am-6pm Mon-Fri, 10am-6pm Sat & Sun) in the north wing of the Kongresshalle helps to put the grounds into some historical context. A stunning walkway of glass cuts diagonally through the complex, ending with an interior view of the congress hall. Inside, the exhibit *Fascination and Terror* examines the rise of the NSDAP (National Socialist German Workers' Party), the Hitler cult, the party rallies and the Nuremberg Trials.

GERMANISCHES NATIONAL MUSEUM
Museum

(www.gnm.de; Kartäusergasse 1; adult/child €6/4; ⏱10am-6pm Tue & Thu-Sun, to 9pm Wed) Spanning prehistory to the early 20th century, the Germanisches National-museum is the country's most important museum of German culture. It features works by German painters and sculptors, an archaeological collection, arms and armour, musical and scientific instru-

Nuremberg for Kids

The **Deutsche Bahn Museum** (below) feeds the kids' obsession for choo-choos.

Käthe Wohlfahrt Christmas shop (www.bestofchristmas.com; Königstrasse 8) is the Nuremberg branch of this year-round Christmas shop.

The **Spielzeugmuseum** (Toy Museum; Karlstrasse 13-15; adult/child €5/3; ⏱10am-5pm Tue-Fri, to 6pm Sat & Sun) has some 1400 sq metres of Matchbox, Barbie, Playmobil and Lego, plus a great play area.

The **Nuremberg Zoo** (📞545 46; www.tiergarten.nuernberg.de; Am Tiergarten 30; adult/child €13.50/6.50; ⏱8am-7.30pm) is an open-air zoo and dolphinarium, with enclosures as close as possible to the animals' natural habitats. Take tram 5 from the Hauptbahnhof.

ments and toys. Among its many highlights is Dürer's anatomically detailed *Hercules Slaying the Stymphalian Birds*.

DEUTSCHE BAHN MUSEUM
Museum

(📞0180-444 22 33; www.db-museum.de; Lessingstrasse 6; adult/child €5/2.50, free with Inter-Rail pass; ⏱9am-5pm Tue-Fri, 10am-6pm Sat & Sun) Germany's first passenger trains ran between here and Fürth, a fact reflected in the unmissable German Railways Museum which explores the history of Germany's legendary rail system.

If you have tots aboard, head straight for the Eisenbahn-Erlebniswelt (Railway World), where lots of hands-on, interactive choo-choo-themed attractions await. Here you'll also find a huge model railway, one of Germany's largest, set in motion every hour by a uniformed controller.

However the real meat of the show are the two halls of locos and rolling stock. The first hall contains Ludwig II's incredible rococo rail carriage, dubbed the 'Versailles of the rails', as well as

Bismarck's considerably less ostentatious means of transport.

ALBRECHT-DÜRER-HAUS   Museum
(Albrecht-Dürer-Strasse 39; adult/child €5/2.50; ⏲10am-5pm Fri-Wed, to 8pm Thu) Dürer, Germany's most famous Renaissance draughtsman, lived and worked at the Albrecht-Dürer-Haus from 1509 until his death in 1528. After a multimedia show, there's an audioguide tour of the four-storey house, which is narrated by 'Agnes', Dürer's wife. Highlights are the hands-on demonstrations in the re-created studio and print shop on the 3rd floor and, in the attic, a gallery featuring copies and originals of Dürer's work.

ALTES RATHAUS   Historic Building
(Rathausplatz 2) Beneath the Altes Rathaus (1616–22), a hulk of a building with lovely Renaissance-style interiors, you'll find the macabre **Lochgefängnisse** (Medieval Dungeons; ☎231 2690; adult/concession €3.50/1.50; ⏲tours 10am-4.30pm Tue-Sun Apr-Oct). This 12-cell death row and torture chamber must be seen on a 30-minute guided tour (held every half-hour) and might easily put you off lunch.

FELSENGÄNGE   Historic Site
(Underground Cellars; www.felsengaenge-nuern berg.de; Bergstrasse 19; tours adult/concession €5/4; ⏲tours 11am, 1pm, 3pm & 5pm Mon-Fri, plus noon, 2pm & 4pm Sat & Sun) Beneath the Albrecht Dürer Monument on Albrecht-Dürer-Platz are the chilly Felsengänge. Departing from the brewery shop at Burg-strasse 19, tours descend to this four-storey subterranean warren, which dates from the 14th century and once housed a brewery and a beer cellar. During WWII, it served as an air-raid shelter. Tours take a minimum of three people. Take a jacket against the chill.

 Tours

English-language **Old Town walking tours** (adult/child €10/free; ⏲1pm May-Oct) are run by the tourist office (p138), and include admission to the Kaiserburg.

GESCHICHTE FÜR ALLE   Cultural Tour
(☎307 360; www.geschichte-fuer-alle.de; adult/concession €7/6.) Intriguing range of themed English-language tours by a non-profit association. The 'Albrecht Dürer' and 'Life in Medieval Nuremberg' tours come highly recommended.

NUREMBERG TOURS   Walking Tour
(www.nurembergtours.com; tours adult/concession €18/16; ⏲11.15am Mon, Wed & Sat Apr-Oct) Four-hour walking and public-transport tours taking in the city centre and the Reichsparteitagsgelände (p135). Groups meet at the entrance to the Hauptbahnhof.

 Sleeping

HOTEL ELCH   Hotel €€
(☎249 2980; www.hotel-elch.com; Irrerstrasse 9; s/d from €75/95; ☎) Tucked up in the antiques quarter, this 14th-century, half-timbered house has morphed into the snuggest, most romantic 12-room gem of a hotel you could imagine. A couple of rooms (2 and 7) have half-timbered walls and ceilings, but modern touches include contemporary art, glazed terracotta bathrooms, rainbow-glass chandeliers and trendy multicoloured elk heads throughout (the name means 'elk').

HOTEL DEUTSCHER KAISER   Hotel €€
(☎242 660; www.deutscher-kaiser-hotel.de; Königstrasse 55; s/d from €89/108; @ ☎) Epicentral in its location, aristocratic in its design and service, this treat of a historic hotel has been in the same family since the turn of the 20th century. Climb the castlelike granite stairs to find rooms of understated simplicity, flaunting oversize beds, Italian porcelain, silk lampshades and real period furniture (Biedermeier and Jugenstil).

ART & BUSINESS HOTEL   Hotel €€
(☎232 10; www.art-business-hotel.com; Gleiss-bühlstrasse 15; s/d €89/115; ☎) You don't have to be an artist or a business person to stay at this new, up-to-the-minute place, a retro sport shoe's throw from the Hauptbahnhof.

From the trendy bar area to the latest in slate bathroom styling, design here is bold, but not overpoweringly so.

PROBST-GARNI HOTEL
Pension €

(☏ 203 433; www.hotel-garni-probst.de; Luitpoldstrasse 9; s/d €56/75; 🛜) A creaky lift from street level takes you up to this realistically priced, centrally located guesthouse, run for 65 years by three generations of Probsts. The 33 gracefully old-fashioned rooms are multihued and high-ceilinged but some are more renovated than others. Furniture in the breakfast room is family made.

HOTEL DREI RABEN
Hotel €€€

(☏ 274 380; www.hotel3raben.de; Königstrasse 63; s/d €130/150; 🛜) The design of this original hotel builds upon the legend of the three ravens perched on the building's chimney stack, who tell stories from Nuremberg lore. Each of the 'mythology' rooms uses decor and art including sandstone-sculpted bedheads and etched-glass bathroom doors to reflect a particular tale, from the life of Albrecht Dürer to the history of the local football club. Junior suites have claw-foot tubs.

LETTE'M SLEEP
Hostel €

(☏ 992 8128; www.backpackers.de; Frauentormauer 42; dm €16-20, r from €50; @ 🛜) A backpacker favourite, this independent hostel is just five minutes' walk from the Hauptbahnhof, with a laundry, colourfully painted dorms and some groovy self-catering apartments. The retro-styled kitchen and common room are great areas to chill; internet, tea and coffee are free, and staff are wired into what's happening around town.

Eating

GOLDENES POSTHORN
Franconian €€

(☏ 225 153; Glöckleinsgasse 2, cnr Sebalder Platz; mains €6-19; ⏱11am-11pm; 🍴) Push open the heavy copper door to find a real culinary treat that has been serving the folk of Nuremberg since 1498. The miniature local sausages are big here, but there's plenty else on the menu including many an obscure rural dish and some vegie options.

BRATWURSTHÄUSLE
German €€

(http://die-nuernberger-bratwurst.de; Rathausplatz 2; meals €6-14; ⏱closed Sun) Seared over a flaming beech-wood grill, the little links sold at this rustic inn arguably set the standards for *Rostbratwürste* across the land.

HÜTT'N
German €€

(Bergstrasse 20; mains €5.50-15; ⏱4pm-midnight Mon-Fri, 11am-12.30am Sat, 11am-10.30pm Sun) Successfully and confusingly relocated from Burgstrasse to Bergstrasse, this local haunt perpetually overflows with admirers of *Krustenschäufele* (roast pork with crackling, dumplings and sauerkraut salad) and the finest bratwurst put to work in various dishes, though menus change daily (Friday is fish day).

The historic Hotel Deutscher Kaiser

CRISTINA FUMI/ALAMY ©

Lochgefängnisse (p136), Nuremberg

MARTIN MOOS/GETTY IMAGES ©

CAFÉ AM TRÖDELMARKT Cafe €
(Trödelmarkt 42; dishes €4-8.50; ⊘9am-6pm
Mon-Sat, 11am-6pm Sun) A gorgeous place
on a sunny day, this multilevel waterfront
cafe overlooks the covered Henkersteg
bridge. It's especially popular for its
continental breakfasts, and has fantastic
cakes, as well as good blackboard lunchtime specials between 11am and 2pm.

**NATURKOSTLADEN
LOTOS** Organic, Buffet €
(www.naturkostladen-lotos.de; Unschlittplatz 1;
dishes €3-6; ⊘noon-6pm Mon-Fri; 🥄) Unclog
arteries and blast free radicals with a blitz
of grain burgers, spinach soup or vegie
pizza at this health-food shop. The fresh
bread and cheese counter is a treasure
chest of nutritious picnic supplies.

ℹ Information

Tourist office (www.tourismus.nuernberg.de)
Hauptmarkt (Hauptmarkt 18; ⊘9am-6pm Mon-
Sat, 10am-4pm Sun May-Oct); Künstlerhaus
(📞233 60; Königstrasse 93; ⊘9am-7pm Mon-
Sat, 10am-4pm Sun)

ℹ Getting There & Away

AIR Nuremberg airport (NUE; www.airport
-nuernberg.de), 5km north of the centre, is served
by regional and international carriers, including
Lufthansa, Air Berlin and Air France. U-Bahn 2
runs every few minutes from the Hauptbahnhof to
the airport (€2.40, 12 minutes). A taxi to/from the
airport will cost you about €16.

TRAIN Connections from Nuremberg:

Berlin €93, five hours, at least hourly

Frankfurt €51, two hours, at least hourly

Munich €52, one hour, twice hourly

Bamberg
0951 / POP 70,000

A disarmingly beautiful architectural
masterpiece with an almost complete
absence of modern eyesores, Bamberg's
entire Altstadt is a Unesco World Heritage
Site and one of Bavaria's unmissables.
Generally regarded as one of Germany's
most attractive settlements, the town is
bisected by rivers and canals and was
built by archbishops on seven hills, earn-
ing it the sobriquet of 'Franconian
Rome'.

Sights

BAMBERGER DOM
Cathedral

(www.erzbistum-bamberg.de; Domplatz; ⊙8am-6pm Apr-Oct, to 5pm Nov-Mar) The quartet of spires of Bamberg's Dom soars above the cityscape. The interior contains superb and often intriguing works of art. In the north aisle, you'll spot the **Lächelnde Engel** (Smiling Angel), who smirkingly hands the martyr's crown to the headless St Denis.

In the west choir is the marble tomb of **Pope Clemens II**, the only papal burial place north of the Alps. Of the several altars, the **Bamberger Altar**, carved by Veit Stoss in 1523, is worth closer inspection. However, the Dom's star attraction is the statue of the knight-king, the **Bamberger Reiter**. Nobody has a clue as to either the name of the artist or the young king on the steed.

ALTES RATHAUS
Historic Building

(Obere Brücke) The best views of the Gothic 1462 Altes Rathaus, which perches on a tiny artificial island between two bridges like a ship in dry dock, are from the small Geyerswörthsteg footbridge across the Regnitz. Look for the cherub's leg sticking out from the fresco on the east side.

For closer views, turning at the end of the Geyerswörthsteg then right again onto Obere Brücke brings you face to facade with the imposing tower, a baroque addition by Balthasar Neumann. It provides access to the precious porcelain and faiences – mostly from Strasbourg and Meissen – housed in the **Sammlung Ludwig Bamberg** (☑871 871; Obere Brücke 1; adult/concession €3.50/2.50; ⊙9.30am-4.30pm Tue-Sun).

NEUE RESIDENZ
Palace

(☑519 390; www.schloesser.bayern.de; Domplatz 8; adult/child €4.50/3.50; ⊙9am-6pm Apr-Sep, 10am-4pm Oct-Mar) The Neue Residenz was home to Bamberg's prince-bishops from 1703 until secularisation in 1802. Forty-five-minute guided tours of the palace take in some 40 stuccoed rooms crammed with furniture and tapestries from the 17th and 18th centuries.

FRÄNKISCHES BRAUEREIMUSEUM
Museum

(☑530 16; www.brauereimuseum.de; Michaelsberg 10f; adult/concession €3/2.50; ⊙1-5pm Wed-Fri, 11am-5pm Sat & Sun Apr-Oct) Located next to the Kloster St Michael, this comprehensive brewery museum exhibits heaps of period mashing, boiling and bottling implements, as well as everything to do with local suds, such as beer mats, tankards, enamel beer signs and lots of documentation and photos.

KLEIN VENEDIG
Neighbourhood

(Little Venice) A row of diminutive, half-timbered cottages once inhabited by fishermen and their families comprises Bamberg's Klein Venedig (Little Venice), which clasps the Regnitz' east bank between Markusbrücke and Untere Brücke. The little homes balance on poles set right into the water and are fronted by tiny gardens and terraces.

Klein Venedig is well worth a stroll but looks at least as pretty from a distance, especially in summer when red geraniums spill from flower boxes. Good vantage points include the Untere Brücke near the Altes Rathaus, and Am Leinritt.

 # Sleeping

HOTEL SANKT NEPOMUK
Hotel €€

(☑984 20; www.hotel-nepomuk.de; Obere Mühlbrücke; r €95-145; 🛜) Aptly named after the patron saint of bridges, this is a classy establishment in a half-timbered former mill right on the Regnitz. It has a superb restaurant (mains €15 to €30) with a terrace, 24 comfy rustic rooms and bikes for hire.

BAROCKHOTEL AM DOM
Hotel €€

(☑540 31; www.barockhotel.de; Vorderer Bach 4; s/d from €77/99; P 🛜) The sugary facade, a sceptre's swipe from the Dom, gives a hint of the baroque heritage and original details within. The 19 rooms have sweeping views of the Dom or over the roofs of the Altstadt, and breakfast is served in a 14th-century vault.

HOTEL
RESIDENZSCHLOSS
Hotel €€€

(☎609 10; www.residenzschloss.com; Untere Sandstrasse 32; r €109-199; [P] 🛜) Bamberg's grandest digs occupy a palatial building formerly used as a hospital. But have no fear, as the swanky furnishings – from the Roman-style steam bath to the flashy piano bar – have little in common with institutional care. High-ceilinged rooms are business standard though display little historical charm.

BACKPACKERS BAMBERG
Hostel €

(☎222 1718; www.backpackersbamberg.de; Heiliggrabstrasse 4; dm €15-18, s/d €27/40; 🛜) Bamberg's backpacker hostel is a funky but well-kept affair, with clean dorms, a fully functional kitchen and a quiet, family-friendly atmosphere. Make sure you let staff know when you're arriving, as it's left unmanned for most of the day.

Eating & Drinking

MESSERSCHMIDT
Franconian €€

(☎297 800; Lange Strasse 41; mains €12-25; ⏱lunch & dinner) Sharpen your molars on platters of roast duck and red cabbage or blood sausage strudel with savoy cabbage enjoyed out on the alfresco terrace overlooking a pretty park, or in the attached wine tavern.

SCHLENKERLA
Franconian €

(☎560 60; Dominikanerstrasse 6; dishes €5-10; ⏱9.30am-11.30pm) At the foot of the cathedral, this local legend is a dark, rustic 14th-century tavern with hefty wooden tables groaning with scrumptious Franconian fare and its own superb *Rauchbier*, poured straight from oak barrels.

KLOSTERBRÄU
Brewery €

(☎522 65; Obere Mühlbrücke 1-3; mains €6-12; ⏱10.30am-11pm Mon-Fri, 10am-11pm Sat, 10am-10pm Sun) This beautiful half-timbered brewery is Bamberg's oldest. It draws *Stammgäste* (regular local drinkers) and tourists alike who wash down filling slabs of meat and dumplings with its excellent range of ales.

❶ Information

Tourist office (☎297 6200; www.bamberg.info; Geyersworthstrasse 5; ⏱9.30am-6pm Mon-Fri, to 4pm Sat, to 2.30pm Sun)

❶ Getting There & Away

Bamberg has the following train connections:

Munich €59, two to 2½ hours, every two hours

Nuremberg €12 to €21, 40 to 60 minutes, four hourly

Würzburg €19, one hour, twice hourly

Bayreuth
🗹0921 / POP 72,600

Even without its Wagner connections, Bayreuth would still be an interesting detour from Nuremberg or Bamberg for its baroque architecture and curious palaces. But it's for the annual **Wagner Festival** that 60,000 opera devotees make a pilgrimage to this neck of the *Wald*.

Bayreuth's glory days began in 1735 when Wilhelmine, sister of King Frederick the Great of Prussia, was forced to marry stuffy Margrave Friedrich. Bored with the local scene, the cultured Anglo-oriented Wilhelmine invited the finest artists, poets, composers and architects in Europe to court. The period bequeathed some eye-catching buildings, still on display for all to see.

Sights

MARKGRÄFLICHES OPERNHAUS
Opera House

(☎759 6922; Opernstrasse 14; tours adult/concession €5.50/4.50; ⏱tours 9am-6pm daily Apr-Sep, occasional weekends Oct-Mar) Designed by Giuseppe Galli Bibiena, a famous 18th-century architect from Bologna, Bayreuth's opera house is one of Europe's most stunningly ornate baroque theatres. Germany's largest opera house until 1871, it has a lavish interior smothered in carved, gilded and marbled wood. However, Richard Wagner considered it too modest for his serious work and conducted here just once. The 45-minute sound-and-light multimedia show is in German only but, even if you don't speak the local lingo, tours are still worth it just to ogle at the show-stopping auditorium.

NEUES SCHLOSS Palace
(☎759 6920; Ludwigstrasse 21; adult/concession €5.50/4.50; ☺9am-6pm daily Apr-Sep, 10am-4pm Tue-Sun Oct-Mar) The Neues Schloss, which opens into the vast **Hofgarten** (admission free; ☺24hr), lies a short distance to the south of the main shopping street, Maxmilianstrasse. A riot of rococo style, the margrave's residence after 1753 features a vast collection of 18th-century porcelain made in Bayreuth. Also worth a look is the Spiegelscherbenkabinett (Broken Mirror Cabinet), which is lined with irregular shards of broken mirror – supposedly Wilhelmine's response to the vanity of her era.

RICHARD WAGNER MUSEUM – HAUS WAHNFRIED Museum
(www.wagnermuseum.de; Richard-Wagner-Strasse 48) In the early 1870s King Ludwig II, Wagner's most devoted fan, gave the great composer the cash to build Haus Wahnfried, a mini-mansion on the northern edge of the Hofgarten. The building now houses the Richard Wagner Museum, but at time of writing this was closed for renovation and would remain that way until at least 2013.

Despite the ongoing building work, you can still sneak around the back of the house to see the unmarked, ivy-covered tomb containing Wagner and his wife Cosima. The sandstone grave of his loving canine companion Russ stands nearby.

FESTSPIELHAUS Opera House
(☎787 80; Festspielhügel 1-2; adult/concession €5/3; ☺tours 10am & 2pm Dec-Apr, 10am, 11am, 2pm & 3pm Sep & Oct, closed Mon & Nov) North of the Hauptbahnhof, the main venue for Bayreuth's annual Wagner Festival is the Festspielhaus, constructed in 1872 with King Ludwig II's backing. The structure was specially designed to accommodate Wagner's massive theatrical sets, with three storeys of mechanical works hidden below stage.

EREMITAGE Park
Around 6km east of the centre lies the Eremitage, a lush park girding the **Altes Schloss** (☎759 6937; adult/concession €4.50/3.50; ☺9am-6pm Apr-Sep), Friedrich and Wilhelmine's summer residence. Visits to the palace are by guided tour only and

Markgräfliches Opernhaus, Bayreuth

H. & D. ZIELSKE/GETTY IMAGES ©

take in the Chinese Mirror room where Countess Wilhelmine penned her memoirs.

Also in the park is horseshoe-shaped Neues Schloss (not to be confused with the one in town), which centres on the amazing mosaic Sun Temple with gilded Apollo sculpture. Around both palaces you'll find numerous grottoes, follies and gushing fountains.

🛏 Sleeping & Eating

HOTEL GOLDENER ANKER   Hotel €€€

(📞787 7740; www.anker-bayreuth.de; Opernstrasse 6; s €98-128, d €148-198; [P] [🛜]) The refined elegance of this hotel, owned by the same family since the 16th century, is hard to beat. It's just a few metres from the opera house, in the pedestrian zone. Many of the rooms are decorated in heavy traditional style with swag curtains, dark woods and antique touches. Parking is €15 a day.

HOTEL GOLDENER HIRSCH   Hotel €€

(📞1504 4000; www.bayreuth-goldener-hirsch. de; Bahnhofstrasse 13; s €65-85, d €85-110; [P] [@] [🛜]) Just across from the train station, the 'Golden Reindeer' looks a bit stuffy from the outside, but once indoors you'll discover crisp, well-maintained rooms with contemporary furniture and unscuffed, whitewashed walls. Some of the 40 rooms have baths. Parking is free.

KRAFTRAUM   Cafe €

(Sophienstrasse 16; mains €6-8; ⏲8am-1am Mon-Fri, from 9am Sat & Sun; [🍴]) This vegetarian eatery has plenty to tempt even the most committed meat eaters, including pastas, jacket potatoes, soups and huge salads. The retroish, shabby-chic interior empties on sunny days when everyone plumps for the alfresco seating out on the cobbles. Tempting weekend brunches (€12.50) always attract a large crowd.

OSKAR   Franconian, Bavarian €€

(📞516 0553; Maximilianstrasse 33; mains €6-15; ⏲8am-1am Mon-Sat, from 9am Sun) At the heart of the pedestrianised shopping boulevard, this multitasking, open-all-hours bar-cafe-restaurant is Bayreuth's busiest eatery. It's good for a busting Bavarian breakfast, a light lunch in the covered garden cafe, a full-on dinner feast in the dark-wood restaurant, or a *Landbier* and a couple of tasty Bayreuth bratwursts anytime you feel.

ℹ Getting There & Away

Most rail journeys between Bayreuth and other towns in Bavaria require a change in Nuremberg:

Munich Change in Nuremberg; €65, 2½ hours, hourly

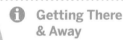

Maisel's Brauerei-und -Büttnerei-Museum, Bayreuth
BRUCE YUANYUE BI/GETTY IMAGES ©

Nuremberg €19, one hour, hourly

Regensburg Change in Nuremberg; €26 to
€41, 2¼ hours, hourly

Coburg

09561 / POP 41,000

Coburg languished in the shadow of
the Iron Curtain during the Cold War,
all but closed in by East Germany
on three sides, but since reunification the town has undergone a
revival. Its proud Veste is one of
Germany's finest medieval fortresses. What's more, some sources
contend that the original hot dog
was invented here.

 Sights & Activities

Coburg's epicentre is the magnificent Markt, a beautifully renovated
square radiating a colourful, aristocratic charm.

VESTE
COBURG   Fortress, Museum
(www.kunstsammlungen-coburg.de;
adult/concession €5/2.50; ⊘9.30am-
5pm daily Apr-Oct, 1-4pm Tue-Sun
Nov-Mar) Towering above Coburg's
centre is a story-book medieval
fortress, the Veste Coburg. It houses
the vast collection of the **Kunstsammlungen**, with works by star
painters such as Rembrandt, Dürer
and Cranach the Elder. The elaborate
Jagdintarsien-Zimmer (Hunting
Marquetry Room) is a superlative
example of carved woodwork.

The **Veste-Express** (one way/return
€3/4; ⊘10am-5pm Apr-Oct), a tourist
train, leaves from the tourist office
(p144) and makes the trip to the
fortress every 30 minutes. Otherwise
it's a steep 3km climb on foot.

SCHLOSS EHRENBURG   Castle
(☎808 832; www.sgvcoburg.de; Schlossplatz;
adult/child €4.50/free; ⊘tours hourly 9am-5pm
Tue-Sun Apr-Sep, 10am-4pm Tue-Sun Oct-Mar)
The lavish Schloss Ehrenburg was once

If You Like...
Beer

Let's face it: you've come to Germany, so
you probably like beer. If you like it as much
to go the extra mile for a special experience,
try these breweries and other storied places
of beery pilgrimage:

1 KLOSTER ANDECHS
(☎08152-376 253; www.andechs.de; admission
free; ⊘8am-6pm Mon-Fri, 9am-6pm Sat, 9.45am-6pm
Sun) Founded in the 10th century, the gorgeous
hilltop monastery of Andechs has long been a place of
pilgrimage, though today more visitors come to slurp
the Benedictines' fabled ales. Soak up the magnificent
views of the purple-grey Alps and forested hills before
plunging into the nearby Bräustüberl, the monks' beer
hall and garden. Andechs is about 45km southwest of
Munich.

2 KLOSTERSCHENKE WELTENBURG
(☎09441-675 70; www.klosterschenke
-weltenburg.de; Asamstrasse 32; ⊘8am-7pm Apr-Nov,
closed Mon-Wed Mar) Klosterschenke Weltenburg has
been brewing its delicious dark beer since 1050. Now
a state-of-the-art brewery, it is a favourite spot for an
excursion, and the comely beer garden can get quite
crowded on warm weekends and holidays. Get there
by boat from Kelheim (about 30km southwest of
Regensburg on the B16) via the Danube Gorge.

3 MAISEL'S BRAUEREI-UND-
BÜTTNEREI-MUSEUM
(☎401 234; www.maisel.com/museum; Kulmbacher
Strasse 40, Bayreuth; tours adult/concession €4/2;
⊘tours 2pm daily) For a fascinating look at the
brewing process, head to this enormous museum
next door to the brewery of one of Germany's top
wheat-beer producers. The 90-minute guided tour
takes you into the bowels of the 19th-century plant,
with atmospheric rooms filled with 4500 beer
mugs and amusing artefacts. Visits conclude with
a glass of cloudy *Weissbier* (wheat beer).

the town residence of the Coburg dukes.
The splendid **Riesensaal** (Hall of Giants)
has a baroque ceiling supported by
28 statues of Atlas.

TIE

Vegetarian **€€€**

(Leopoldstrasse 14; mains €15-23; ⏰from 5pm Tue-Sun;) Heavenly (if pricey) food is crafted from fresh organic ingredients at this vegetarian restaurant, where the focus is firmly on the food and not gimmicky decor. Dishes range from vegetarian classics to Asian inspirations, with the odd fish or meat dish for the unconverted.

 Sleeping & Eating

ROMANTIK HOTEL
GOLDENE TRAUBE

Hotel **€€**

(☎8760; www.goldenetraube.com; Am Viktoriabrunnen 2; s €89-99, d €109-129; **P** 🛜) Owner Bernd Glauben is president of the German Sommelier's Union, and you can taste and buy over 400 wines in the charming hotel wine bar. These can also be sampled in the two eateries, the Michelin-starred Esszimmer and the less fancy Victora Grill. Rooms are splashed with bright Mediterranean yellows and oranges or else decked out Laura Ashley–style.

RATSKELLER

Franconian **€**

(Markt 1; mains €4.50-13.50; ⏰10am-midnight) Munch on regional dishes from Thuringia and Franconia while kicking back on well-padded leather benches under the heftily vaulted ceiling of Coburg's spectacular town hall.

ℹ Information

Tourist office (☎898 000; www.coburg-tourist .de; Herrengasse 4; ⏰9am-6.30pm Mon-Fri, 10am-3pm Sat, 10am-2pm Sun Apr-Oct, 9am-5pm Mon-Fri, 10am-3pm Sat Nov-Mar)

ℹ Getting There & Away

Coburg has the following train connections:

Bamberg €11.10, 40 minutes, hourly

Bayreuth €16.40, 1½ hours, hourly

Nuremberg €21.50, 1¾ hours, hourly

Regensburg

📞 0941 / POP 135,500

A Roman settlement completed under Emperor Marcus Aurelius, Regensburg was the first capital of Bavaria, the residence of dukes, kings and bishops, and for 600 years imperial free city. Two millennia of history bequeathed the city some of the region's finest architectural heritage, a fact recognised by Unesco in 2006. Though big on the historical wow factor, today's Regensburg is a laid-back and unpretentious sort of place, and a good springboard into the wider region.

Sights

DOM ST PETER Church

(Domplatz; ⊙6.30am-6pm Apr-Oct, to 5pm Nov-Mar) It takes a few seconds for your eyes to adjust to the dim interior of Regensburg's soaring landmark, the Dom St Peter, one of Bavaria's grandest Gothic cathedrals. Impressive features inside are the kaleidoscopic stained-glass windows above the choir and in the south transept and the intricately gilded altar.

ALTES RATHAUS & REICHSTAGSMUSEUM

Historic Building

(Rathausplatz; adult/concession €7.50/4; ⊙English tours 3pm Apr-Oct, 2pm Nov-Mar) The seat of the Reichstag for almost 150 years, the Altes Rathaus is now home to Regensburg's mayors and the **Reichstagsmuseum**. Tours take in not only the lavishly decorated **Reichssaal** (Imperial Hall), but also the original **torture chambers** in the basement.

STEINERNE BRÜCKE Bridge

An incredible feat of engineering for its day, Regensburg's 900-year-old Steinerne Brücke (Stone Bridge) was at one time the only fortified crossing of the Danube.

Regensburg

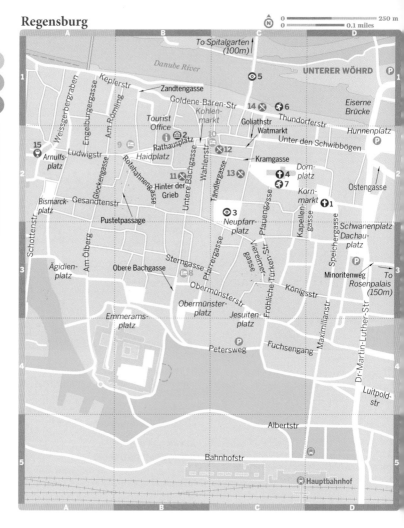

Danube River

ALTE KAPELLE   Church

(Alter Kornmarkt 8) South of the Dom, the humble exterior of the graceful Alte Kapelle belies the stunning interior with its rich rococo decorations. The core of the church, however, is about 1000 years old, although the Gothic vaulted ceilings were added in the Middle Ages.

DOCUMENT
NEUPFARRPLATZ   Historic Site

(507 3454; Neupfarrplatz; adult/concession €5/2.50; tours 2.30pm Thu-Sat Sep-Jun,

Thu-Mon Jul & Aug) Excavations in the mid-1990s revealed remains of Regensburg's once-thriving 16th-century Jewish quarter, along with Roman buildings, gold coins and a Nazi bunker. The subterranean Document Neupfarrplatz only provides access to a small portion of the excavated area, but tours feature a nifty multimedia presentation (in German) about the square's history.

Purchase tickets from Tabak Götz at Neupfarrplatz 3.

Regensburg

 Tours

SCHIFFFAHRT KLINGER — Boat Tour
(☎521 04; www.schifffahrtklinger.de) Offers short cruises (50 minutes) on the Danube (adult/child €7.50/4.80, hourly from 9am to 4pm, April to late October) and to the Walhalla monument (see p148; adult/child single €7.50/4.80, return €11/6.80; at 10.30am and 2pm, 45 minutes each way plus a one-hour stop at the monument).

TOURIST TRAIN TOURS — Train Tour
(departs Domplatz; adult/family €8/19; ⊘8 tours daily) Multilingual tourist train tours of the city centre take 45 minutes to complete a circuit from the south side of the cathedral.

 Sleeping

PETIT HOTEL ORPHÉE — Hotel €€
(☎596 020; www.hotel-orphee.de; Wahlenstrasse 1; s €35-125, d €70-135) Behind a humble door in the heart of the city lies a world of genuine charm, unexpected extras and real attention to detail. Another somewhat grander branch of the hotel is located above the Café Orphée (p148).

HOTEL GOLDENES KREUZ — Hotel €€
(☎558 12; www.hotel-goldeneskreuz.de; Haidplatz 7; r €75-125; ☎) Surely the best deal in town, the nine fairy-tale rooms each bear the name of a crowned head and are fit for a kaiser. Huge mirrors, dark antique and Bauhaus furnishings, four-poster beds, chubby exposed beams and parquet flooring produce a stylishly aristocratic opus in leather, wood, crystal and fabric.

BROOK LANE HOSTEL — Hostel €
(☎696 5521; www.hostel-regensburg.de; Obere Bachgasse 21; dm/s/d from €16/40/50, apt per person €55; ☎) Regensburg's only backpacker hostel has it's very own convenience store, which doubles up as reception, but isn't open 24 hours, so late landers should let staff know in advance. Dorms do the minimum required, but the apartments and doubles here are applaudable deals.

 Eating

HAUS HEUPORT — International €€
(☎599 9297; Domplatz 7; mains €7-23; ⊘from 9am; ☑) Enter an internal courtyard (flanked by stone blocks where medieval torches were once extinguished) and climb up the grand old wooden staircase to this space-rich Gothic dining hall for eye-to-eye views of the Dom and an internationally flavoured culinary celebration.

Detour:
Walhalla

Modelled on the Parthenon in Athens, the Walhalla is a breathtaking Ludwig I monument dedicated to the giants of Germanic thought and deed. Marble steps seem to lead up forever from the banks of the Danube to this dazzling marble hall, with a gallery of 127 heroes in marble. The latest addition (2009) was romantic poet Heinrich Heine, whose works were set to music by Strauss, Wagner and Brahms.

To get there take the Danube Valley country road (unnumbered) 10km east from Regensburg to the village of Donaustauf, then follow the signs. Alternatively, you can take a two-hour boat cruise with Schifffahrt Klinger (p147), which includes a one-hour stop at Walhalla, or bus 5 from Regensburg Hauptbahnhof.

HISTORISCHE WURSTKUCHL
German €

(Thundorfer Strasse 3; 6 sausages €7.80; ⊙daily 8am-7pm) Completely submerged several times by the Danube's fickle floods, this titchy eatery has been serving the city's traditional finger-sized sausages, grilled over beechwood and dished up with sauerkraut and sweet grainy mustard, since 1135, making it the world's oldest sausage kitchen.

CAFÉ ORPHÉE
French €€

(☎529 77; Untere Bachgasse 8; mains €7-18; ⊙9am-1am) Claiming to be the Frenchiest bistro east of the Rhein, this visually pleasing eatery, bedecked in red velvet, dark wood and mirrors aplenty, does make you feel as though you've been teleported to 1920s Paris.

ROSENPALAIS
Bavarian €€€

(☎0170 880 1333; Minoritenweg 20; mains €12-32; ⊙dinner Tue-Sat) If it's posh nosh you're after, try this refined place ocupying a pinkish palace just off Dachauplatz and serving a well-heeled gourmet clientele.

DAMPFNUDEL ULI
Cafe €

(☎532 97; Watmarkt 4; dishes under €5; ⊙10.01am-6.01pm Wed-Fri, to 3.01pm Sat) This quirky little noshery serves a mean Dampfnudel (steamed doughnut) with custard in a photo- and stein-filled Gothic chamber at the base of the Baumburger Tower.

🍷 Drinking

SPITALGARTEN
Beer Garden

(St Katharinenplatz 1) A veritable thicket of folding chairs and slatted tables by the Danube, this is one of the best places in town for some alfresco quaffing.

KNEITINGER
Pub

(Arnulfsplatz 3) This quintessential Bavarian brewpub is the place to go for some hearty home cooking, delicious house suds and outrageous oompah frolics. It's been in business since 1530.

ℹ Information

Tourist office (www.regensburg.de; Altes Rathaus; ⊙9am-6pm Mon-Fri, to 4pm Sat & Sun)

ℹ Getting There & Away

CAR Regensburg is about an hour's drive southeast of Nuremberg and northwest of Passau via the A3 autobahn. The A93 runs south to Munich.

TRAIN Connections from Regensburg:

Munich €25.20, 1½ hours, hourly

Nuremberg €19, one to two hours, hourly

Passau From €22 to €27, one to 1½ hours, hourly or change in Plattling

Passau

0851 / POP 50,600

Water has quite literally shaped the picturesque town of Passau on the border with Austria. Its Altstadt is stacked atop a narrow peninsula that jabs its sharp end into the confluence of three rivers: the Danube, Inn and Ilz. The rivers brought wealth to Passau, which for centuries was an important trading centre, especially for Bohemian salt, central Europe's 'white gold'. Christianity, meanwhile, generated prestige as Passau evolved into the largest bishopric in the Holy Roman Empire.

 ## Sights

DOM ST STEPHAN   Church

(⊙6.30am-7pm) The green onion domes of Passau's Dom St Stephan float serenely above the town's silhouette. There's been a church in this spot since the late 5th century, but what you see today is much younger thanks to the Great Fire of 1662, which ravaged much of the medieval town, including the ancient cathedral. The rebuilding job went to a team of Italians, notably the architect Carlo Lurago and the stucco master Giovanni Battista Carlone. The result is a rather top-heavy baroque interior with a pious mob of saints and cherubs gazing down at the congregation from countless cornices, capitals and archways.

The building's acoustics are perfect for its pièce de résistance, the world's largest organ above the main entrance, which contains an astonishing 17,974 pipes. Half-hour **organ recitals** take place at noon daily Monday to Saturday (adult/child €4/2) and at 7.30pm on Thursday (adult/child €5/3) from May to October and for a week around Christmas. Show up at least 30 minutes early to ensure you get a seat.

VESTE OBERHAUS   Fortress

(www.oberhausmuseum.de; adult/concession €5/4; ⊙9am-5pm Mon-Fri, 10am-6pm Sat & Sun mid-Mar–mid-Nov) A 13th-century defensive fortress, built by the prince-bishops, Veste Oberhaus towers over Passau with patriarchal pomp. Not surprisingly, views of the city and into Austria are superb from up here.

Inside the bastion is the **Oberhausmuseum**, a regional history museum

Dom St Stephan

WIDMANN WIDMANN/GETTY IMAGES ©

where you can uncover the mysteries of medieval cathedral building, learn what it took to become a knight and explore Passau's period as a centre of the salt trade. Displays are labelled in English.

PASSAUER GLASMUSEUM Museum
(☎ 350 71; www.glasmuseum.de; Hotel Wilder Mann, Am Rathausplatz; adult/concession €5/4; ⏰ 10am-5pm) Opened by Neil Armstrong, of all people, Passau's warrenlike glass museum is filled with some 30,000 priceless pieces of glass and crystal from the baroque, classical, art nouveau and art deco periods. Much of what you see hails from the glassworks of Bohemia, but there are also works by Tiffany and famous Viennese producers. Be sure to pick up a floor plan as it's easy to get lost.

 Sleeping

HOTEL SCHLOSS ORT Boutique Hotel €€
(☎ 340 72; www.schlosshotel-passau.de; Im Ort 11; s €68-98, d €97-156; P) This 800-year-old medieval palace by the Inn conceals a tranquil boutique hotel, stylishly done out with polished timber floors, crisp white cotton sheets and wrought-iron bedsteads. Many of the 18 rooms enjoy river views and breakfast is served in the vaulted restaurant.

HENDLHOUSEHOTEL Hotel €
(☎ 330 69; www.hendlhousehotel.com; Grosse Klingergasse 17; s/d €55/78) With their light, unfussy decor and well-tended bathrooms, the 15 pristine rooms at this Altstadt new boy offer a high quality to price ratio. Buffet breakfast is served in the downstairs restaurant.

 Eating & Drinking

HEILIG-GEIST-STIFTS-SCHENKE Bavarian €€
(☎ 2607; Heilig-Geist-Gasse 4; mains €9.50-20; ⏰ closed Wed) Not only does the 'Holy Spirit Foundation' have a succession of walnut-panelled rooms, a candlelit cellar (open from 6pm) and a vine-draped garden, but the food is equally inspired. Specialities include *Spiessbraten* (marinated meat licked by a beechwood fire) and fish plucked live from the concrete trough.

DIWAN Cafe €€

(📞490 3280; Niebelungenplatz 1, Stadtturm; mains €7.20-10.50; ⏰9am-7pm Mon-Thu, to midnight Fri & Sat, 1-6pm Sun) Climb aboard the high-speed lift from street level to this trendy, high-perched cafe-lounge, with by far the best views in town. From the tangled rattan and plush cappuccino-culture sofas you can see it all – the Dom, the rivers, the fortress – while you tuck into the offerings of the changing seasonal menu.

ZUM GRÜNEN BAUM Organic €€

(📞356 35; Höllgasse 7; mains €7.50-16.50; ⏰10am-1am; 🍴) Take a seat under the chandelier made from cutlery to savour risottos, goulash, schnitzel and soups, prepared as far as possible using organic ingredients. Cosy, friendly and tucked away in the atmospherically narrow lanes between the river and the Residenzplatz.

ℹ Information

Tourist office (📞955 980; www.passau.de) Altstadt (Rathausplatz 3; ⏰8.30am-6pm Mon-Fri, 9am-4pm Sat & Sun Easter–mid-Oct, 8.30am-5pm Mon-Thu, 8.30am-4pm Fri mid-Oct–Easter); Hauptbahnhof (Bahnhofstrasse 28; ⏰9am-5pm Mon-Fri, 10.30am-3.30pm Sat & Sun Easter-Sep, reduced hours Oct-Easter)

ℹ Getting There & Away

BUS Buses leave at 7.45am and 4.45pm to the Czech border village of Železná Ruda (2½ hours), from where there are connections to Prague.

TRAIN Connections from Passau:

Munich €32.70, 2¼ hours, hourly

Nuremberg €46, 2¼ hours, every two hours

Regensburg €27, one hour, every two hours or change in Plattling

Stuttgart & the Black Forest

If one word could sum up Germany's southwesternmost region, it would be inventive. Baden-Württemberg gave the world relativity (Einstein), DNA (Miescher) and the astronomical telescope (Kepler). It was here that Bosch invented the spark plug; Gottlieb Daimler, the gas engine; and Count Ferdinand, the Zeppelin. And where would we be without Black Forest cake, cuckoo clocks and the ultimate beer food, the pretzel?

Beyond the high-tech, urbanite pleasures of 21st-century Stuttgart lies a region still ripe for discovery. On the city fringes country lanes roll to vineyards and lordly baroque palaces, spa towns and castles steeped in medieval myth. Swinging south, the Black Forest (*Schwarzwald* in German) looks every inch the Grimm fairy-tale blueprint. Hills rise sharp and wooded above steeples, half-timbered villages and a crochet of tightly woven valleys. It is a perfectly etched picture of sylvan beauty; a landscape refreshingly oblivious to time and trends.

Giant cuckoo clock, Schonach (p177)
INGOLF POMPE/GETTY IMAGES ©

Stuttgart & the Black Forest

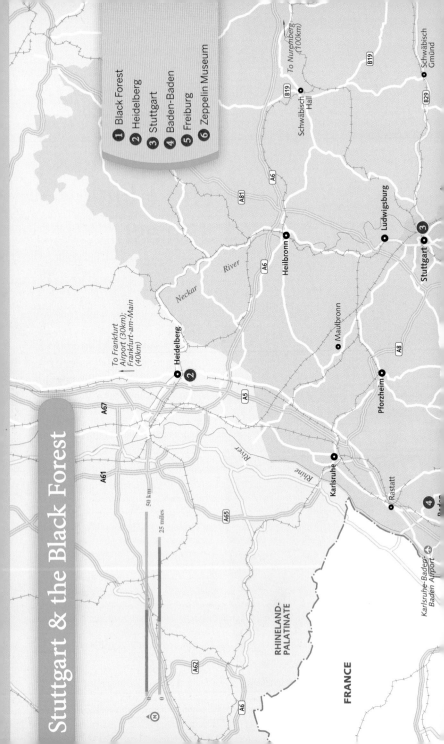

Legend	
1	Black Forest
2	Heidelberg
3	Stuttgart
4	Baden-Baden
5	Freiburg
6	Zeppelin Museum

To Nuremberg (100km)

B19

Schwäbisch Gmünd

B29

B19

Schwäbisch Hall

A6

A81

Ludwigsburg

A6

Heilbronn

3 Stuttgart

Neckar River

Maulbronn

To Frankfurt Airport (30km); Frankfurt-am-Main (40km)

Heidelberg **2**

A5

A8

Pforzheim

A67

Rhine River

Karlsruhe

A61

Rastatt

50 km

4

25 miles

A65

Karlsruhe-Baden-Baden Airport

RHINELAND-PALATINATE

A62

A6

FRANCE

N

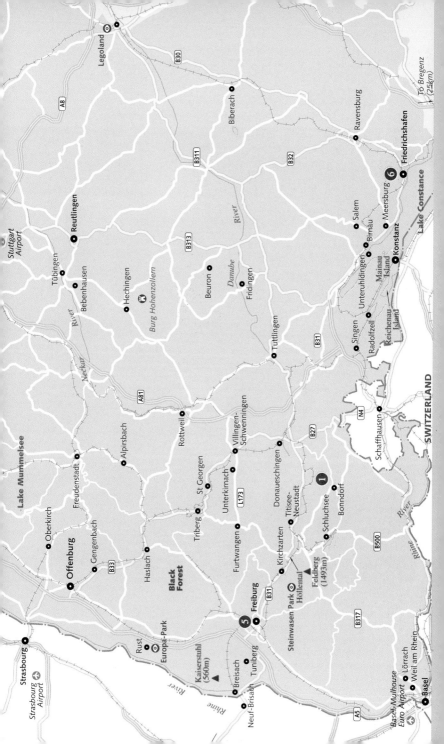

Stuttgart & the Black Forest's Highlights

① Be Bewitched by the Black Forest

I'm always amazed by the deepness and narrowness of the valleys, the soft landscape with green meadows paired with tradition-filled culture and well-preserved architecture. I love taking a walk on a foggy day in a fir forest in the central part of the mountain range. The woods are old, dark and filled with magic. Above: Schauinsland (p181); Top Right: Open-air museum Vogtsbauernhof, Gutach; Bottom Right: Schauinslandbahn (p181)

Need to Know

TOP TIP Avoid school holidays (p392) **LET A GUIDE GUIDE YOU** So you don't miss the most beautiful corners, local history, nature and traditions. **For further coverage, see p173**

Black Forest Don't Miss List

BY ÓSCAR HERNÁNDEZ CABALLERO,
BLACK FOREST MIDDLE-NORTH
NATURAL PARK GUIDE

1 WALK THE WUTACHSCHLUCHT

Take a day to walk the Wutachschlucht gorge (p181) of the river Wutach, in the south. It's the most well-preserved section of the Black Forest and one of the rare places where you can find limestone.

2 SCOOT DOWN SCHAUINSLAND

From the top of the Schauinsland (p181), near Freiburg, you can try a downhill scooter track. Take the cable car up and have a walk around the top – be sure to investigate the viewing tower. Just ask at the cable car station and they'll set you up.

3 EXPLORE A HISTORIC OPEN-AIR MUSEUM

Head to the open-air museum (p176) at the Vogtsbauernhof in Gutach. You can see a variety of traditional Black Forest farms from the 16th century and see how people lived before electricity and cars. You can even try traditional food like smoked ham and Black Forest cake in the restaurant (if you ask, they show you how they make the latter!).

4 TAKE A DRIVE

I highly recommend the Freudenstadt to Baden-Baden portion of the Schwarzwald-Hochstrasse B500 (p182)– it's particularly picturesque, and look out for the messy (but interesting) part that still shows signs of the 1999 hurricane Lothar. One of my other favourite drives is the Deutsche Uhrenstrasse (p182), which passes through the central portion of the mountain range and the land of the cuckoo clocks.

Fall in Love with Heidelberg

With its castle ruin, the oldest university in Germany and the surrounding hills, Heidelberg (p170) enchants with a fascinating mixture of history, vibrant modern life and nature. It's a magical place with a romantic, bustling and international ambience. But it's impossible to truly explain 'magic': come and experience it yourself!

3 Feel the Thrill of Fast Cars

Car lovers will go mad in Stuttgart, which is home to two car museums. At the Mercedes-Benz museum (p165), look out for legends like the 1888 Daimler Riding Car, the world's first gasoline-powered vehicle. The Porsche Museum (p165) takes you through the history of Porsche from its 1948 beginnings – break to glimpse the 911 GTI that won Le Mans in 1998. Porsche Museum, Stuttgart

Take to the Waters

After hiking all those high peaks, you deserve to unwind, give your muscles a rest and take a moment to relax in Baden-Baden (p173), the swish spa town that heals the mind and the skin. Forget your troubles, close your eyes, and let the curative water soothe your muscles and your worries in Germany's most renowned waters. Caracalla Therme (p175), Baden-Baden

Explore Lively Freiburg

It's tough to put your finger on why Freiburg (p177) has such a fun and relaxing feel – maybe it's the large student population, or maybe it's the gorgeous, soothing, ubiquitous red-sandstone buildings, most notably the soaring Gothic Münster on the town square. Contemplate it all at one of Freiburg's fine watering holes.

Get 'High' at the Zeppelin Museum

Get the scoop on the airships that first took flight in 1900 under the stewardship of Count Ferdinand von Zeppelin at this museum (p185). There's even a mock-up of a 33m section of the *Hindenburg*, the largest airship ever built. Outfitted as luxuriously as an ocean liner, it tragically burst into flames during landing in 1937.

Stuttgart & the Black Forest's Best...

Freebies

o **Schlossgarten** (p164) Stuttgart's palace gardens are a remarkable sanctuary of greenery

o **Münster** (p178) Freiburg's magnificent minster has a mesmerising high altar and stained-glass windows

o **Trinkhalle** (p174) (Pump Room) Bring your own bottle and fill it up with medicinal mineral water in Baden-Baden

Heart-Pumping Hikes

o **Winzerweg** (p182) (Wine Growers' Trail) Fifteen kilometres of forests and vineyards through the Kaiserstuhl

o **Schattenmühle to Wutachmühle** (p182) This 13km-long path is the best place to view the dramatic gorge

o **Kaiserstuhl-Tour** (p182) This 55km-long circuit is for hard-core hikers only

Lazy Rides

o **Kaiserstuhlbahn** (p182) (Kaiserstuhl train) Head up into wine country for a relaxing loop around volcanic hills

o **Schauinslandbahn** (p181) (cable car) Enjoy the 3.6km ride and fabulous Black Forest views

o **Schlossbergbahn** (p179) Newly restored, this one takes to Freiburg's 'upper story'

o **Bergbahn** (p172) Trundle up this Heidelberg hill in an antique rail car

Need to Know

Regional Eateries

◦ **Rathausglöckel** (p175) Serves the gamut of hearty fare in an woodsy, olde-worlde setting

◦ **Englers Weinkrügle** (p180) Offers local fish with local wine, and various other mouth-watering concoctions

◦ **Café Schäfer** (p177) For a decadent slice of *Schwarzwälder Kirschtorte* (Black Forest gateau), made according to the original recipe

◦ **Weinstube Frey** (p187) For freshly caught Lake Constance trout

ADVANCE PLANNING

◦ **One month before** Book a guide for an unforgettable hike through the Black Forest – contact the regional tourist offices for names and numbers.

◦ **Several weeks in advance** Book a table at trendy and Michelin-starred restaurants.

◦ **One week before** Check the weather forecast and make sure you pack accordingly.

RESOURCES

◦ **Schwarzwaldverein** (www.schwarzwaldverein.de) The Schwarzwaldverein is Germany's first hiking club.

◦ **State Tourist Board** (www.tourismus-bw.de) Stuttgart and the Black Forest are within the state of Baden-Württemberg.

GETTING AROUND

◦ **Air** Flights to the region serve Stuttgart, Karlsruhe-Baden-Baden and Basel-Mulhouse EuroAirport.

◦ **Boat** Bodensee-schifffahrt (www .bodenseeschifffahrt .at) and Bodensee-Schiffsbetriebe (www .bsb-online.com) link the ports on Lake Constance.

◦ **Car** The main north–south autobahn is the A5 from Baden-Baden south to Freiburg. The A81 runs south from Stuttgart to Lake Constance, while the A8 links Stuttgart to Karlsruhe, Ulm and Munich.

◦ **Train** Save on train fares with the good-value Baden-Württemberg Ticket available at train stations and online (www .bahn.de).

BE FOREWARNED

◦ **Museums** Many are closed on Mondays.

◦ **Public transport** Travelling around the Black Forest can be slow, and long-distance trips (for instance Freiburg to Konstanz) may involve several changes. Use www.efa-bw.de or www .bahn.de for trip planning.

◦ **Limited bus service** Some commuter-geared regional buses don't run in the evenings and on weekends.

◦ **Ongoing roadworks** Traffic jams often clog the A5 from Baden-Baden to Freiburg; check www.swr .de for up-to-date traffic news.

Stuttgart & the Black Forest Itineraries

Explore storied towns like Heidelberg, Baden-Baden and Freiburg, then let winding backroads take you through the Black Forest's misty vales, fairy-tale woodlands and villages that ooze earthy authenticity.

3 DAYS

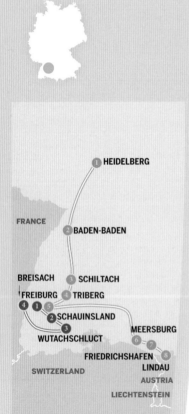

FREIBURG & AROUND

A Black Forest Immersion

The southern Black Forest serves up some of Germany's most enigmatic scenery. Base yourself in student-flavoured **(1) Freiburg** and spend the morning visiting the glorious minster and getting lost amid tangled cobbled lanes. In the afternoon, take the 3.6km cable car ride to the **(2) Schauinsland peak** for knockout views of the Alps, the Rhine Valley and the Black Forest. Are you itching to grab your walking boots and delve into this emerald expanse? If so, spend the next day exploring the wild beauty of the narrow **(3) Wutachschlucht** (Wutach Gorge), carved by the eponymous sprightly river, flanked by ferns and wild orchids. Return to Freiburg and treat yourself to a well-deserved wine tavern dinner. This should whet your appetite for the following day's adventure to the Kaiserstuhl, one of Germany's most celebrated wine-growing regions, near **(4) Breisach**. Blessed with the country's warmest and sunniest climate, it produces wonderfully crisp *Grauburgunder* (Pinot gris) and rich *Spätburgunder* (Pinot noir). Stop by the Breisach tourist office to find out about cellar tours and wine tastings.

Top: Schauinslandbahn (p181), Schauinsland;
Right: Triberger Wasserfälle (p177), Triberg

5 DAYS

HEIDELBERG TO LINDAU

City to the Sea

Done as a road trip, this whirlwind itinerary lets you quickly sample the region's block-buster destinations. Start off in **(1) Heidelberg**, where the romantically ruined castle, a stroll along Philosophenweg and an evening in a student tavern are must-dos. The next day, steer south to swish **(2) Baden-Baden** to revel in its refined air, wallow in its therapeutic baths and challenge Lady Luck in its glamorous casino. On day three plunge on into the Black Forest via the scenic Schwarzwald-Hochstrasse and on to the half-timbered gem of **(3) Schiltach** and the cuckoo-clock capital of **(4) Triberg**. Take time to visit the latter's dreamy waterfall, marvel at the two timepieces that claim to be the world's largest cuckoo clock and, of course, indulge in a slice of Black Forest cake in the village where it was invented. Continue to delightful **(5) Freiburg** to absorb its ample charms (also see the three-day itinerary), then drive east towards Lake Constance to take in enchanting **(6) Meersburg**, and study up on Zeppelin airships in **(7) Friedrichshafen**, before wrapping up your epic journey in lovely **(8) Lindau**.

Discover Stuttgart & the Black Forest

STUTTGART

♪ 0711 / POP 581,100

Ask many Germans their opinion of Stuttgarters and they will go off on a tangent: they are road hogs behind a Mercedes wheel, speeding along the autobahn; they are sharp-dressed executives with a Swabian drawl; they are tight-fisted homebodies who slave away to *schaffe, schaffe, Häusle baue* (work, work, build a house). So much for the stereotypes.

The real Stuttgart is less superficial than the legend. True, some good-living locals like their cars fast and their restaurants fancy but most are just as happy getting their boots dirty in the surrounding vine-clad hills and hanging out with friends in the rustic confines of a *Weinstube* (wine tavern).

 Sights

SCHLOSSGARTEN   Garden
East of the station, the fountain-dotted **Mittlerer Schlossgarten (Middle Palace Garden)** draws thirsty crowds to its beer garden in summer. The **Unterer Schlossgarten (Lower Palace Garden)** is a ribbon of greenery rambling northeast to the Neckar River and the **Rosensteinpark**, home to the zoo. Sitting south, the **Oberer Schlossgarten** (Upper Palace Garden) is framed by eye-catching landmarks like the columned **Staatstheater** (State Theatre) and the ultramodern glass-clad **Landtag** (State Parliament).

SCHLOSSPLATZ   Square
Rising majestically above the square is the exuberant three-winged **Neues Schloss**. Duke Karl Eugen von Württem-

Mercedes-Benz Museum, Stuttgart
DAVID PEEVERS/GETTY IMAGES ©

berg's answer to Versailles, the baroque-neoclassical royal residence now houses state government ministries.

STAATSGALERIE Gallery
(www.staatsgalerie-stuttgart.de; Konrad-Adenauer-Strasse 30-32; adult/concession €5.50/4, special exhibitions €10/8, Wed & Sat free; ⏰10am-6pm Tue-Sun, to 8pm Tue & Thu) The neoclassical-meets-contemporary Staatsgalerie bears British architect James Stirling's curvy, colourful imprint. Alongside big-name exhibitions, the gallery harbours a phenomenal collection of 20th-century art, showcasing works by Rembrandt, Picasso, Monet, Dalí and pop idols Warhol and Lichtenstein.

MERCEDES-BENZ MUSEUM Museum
(www.museum-mercedes-benz.com; Mercedes-strasse 100; adult/concession €8/4; ⏰9am-6pm Tue-Sun; 🚆Neckarpark) A futuristic swirl on the cityscape, the Mercedes-Benz Museum takes a chronological spin through the Mercedes empire. Look out for legends like the 1885 Daimler Riding Car, the world's first gasoline-powered vehicle, and the record-breaking Lightning Benz that hit 228km/h on Daytona Beach in 1909. There's a free guided tour in English at 11am.

PORSCHE MUSEUM Museum
(www.porsche.com; Porscheplatz 1; adult/concession €8/4; ⏰9am-6pm Tue-Sun; 🚆Neuwirtshaus) Like a pearly white spaceship preparing for lift-off, the barrier-free Porsche Museum is every little boy's dream. Groovy audioguides race you through the history of Porsche from its 1948 beginnings. Break to glimpse the 911 GT1 that won Le Mans in 1998.

 Tours

Sightseeing tours feature **Hop-on, Hop-off Bus Tours** (adult/concession €18/15; ⏰11am Apr-Oct), which depart roughly hourly from 11am to 6pm from Schloss-platz and trundle past city icons like the Fernsehturm and Mercedes-Benz Museum.

 Sleeping

KRONEN HOTEL Hotel €€€
(🕿225 10; www.kronenhotel-stuttgart.de; Kronenstrasse 48; s €108-120, d €149-180; P ❄ @ 🛜) Right in the lap of König-strasse, the Kronen outclasses most of Stuttgart's hotels with its terrific location, good-natured team, well-appointed rooms and funkily lit sauna.

HOTEL AZENBERG Hotel €€
(🕿225 5040; www.hotelazenberg.de; Seestrasse 114-116; s €70-105, d €85-120; P 🛜 ♿; 🚌43) This family-run pick has individually designed quarters with themes swinging from English country manor to Picasso. There's a pool, tree-shaded garden and mini spa for relaxing moments. Take bus 43 from Stadtmitte to Hölderlinstrasse.

HOTEL AM SCHLOSSGARTEN Luxury Hotel €€€
(🕿202 60; www.hotelschlossgarten.com; Schill-erstrasse 23; s €132-167, d €167-187; P ❄ 🛜) Sidling up to the Schloss, this hotel has handsome, park-facing rooms, which flaunt the luxuries that justify the price tag. Book a table at Michelin-starred Zirbelstube (tasting menus €109 to €139) for classy French dining in subtly lit, pine-panelled surrounds.

 Eating

IRMA LA DOUCE Mediterranean €€€
(🕿470 4320; www.irmaladouce.de; Katharinen-strasse 21b; lunch €11-14, dinner €25-39.50; ⏰closed lunch Sat & Sun) An ornate fireplace and chandeliers cast flattering light across the polished wood, bookshelves and paintings at this 19th-century bistro. Inspired by the seasons and herby Mediterranean flavours, the menu might star such delicacies as quail breast on wild garlic and roast Iberian pork with spinach gnocchi.

DÉLICE Modern European €€€
(🕿640 3222; www.restaurant-delice.de; Haupt-stätter Strasse 61; 5-course tasting menu €90; ⏰6.30pm-midnight Mon-Fri) At this vaulted Michelin-starred restaurant, natural,

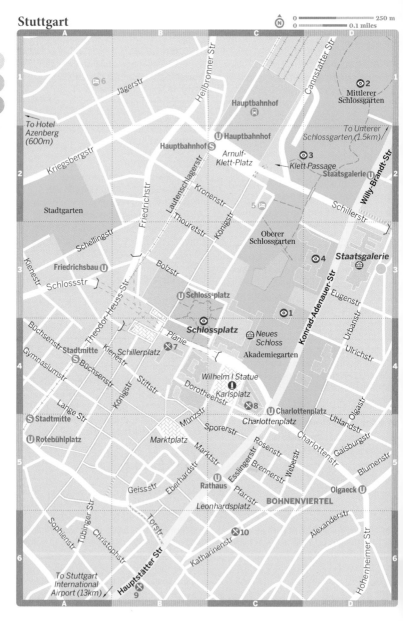

Stuttgart

integral flavours sing in specialities like medley of tuna with lemon vinaigrette and fried egg with parsnips and Périgord truffles. The sommelier will talk you through the award-winning riesling selection.

AMADEUS Swabian €€
(☎ 292 678; Charlottenplatz 17; mains €9.50-22.50; ☺ daily) Once an 18th-century orphanage dishing up gruel, this chic, bustling restaurant now serves glorious Swabian

Stuttgart

food such as *Maultaschen* (pork and spinach ravioli) and riesling-laced *Kutteln* (tripe). The terrace is a big draw in summer.

ALTE KANZLEI German €€
(☏ 294 457; Schillerplatz 5a; mains €10.50-20.50; ☉ daily) Empty tables are gold-dust rare at this convivial, high-ceilinged restaurant on Schillerplatz. Feast on Swabian favourites like *Spannferkel* (roast suckling pig) and *Flädlesuppe* (pancake soup), washed down with regional tipples.

Information

Tourist office (☏ 222 8100; www.stuttgart-tourist.de; Königstrasse 1a; ☉ 9am-8pm Mon-Fri, 9am-6pm Sat, 11am-6pm Sun) The staff can help with room bookings for a €3 fee and public transport enquiries. Has a list of vineyards open for tastings.

Getting There & Away

Air

Stuttgart International Airport (www.stuttgart-airport.com), a major hub for Germanwings (www.germanwings.com), is 13km south of the city. S2 and S3 trains take about 30 minutes to get from the airport to the Hauptbahnhof (€3.50).

Car & Motorcycle

The A8 from Munich to Karlsruhe passes Stuttgart, often abbreviated to 'S' on highway signs, as does the A81 from Singen (near Lake Constance) to Heilbronn and Mannheim.

Train

IC and ICE destinations include Berlin (€135, 5½ hours), Frankfurt (€59, 1¼ hours) and Munich (€49 to €54, 2¼ hours).

AROUND STUTTGART

Tübingen
☏ 07071 / POP 88,360

Liberal students and deeply traditional *Burschenschaften* (fraternities) singing ditties for beloved Germania, eco-warriors, artists and punks – all have a soft spot for this bewitchingly pretty Swabian city, where cobbled lanes lined with half-timbered town houses twist up to a turreted castle. It's about 40km south of Stuttgart.

Sights

SCHLOSS HOHENTÜBINGEN Castle
(Burgsteige 11; museum adult/concession €5/3; ☉ castle 7am-8pm daily, museum 10am-5pm Wed-Sun to 7pm Thu) On its perch above Tübingen, this turreted 16th-century castle has a terrace overlooking the Neckar and the Altstadt's triangular rooftops to the vine-streaked hills beyond. An ornate Renaissance gate leads to the courtyard and the laboratory where Friedrich Miescher discovered DNA in 1869.

AM MARKT Square
Half-timbered town houses frame the Altstadt's main plaza Am Markt, a much-loved student hang-out. Rising above it is the 15th-century **Rathaus** (Town Hall), with a riotous baroque facade and an astronomical clock. Statues of four women representing the seasons grace the **Neptune Fountain** opposite. Keep an eye out for **No 15**, where a white window frame identifies a secret room where Jews hid in WWII.

YOSHIHIRO TAKADA/A COLLECTIONRF/GETTY IMAGES ©

Eating

NECKARMÜLLER Brewpub €€

(📞278 48; Gartenstrasse 4; mains €7.50-15;
🕙10am-1am) Overlooking the Neckar, this
cavernous microbrewery is a summertime magnet for its chestnut-shaded
beer garden. Come for home brews by
the metre and beer-laced dishes from
(tasty) Swabian roast to (interesting)
tripe stew.

WURSTKÜCHE German €€

(📞927 50; Am Lustnauer Tor 8; mains
€9-17.50; 🕙11am-midnight daily) The rustic,
wood-panelled Wurstküche brims with
locals quaffing wine and contentedly
munching *Schupfnudeln* (potato
noodles) and *Spanpferkel* (roast
suckling pig).

❶ Information

Tourist office (📞913 60; www.tuebingen-info
.de; An der Neckarbrücke 1; 🕙9am-7pm Mon-Fri,
10am-4pm Sat, plus 11am-4pm Sun May-Sep)

❶ Getting There & Around

Tübingen is an easy train ride from Stuttgart
(€12.20, one hour, twice an hour) and Villingen
(€21, 1½ to two hours, hourly) in the Black Forest.

Ulm

📞 0731 / POP 122,800

Starting with the statistics, Ulm has the
crookedest house (as listed in *Guinness
World Records*) and one of the narrowest
(4.5m wide), the world's oldest zoomor-
phic sculpture (aged 30,000 years) and
tallest cathedral steeple (161.5m high) and
is the birthplace of the physicist, Albert
Einstein. Relatively speaking, of course.

Superlatives aside, this idiosyncratic
city will win your affection with everyday
encounters; particularly in summer when
your chain sings as you pedal along the
Danube and the Fischerviertel's beer
gardens hum with animated chatter.

◎ Sights

FREE MÜNSTER Cathedral

(www.ulmer-muenster.de; Münsterplatz; organ
concerts €3.50-6, tower adult/concession
€4/2.50; 🕙9am-7.45pm, to 4.45pm in winter)

Ooh, it's so big...first-time visitors gush as they strain their neck muscles gazing up to the Münster. It is. And rather beautiful. Celebrated for its 161.5m-high steeple, the world's tallest, this Goliath of cathedrals took a staggering 500 years to build from the first stone laid in 1377. Only by puffing up 768 spiral steps to the 143m-high viewing platform of the **tower** can you appreciate the Münster's dizzying height.

MARKTPLATZ Square

Lording it over the Marktplatz, the 14th-century, step-gabled **Rathaus** sports an ornately painted Renaissance facade and a gilded astrological clock. Inside there is a replica of Berblinger's flying machine.

 Eating

ZUR FORELLE German €€€

(639 24; Fischergasse 25; mains €12-22; daily) Since 1626, this low-ceilinged tavern has been convincing wayfarers (Einstein included) about the joys of seasonal Swabian cuisine.

ZUNFTHAUS DER SCHIFFLEUTE German €€€

(175 5771; www.zunfthaus-ulm.com; Fischergasse 31; mains €10-19; daily) Looking proudly back on a 600-year tradition, this timber-framed restaurant sits by the river. The menu speaks of a chef who loves his region, with Swabian faves like *Katzagschroi* (beef, onions, egg and fried potatoes) and meaty one-pot *Schwäbisches Hochzeitssüppchen*.

ℹ Information

Tourist office (161 2830; www.tourismus.ulm .de; Münsterplatz 50, Stadthaus; 9am-6pm Mon-Fri, 9am-4pm Sat, 11am-3pm Sun)

ℹ Getting There & Away

Ulm, about 90km southeast of Stuttgart and 150km west of Munich, is near the intersection of the north–south A7 and the east–west A8.

Ulm is well-served by ICE and EC trains; major destinations include Stuttgart (€18.10 to €25, 56 minutes to 1¼ hours, several hourly) and Munich (€30 to €36, 1¼ hours, several hourly).

Kloster Maulbronn

Billed as the best-preserved medieval monastery north of the Alps, the one-time Cistercian monastery **Kloster Maulbronn** (Maulbronn Monastery; 07043-926 610; www .schloesser-und-gaerten.de; adult/concession/ family €6/3/15; 9am-5.30pm Mar-Oct, 9.30am-5pm Tue-Sun Nov-Feb) was founded by Alsatian monks in 1147, born again as a Protestant school in 1556 and designated a Unesco World Heritage Site in 1993. Its famous graduates include the astronomer Johannes Kepler. Aside from the Romanesque-Gothic portico in the **monastery church** and the weblike vaulting of the **cloister**, it's the insights into monastic life that make this place so culturally stimulating.

Maulbronn is 30km east of Karlsruhe and 33km northwest of Stuttgart, near the Pforzheim Ost exit on the A8.

Burg Hohenzollern

Rising dramatically from an exposed crag, its medieval battlements and silver turrets often veiled in mist, **Burg Hohenzollern** (www.burg-hohenzollern.com; tour adult/concession €10/8, grounds admission only adult/concession €5/4; tour 10am-5.30pm, to 4.30pm Nov–mid-Mar) is impressive from a distance but up close it looks more contrived. Dating to 1867, this neo-Gothic castle is the ancestral seat of the Hohenzollern family, the first and last monarchical rulers of the short-lived second German empire (1871–1918).

History fans should take a 35-minute German-language **tour**, which takes in towers, overblown salons replete with stained glass and frescoes, and the dazzling *Schatzkammer* (treasury). The **grounds** command tremendous views over the Swabian Alps.

Frequent trains link Tübingen, 28km distant, with Hechingen (€4.40, 25 minutes, one or two an hour), about 4km northwest of the castle.

HEIDELBERG

Germany's oldest and most famous university town is renowned for its baroque Altstadt, lively university atmosphere, excellent pubs and evocative half-ruined castle, which draw 3½ million visitors a year. They are following in the footsteps of the late 18th- and early 19th-century romantics, most notably the poet Goethe. Less-starry eyed was Mark Twain, who in 1878 began his European travels with a three-month stay in Heidelberg, recounting his bemused observations in *A Tramp Abroad*.

 ## Sights

MARKTPLATZ   Square
The Marktplatz is the focal point of Altstadt street life. The central trickling **Hercules fountain** – that's him up on top of the pillar – is where petty criminals were chained and left to face the mob in the Middle Ages. Across the street at Haupstrasse 190 stands the baroque **Hofapotheke (Court Pharmacy)**, built in the early 1700s and still sporting a gilded coat-of-arms.

HEILIGGEISTKIRCHE   Church
(Marktplatz; spire adult/student €2/1; ⊙11am-5pm Mon-Sat, 12.30-5pm Sun & holidays mid-Mar–Oct, 11am-3pm Fri & Sat, 12.30-3pm Sun Nov–mid-Mar) Heidelberg's most famous church, the Gothic-style Church of the Holy Spirit, was built from 1398 to 1441. Starting in 1706 it was used by both Catholics and Protestants, with a wall separating the two congregations; since 1936 it's been Protestant. For a bird's-eye view of Heidelberg, climb 208 stairs to the top of the **spire**.

STUDENTENKARZER   Historic Site
(Augustinergasse 2; adult/student incl Universitäts Museum €3/2.50; ⊙10am-6pm Tue-Sun Apr-Sep, 10am-4pm Tue-Sat Oct-Mar) From 1823 to 1914, students convicted of misdeeds such as public inebriation, loud nocturnal singing, freeing the local pigs or duelling were sent to the Student Jail, where they were 'inkarzerated' for at least 24 hours and, for the first two days, fed only bread and water. Judging by the inventive graffiti and creative inscriptions, some found their stay highly entertaining.

ALTE BRÜCKE   Bridge
(Karl-Theodor-Brücke; Neckarstaden) The 200m-long 'Old Bridge', built in 1788, connects the Altstadt with the river's right bank and the **Schlangenweg** (Snake Path), whose switchbacks head up the hill to the **Philosophenweg** (Philosophers' Way).

PHILOSOPHENWEG   Trail
Passing through steep fields and orchards on the slopes across the river from the Altstadt, the Philosophers' Way commands panoramic views of the Schloss as it wends its way through the forest to various monuments, towers, ruins, a beer garden and the **Thingstätte**, a Nazi-era amphitheatre.

 ## Tours

The tourist office runs English-language **walking tours** (adult/concession €7/5; ⊙10.30am Fri & Sat Apr-Oct) of the Altstadt; departures are from the Marktplatz (Rathaus) tourist office.

Heidelberg

0 — 200 m
0 — 0.1 miles

Neckar River

Neckarstaden

To Theodor-Heuss-Brücke (500m);
Bismarckplatz (600m)

Neuenheimer Landstr

Alte Brücke
(Karl-Theodor-
Brücke)

To Schangenweg (150m);
Philosophenweg (400m)

Am Hackteufel

Neckarmünzplatz

Leyergasse

Hauptstr

Heiliggeiststr

Karlstr

Karlsplatz

Mönchgasse

Obere Neckarstr

Kornmarkt

Marktplatz

Tourist
Office

Mittelbadgasse

Krämergasse

Steingasse

Haspelgasse

Ingrimstr

Heiliggeistkirche

Kettengasse

Dreikönigstr

Untere Str

Hauptstr

Lauerstr

Kleine Mantelgasse

Augustinergasse

Merianstr

Jesuitenviertel

Zwingerstr

Studentenkarzer

Universitäts-
platz

Grabengasse

Grosse Mamtlgasse

Heumarkt

Sandgasse

Theaterstr

Friedrichstr

Bauamtsgsssse

Plöck

Untere Neckarstr

Bienenstr

Karpfengasse

Märzgasse

Friedrich-Ebert-Anlage

To Hauptbahnhof (2km)

Schlossberg

Neue Schlossstr

Unter-Fauler Pelz

Oberer Fauler Pelz

Neue Schlossstr

Funicular Railway

Burgweg

Schloss

Schlossgarten

171

TAKASHI HAGIHARA/AMANAIMAGESRF/GETTY IMAGES ©

Don't Miss Schloss Heidelberg

Sticking up above the Altstadt like a picture-book pop-up, Heidelberg's ruined Schloss is one of the most romantic spots in Germany. Palatinate princes, stampeding Swedes, rampaging French, Protestant reformers and lightning strikes – this Renaissance castle has seen the lot. Its tumultuous history, lonely beauty and changing moods helped inspire the German Romantic movement two centuries ago.

With a capacity of about 228,000L, the mid-18th-century **Grosses Fass** (Great Wine Barrel), shaped from 130 oak trees, is the world's largest wine cask. Describing it as being 'as big as a cottage', Mark Twain bemoaned its emptiness and mused on its possible functions as a dance floor and a gigantic cream churn.

To reach the red-sandstone castle, perched about 80m above the Altstadt, you can either hoof it up the steep, cobbled Burgweg in about 10 minutes, or take the Bergbahn, opened in 1890, from the Kornmarkt station.

NEED TO KNOW

www.schloss-heidelberg.de; adult/child incl Bergbahn €5/3, audioguides €4, 1½ hours; 24hr, ticket required 8am-5.30pm

Sleeping

HIP HOTEL Boutique Hotel €€€
(**208 79; www.hip-hotel.de; Hauptstrasse 115; s €135-180, d €150-210, breakfast €12;**) Snooze in a Fijian beach shack complete with sandy bay, a woodsy Canadian hunter's cottage, or a topsy-turvy Down Under room where everything (paintings, doors, bed) is upside down. In an age in which cities are awash in 'theme hotels', this 27-room place is both genuinely creative and heaps of fun.

ARTHOTEL Boutique Hotel €€
(**650 060; www.arthotel.de; Grabengasse 7; d without breakfast €115-198;**) If you're in the mood to experience 21st-century German interior design at its most stylish,

the Arthotel won't disappoint. The red and black lobby, lit by a wall of windows, sets the tone, while the 24 rooms, equipped with huge bathrooms, are spacious and cleanly minimalist – except for three, which come with painted ceilings that date from 1790.

Eating & Drinking

ZUR HERRENMÜHLE German €€€
(☎602 909; www.herrenmuehle-heidelberg .de; Hauptstrasse 237-239; mains €14.50-28.50; ⏰6-10pm Mon-Sat) A flour mill from 1690 has been turned into an elegant and highly cultured place to enjoy traditional 'country house' cuisine, including fish, under 300-year-old wood beams, a candle flickering romantically at each table.

KULTURBRAUEREI Cafe €€
(☎502 980; Leyergasse 6; mains €10.50-26.50; ⏰7am-11pm or later) With its wood-plank floor, black iron chandeliers and time-faded ceiling frescoes, this microbrewery – in a hall that dates from 1903 – is an atmospheric spot to tuck into salad, soup or regional dishes such as *Schäufele* (pork shoulder) with sauerkraut (€10.50), or to quaff home-brews in the beer garden.

WIRTHAUS ZUM SEPP'L German €€
(Hauptstrasse 217; mains €11.90-24.50; ⏰5pm-12.30am Tue-Sat) Heidelberg's most historic student pub has black-and-white frat photos on the dark wooden walls and names carved into the tables, though these days students are outnumbered by tourists. Dishes are a mix of German and Italian.

 Information

Tourist office (☎194 33, 584 4444; www .heidelberg-marketing.de) Has loads of useful information and sells a handy walking tour map (€1.50). The **Hauptbahnhof** (Willy-Brandt-Platz 1; ⏰9am-7pm Mon-Sat, 10am-6pm Sun & holidays Apr-Oct, 9am-6pm Mon-Sat Nov-Mar) branch is right outside the train station; the **Marktplatz** (Marktplatz 10; 8am-5pm Mon-Fri, 10am-5pm Sat) branch is inside the red-sandstone Rathaus.

Getting There & Away

From the **Hauptbahnhof** (Willy-Brandt-Platz), 3km west of the Schloss, there are at least hourly train services to/from Frankfurt (€16.40 to €27, one hour to 1½ hours) and Stuttgart (€21.20 to €37, 40 minutes to 1½ hours).

The fastest way to get to Frankfurt airport (€23, one hour, every hour or two) is to take the eight-seat **Lufthansa's Airport Shuttle** (☎06152-976 9099; www.transcontinental -group.com).

THE BLACK FOREST
Baden-Baden
☎07221 / POP 54,500

'So nice that you have to name it twice', enthused Bill Clinton about Baden-Baden, whose air of old-world luxury and curative waters have attracted royals – Obama and Bismarck, Queen Victoria and Victoria Beckham included. 'Nice', however, could never convey the amazing grace of this Black Forest town, with its grand colonnaded buildings and whimsically turreted art nouveau villas spread across the hillsides and framed by forested mountains.

And with its temple-like thermal baths – which put the *Baden* (bathe) in Baden – and palatial casino, the allure of this grand dame of German spa towns is as timeless as it is enduring.

Sights & Activities

KURHAUS & CASINO Landmark
(www.kurhaus-baden-baden.de; Kaiserallee 1; guided tour €5; ⏰guided tour 9.30am-11.30am daily) Corinthian columns and a frieze of mythical griffins grace the belle époque facade of the Kurhaus, which towers above well-groomed gardens. An alley of chestnut trees, flanked by two rows of boutiques, links the Kurhaus with Kaiserallee.

Inside is the sublime **casino** (www.casino -baden-baden.de; admission €5; ⏰2pm-2am Sun-Thu, 2pm-3am Fri & Sat), which seeks

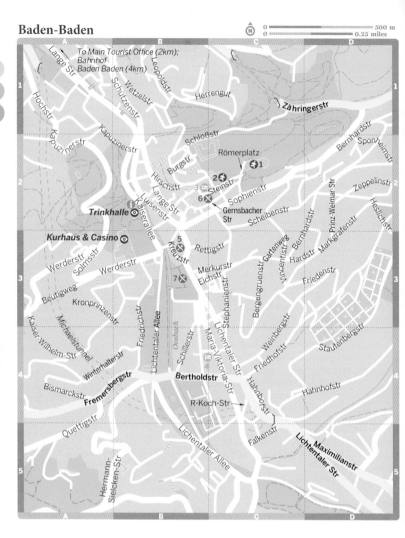

to emulate – indeed, outdo – the gilded splendour of Versailles.

TRINKHALLE
Landmark

(Pump Room; Kaiserallee 3; ⏰10am-5pm Mon-Sat, 2-5pm Sun) Standing proud above a manicured park, this neoclassical pump room was built in 1839 as an attractive addition to the Kurhaus. The 90m-long portico is embellished with 19th-century frescoes of local legends. Baden-Baden's elixir of youth, some say, is the free curative mineral water that gushes from a faucet linked to the Friedrichsbad spring.

FRIEDRICHSBAD
Spa

(☎275 920; www.roemisch-irisches-bad.de; Römerplatz 1; 3hr ticket €23, incl soap-and-brush massage €33; ⏰9am-10pm, last admission 7pm) If it's the body of Venus and the complexion of Cleopatra you desire, abandon modesty (and clothing) to wallow in thermal waters at this sumptuous 19th-century spa. As Mark Twain put it: 'after 10 minutes you forget time; after 20

Baden-Baden

Top Sights

Activities, Courses & Tours

Sleeping

Eating

minutes, the world', as you slip into the regime of steaming, scrubbing, hot-cold bathing and dunking in the Roman-Irish bath. With its cupola, mosaics and Carrera marble pool, the bathhouse is the vision of a neo-Renaissance palace.

CARACALLA THERME Spa

(www.caracalla.de; Römerplatz 11; 2/3/4hr €14/17/20; 8am-10pm, last admission 8pm) If you would prefer to keep your bathing togs on, this glass-fronted spa has a cluster of indoor and outdoor pools, grottos and surge channels, making the most of the mineral-rich spring water. For those who dare to bare, saunas range from the rustic 'forest' to the roasting 95°C 'fire' variety.

Sleeping

HOTEL BELLE EPOQUE Luxury Hotel **€€€**

(300 660; www.hotel-belle-epoque.de; Maria-Viktoria-Strasse 2c; s €170-245, d €225-299;) Nestling in manicured parkland, this neo-Renaissance villa is one of Baden-Baden's most characterful five-star pads. Antiques lend a dash of old-world opulence to the individually designed rooms. Rates include high tea, with scones and cakes and fine brews served on the terrace or by the fireplace.

HOTEL AM MARKT Historic Hotel **€**

(270 40; www.hotel-am-markt-baden.de; Marktplatz 18; s €37-53 d €70-92; P @) Sitting pretty in front of the Stiftskirche, this 250-year-old hotel has 23 homely, well-kept rooms. It's quiet up here apart from your wake-up call of church bells, but then you wouldn't want to miss out on the great breakfast.

Eating

RATHAUSGLÖCKEL German **€€**

(906 10; Steinstrasse 7; mains €10-16; 6-11pm Mon-Sat, 11.30am-2pm & 6-11pm Sun, closed Wed;) Strong on old-school charm, this low-beamed tavern is cosily clad in dark wood and oil paintings. Historic regional and German dishes are on the menu, from *Himmel und Erde* (black pudding, mashed potatoes, apple sauce and fried onions) to stuffed quail with *Schupfnudeln* (stubby potato noodles with sauerkraut).

RIZZI Italian **€€€**

(258 38; Augustaplatz 1; mains €18-25; noon-1am) A summertime favourite, this pink villa's tree-shaded patio faces Lichtentaler Allee. Italian-influenced dishes like osso buco (veal shanks braised with vegetables, garlic and wine) and scallops with truffle mash pair well with local wines.

CAFÉ KÖNIG Cafe **€**

(Lichtentaler Strasse 12; cake €3.50-5; 9.30am-6.30am Mon-Sat, 10.30am-6.30pm Sun) Liszt and Tolstoy once sipped coffee at this venerable cafe, which has been doing a brisk trade in Baden-Baden's finest cakes, tortes, pralines and truffles for 250 years.

Information

Branch tourist office (Kaiserallee 3; 10am-5pm Mon-Sat, 2-5pm Sun) In the Trinkhalle.

Main tourist office (275 200; www.baden-baden.com; Schwarzwaldstrasse 52; 9am-6pm Mon-Sat, 9am-1pm Sun) Situated 2km northwest of the centre. If you're driving from the northwest (from the A5) this place is on the way into town.

JUERGEN STUMPE/GETTY IMAGES ©

ⓘ Getting There & Away

Karlsruhe-Baden-Baden airport (Baden Airpark; www.badenairpark.de), 15km west of town, is linked to London and other European cities by Ryanair.

Baden-Baden is close to the A5 (Frankfurt–Basel autobahn) and is the northern starting point of the zigzagging Schwarzwald-Hochstrasse, which follows the B500.

Twice-hourly destinations include Freiburg (€19.20 to €28, 45 to 90 minutes) and Karlsruhe (€10 to €15, 15 to 30 minutes).

Gutach

The **Schwarzwälder Freilichtmuseum** (www.vogtsbauernhof.org; adult/concession/child/family €8/7/4.50/18; ⏱9am-6pm late Mar–early Nov, to 7pm Aug) spirals around the Vogtsbauernhof, an early-17th-century farmstead. Farmhouses shifted from their original locations have been painstakingly reconstructed, using techniques such as thatching and panelling, to create this authentic farming hamlet and preserve age-old Black Forest traditions. It's a great place for families.

Schiltach

☏ 07836 / POP 3880

Sitting smugly at the foot of wooded hills and on the banks of the Kinzig and Schiltach Rivers, medieval Schiltach looks too perfect to be true. The meticulously restored half-timbered houses, which once belonged to tanners, merchants and raft builders, are a riot of crimson geraniums in summer.

Sights

ALTSTADT   Neighbourhood
Centred on a trickling fountain, the sloping, triangular **Marktplatz** is Schiltach at its picture-book best. The frescoes of the step-gabled, 16th-century **Rathaus** opposite depict scenes from local history. Clamber south up **Schlossbergstrasse**, pausing to notice the plaques that denote the trades of one-time residents, such as the *Strumpfstricker* (stocking weaver) at No 6, and the sloping roofs where tanners once dried their skins. Up top there are views over Schiltach's red rooftops.

Information

Tourist office (☎5850; www.schiltach.de; Marktplatz 6; ☺9am-noon & 2-4pm Mon-Thu, 9am-noon Fri) In the Rathaus; can help find accommodation and offers free internet access.

Triberg
☎ 0722 / POP 5000

Home to Germany's highest waterfall, heir to the original 1915 Black Forest gateau recipe and nesting ground of the world's biggest cuckoos, Triberg leaves visitors reeling with superlatives.

Sights

TRIBERGER WASSERFÄLLE   Waterfall
(adult/concession €3.50/3; ☺Mar–early Nov, 25-30 Dec) Niagara they ain't but Germany's highest waterfalls do exude their own wild romanticism. The Gutach River feeds the seven-tiered falls, which drop a total of 163m. It's annoying to have to pay to experience nature but the fee is at least worth it.

**WELTGRÖSSTE
KUCKUCKSUHR**   Landmark
Triberg is Germany's undisputed cuckoo-clock capital. Two timepieces claim the title of world's largest cuckoo clock, giving rise to the battle of the birds.

To the casual observer, the biggest is undeniably the commercially savvy **Eble Uhren–Park** (www.uhren-park.de; Schonachbach 27; admission €2; ☺9am-6pm Mon-Sat, 10am-6pm Sun), listed in the *Guinness World Records*, on the B33 between Triberg and Hornberg.

At the other end of town in Schonach is its underdog **rival** (Untertalstrasse 28; adult/concession €1.20/0.60; ☺9am-noon & 1-6pm), nestled inside a snug chalet and complete with gear-driven innards. This giant timepiece – unable to compete in size alone – has taken to calling itself the world's oldest, largest cuckoo clock. It was built in the 1980s.

Sleeping & Eating

PARKHOTEL
WEHRLE   Historic Hotel €€€
(☎860 20; www.parkhotel-wehrle.de; Hauptstrasse 51; s €95-105, d €149-169, mains €12-23; P 🛜 ♨) Hemingway once waxed lyrical about this 400-year-old hotel and it remains a rustically elegant place to stay today. All guests get free entry to the hotel's Sanitas Spa. The well-regarded restaurant serves seasonal delicacies like gilthead sea bream with market-fresh veg and oxtail jus in wood-panelled, softly lit surrounds.

CAFÉ SCHÄFER   Bakery €
(www.cafe-schaefer-triberg.de; Hauptstrasse 33; cake €3-4; ☺9am-6pm Mon-Fri, 8am-6pm Sat, 11am-6pm Sun, closed Wed) The Black Forest cake here is the real deal and confectioner Claus Schäfer has Josef Keller's original 1915 recipe for *Schwarzwälder Kirschtorte* to prove it: layers of moist sponge, fresh cream and sour cherries, with a mere suggestion of Kirsch (cherry brandy) and heavenly dusting of chocolate.

Information

Tourist office (☎866 490; www.triberg.de; Wahlfahrtstrasse 4; ☺10am-5pm Oct-Apr, 10am-6pm May-Sep) Inside the Schwarzwald-Museum, 50m uphill from the river.

Getting There & Away

The Schwarzwaldbahn train line loops southeast to Konstanz (€23.30, 1½ hours, hourly), and northwest to Offenburg (€11.10, 46 minutes, hourly).

Freiburg
☎ 0761 / POP 224,190

Sitting plump at the foot of the Black Forest's wooded slopes and vineyards, Freiburg is a sunny, cheerful university town; its medieval Altstadt a story-book tableau of gabled town houses, cobblestone lanes and cafe-rimmed plazas. Party-loving students spice up the local nightlife and give Freiburg its carefree air.

STUTTGART & THE BLACK FORREST TRIBERG

177

If You Like...
Amusement Parks

1 STEINWASEN PARK
(www.steinwasen-park.de; Steinwasen 1; adult/concession €19/16; ⏰9am-6pm, closed early Nov–late Mar) Buried deep in the forest, the nature-focused Steinwasen Park is a big hit with families. A trail weaves past animal-friendly enclosures home to wild boar, ibex and burrowing marmots. One of the top attractions is a 218m-long hanging bridge, one of the world's longest. Not to be outdone by its rival, Europa-Park, Steinwasen has introduced whizzy rides such as Gletscherblitz and River Splash.

2 EUROPA-PARK
(www.europapark.de; adult/concession €37.50/33; ⏰9am-6pm Apr–early Nov, 11am-7pm late Nov–early Jan) Germany's largest theme park, 35km north of Freiburg near Rust, is Europe in miniature. Get soaked fjord-rafting in Scandinavia before nipping across to England to race at Silverstone, or Greece to unravel the mysteries of Atlantis. Aside from white-knuckle thrills, Welt der Kinder amuses tots with labyrinths and Viking ships. When Mickey waltzed off to Paris, Europa-Park even got their own mousy mascot, Euromaus. Shuttle buses (hourly in the morning) link Ringsheim train station, on the Freiburg–Offenburg line, with the park. By car, take the A5 exit Rust (57b).

3 LEGOLAND
(www.legoland.de; adult/concession €38/34; ⏰10am-btwn 6pm & 8pm Apr–early Nov) A sure-fire kid-pleaser, Legoland Deutschland is a pricey Lego-themed amusement park, with shows, splashy rides and a miniature world built from 25 million Lego bricks. It's in Günzburg, 37km east of Ulm, just off the A8.

◎ Sights & Activities

MÜNSTER   Cathedral
(Münsterplatz; tower adult/concession €1.50/1; ⏰10am-5pm Mon-Sat, 1pm-7.30pm Sun, tower 9.30am-5pm Mon-Sat, 1-5pm Sun) Freiburg's 11th-century Münster is the monster of all minsters, a red-sandstone giant that looms above the half-timbered facades framing the square. The main portal is adorned with sculptures depicting scenes from the Old and New Testaments. Square at the base, the sturdy tower becomes an octagon higher up and is crowned by a filigreed 116m-high spire. Inside the Münster, the kaleidoscopic stained-glass windows dazzle. The **high altar** features a masterful triptych of the coronation of the Virgin Mary by Hans Baldung.

RATHAUSPLATZ   Square
(Town Hall Square) Freiburg locals hang out by the fountain in chestnut-shaded Rathausplatz. On its western side, note the red-sandstone, step-gabled **Neues Rathaus (New City Hall)**.

Across the way is the mid 16th-century **Altes Rathaus (Old City Hall; Universtitatstrasse)**, a flamboyant, ox-blood red edifice, embellished with gilt swirls and crowned by a clock and a fresco of the twin-headed Habsburg eagle.

On its northern side, the medieval **Martinskirche** demands attention with its covered cloister. Once part of a Franciscan monastery, the church was severely damaged in WWII; it was rebuilt in the ascetic style typical of this mendicant order.

AUGUSTINERMUSEUM   Museum
(Augustinerplatz 1; adult/concession €6/4; ⏰10am-5pm Tue-Sun) Following a recent makeover, this beautiful Augustinian monastery, with origins dating back to 1278, once again showcases a prized collection of medieval, baroque and 19th-century art. Baldung, Matthias Grünewald and Cranach masterpieces grace the gallery and the medieval stained glass ranks among Germany's finest.

HISTORISCHES KAUFHAUS   Landmark
(Münsterplatz) Facing the Münster's south side and embellished with polychrome tiled turrets is the arcaded brick-red Historisches Kaufhaus, an early-16th-century

merchants' hall. The coats of arms on the oriels and the four figures above the balcony symbolise Freiburg's allegiance to the House of Habsburg.

CITY GATES   Historic Building

Freiburg has two intact medieval gates, one of which is the **Martinstor** (Martin's gate) rising above Kaiser-Joseph-Strasse. The other is the 13th-century **Schwabentor** on the Schwabenring, a massive city gate with a mural of St George slaying the dragon and tram tracks running under its arches.

SCHLOSSBERG   Viewpoint, Walk

(Schlossbergring; cable car one way/return €2.80/5; ☺9am-10pm, shorter hours in winter) The forested Schlossberg dominates Freiburg. Take the footpath opposite the Schwabentor, leading up through sun-dappled woods, or hitch a ride on the recently restored **Schlossbergbahn** cable car.

 Tours

If you want to explore the Altstadt at your own pace, 2½-hour audioguides are available at the tourist office for €9.

FREIBURG KULTOUR   Guided Tour

(www.freiburg-kultour.com; Rathausplatz 2-4; adult/concession €8/6; ☺11.30am Sat) Based in the tourist office, Kultour offers 1½- to two-hour walking tours of the Altstadt and Münster in English.

Sleeping

HOTEL OBERKIRCH

Historic Hotel €€€

(☎202 6868; www.hotel-oberkirch.de; Münsterplatz 22; s €102-123, d €155-169; P) Wake up to Münster views at this green-shut-tered hotel. It's as though Laura Ashley has been let loose in the country-style rooms with floral wallpaper and half-canopies over the beds. The dark-wood **tavern** (mains €13 to €23) downstairs does a roaring trade in hearty Badisch fare like venison ragout with *Knödel* (dumplings).

**HOTEL
SCHWARZWÄLDER HOF**   Hotel €€

(☎380 30; www.schwarzwaelder-hof.eu; Herrenstrasse 43; s/d/tr €65/99/120; @) This bijou hotel has an unrivalled style-for-euro ratio. A wrought-iron staircase sweeps up to snazzy rooms that are temples to chalk whites and chocolate browns. Some have postcard views of the Altstadt.

**HOTEL
MINERVA**   Hotel €€

(☎386 490; www.minerva-freiburg.de; Poststrasse 8; s €85-100, d €115-150; P �) All curvaceous windows and polished wood, this art nouveau charmer is five minutes' trudge from the Altstadt. The convivial rooms are painted in sunny shades and feature free wi-fi. The sauna is another plus.

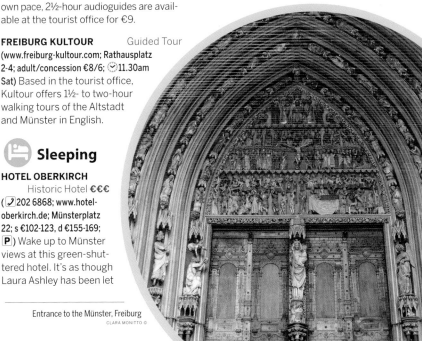

Entrance to the Münster, Freiburg
CLARA MONITTO ©

Freiburg

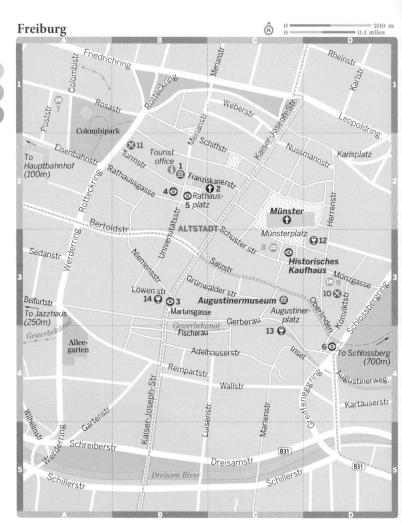

 Eating

ZIRBELSTUBE French €€€
(☎ 210 60; www.colombi.de; Rotteckring 16; mains €32-49; ☺ Wed-Sun) Freiburg's bastion of fine dining is this candlelit restaurant, decorated in warm Swiss pine. A chef of exacting standards, Alfred Klink allows each ingredient to shine in specialities like poussin with Périgord truffles and Dover sole with caramelised capers, perfectly matched with top wines.

ENGLERS WEINKRÜGLE German €€
(☎ 383 115; Konviktstrasse 12; mains €9-16; ☺ Tue-Sun) A warm, woody Baden-style *Weinstube* (wine tavern) with wisteria growing out front and regional flavours on the menu. The trout in various guises (for instance with riesling or almond-butter sauce) is delicious.

Drinking &
Entertainment

HAUSBRAUEREI
FEIERLING   Beer Garden
(Gerberau 46; ⏰11am-midnight, to 1am Fri & Sat
Mar-Oct) This stream-side beer garden is a
relaxed spot to quaff a cold one under the
chestnut trees in summer. Pretzels and
sausages (snacks €3 to €7) soak up the
malty brews.

SCHLAPPEN   Pub
(Löwenstrasse 2; ⏰11am-btwn 1am & 3am
Mon-Sat, 3pm-1am Sun) With its jazz-themed
back room and poster-plastered walls,
this pub is a perennial favourite.

ALTE WACHE   Wine Bar
(Münsterplatz 38; ⏰10am-7pm Mon-Fri, 10am-
4pm Sat) Right on the square, this 18th-
century guardhouse serves local Müller-
Thurgau and Pinot noir wines at the tasting
tables. If they sharpen your appetite, order
a tasting plate of cheese and olives.

JAZZHAUS   Live Music
(☎349 73; www.jazzhaus.de; Schnewlinstrasse
1) Under the brick arches of a wine cellar,
this venue hosts first-rate jazz, rock and
world music concerts (€15 to €25) at
7.30pm or 8pm at least three nights a
week (see the website for details).

❶ Information

Tourist office (☎388 1880; www.freiburg.de;
Rathausplatz 2-4; ⏰8am-8pm Mon-Fri, 9.30am-
5pm Sat, 11am-4pm Sun)

❶ Getting There & Away

The Frankfurt–Basel A5 passes just west of
Freiburg. The scenic B31 leads east through the
Höllental to Lake Constance. The B294 goes
north into the Black Forest. Freiburg is on a major
north–south rail corridor with frequent departures
for destinations such as Basel (€16.40 to €24.20,
42 to 69 minutes) and Baden-Baden (€19.20 to
€28, 45 minutes to 1½ hours).

Around Freiburg
Schauinsland

Freiburg seems tiny as you drift up above
the city and a tapestry of meadows and
forest on the **Schauinslandbahn** (adult/
concession return €12/11, one-way €8.50/8;
⏰9am-5pm, to 6pm Jul-Sep) to the 1284m
Schauinsland peak (www.bergwelt-schauin
sland.de). The lift provides a speedy link
between Freiburg and the Black Forest high-
lands. It's about 10km southeast of town.

Wutachschlucht

This wild gorge, carved out by a fast-
flowing river and flanked by near-vertical
rock faces, lies near Bonndorf, about

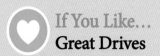

If You Like…
Great Drives

Spoiled with pastoral settings of fir-cloaked hills, peaceful river valleys, crystalline lakes, dense forests and other equally lyrical landscapes, there's no better way to appreciate the Black Forest's beauty than by careening along its many scenic routes.

1 SCHWARZWALD-HOCHSTRASSE
(Black Forest Hwy; www.schwarzwaldhochstrasse .de) Swoon over views of the mist-wreathed Vosges Mountains, heather-flecked forests and glacial lakes like Mummelsee on this meandering 60km road from Baden-Baden to Freudenstadt on the B500.

2 BADISCHE WEINSTRASSE
(Baden Wine Rd; www.deutsche-weinstrassen.de) From Baden-Baden south to Lörrach, this 160km-long route corkscrews through the red-wine vineyards of Ortenau, the Pinot noir of Kaiserstuhl and Tuniberg, and the white-wine vines of Markgräflerland.

3 SCHWARZWALD-TÄLERSTRASSE
(Black Forest Valley Rd) What scenery! Twisting 100km from Rastatt to Alpirsbach, this road dips into the forest-cloaked hills and half-timbered towns of the Murgtal and Kinzigtal valleys.

4 DEUTSCHE UHRENSTRASSE
(German Clock Rd; www.deutscheuhrenstrasse .de) A 320km-long loop starting in Villingen-Schwenningen that revolves around the story of clockmaking in the Black Forest. Stops include Furtwangen and cuckoo-crazy Triberg.

50km southeast of Freiburg. The best way to experience its unique microclimate, where you might spot orchids, ferns, rare butterflies and lizards, is on this trail leading from Schattenmühle to Wutachmühle. For more details, visit the website www .wutachschlucht.de (in German).

Kaiserstuhl

About 30km west of Freiburg (via the A5 and B31), these low-lying volcanic hills in the Upper Rhine Valley yield highly quaffable wines including fruity *Spätburgunder* (Pinot noir) and *Grauburgunder* (Pinot gris) varieties.

The grapes owe their quality to a unique microclimate, hailed as Germany's sunniest, and fertile loess (clay and silt) soil that retains heat during the night. Nature enthusiasts should look out for rarities like sand lizards, praying mantis and European bee-eaters.

The **Breisach tourist office** (📞940 155; Marktplatz 16; 🕑9am-12.30pm & 1.30-6pm Mon & Wed-Fri, 10am-3pm Sat) can advise on cellar tours, wine tastings, bike paths like the 55km **Kaiserstuhl-Tour** circuit, and trails such as the **Winzerweg** (Wine Growers' Trail), an intoxicating 15km hike from Achkarren to Riegel.

The **Kaiserstuhlbahn** does a loop around the Kaiserstuhl. Stops (where you may have to change trains) include Sasbach, Endingen, Riegel and Gottenheim.

LAKE CONSTANCE

Nicknamed the *Schwäbische Meer* (Swabian Sea), Lake Constance is Central Europe's third largest lake and it straddles three countries: Germany, Austria and Switzerland. Formed by the Rhine Glacier during the last ice age and fed and drained by that same sprightly river today, this whopper of a lake measures 63km long, 14km wide and up to 250m deep.

ℹ️ Getting There & Around

The most enjoyable way to cross the lake is by ferry. Konstanz is the main hub but Meersburg and Friedrichshafen also have ferry ports.

Although most towns have a train station (Meersburg is an exception), in some cases buses provide the only land connections. Euregio Bodensee (www.euregiokarte.com), which groups all Lake Constance-area public transport, publishes a free *Fahrplan* with schedules for all train, bus and ferry services.

The Euregio Bodensee Tageskarte (www .euregiokarte.com) gets you all-day access to land transport around Lake Constance, including areas in Austria and Switzerland. It's sold at train stations and ferry docks. It costs €16.50/22/29 for one/two/all zones.

Konstanz

 07531 / POP 84,690

Sidling up to the Swiss border, bisected by the Rhine and outlined by the Alps, Konstanz sits prettily on the northwestern shore of Lake Constance. When the sun comes out to play, Konstanz is a feel-good university town with a lively buzz and upbeat bar scene, particularly in the cobbled Altstadt and the harbour where the voluptuous *Imperia* turns.

Sights

MÜNSTER Cathedral
(tower adult/child €2/1; ⊙10am-6pm Mon-Sat, 10am-6pm Sun, tower 10am-5pm Mon-Sat, 12.30am-5.30pm Sun) Crowned by a filigree spire and looking proudly back on 1000 years of history, the sandstone Mün-ster was the church of the diocese of Konstanz until 1821. Standouts include the 15th-century **Schnegg**, an ornate spiral staircase in the northern transept, to the left of which a door leads to the 1000-year-old **crypt**. On cloudless days, it's worth ascending the **tower** for broad views over the city and lake.

NIEDERBURG
Neighbourhood
Best explored on foot, Kon-stanz' cobbled heart, Nieder-burg, stretches north from the Münster to the Rhine. The twisting cobbled lanes lined with half-timbered town houses are the place to snoop around galleries, antique shops and 13th-century **Kloster Zoffingen** (Brückengasse 15), Konstanz' only remaining convent, still in the hands of Dominican nuns.

LAKEFRONT Harbour
At the merest hint of a sunray, the tree-fringed, sculpture-dotted lakefront promenade lures inline skaters, cyclists, walkers and ice-cream-licking crowds.

Look out for the white dormered **Konzilgebäude** (Council Building), built in 1388, which served as a granary and warehouse before Pope Martin V was elected here in 1417. Today it's a conference and concert hall.

The nearby **Zeppelin Monument** shows the airship inventor Count Ferdinand von Zeppelin in an Icarus-like pose. He was born in 1838 on the Insel, an islet a short stroll north through the flowery **Stadtgarten** park, where there's a **children's playground**.

Sleeping

VILLA BARLEBEN Historic Hotel €€€
(942 330; www.hotel-barleben.de; Seestrasse 15; s €135-230, d €195-255;) Gregariously elegant, this 19th-century villa's sunny rooms and corridors are sprinkled with

Konstanz, Lake Constance
ELFI KLUCK/GETTY IMAGES ©

antiques and ethnic art. The rambling lakefront gardens are ideal for dozing in a *Strandkorb* (wicker beach lounger), G&T in hand, or enjoying lunch on the terrace.

HOTEL BARBAROSSA   Historic Hotel €€

(☏128 990; www.barbarossa-hotel.com; Obermarkt 8-12; s €55-75, d €95-130; 🛜) This 600-year-old patrician house harbours parquet-floored, individually decorated rooms, which are bright and appealing, if a tad on the small side. The terrace has views over Konstanz' rooftops and spires.

RIVA   Boutique Hotel €€€

(☏363 090; www.hotel-riva.de; Seestrasse 25; s €110-150, d €200-240; P 🛜 ♨) This ultra-chic contender has crisp white spaces, glass walls and a snail-like stairwell. Zen-style rooms with hardwood floors feature perks including (like it!) free minibars. The rooftop pool and Mediterranean-style restaurant (mains €18 to €25) overlook the lake.

Eating

MÜNSTERHOF   German €€€

(☏363 8427; Münsterplatz 3; mains €8.50-17; ⏱daily; 🍴👶) Tables set up in front of the Münster, a slick bistro interior and a lunchtime buzz have earned Münsterhof a loyal local following.

VOGLHAUS   Cafe €

(Wessenbergstrasse 8; light meals €2.50-6; ⏱9am-6.30pm Mon-Sat, 11am-6pm Sun; 🍴) Locals flock to the 'bird house' for its chilled vibe and contemporary wood-and-stone interior, warmed by an open fire in winter.

ZEITLOS   German €

(St Stephansplatz 25; snacks €4-10; ⏱10am-1am Mon-Sat, 10am-6pm Sun) Behind Stephanskirche, this beamed, stone-walled bistro overflows with regulars. It's a cosy spot for brunch or filling snacks like *Wurstsalat* (sausage salad) and *Maultaschen*, the local take on ravioli. Sit in the ivy-draped courtyard in summer.

ⓘ Information

Tourist office (☏133 030; www.konstanz -tourismus.de; Bahnhofplatz 43; ⏱9am-6.30pm Mon-Fri, 9am-4pm Sat, 10am-1pm Sun Apr-Oct, 9.30am-6pm Mon-Fri Nov-Mar)

ⓘ Getting There & Away

By car, Konstanz can be reached via the B33, which links up with the A81 to and from Stuttgart near Singen. Konstanz' Hauptbahnhof is the southern terminus of the scenic Schwarzwaldbahn, which trundles hourly through the Black Forest.

Meersburg

☏ 07532 / POP 5625

Tumbling down vine-streaked slopes to Lake Constance and crowned by a perkily turreted medieval castle, Meersburg lives up

Lake Constance (p182)
DAVID C TOMLINSON/GETTY IMAGES ©

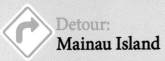

Detour:
Mainau Island

Jutting out over the lake and bursting with flowers, the lusciously green islet of **Mainau** (www.mainau.de; adult/concession €16.90/9.50; ☉sunrise-sunset) is a 45-hectare Mediterranean garden dreamed up by the Bernadotte family, relatives of the royal house of Sweden.

Around two million visitors flock here every year to admire sparkly lake and mountain views from the **baroque castle**, and wander sequoia-shaded avenues and hothouses bristling with palms and orchids. Crowd-pullers include the **Butterfly House**, where hundreds of vivid butterflies flit amid the dewy foliage, an **Italian Cascade** integrating patterned flowers with waterfalls, and a **petting zoo**. Tulips and rhododendrons bloom in spring, hibiscus and roses in summer. Avoid weekends when the gardens get crowded.

You can drive, walk or cycle to Mainau, 8km north of Konstanz. Take bus 4 from Konstanz' train station or hop aboard a passenger ferry.

to all those clichéd knights-in-armour, damsel-in-distress fantasies.

Looking across the Lake Constance from its lofty perch, the **Altes Schloss** (adult/concession €8.50/6.50; ☉9am-6.30pm Mar-Oct, 10am-6pm Nov-Feb) is an archetypal medieval stronghold, complete with keep, drawbridge, knights' hall and dungeons. Founded by Merovingian king Dagobert I in the 7th century, the fortress is among Germany's oldest, which is no mean feat in a country with a lot of castles.

The **tourist office** (☎440 400; www .meersburg.de; Kirchstrasse 4; ☉9am-12.30pm & 2-6pm Mon-Fri, 10am-3pm Sat, 10am-1pm Sun, shorter hours in winter) is housed in a one-time Dominican monastery. Internet access costs €3 per hour.

ⓘ Getting There & Away

Meersburg, which lacks a train station, is 18km west of Friedrichshafen. From Monday to Friday, eight times a day, express bus 7394 makes the trip to Konstanz (€3.25, 40 minutes) and Friedrichshafen (€3.10, 26 minutes). Bus 7373 connects Meersburg with Ravensburg (€5, 40 minutes, four daily Monday to Friday, two Saturday). Meersburg's main bus stop is next to the church.

ⓘ Getting Around

The best and only way to get around Meersburg is on foot. Even the large pay car park near the car-ferry port (€1.20 per hour) is often full in high

season. You might find free parking north of the old town along Daisendorfer Strasse.

Hire bikes at **Hermann Dreher** (☎5176; Stadtgraben 5; per day €4.50; ☉rental 9am-noon), down the alley next to the tourist office.

Friedrichshafen
☎ 07541 / POP 59,000

Zeppelins, the cigar-shaped airships that first took flight in 1900 under the stewardship of high-flying Count Ferdinand von Zeppelin, will forever be associated with Friedrichshafen. An amble along the flowery lakefront promenade and a visit to the museum that celebrates the behemoth of the skies are the biggest draws of this industrial town, which was heavily bombed in WWII and rebuilt in the 1950s.

◉ Sights & Activities

LAKEFRONT   Promenade
A promenade runs through the lakefront, sculpture-dotted **Stadtgarten** park along Uferstrasse, a great spot for a picnic or stroll. Pedal and electric **boats** can be rented at the Gondelhafen (€9 to €23 per hour).

ZEPPELIN MUSEUM   Museum
(www.zeppelin-museum.de; Seestrasse 22; adult/concession €7.50/4; ☉9am-5pm daily May-Oct, 10am-5pm Tue-Sun Nov-Apr) Near the

185

Left: Zeppelin Museum (p185), Friedrichshafen;
Right: Lindau harbour, Lake Constance
(LEFT)WALTER BIBIKOW/GETTY IMAGES ©; (RIGHT) ROLFO/GETTY IMAGES ©

eastern end of Friedrichshafen's lakefront promenade, Seestrasse, is the Zeppelin Museum, housed in the Bauhaus-style former Hafenbahnhof, built in 1932.

The centrepiece is a full-scale mock-up of a 33m section of the *Hindenburg* (LZ 129), the largest airship ever built, measuring an incredible 245m long and outfitted as luxuriously as an ocean liner. The hydrogen-filled craft tragically burst into flames, killing 36, while landing in New Jersey in 1937.

Other exhibits provide technical and historical insights, including an original motor gondola from the famous *Graf Zeppelin*, which made 590 trips and travelled around the world in 21 days in 1929.

Sleeping

HOTEL RESTAURANT MAIER   Hotel €€
(☎ 4040; www.hotel-maier.de; Poststrasse 1-3, Friedrichshafen-Fischbach; s €59-95, d €89-120;

P) The contemporary, light-drenched rooms are immaculately kept at this family-run hotel, 5km west of Friedrichshafen and an eight-minute hop on the train. The mini spa invites relaxing moments, with its lake-facing terrace, steam room and sauna.

ℹ Information

Tourist office (☎ 300 10; www.friedrichshafen .info; Bahnhofplatz 2; ⏱ 9am-1pm & 1-6pm Mon-Fri, 9am-1pm Sat) On the square outside the Stadtbahnhof. Has a free internet terminal. Can book accommodation and Zeppelin flights.

Lindau

☎ 08382 / POP 24,800

Cradled in the southern crook of the Lake Constance and almost dipping its toes into Austria, Lindau is a good-looking, outgoing little town, with a candy-coloured postcard of an Altstadt, clear-

day Alpine views and lakefront cafes that use every sunray to the max.

 Sights

SEEPROMENADE   Promenade
In summer the harbourside promenade has a happy-go-lucky air, with its palms, bobbing boats and folk sunning themselves in pavement cafes.

ALTES RATHAUS   Landmark
(Old Town Hall; Bismarckplatz) Lindau's biggest architectural stunner is the 15th-century, step-gabled Altes Rathaus, a frescoed frenzy of cherubs, merry minstrels and galleons.

PETERSKIRCHE   Church
(Schrannenplatz; ☉daily) Looking back on a 1000-year history, this enigmatic church is now a war memorial, hiding exquisite time-faded frescoes of the Passion of Christ by Hans Holbein the Elder.

 Eating & Drinking

WEINSTUBE FREY   German €€€
(☎947 9676; Maximilianstrasse 15; mains €13-22; ☉closed Mon) This 500-year-old wine tavern oozes Bavarian charm in its wood-panelled tavern full of cosy nooks. Waiters in traditional outfits serve up regional wines and fare such as beer-battered Lake Constance trout. Sit on the terrace when the sun's out.

ℹ **Information**

Tourist office (☎260 030; www.lindau.de; Alfred-Nobel-Platz 1; ☉10am-6pm Mon-Sat, 10am-1pm Sun, shorter hours in low season)

ℹ **Getting There & Away**

Lindau is on the B31 and is connected to Munich by the A96. The precipitous **Deutsche Alpenstrasse** (German Alpine Rd), which winds giddily eastward to Berchtesgaden, begins here.

Lindau is at the eastern terminus of the train line, which goes along the lake's north shore via Friedrichshafen (€5.50, 20 minutes) westward to Radolfzell.

Frankfurt & the Rhineland

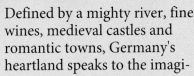

Defined by a mighty river, fine wines, medieval castles and romantic towns, Germany's heartland speaks to the imagination. Posh and modern Frankfurt may seem all buttoned-up at first, but further exploration will reveal a laid-back metropolis with flowery parkland, fabulous museums and pulsating nightlife.

Just an hour west – past the cathedral city of Mainz (where Gutenberg invented printing) – flows the Romantic Rhine, whose legend-shrouded landscapes have drawn artists and tourists since the early 19th century. Vineyards stretch along the steep hillsides above the serpentine Moselle River.

But it's the mighty Rhine that's shaped this region more than anything else, providing a vital link between such cosmopolitan centres as Roman-founded Cologne, art-world star Düsseldorf and Bonn, with its Beethoven legacy. Away from the river, Aachen still echoes the beat of the Holy Roman Empire and Charlemagne.

Frankfurt am Main (p200)

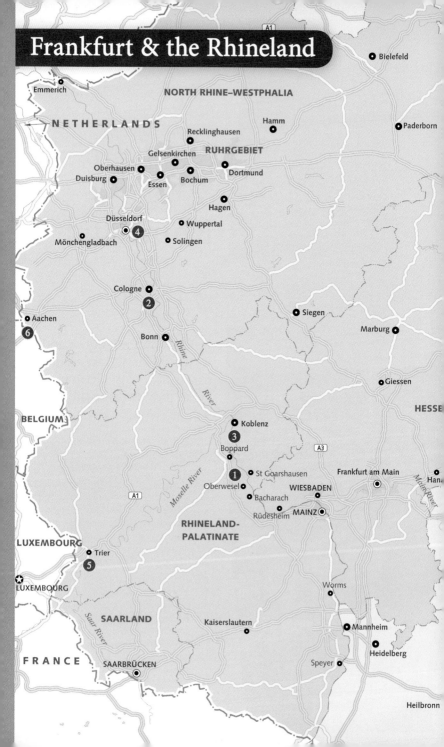

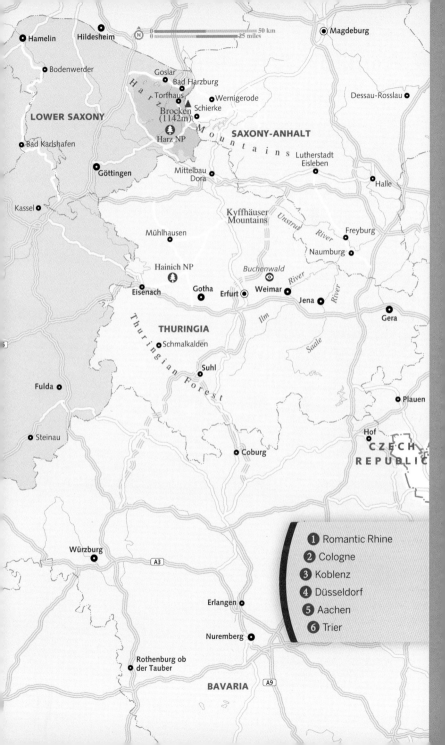

Frankfurt & the Rhineland Highlights

1

Ramble Along the Romantic Rhine

The Romantic Rhine (p213), the river's prettiest stretch between Koblenz and Rüdesheim, is a magical land where half-timbered villages are serenaded by medieval castles. Nature, history and humankind have collaborated to create a delightful landscape of great beauty and complexity.

Above: Rhine River, Bacharach; Top Right: Medieval fortifications, Bacharach; Bottom Right: Burg Katz and Loreley Rock (p217), St Goarshausen

Need to Know

TRAVEL TIP Take the boat one way and come back by train. **SPEND** At least one full day in the valley. **BEST TIME** spring and fall. For further details, see p213

Romantic Rhine Don't Miss List

BY WOLFGANG BLUM, CERTIFIED NATURE & LANDSCAPE GUIDE

1 CASTLES GALORE

There are two castles that should not be missed: Pfalzgrafenstein (p216) near Kaub, and the Marksburg (p219) near Braubach. Both have never been destroyed. The Marksburg gives you a palpable sense of what daily life was like in the days of knights and chivalry. Pfalzgrafenstein is a classic toll castle on a rocky island in the middle of the Rhine.

2 MUSEUM AM STROM

This museum (p215) is dedicated to Hildegard von Bingen, an abbess and one of the most important women of the Middle Ages. The Vatican canonised her in 2012. The museum portrays the life of this remarkable woman and also traces the history of the Romantic Rhine region.

3 VIEWS

The most famous views are those from the Germania memorial (at Assmannshausen) above Rüdesheim and from the legend-shrouded Loreley Rock (p217) near St Goarshausen. But actually many of the castles also offer vistas that are no less impressive.

4 FORTIFIED VILLAGES

Soak up the spirit of the Middle Ages when walking along the fortifications that hem in several of the Rhine villages. The nicest of these are Bacharach (p216) and Oberwesel. Both have compact historic centres with colourfully painted half-timbered houses impressive churches and mighty castles standing sentinel over the valley.

5 KLOSTER EBERBACH

The Eberbach monastery (p215) is one of the most important medieval monasteries in Germany. It sits right next to the largest wine estate in Germany, the state-of-the-art Hessische Staatsweingüter (Hessian State Wineries). The contrast between high-tech and tradition is a truly memorable experience. And by the way, the monastery gained world-wide fame as a film location for *The Name of the Rose* starring Sean Connery.

Admire the Grandeur of Cologne's Cathedral

The Kölner Dom (p229) is much more than just a city landmark. It was planned as the largest cathedral in central Europe and ended up being a perfect expression of the Gothic architectural style rooted in medieval France. It reflects the long history of the country better than any other structure in Germany.

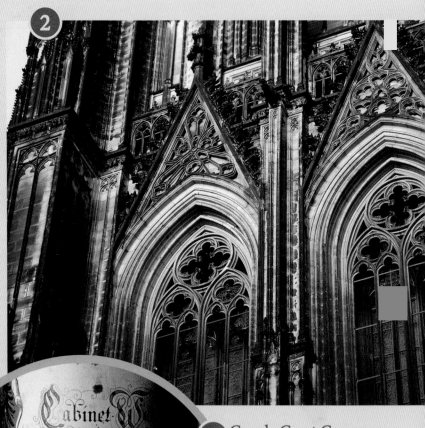

Guzzle Great Grapes

Some of Germany's finest vintages grow along the Rhine and Moselle River valleys that meet in Koblenz (p219). Terraced vineyards surge skyward in columned symmetry, sheltering the vines from fierce winds, while the slate-rich soil stores up the sun's energy – conditions ideal for the noble riesling grape. Sample it in cosy taverns or at ancient wine estates.

IONAS KALTENBACH/GETTY IMAGES ©

Party in Düsseldorf's Old Town  4

Nicknamed the 'longest bar in the world', the warren of lanes that is Düsseldorf's Altstadt (p231) is tailor-made for letting your hair down. Sure, there are plenty of fancy bars, hopping night clubs, riverside cafes and chic lounges, but to soak up the true Rhenish spirit, sample the local brew known as *Altbier* in a traditional pub.

5

Channel Charlemagne in Aachen

Sharing a border with Belgium and the Netherlands, Aachen (p238) exudes international flair rooted in the 8th century when Charlemagne made it the capital of his vast Frankish empire. Pay your respects to the 'father of Europe', who is buried in the magnificent cathedral he founded in 800. Don't forget to sample the local speciality called *Printen*, a spicy, gingery cookie.

6

Revel in Roman Trier

Cologne, Bonn, Mainz and Trier all started out as Roman military camps founded by the Romans in the 1st century BC when the Rhine and Moselle formed the empire's northern frontier. Trier (p223), Germany's oldest city, boasts some the best-preserved remnants in Europe from this era, including a town gate, an amphitheatre and thermal baths. Porta Nigra (p224), Trier

Frankfurt & the Rhineland's Best...

Heavenly Heights

○ **Festung Ehrenbreitstein** (p219) Mighty castle perched above the Rhine and Moselle

○ **Kölner Dom** (p229) Climb the tower for the ultimate exercise fix

○ **Niederwald Denkmal** (p214) Join Germania in surveying its domain above Rüdesheim

○ **Vierseenblick** (p218) Unique views from the hills above Boppard

Traditional Taverns

○ **Am Knipp** (p241) Serving hearty tummy fillers in Aachen since 1698

○ **Päffgen** (p230) Pouring Cologne's *Kölsch* beer for over a century

○ **Weinstube Hottum** (p211) Tasty Mainz wines and specialities

○ **Zum Gequetschten** (p238) Carnivore heaven in Bonn

Fairy-Tale Fancies

○ **Bacharach** (p216) Half-timbered medieval time warp with great wine taverns

○ **Beilstein** (p220) Higgledy-piggledy village nicknamed 'Sleeping Beauty of the Moselle'

○ **Burg Eltz** (p220) Turreted beauty dreamily cradled by a dense forest

○ **Loreley Rock** (p217) Home of the legendary lady whose beauty lured sailors to their deaths

Hilltop Castles

○ **Burg Rheinfels** (p218)
Robber-baron hang-out
honeycombed with secret
tunnels

○ **Festung Ehrenbreitstein**
(p219) One of Europe's
largest fortifications

○ **Marksburg** (p219)
A Rhine castle that was
never destroyed

: The Marksburg (p219) near Braubach; Above:
ving platform at Festung Ehrenbreitstein (p219)

Need to Know

ADVANCE PLANNING

○ **As early as possible**
If Frankfurt is hosting any
major trade fairs during
your visit then book your
hotel now. Same goes if
you're visiting Cologne,
Bonn, Aachen, Mainz or
Düsseldorf during Carnival,
or the Moselle and Rhine
villages in summer.

○ **One month before**
Order concert tickets
for Düsseldorf's Tonhalle
or Cologne's Kölner
Philharmonie.

RESOURCES

○ **Messe Frankfurt**
(www.messefrankfurt.com)
A list of trade fairs in
Frankfurt

○ **Welterbe-Mittelrheintal**
(www.welterbe-mittelrheintal
.de) Comprehensive
information about the
Unesco-listed Romantic
Rhine

○ **Romantic Germany**
(www.romantic-germany.info)
Information about wine
festivals along the Rhine
and Moselle Rivers

○ **Deutsche Weine** (www
.deutscheweine.de) In-depth
information about German
grape-growing areas

GETTING AROUND

○ **Boat** Köln-Düsseldorfer
(www.k-d.com) and
local operators link
villages along the Rhine
and Moselle from April to
October.

○ **Car** Your own wheels
are a pain in the cities,
but useful, though not
essential, when exploring
the Rhine and Moselle
River valleys. Note that
heavy traffic can be an
issue in summer.

○ **Train** Great for getting
around with practically
all destinations served.
Check at a train station
or www.bahn.de for deals
such as the Hessenticket,
the Rheinland-Pfalz-Ticket
and the Schöner TagTicket,
which are especially handy
for small groups.

BE FOREWARNED

○ **Frankfurt train station**
The area northeast of the
Hauptbahnhof is a base for
Frankfurt's trade in sex and
illegal drugs. Elbestrasse
and Taunusstrasse form
part of the main red-light
district.

○ **Off-season travel** The
villages along the Rhine,
Moselle and the German
Wine Road are pretty
much deserted from
November to February.

○ **Room rates and
availability** Rooms are
scarce and rates skyrocket
in the entire region
during big trade shows in
Frankfurt, Cologne and
Düsseldorf.

197

Frankfurt & the Rhineland Itineraries

Along the prettiest stretch of the Rhine, this region packs big cities and higgledy-piggledy villages, Roman ruins and medieval castles, postmodern skyscrapers and world-class museums into one neat package.

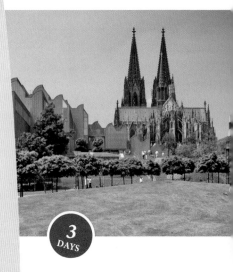

3 DAYS

DÜSSELDORF TO BONN

Arty Trio

The 'trio' in question are the neighbouring cities of Düsseldorf, Cologne and Bonn, whose world-class museums deliver a fine survey of what's been going on in the Western art world for, oh, the past 700 years or so. All three are linked several times hourly by regional S-Bahn trains. In **(1) Düsseldorf** start off at the K20 Grabbeplatz to admire 20th-century art from Picasso to Pollock, then skip over to the K21 Ständehaus where Andreas Gursky, Tony Cragg (now director of the city's prestigious art academy) and Nam June Paik are main players.

The next day, in **(2) Cologne,** don't miss the Wallraf-Richartz-Museum, graced by Old Masters like Rembrandt, key impressionists like Monet, and Romantic heavyweights like Caspar David Friedrich. Meanwhile at the nearby Museum Ludwig, the spotlight is on postmodern art, especially American pop art.

Spend day three in **(3) Bonn**, where the Kunstmuseum Bonn has important 20th-century German art by Macke, Beuys and Kiefer. It's part of the city's 'Museum Mile', so if you're in the mood for more, check out the latest exhibits in the adjacent museums.

Left: Wallraf-Richartz-Museum (p228), Cologne;
Right: Altes Haus (p216), Bacharach
(TOP LEFT) WERNER OTTO/ALAMY ©: (TOP RIGHT) H & D ZIELSKE/GETTY IMAGES ©

5 DAYS

FRANKFURT TO COLOGNE

Romancing the Rhine

Start in **(1) Frankfurt am Main** and let this journey of grand architecture, absorbing history, world-class art and fine wine unfurl. Ride the Ebbelwei-Express tram past all the major sights, then head to Museumsufer (Museum Embankment) for fabulous city skyline views and a culture fix in your favourite riverside museum. Wrap up with an earthy meal in a Sachsenhausen apple wine tavern.

The next day, move on to real wine by sampling Germany's top rieslings in **(2) Rüdesheim** or in the atmospheric Eberbach monastery. Catch a boat and drift past steep vineyards and castle-crowned cliffs to half-timbered **(3) Bacharach** to fall asleep among the vines.

Boat travel is also ideal for appreciating the dramatically narrowing river valley further north, especially around the fabled Loreley Rock. Disembark in **(4) St Goarshausen** and catch the train to **(5) Braubach** for a spin around the Marksburg, the best-preserved and most evocative Rhine castle.

Spend the night here or in **(6) Koblenz**, then train it to **(7) Cologne** to be awed by its cathedral, museums (chocolate, art, Romans – take your pick!) and *Kölsch* beer.

Discover Frankfurt & the Rhineland

Römer, Frankfurt am Main
SANDRA RACCANELLO/GRAND TOUR/GRAND TOUR/CORBIS ©

FRANKFURT AM MAIN

♪ 069 / POP 680,000

Unashamedly high-rise, Frankfurt-on-the-Main (pronounced 'mine') is unlike any other German city. Bristling with jagged skyscrapers, 'Mainhattan' – the focal point of a conurbation with some 5 million inhabitants – is a true capital of finance and business, home base for one of the world's largest stock exchanges as well as the European Central Bank. It also hosts some of Europe's most important trade fairs, including the largest book and motorcar fairs anywhere.

Yet Frankfurt consistently ranks as one of the world's most liveable cities, with a rich collection of museums (second in Germany only to Berlin's), lots of parks and greenery, a lively student scene, excellent public transport, fine dining and plenty to do in the evening.

Sights & Activities

FRANKFURTER DOM Cathedral
(Frankfurt Cathedral; www.dom konzerte.de; Domplatz 14; ⊘church 9am-noon & 2.30-8pm) Dominated by an elegant Gothic **tower** (95m), begun in the 1400s and completed in the 1860s, Frankfurt's red sandstone cathedral is an island of calm amid the bustle of the city centre. From 1356 to 1792, the Holy Roman Emperors were elected (and, after 1562, consecrated and crowned) in the **Wahlkapelle** and the adjacent transept, now the site of a modern high altar. The structure was rebuilt both after an 1867 fire and after the bombings of 1944, which left it a burnt-out shell.

For a bit of background on the Dom's history and architecture, look around for a shelf with the brochure *Welcome to the Cathedral*.

The **Dommuseum** (cathedral museum; www.dommuseum-frankfurt.de; adult/student €3/2, tours adult/student €4/2; ◷10am-5pm Tue-Fri, 11am-5pm Sat, Sun & holidays, tours 3pm Tue-Sun except during weddings), to the left as you enter the cathedral, has a small collection of precious liturgical objects and sells tickets for Dom tours (in German).

RÖMERBERG   Plaza
(☒Dom/Römer) The Römerberg is Frankfurt's old central square. Buildings from the 14th and 15th centuries, reconstructed after the war, give an idea of how beautiful the city's medieval core once was. In the centre is the **Gerechtigkeitsbrunnen** (Font of Justice); in 1612, at the coronation of Matthias, the fountain ran with wine!

RÖMER   Historic Building
(Römerberg; ☒Dom/Römer) The old town hall, or Römer, in the northwestern corner of Römerberg, consists of three step-gabled 15th-century houses that were little more than shells at the end of the war. In the time of the Holy Roman Empire, it was the site of celebrations during the election and coronation of emperors; today it houses the office of Frankfurt's mayor and serves as the registry office.

Reached from Limpurgerstrasse (around the south side of the building), the barrel-vaulted **Kaisersaal** (Emperor's Hall; adult/child €2/0.50; ◷10am-1pm & 2-5pm, closed during events) is adorned with the mid-19th-century portraits of 52 rulers who made their mark between the 8th century and 1806. Access is via a fine little courtyard and a spiral staircase made of carved red sandstone.

ZEIL   Pedestrian Mall
For some truly grand (window) shopping, stroll along the pedestrianised Zeil, Frankfurt's great commercial precinct, which is unendingly animated by day and brightly lit by night. It is anchored to the east by a public square known as **Konstabler-wache** (☒Konstablerwache) and to the west

by a square called **An der Hauptwache** (☒Hauptwache), named after a baroque-style building (now a cafe) that once housed the city's main guardhouse. West of there, you can continue through the pedestrianised restaurant district known as **Fressgass'** (officially Biebergasse, Kalbächer Gasse and Grosse Bockenheimer Strasse) to the Alte Oper.

ALTE OPER   Opera House
(Opernplatz 1; ☒Alte Oper) Inaugurated in 1880, the Italian Renaissance-style Alte Oper anchors the western end of the Zeil-Fressgass' pedestrian zone. Burnt out in 1944, it narrowly avoiding being razed and replaced with 1960s cubes and was finally reconstructed (1976-81) to resemble the original, its ornate facade graced with statues of Goethe and Mozart. Except for the mosaics in the lobby, the interior (closed except during concerts) is modern.

MAIN TOWER   Skyscraper
(www.maintower.de; Neue Mainzer Strasse 52-58; elevator adult/child/family €5/3.50/13.50; ◷10am-9pm Sun-Thu, to 11pm Fri & Sat late-Mar–late-Oct, closes 2hr earlier late-Oct–late-Mar, cocktail lounge 9pm-midnight or 1am Tue-Sat; ☒Alte Oper) A good place to get a feel for 'Mainhattan' is 200m above street level, on the **observation platform** of the 56-storey Main Tower.

STÄDEL MUSEUM   Museum
(www.staedelmuseum.de; Schaumainkai 63; adult/student/family €12/10/20, child under 12yr free; ◷10am-5pm Tue & Fri-Sun, to 9pm Wed & Thu; ☒Schweizer Platz) Founded in 1815, this world-renowned institution has a truly outstanding collection of works by 14th- to 20th-century painters, including Botticelli, Dürer, Van Eyck, Rembrandt, Renoir, Rubens, Vermeer and Cézanne, plus Frankfurt natives such as Hans Holbein. The contemporary art section reopened in 2012 after extensive renovations. The Städel is the biggest draw among the dozen or so repositories along the Museumsufer (Museum Embankment)on the southern Main River bank between Friedensbrücke and Eiserner Steg.

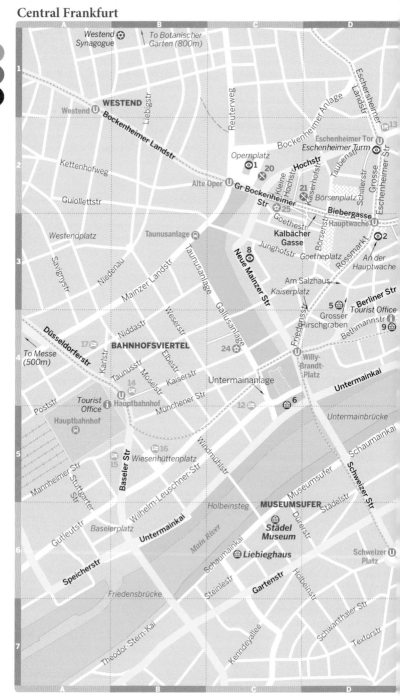

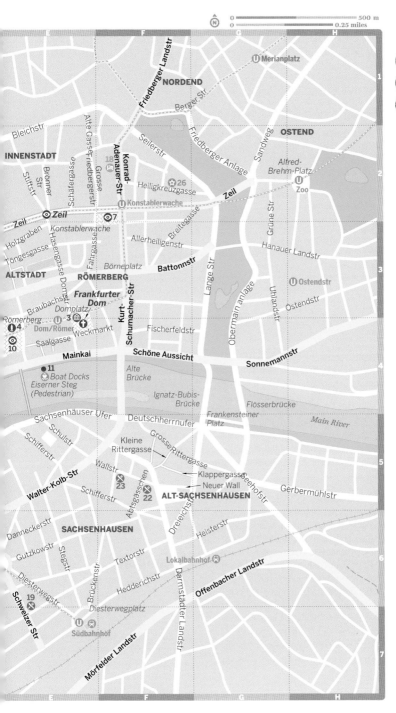

INNENSTADT

Bleichstr

Brönner Str

Stiftstr

Schäfergasse

Alte Gasse

Friedberger Str

Grosse

Friedberger Str

Holzgraben

Zeil

Zeil

Konstablerwache

Hasengasse

Töngesgasse

ALTSTADT

RÖMERBERG

Braubachstr

Domstr

Domplatz

Römerberg

Dom/Römer

Saalgasse

Weckmarkt

Frankfurter Dom

Fahrgasse

Börneplatz

Battonnstr

Allerheiligenstr

Breitegasse

NORDEND

Friedberger Landstr

Seilerstr

Berger Str

Konrad-Adenauer-Str

Heiligkreuzgasse

Friedberger Anlage

Zeil

Konstablerwache

26

7

Kurt-Schumacher-Str

Fischerfeldstr

Lange Str

OSTEND

Merianplatz

Sandweg

Alfred-Brehm-Platz

Zoo

Grüne Str

Hanauer Landstr

Obermain anlage

Ostendstr

Uhlandstr

Ostendstr

18

Mainkai

Schöne Aussicht

Sonnemannstr

11

Boat Docks

Eiserner Steg

(Pedestrian)

Alte Brücke

Ignatz-Bubis-Brücke

Deutschherrnufer

Frankensteiner Platz

Flösserbrücke

Main River

4

10

Sachsenhäuser Ufer

Schulstr

Schifferstr

Walter-Kolb-Str

Schifferstr

Wallstr

Kleine Rittergasse

Grosse Rittergasse

Abtsgässchen

23

22

Klappergasse

Neuer Wall

Seehofstr

Gerbermühlstr

ALT-SACHSENHAUSEN

Danneckerstr

SACHSENHAUSEN

Gutzkowstr

Stegstr

Brückenstr

Textorstr

Dreieichstr

Heisterstr

Lokalbahnhof

Darmstädter Landstr

Offenbacher Landstr

Diesterwegstr

Schweizer Str

19

Hedderichstr

Diesterwegplatz

Südbahnhof

Mörfelder Landstr

Central Frankfurt

LIEBIEGHAUS   Museum

(www.liebieghaus.de; Schaumainkai 71; adult/student & senior/family €7/5/16, child under 12yr free; ⏰10am-6pm Tue-Sun, to 9pm Wed & Thu) *The* place to come to see sculpture. Housed in a gorgeous 1890s villa, the superb collection encompasses Greek, Roman, Egyptian, medieval, Renaissance and baroque works, plus some items from East Asia.

GOETHE-HAUS   Historic Building

(www.goethehaus-frankfurt.de; Grosser Hirschgraben 23-25; adult/student/family €7/3/11; ⏰10am-6pm Mon-Sat, 10am-5.30pm Sun; ®Willy-Brandt-Platz) Completely rebuilt after the war (only the cellar survived Allied bombing), the birthplace of Johann Wolfgang von Goethe (1749-1832) is furnished in the haut-bourgeois style of Goethe's time, based on an inventory taken when Goethe's family sold the place. The **Gemäldegalerie** (in the same building as the ticket counter) displays 18th-century paintings.

JÜDISCHES MUSEUM   Museum

(Jewish Museum; www.jewishmuseum.de; Untermainkai 14-15; adult/child €4/2, incl same-day entry to Museum Judengasse €5/2.50; ⏰10am-5pm Tue-Sun, to 8pm Wed; ®Willy-Brandt-Platz) Nine centuries of Jewish life in Frankfurt are explored with chronologically arranged artefacts, paintings (including a Matisse confiscated by the Nazis), photographs and documents. Housed in the one-time residence of the Rothschild family. In 1933, Frankfurt's Jewish community, with 30,000 members, was Germany's second-largest.

 Tours

Run by Frankfurt's public transport company, the **Ebbelwei-Express** (Apple Wine Express; www.ebbelwei-express.com; adult/child under 14yr €7/3; ⏰half-hourly 1.30-5.30pm Sat, Sun & holidays Apr-Oct & Sat Nov-Mar, approx hourly 1.30-5pm Sun & holidays Nov-Mar) is a historic tram whose 70-minute circuit takes in both banks of the Main between the Zoo and the Messe. Jump on at any stop marked with the letters EE. As you'd expect, the price includes apple wine or juice and pretzels.

TOURIST OFFICE Walking Tours
(www.frankfurt-tourismus.de; Römerberg 27; adult/child 4-14yr/student €12/6/10; ☺tours depart 2.30pm; 🚊Dom/Römer) Two-hour walking tours of the city start every day at the Römer tourist office; no need to reserve ahead.

PRIMUS LINIE Boat Tours
(www.primus-linie.de; Mainkai, Altstadt; ☺hourly 11am-5pm Mon-Sat, half-hourly 11am-6.30pm Sun & holidays Apr-Oct, also Sat & Sun Mar; 🚊Dom/Römer) Runs 50-minute sightseeing cruises (adult €8.40) both upstream and down; for the best skyline views, take the full 100-minute circuit (€10.40). The dock is across the Eisener Steg from the Museumsufer.

 Sleeping

When it comes to accommodation prices, supply and demand reign supreme in Frankfurt. The city's hotels cater mainly to business travellers and so tend to drop rates on weekends (Friday, Saturday and Sunday nights), on holidays and in July and August. But during major trade fairs, prices can triple or even quadruple, with modest doubles going for €300 or more. The easiest way to find out if your trip coincides with one of the larger fairs is go to almost any hotel website and plug in specific dates. Sky-high prices mean that you've got a big *Messe* on your hands.

To avoid paying a fortune for accommodation during trade fairs, many travellers stay outside the city and commute using Frankfurt's fast, easy-to-use public transport system. In neighbouring cities such as Darmstadt, Wiesbaden and Mainz, which are an hour or less by S-Bahn from the fairgrounds, prices rise by only a few tens of per cent during even the largest fairs, and each has a lot more to offer visitors than the suburbs out by the airport.

Major hotel chains with outposts in Frankfurt include Hilton, Holiday Inn, Ibis, Intercontinental, Le Méridien, Mercure, Mövenpick (on the Messe grounds), Ramada and Sheraton.

The **tourist office** (www.frankfurt -tourismus.de) has a free hotel booking

Römerberg (p201), Frankfurt am Main

RAIMUND KOCH/GETTY IMAGES ©

service but arranges private rooms only during trade fairs. At the airport, help with hotel reservations (including during trade fairs) is available from **Hotels & Tours** (6907 0402; https://hotels.frankfurt-airport .de; Terminal 1, Arrival Hall B; 7am-10.30pm).

You can find furnished rooms and apartments through a *Mitwohnzentrale* (accommodation finding service), such as www.city-residence.de and www .mitwohnzentrale-mainhattan.de (in German; free registration required).

TWENTY-FIVE HOURS
Boutique Hotel €€

(25h; 256 6770; www.25hours-hotels.com; Niddastrasse 58; d without breakfast weekday/ weekend from €107/77, during fairs up to €390; @ ; Frankfurt Hauptbahnhof) Inspired by Levi's (yes, the jeans), the 76 rooms are themed by decade, with each floor representing 10 years between the 1930s and 1940s (calm, conservative colours) through the 1980s (brace yourself for tiger-print walls and optical-illusion carpets). The staff are young and friendly; clients often come from creative

sectors of the economy. In the basement Musik-Raum (music room), designed by Gibson, guests are welcome to jam on the drums and guitars. The roof terrace offers skyline views.

FLEMING'S HOTEL
Historic Hotel €€€

(0800-373 7700, 427 2320; www.flemings -hotels.com; Eschenheimer Tor 2; d without breakfast from €168, during fair €398; @ ; Eschenheimer Tor) Classic 1950s elegance stretches from the stainless steel, neon and black-and-white marble of the lobby all the way up to the 7th-floor panoramic restaurant, linked by a rare, hop-on-hop-off Paternoster elevator/lift. The sexy, see-through showers, set in the middle of the room, are not for the prudish.

LE MÉRIDIEN PARKHOTEL
Luxury Hotel €€€

(26970; www.lemeridienparkhotelfrankfurt .com; Wiesenhüttenplatz 28-38; s weekday/ weekend from €139/125, d weekday/weekend €199/145, during fairs up to €600; P @ ; Frankfurt Hauptbahnhof) Midway between the train station and the river, this stylish luxury hotel has 80 rooms in an ornate Wilhelmian-era structure, built in 1905 with high ceilings and broad hallways, and another 217 rooms in its modern business wing. The former are decorated with English-style antiques and have marble bathrooms, while the latter come with light-coloured wood furnishings and, sometimes, great skyline views.

ADINA APARTMENT HOTEL
Hotel €€

(247 4740; www.adina.eu; Wilhelm-Leuschner-Strasse 6; d without breakfast from €84-135, during fairs up to €377; ; Willy-Brandt-Platz) If you'd like to do some of your own cooking and have a bit more space, or are travelling with kids, it's well worth consider-ing the Adina's studio, one

Kaiserdom, Speyer

and two-bedroom apartments, all with kitchenettes.

FRANKFURT HOSTEL Hostel €
(📞247 5130; www.frankfurt-hostel.com; Kaiserstrasse 74, 3rd fl; dm €19-25, s/d from €35/45, during fairs up to €80/100; @🛜; 🚉Frankfurt Hauptbahnhof) Popular with young travellers (and families, too), this lively, 200-bed establishment is a great place to meet other travellers. Reached via a pre-war marble-and-tile lobby and a mirrored lift, this 200-bed hostel has a chill-out area for socialising, a small shared kitchen, squeaky wooden floors and free, all-you-can-eat spaghetti, served nightly at 8pm. Dorm rooms, two of which are women-only, have three to 10 metal bunks. Use of lockers is free (deposit required for the key).

HOTEL EXCELSIOR Hotel €
(📞256 080; www.hotelexcelsior-frankfurt .de; Mannheimer Strasse 7-9; s/d from €61/75, during fairs €199/239; 🅿@🛜; 🚉Frankfurt Hauptbahnhof) Behind a light-green facade, this 197-room place offers excellent value, with a free business centre, free landline phone calls throughout Germany, and free coffee, tea, fruit and cakes in the lobby.

WESTIN GRAND Business Hotel €€€
(📞29810; www.westin.com; Konrad-Adenauer -Strasse 5-7; d €200-300, ste €500-1500; 🅿✳@🛜♒; 🚉Konstablerwache) An international-standard business hotel whose 371 rooms, large and very comfortable, come with sparkling marble bathrooms. There's a candle-lit bar in the classy, granite-floored lobby, which displays two classic motorcars.

 Eating & Drinking

The pedestrianised avenue linking the Alte Oper and the western end of the Zeil – officially called Kalbächer Gasse and Grosse Bockenheimer Strasse – is known affectionately as Fressgass' because of its generous selection of eater-

If You Like…
Grand Cathedrals

If you've been in awe of the cathedrals in Aachen, Cologne and Mainz, you might also delight in these houses of worship.

1 KAISERDOM, WORMS
(www.wormser-dom.de; Worms; ⊙9am-6pm Apr-Oct, 10am-5pm Nov-Mar, closed during Sun morning Mass) Some 45km south of Mainz, Worms is dominated by the four towers and two domes of the some 900-year-old late-Romanesque Kaiserdom. Its lofty dimensions impress as much as the lavish canopied high altar (1742) by baroque master Balthasar Neumann.

2 KAISERDOM, SPEYER
(Speyer; crypt adult/child €3/free; ⊙9am-7pm Mon-Sat, 11.30am-5.30pm Sun Apr-Oct, 9am or 10am-5pm daily Nov-Mar) Construction of Speyer's extraordinary Romanesque cathedral began in 1030, resulting in a interior that is startling for its austere, dignified symmetry and a darkly festive crypt , whose candy-striped Romanesque arches recall Moorish architecture. It's a Unesco World Heritage Site and about 45km south of Worms.

3 DOM ST PAUL, MÜNSTER
(www.paulusdom.de; Domplatz, Münster; ⊙6.30am-6pm Mon-Sat, to 7.30pm Sun) Richly carved sculptures of the apostles greet you upon entering Münster's massive twin-towered cathedral. Inside, pay your respects to St Christopher, the patron saint of travellers, then focus your attention on the marvelous 16th-century astronomical clock. The town is about 120km north of Düsseldorf.

4 DOM, PADERBORN
(Markt 17, Paderborn; ⊙10am-6.30pm) Highlights of Paderborn's mighty Dom include the delicate high altar, the pompous memorial tomb of 17th-century bishop Dietrich von Fürstenberg and the endearing Dreihasenfenster (Three Hares' Window), which has tracery depicting three hares, ingeniously arranged so that each has two ears, even though there are only three ears in all. Paderborn is about 105km southwest of Hanover.

Apple wine tavern, Frankfurt am Main

INGOLF POMPE/GETTY IMAGES ©

ies. Frankfurt's biggest cluster of places to drink and eat is in Sachsenhausen's northeastern corner, in an area called Alt-Sachsenhausen.

FLEMING'S CLUB   International €€€

(☎427 2320; www.flemings-hotels.com; Eschenheimer Tor 2; mains €14-58; � 6am-llpm; 🛜; 🚇Eschenheimer Tor) Great city views and equally great food await at this 7th floor restaurant and bar, reached from the lobby of Fleming's Hotel via a Paternoster lift/elevator that will make you feel like you're in a 1930s movie.

ADOLF WAGNER   Apple Wine Tavern €€

(☎612 565; www.apfelwein-wagner.com; Schweizer Strasse 71; mains €4.50-13.90; � 11am-midnight; 🍴; 🚇Südbahnhof) Opened in 1931, this warm, woody tavern specialises in local dishes such as *handkäse mit Musik* (€2.90), *Grüne Sosse* (€8.20) and *Würstchen mit Sauerkraut* (sausage with sauerkraut; €4.50).

DIE LEITER   French & Italian €€€

(☎292 121; www.dieleiter.de; Kaiserhofstrasse 11; mains €19.50-29.50; �noon-3pm & 6-11pm Mon-Fri, noon-11pm Sat; 🚇Opernplatz) Dine on veal, steak and fish amid old-world, bistro-style elegance. The chef, who hails from Vienna, is deft with his signature French and Italian dishes but is especially proud of his 'Original Wiener Schnitzel'.

LOBSTER   Bistro €€€

(☎612 920; www.lobster-weinbistrot.de; Wallstrasse 21; mains €15-20; � 6pm-1am Mon-Sat, hot dishes until 10.30pm; 🚇Südbahnhof) In a one-time grocery and milk shop from the 1950s, this cosy, friendly 'wine bistro' is renowned for mouth-watering meat and fish dishes that are 'a little bit French'; offerings are listed on chalkboards.

FICHTE KRÄNZI   Apple Wine Tavern €€

(☎612 778; www.fichtekraenzi.de; Wallstrasse 5; mains €7.20-15.50; � 5-11pm; 🍴; 🚇Lokalbahnhof) Founded in 1849, Fichte Kränzi is an authentic Frankfurt *Lokal* (pub) with wood-panelled walls, smoke-stained murals, long tables, long benches and great atmosphere. Serves a good selection of German and Frankfurt-style favourites, including *Handkäse mit Musik*, schnitzel and apple strudel.

BRASSERIE Bistro €€

(9139 8634; Opernplatz 8; mains €11.50-26.80; 10am-1am; Opernplatz) One of four cosy little eateries facing the east side of the Alte Oper, Brasserie serves red meat, fish and pasta of German, Italian and French inspiration. The front terrace affords fine views of the Alte Oper and surrounding skyscrapers.

 Entertainment

Frankfurt is a cultural magnet for the whole Rhine-Main region, and this is reflected in the variety, verve and velocity of its concerts, clubs and cabarets. Thursday is a big night out for workers who commute to Frankfurt for the week and go 'home' on Friday with drooping eyelids, scuffed dance shoes and wretched hangovers. Several dance clubs have summertime beach clubs along the Main River.

Several entertainment magazines (in German), available at newsstands and kiosks (or online), provide day-by-day listings of cultural events and nightlife, including lesbian and gay venues: comprehensive *Journal Frankfurt* (www.journal-frankfurt.de; €1.80), *Prinz Frankfurt* (http://frankfurt.prinz.de; €2.90), student-oriented *Frizz* (www.frizz-frankfurt.de; free) and *Strandgut* (www.strandgut.de; free).

TIGERPALAST Cabaret

(restaurant 9200 2225, tickets 920 0220; www.tigerpalast.com; Heiligkreuzgasse 16-20; adult €58.75-64.25, child half-price; shows 7pm & 10pm Tue-Thu, 7.30pm & 10.30pm Fri & Sat, 4.30pm & 8pm Sun, closed mid-Jun-mid-Aug; Konstablerwache) A top venue for cabaret and *Varieté* theatre, with programs that often include acrobats and circus and magic performances. Hugely enjoyable even if you don't speak German.

JAZZKELLER Jazz

(www.jazzkeller.com; Kleine Bockenheimer Strasse 18a; admission €5-25; 8pm-2am Tue-Thu, 10pm-3am Fri, 9pm-2am Sat, 8pm-1am Sun; Alte Oper) A great jazz venue with mood, since 1952. Check out the walls for photos of jazz greats who've played here over the years.

ENGLISH THEATRE Theatre

(2423 1620; www.english-theatre.org; Kaiserstrasse 34, entrance on Gallusanlage; tickets €22-47; season runs late Aug-Jun, box office noon-6pm Mon, 11am-6.30pm Tue-Fri, 3-6.30pm Sat, 3-5pm Sun; Willy-Brandt-Platz) Continental Europe's largest English-language theatre company stages first-rate plays and musicals, with top actors hired after casting calls in London and New York.

 Information

Tourist Information

Tourist office (2123 8800, for hotel reservations 2123 0808; www.frankfurt-tourismus.de) The Hauptbahnhof branch (8am-9pm Mon-Fri, 9am-6pm Sat, Sun & holidays; Frankfurt Hauptbahnhof) is behind track 13 at the far end of the barrel-vaulted hall; the Altstadt branch (Römerberg 27, inside Römer, Altstadt; 9.30am-5.30pm Mon-Fri, 9.30am-4pm Sat, Sun & holidays; Dom/Römer) is very helpful, with oodles of useful information and brochures.

Getting There & Away

Air

Frankfurt Airport (FRA; www.frankfurt-airport.com), 12km southwest of downtown, is Germany's busiest airport. S-Bahn lines S8 and S9 shuttle between the airport's regional train station, Flughafen Regionalbahnhof, and the city centre (one-way €4.10, 15 minutes). A taxi from the airport to the city centre costs about €27 (a bit more from 10pm to 6am).

Train

The Hauptbahnhof, about 1km west of the Altstadt and 1km southeast of the Messe, handles more departures and arrivals than any other station in Germany, which means that there are convenient trains to pretty much everywhere, including Berlin (€118, four hours).

If You Like…
Art World Stars

If you've feasted your eyes on classic canvasses at Düsseldorf's Kunstsammlung or Cologne's Museum Ludwig, capture further artistic eye candy at these nearby fine-art repositories.

1 **MUSEUM FOLKWANG**
(☎884 5314; www.museum-folkwang.de; Goethestrasse 41, Essen; adult/child €5/3.50; ⏰10am-6pm Tue-Sun, to 10.30pm Fri) This venerable museum in Essen (about 40km northeast of Düsseldorf via the A44/52 autobahns) is a highly respected showcase of such 19th- and 20th-century masters as Gauguin, Caspar David Friedrich and Mark Rothko. Since 2011 it is housed in sparkling new digs by British star architect David Chipperfield.

2 **DORTMUNDER U**
(www.dortmunder-u.de; Leonie-Reygers-Terrasse, Dortmund; ⏰Tue-Wed & Sat-Sun 11am-6pm, to 8pm Thu-Fri) You can see it from afar – the golden 'U' atop the tower of the defunct Union Brauerei. Once one of Dortmund's largest and most famous breweries, this protected landmark is now home to the **Museum am Ostwal** (www.museumamostwall.dortmund.de; Dortmunder U, Leonie-Reygers-Terrasse; adult/child €5/2.50)l, with its impressive range of 20th- and 21st-century headliners, including Macke, Nolde, Beuys and Paik. Dortmund is about 80km northeast of Düsseldorf via the A46 and A1 autobahns.

3 **MUSEUM KÜPPERSMÜHLE**
(☎3019 4811; www.museum-kueppersmuehle.de; Philosophenweg 55, Duisburg; adult/child €6/free, incl special exhibit €8/free; ⏰2-6pm Wed, 11am-6pm Thu, Sat & Sun) From Baselitz to Kiefer to Richter, all the big names from post-WWII German art are on display in this mill storage building converted by Swiss Pritzker Prize–winning architects Herzog & de Meuron. Duisburg is 30km north of Düsseldorf via the A59.

Mainz
☎06131 / POP 199,000

Mainz has a sizable university, fine pedestrian precincts and a certain *savoir vivre* whose origins go back to Napoléon occupation (1797–1814). Strolling along the Rhine and sampling local wines in a half-timbered Altstadt tavern are as much a part of any Mainz visit as viewing the fabulous Dom, Chagall's ethereal windows in St-Stephan-Kirche, or the first printed Bible in the Gutenberg Museum, a bibliophile's paradise.

◉ Sights

DOM ST MARTIN   Church
(Marktplatz; ⏰9am-6.30pm Mon-Fri, 9am-4pm Sat, 12.45-3pm & 4-6.30pm Sun & holidays Mar-Oct, to 5pm Sun-Fri & to 3pm Sat Nov-Feb) Topped by an octagonal tower, Mainz' world-famous cathedral, built of deep red sandstone in the 12th century, is quintessentially Romanesque. Inside, a pink-hued solemnity pervades the nave, which, surprisingly, has a choir at each end. The grandiose, wall-mounted memorial tombstones form a veritable portrait gallery of archbishops and other 13th- to 18th-century powermongers, many portrayed alongside their personal putti.

GUTENBERG MUSEUM   Museum
(www.gutenberg-museum.de; Liebfrauenplatz 5; adult/child €5/3; ⏰9am-5pm Tue-Sat, 11am-5pm Sun) A heady experience for anyone excited by books, the Gutenberg Museum takes a panoramic look at the technology that made the world as we know it possible. Highlights include very early printed masterpieces – kept safe in a walk-in vault – such as three extremely rare (and valuable) examples of Gutenberg's original 42-line Bible.

ST-STEPHAN-KIRCHE   Church
(Kleine Weissgasse 12; ⏰10am-4.30 or 5pm) This would be just another Gothic church rebuilt after WWII were it not for the nine brilliant, stained-glass windows created by the Russian-Jewish artist Marc Chagall (1887-1985) in the final years of his life.

Bright blue and imbued with a mystical, meditative quality, they serve as a symbol of Jewish-Christian reconciliation.

 Tours

The tourist office runs **walking tours** (adult/student/family €7/4/15; ⏱2pm Sat year-round, also at 2pm Mon, Wed, Fri & Sun May-Oct) of the city in English and German.

 Sleeping

HOTEL HOF EHRENFELS Hotel €€
(☎971 2340; www.hof-ehrenfels.de; Grebenstrasse 5-7; s/d/tr €80/100/120, €10 less Fri-Sun) Just steps from the cathedral, this 22-room place, housed in a 15th-century, one-time Carmelite nunnery, has Dom views that are hard to beat.

HOTEL SCHWAN Hotel €€
(☎144 920; www.mainz-hotel-schwan.de; Liebfrauenplatz 7; s/d €87/114, during fairs €98/149; 📶) You can't get any more central than this family-run place, around since 1463. The 22 well-lit rooms have baroque-style furnishings.

 Eating & Drinking

Cheap eateries can be found near the Hauptbahnhof (eg along Bahnhof-strasse) and, south of the Dom, along Augustinerstrasse.

ZUR KANZEL French €€€
(☎237 137; www.zurkanzel.de; Grebenstrasse 6; mains €11.50-21.50; ⏱5pm-1am Mon-Fri, noon-3pm & 6pm-1am Sat) A classy place with a distinctly French flair and a lovely courtyard, this *Weinstube* (wine bar) serves upmarket French and regional cuisine, including dishes made with *grüne Sosse* (light sauce made with fresh herbs, sour cream and soft white cheese).

WEINSTUBE HOTTUM German €€
(☎223 370; Grebenstrasse 3; mains €7.80-15.50; ⏱4pm-midnight, may close earlier Jul & Aug) This eight-table wine tavern has a cosy, traditional atmosphere and a menu – half of which appears on a tiny slate tablet – with regional dishes such as *Saumagen* (pig's stomach stuffed with meat, potatoes and spices, then boiled, sliced and briefly fried) and *Winzersteak* (vintner-style pork steak).

EISGRUB-BRÄU Beer Tavern €
(☎221 104; www.eisgrub.de; Weissliliengasse 1a; weekday lunch €5.90, mains €8.40-18.90; ⏱11.30am-midnight Mon-Fri, 9am-midnight Sat & Sun) Grab a seat in this down-to-earth microbrewery's warren of vaulted chambers, and order a mug of *Dunkel* (dark) or *Hell* (light). The Monday-to-Friday lunch (€5.90) and the weekend breakfast buffet (€6.90; available 9am to 11.30am) offer great value.

HEILIGGEIST Cafe €€
(www.heiliggeist-mainz.de; Mailandsgasse 11; mains €9.80-19.80; ⏱4pm-1am Mon-Fri, 9am-1am or 2am Sat, Sun & holidays) Sit beneath the soaring

Dom St Martin, Mainz
YOSHIHIRO TAKADA/A COLLECTIONRF/GETTY IMAGES ©

Gothic vaults of a 15th-century hospital and enjoy a beer, glass of wine, snack or full meal from a menu filled with dishes of German and Italian inspiration. On weekends breakfast is served until 4pm.

 ## ⭐ Entertainment

Mainz has exceptionally rich and varied cultural offerings.

Four free monthly mags, available at the tourist office and in cafes and pubs, have listings (in German) of cultural events: *Frizz* (www.frizz-mainz.de), *Der Mainzer* (www.dermainzer.net), *Sensor* (www.sensor-magazin.de) and *Stuz* (www.stuz.de).

Tickets for most events can be purchased at the tourist office.

KUZ Live Music
(✆ 286 860; www.kuz.de; Dagobertstrasse 20b) Concerts by German and international bands, dance parties, theatre for kids… the happening *KulturZentrum* (cultural centre) has something for almost everyone. Housed in a red-brick building that began life in the 19th century as a military laundry.

FRANKFURTER HOF Live Music
(✆ 220 438; www.frankfurter-hof-mainz.de; Augustinerstrasse 55) Hosts and organises concerts both by up-and-coming artists and by big-name international acts such as Chris de Burgh. Some events take place at other venues around the city.

STAATSTHEATER Performing Arts
(✆ 285 1222; www.staatstheater-mainz.com; Gutenbergplatz 7) The state theatre stages plays, opera and ballet. Students get significant discounts.

ℹ Information

Tourist office (✆ 286 210; www.touristik-mainz.de; Brückenturm am Rathaus; ⏰ 9am-6pm Mon-Fri, 10am-4pm Sat, 11am-3pm Sun)

ℹ Getting There & Away

From the Hauptbahnhof, S-Bahn line S8 goes via Frankfurt airport to Frankfurt's Hauptbahnhof (€7.30, 35-42 minutes, several times hourly).

A major rail hub, Mainz's Hauptbahnhof has at least hourly regional services to Bingen (€6.20, 15 to 40 minutes) and other Romantic Rhine towns, Koblenz (€18.10 to €21, 50 to 90 minutes), Saarbrücken (€21, 2¼ hours) and Worms (€8.30, 26 to 43 minutes).

Gutenberg Museum (p210), Mainz

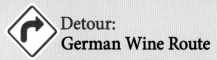

Detour:
German Wine Route

The **Deutsche Weinstrasse** (www.deutsche-weinstrasse.de), inaugurated in 1935, is a collection of roughly parallel rural roads, only sporadically signposted, that wend their way through the heart of the Palatinate (Pfalz), a region of vine-covered hillsides, gentle forests, ruined castles, picturesque hamlets and welcoming wine estates. Starting in Bockenheim, about 15km west of Worms, it winds south – through Germany's largest contiguous winegrowing area – for 85km to Schweigen-Rechtenbach, on the French border (adjacent to the Alsatian town of Wissembourg). Especially pretty towns and villages include (from north to south) **Freinsheim**, **Kallstadt**, **Bad Dürkheim**, **Forst**, **Deidesheim**, **Meilkammer** and **Rhodt**. Hiking and cycling options are legion.

Blessed with a moderate climate that allows almonds, figs, kiwi fruit and even lemons to thrive, the German Wine Route is especially pretty during the spring bloom (March to mid-May). **Weinfeste** (wine festivals) run from March to mid-November (especially on the weekends). The grape harvest (September and October) is also a particularly eventful time to visit.

In part because of its proximity to France, the Palatinate is a renowned culinary destination, with restaurants serving everything from gourmet German nouvelle cuisine to traditional regional specialities such as *Saumagen*. Tourist offices can supply lists of visitable wineries.

The German Wine Route is most easily explored by car.

THE ROMANTIC RHINE VALLEY

Between Rüdesheim and Koblenz, the Rhine cuts deeply through the Rhenish slate mountains, meandering between hillside castles and steep fields of wine to create a magical mixture of beauty and legend. Idyllic villages appear around each bend, their neat half-timbered houses and Gothic church steeples seemingly plucked from the world of fairy tales.

High above the river and the rail lines that run along each bank are the famous medieval castles, some ruined, some restored, all mysterious and vestiges of a time that was anything but tranquil. In 2002 Unesco designated these 67km of riverscape, more prosaically known as the **Oberes Mittelrheintal** (Upper Middle Rhine Valley; www.welterbe-mittelrheintal.de), as a World Heritage Site.

ℹ Getting Around

Boat

River travel is a relaxing and very romantic way to see the castles, vineyards and villages of the Romantic Rhine.

From about Easter to October (winter services are very limited), passenger ships run by Köln-Düsseldorfer (KD;  0221-2088 318; www.k-d.com) link Rhine villages on a set timetable. You can travel to the next village or all the way from Mainz to Koblenz (€55.40, downstream/upstream 5½/8 hours). Other companies:

Bingen-Rüdesheimer (www.bingen-ruedesheimer.com)

Hebel Linie (www.hebel-linie.de)

Loreley Linie (www.loreley-linie.com)

Rössler Linie (www.roesslerlinie.de)

Train

Villages on the Rhine's left bank (eg Bingen, Bacharach, Oberwesel and Boppard) are served hourly by local trains on the Koblenz-Mainz run, inaugurated in 1859.

Right-bank villages such as Rüdesheim, Assmannshausen, Kaub, St Goarshausen and Braubach are linked hourly to Koblenz' Hauptbahnhof and Wiesbaden by the RheingauLinie, operated by Vias.

Car Ferry

Since there are no bridges over the Rhine between Koblenz and Mainz (though there are controversial plans to build one near St Goar, possibly endangering the area's Unesco World Heritage status), the only way to cross the river along this stretch is by *Autofähre* (car ferry).

The following services, listed from south to north, operate every 15 or 20 minutes during the day and every 30 minutes early in the morning and late at night:

Bingen-Rüdesheim (www.bingen-ruedesheimer .com/rheinfaehren; ⏰6 or 7am-9.45pm Nov-Apr, to midnight or later May-Oct)

Niederheimbach-Lorch (www.mittelrhein -faehre.de; ⏰6am-6.50pm Nov-Mar, to 7.50pm Apr-Oct)

Boppard-Filsen (www.faehre-boppard.de; ⏰6.30am-8pm Oct-Mar, to 9pm Apr, May & Sep, to 10pm Jun-Aug)

Oberwesel-Kaub (www.faehre-kaub.de; ⏰6 or 8am-6.50pm Oct-Mar, to 7.50pm Apr-Sep)

St Goar-St Goarshausen (www.faehre-loreley .de; ⏰5.30 or 6am-midnight)

Rüdesheim

☎ 06722 / POP 10,000

Rüdesheim, part of the Rheingau wine region (famous for its superior rieslings), is deluged by some three million day-tripping coach tourists a year. Depending on how you look at it, the town centre – and especially its most famous feature, an alley know as Drosselgasse – is either a 'mass tourism nightmare from hell' or a lot of silly, kitschy, colourful fun.

👁 Sights & Activities

DROSSELGASSE Alley
Drosselgasse, a tunnel-like alley so overloaded with signs that it looks like it could be in Hong Kong (some of the signs are, in fact, in Chinese), is the Rhine at its most colourfully touristic – bad German pop wafts out of the pubs, which are filled with rollicking crowds. The **Oberstrasse,** at the top of Drosselgasse, is similarly overloaded with eateries and drinkeries, though to get away from the drunken madness all you have to do is wander a few blocks in any direction.

SIEGFRIED'S MECHANISCHES MUSIKKABINETT Museum
(www.smmk.de; Oberstrasse 29; tour adult/student €6/3; ⏰10am-6pm Mar-Dec) Has a fun and often surprising collection of 18th- and 19th-century mechanical musical instruments that play themselves as you're shown around. Situated 50m to the left from the top of Drosselgasse.

Drosselgasse, Rüdesheim

NIEDERWALD DENKMAL

For a stunning panorama, head up to the Niederwald Denkmal (inaugurated 1883), a bombastic monument on the wine slopes west of town starring **Germania** and celebrating the creation of the German Reich in 1871. You can walk up via the vineyards – trails, including one that begins at the western end of Oberstrasse, are signposted – but it's faster to glide above the vineyards aboard the **Seilbahn cable car** (Kabinenbahn; www.seilbahn-ruedesheim.de; Oberstrasse 30; adult/5-13yr one-way €4.50/2, return €6.50/3; ⊙late Mar-11 Nov & late Nov-23 Dec).

 Information

Tourist Office (📞906 150; www.ruedesheim .de; Rheinstrasse 29a; ⊙8.30am-6.30pm Mon-Fri & 10am-4pm Sat, Sun & holidays Apr-Oct, 11am-4.30pm Mon-Fri Nov-Mar)

Getting There & Away

Rüdesheim is connected to Bingen by passenger and car ferries.

Bingen
📞 06721 / POP 24,600

Thanks to its strategic location at the confluence of the Nahe and Rhine Rivers, Bingen has been coveted by warriors and merchants since its founding by the Romans in 11 BC. These days it's an attractive, flowery town that's less touristy – and less cute – than its smaller neighbours.

 Sights

MUSEUM AM STROM   Museum
(Museumsstrasse 3; adult/concession/family €3/2/6; ⊙10am-5pm Tue-Sun) On the riverside promenade, this museum – in a one-time power station – has worthwhile exhibits on Rhine romanticism, both engraved and painted, and on the life and achievements of Hildegard von Bingen. Another highlight is a set of surgical instruments – from scalpels and cupping glasses to saws – left behind by a Roman doctor in the 2nd century AD.

Detour:
Kloster Eberbach

If you saw the 1986 film *The Name of the Rose*, starring Sean Connery, you've already seen parts of this one-time Cistercian **monastery** (www.kloster-eberbach.de; adult/student incl audioguide €6.50/4.50; ⊙10am-6pm Apr-Oct, 11am-5pm Nov-Mar), in which many of the interior scenes were shot. Dating from as far back as the 12th century and once home to 150 or more monks and perhaps 400 lay brothers, this graceful complex – in an idyllic little valley – went through periods as a lunatic asylum, jail, sheep pen and accommodation for WWII refugees. Today visitors can explore the 13th- and 14th-century **Kreuzgang** (cloister), the monks' baroque **refectory** and their vaulted Gothic **Monchdormitorium** (dormitory), as well as the austere Romanesque **Klosterkirche** (basilica).

Kloster Eberbach is about 20km northeast of Rüdesheim (towards Wiesbaden).

MÄUSETURM   Castle
(⊙closed to the public) The Mouse Tower, on an island near the confluence of the Nahe and Rhine, is where – according to legend – Hatto II, the 10th-century archbishop of Mainz, was devoured alive by mice as punishment for his oppressive rule. In fact, the name is probably a mutation of *Mautturm* (toll tower), which reflects the building's medieval function.

Sleeping & Eating

HOTEL-CAFÉ KÖPPEL   Hotel €
(📞147 70; www.hotel-koeppel.de; Kapuzinerstrasse 12; s/d from €48/78; 🛜) In the heart of town across from the Kapuzinerkirche, this place is above a stylish *Konditorei*

(cake cafe) whose products will make your eyes go wide. The 22 rooms are quiet, modern and attractive, decorated in calming, lighter hues. The hotel entrance is around the side.

 Information

Tourist office (☎184 205; www.bingen.de; Rheinkai 21; ☺9am-6pm Mon-Fri, 9am-5pm Sat Easter-Oct, 10am-1pm Sun May-Oct, 9am-4pm Tue-Thu, to 6pm Mon, to 1pm Fri Nov-Easter)

❶ Getting There & Away

Bingen has two train stations: the Hauptbahnhof, just west of the Nahe in Bingerbrück; and the more central Bahnhof Bingen Stadt, just east of the town centre.

Passenger ferries to Rüdesheim leave from the town centre's riverfront promenade; car ferries dock about 1km upriver (east) from the centre.

Burg Reichenstein

Looming above the village of Trechtingshausen, mighty **Burg Reichenstein** (☎06721-6117; www.burg-reichenstein.de; adult/under 12yr €4.50/3; ☺10am-6pm Tue-Sun Mar–mid-Nov, call for winter hours) harbours a lavish collection of furnishings, armour, hunting trophies and even cast-iron oven slabs. It also has rooms for rent (doubles cost €94 to €153). Situated 8km downriver from Bingen.

Bacharach

☎06743 / POP 2250

One of the prettiest of the Rhine villages, tiny Bacharach – 24km downriver from Bingen – conceals its considerable charms behind a 14th-century wall. From the B9, go through one of the thick arched gateways under the train tracks and you'll find yourself in a medieval old town graced with half-timbered mansions such as the **Altes Haus,** the **Posthof** and the off-kilter **Alte Münze** – all are along Oberstrasse, the main street, which runs parallel to the Rhine, and all now house places to eat, drink and be merry.

Sights & Activities

STADTMAUER RUNDWEG Walking
The best way to get a sense of the village and its hillside surrounds is to take a stroll on top of the walls – it's possible to walk almost all the way around the centre. The **lookout tower** on the upper section of the wall affords panoramic views. The filigreed ruins of the Gothic **Wernerkapelle** were built between 1289 and 1430; the 12th-century **Burg Stahleck** is now a hostel.

🛏 Sleeping & Eating

RHEIN HOTEL Hotel €€
(☎1243; www.rhein-hotel-bacharach.de; Langstrasse 50; s €39-65, d €78-130; ❄️🛜) Right on the town's medieval ramparts, this very welcoming, family-run hotel has 14 well-lit rooms with original artwork and compact bathrooms. The restaurant specialises in regional dishes such as *Rieslingbraten* (riesling-marinated braised beef).

ZUM GRÜNEN BAUM Wine Bar
(Oberstrasse 63; snacks & light meals €2.90-9.80; ☺noon-11pm except Thu) An unpretentious wine tavern serving some of Bacharach's best whites, 18 of them by the glass (€2.90-4.10). Order the *Weinkarussel* (€19.50) and you can sample 15 of them!

❶ Information

Tourist office (☎919 303; www.rhein-nahe-touristik.de; Oberstrasse 45; ☺9am-5pm Mon-Fri, 10am-3pm Sat, Sun & holidays Apr-Oct, 9am-1pm Mon-Fri Nov-Mar)

Kaub

Across the river from Bacharach and about 8km upriver from Loreley, near the village of Kaub, stands the fairly-tale **Pfalzgrafenstein** (www.burg-pfalzgrafenstein.de; adult/under 18yr/family €3/1.50/6; ☺10am-6pm Tue-Sun Apr-Oct, to 5pm Mar, 10am-5pm Sat & Sun Nov, Jan & Feb, closed Dec), a boat-shaped toll castle perched on a narrow island – perfect for picnics –

STEINER STEINER/GETTY IMAGES ©

in the middle of the Rhine. To get out to there, hop on a **Fährboot** (ferry boat; adult/4-11yr/family €2.50/1/6) next to the Kaub car ferry dock; there are departures every half-hour.

Loreley & St Goarshausen

🎵 06771 / POP 1300

Loreley, the most fabled spot along the Rhine, is an enormous, almost vertical slab of slate that owes its fame to a mythical maiden whose siren songs are said to have lured sailors to their death in the treacherous currents. A **sculpture** of the blonde, buxom beauty in question perches lasciviously below the outcrop, at the very tip of a narrow breakwater jutting into the Rhine.

Sights & Activities

**LORELEY
BESUCHERZENTRUM** Visitors Centre
(🎵 599 093; www.loreley-besucherzentrum.de; adult/student €2.50/1.50; ⏲10am-6pm Apr-Oct, 10am-5pm Mar, 11am-4pm Sat & Sun Nov-Feb)
On the edge of the agricultural plateau stretching away from the cliff, Loreley's Visitors Centre takes an engaging, inter-active look at the region's geology, flora and fauna, shipping and winemaking; the Loreley myth; and early Rhine tourism (signs are in English and German).

BURG KATZ & BURG MAUS Castles
Flanking St Goarshausen are two rival castles. Burg Peterseck was built by the archbishop of Trier in an effort to counter the toll practices of the powerful Katzenelnbogen family. In a show of medieval muscle flexing, the latter responded by building a much bigger castle high on the other side of town, Burg Neukatzenelnbogen, which became known as **Burg Katz** (Cat Castle; ⏲closed to the public). And so, to highlight the obvious dominance of the Katzenelnbogens, Burg Peterseck was soon nicknamed **Burg Maus** (Mouse Castle; ⏲closed to the public).

❶ Getting There & Away

The Loreley outcrop can be reached:
By car It's a 4km uphill drive from St Goarshausen; parking costs €2.

By shuttle bus One way from St Goarshausen's Marktplatz costs €2.65; runs hourly from 10am to 5pm April to October.

On foot The Treppenweg, a strenuous, 400-step stairway, begins about 2km upriver from St Goarshausen at the base of the breakwater.

St Goar

A car ferry connects St Goarshausen with its twin across the river, St Goar, which is lorded over by the sprawling ruins of **Burg Rheinfels** (www.st-goar.de; adult/child €4/2; ◷9am-6pm mid-Mar–early Nov, 11am-5pm Sat & Sun in good weather early Nov–mid-Mar), once the mightiest fortress on the Rhine. Built in 1245 by Count Dieter V of Katzenelnbogen as a base for his toll-collecting operations, its size and labyrinthine layout – guard towers, battlements, casemates, subterranean galleries – are truly astonishing. The views are stupendous.

Boppard

☑ 06742 / POP 15,750

Thanks to its scenic location on a horseshoe bend in the river – and the fact that the riverfront and historic centre are both on the same side of the train tracks – Boppard (pronounced bo-*part*) is one of the Romantic Rhine's prettiest and most enjoyable getaways.

◉ Sights & Activities

MARKTPLATZ   Square

(food market 8am-1pm Fri) Just off Boppard's main commercial street, the pedestrianised, east-west oriented **Oberstrasse**, is the ancient Marktplatz, whose modern fountain is a favourite local hang-out. Still home to a weekly **food market**, it's dominated by the pointy twin towers of the late Romanesque **Severuskirche** (◷8am-6pm) an elegant 13th-century Catholic church built on the site of Roman military baths. Inside are polychrome wall paintings, a hanging cross from 1225 (in the choir) and spiderweb-like vaulted ceilings.

VIERSEENBLICK   Hiking

The peculiar geography of the Four-Lakes-View panoramic outlook creates the illusion that you're looking at four separate lakes rather than a single river. The nearby **Gedeonseck** affords views of the Rhine's hairpin curve. To get up there you can either hike or – to save 240 vertical metres – take the 20-minute **Sesselbahn** (chairlift; www.sesselbahn-boppard.de; adult/child under

Burg Rheinfels, St Goar

14yr return €7/4.50, up only €4.20/3, bicycle €1.50; ☉10am-5 or 6pm Apr-Oct) over the vines from the upriver edge of town.

FREE **RÖMER-KASTELL**   Archaeology
(Roman Fort; cnr Angertstrasse & Kirchgasse; ☉24hr) A block south of the Marktplatz, the Roman Fort (also known as the Römerpark) has 55m of the original 4th-century Roman wall and graves from the Frankish era (7th century). A wall panel shows what the Roman town of Bodo-brica looked like 1700 years ago.

Sleeping & Eating

HOTEL GÜNTHER   Hotel €€
(📞890 90; www.hotelguenther.de; Rheinallee 40; s/d from €72/82, cheaper Nov-Apr; ☉closed most of Dec; @🖥) Watch boats and barges glide along the mighty Rhine from your balconied room at this bright, welcoming waterfront hotel. It's owned by an American fellow and his German wife, which makes communication a cinch – and explains why the breakfast buffet includes peanut butter.

Drinking

WEINHAUS HEILIG GRAB   Wine Bar
(www.heiliggrab.de; Zelkesgasse 12; snacks €3.50-7; ☉3-11pm or later Wed-Mon) Across the street from the Hauptbahnhof, Boppard's oldest wine tavern offers a cosy setting for sipping 'Holy Sepulchre' rieslings. When it's warm, you can sit outside under the chestnut trees. Also has snacks and five **rooms for rent** (doubles €59 to €79).

ℹ Information

Tourist office (📞3888; www.boppard-tourismus .de; Marktplatz; ☉9am-6.30pm Mon-Fri, 10am-2pm Sat May-Sep, 9am-5pm Mon-Fri Oct-Apr)

Braubach
📞02627 / POP 3050

Framed by forested hillsides, vineyards and Rhine-side rose gardens, the 1300-year-old town of Braubach, about 8km south of Koblenz on the right bank,

is centred on the small, half-timbered **Marktplatz.** High above are the dramatic towers, turrets and crenellations of the 700-year-old **Marksburg,** (📞206; www .marksburg.de; adult/student/6-18yr €6/5/4; ☉10am-5pm mid-Mar-Oct, 11am-4pm Nov-mid-Mar) one of the area's most interesting castles because, unique among the Rhine fortresses, it was never destroyed. Tours (often held in English at noon and 4pm – call for details) take in the citadel, the Gothic hall and the large kitchen, plus a grisly torture chamber, with its hair-raising assortment of pain-inflicting nasties.

Koblenz
📞0261 / POP 106,000

The modern, flowery, park-filled city of Koblenz sits at the confluence of the Rhine and Moselle Rivers. Its roots go all the way back to the Romans, who founded a military stronghold here (calling it Confluentes) because of the site's supreme strategic value.

Sights

DEUTSCHES ECK   Plaza
At the point of confluence of the Moselle and the Rhine, the 'German Corner' is dominated by a **statue of Kaiser Wilhelm I** on horseback, in the bombastic style of the late 19th century.

FESTUNG EHRENBREITSTEIN   Fortress
(www.diefestungehrenbreitstein.de; adult/child €6/3; ☉10am-6pm Apr-Oct, to 5pm Nov-Mar) On the right bank of the Rhine opposite the Deutsches Eck, looming 118m above the river, the mighty Ehrenbreitstein Fortress proved indestructible to all but Napoléonic troops, who levelled it in 1801. A few years later the Prussians, to prove a point, rebuilt it as one of Europe's mightiest fortifications. Today, its once-top-secret ramparts offer excellent views.

By far the most spectacular way to get up there from the city centre is to take the 850m-long **Seilbahn** (aerial cable car; www .seilbahn-koblenz.de; adult/6-14yr return €8/4, incl fortress €11.20/5.60; bicycle one-way €3; ☉10am-6pm or 7pm Apr-Oct, to 5pm Nov-Mar) from near the Deutsches Eck. Intended, like the Eiffel Tower, to be temporary, it's theoretically going to be dismantled in 2013 to avoid running foul of Unesco's World Heritage designation.

Sleeping & Eating

HOTEL MORJAN
Hotel €€

(☎ 304 290; www.hotel-morjan.de; Konrad Adenauer Ufer; s/d €65/95, with Rhine view €10 more; P@⊠) In a great spot facing the Rhine about 300m south of the Deutsches Eck, this late-20th-century hotel has 42 bright rooms, half with river views. Some of Koblenz' loveliest gardens are right nearby.

CAFE MILJÖÖ
Cafe €€

(www.cafe-miljoeoe.de; Gemüsegasse 12; mains €7.90-11.90; ⊙9am-1am or later; ⊠) 'Milieu' (pronounce it like the French) is a cosy cafe-restaurant with fresh flowers, changing art exhibits, salads, healthy mains and a great selection of coffees, teas and homemade cakes. Breakfast is available until 5pm.

❶ Information

The Tourist office (www.touristik-koblenz.de) has a branch at the Hauptbahnhof (☎313 04; Bahnhofplatz 17; ⊙9am-6pm Mon-Fri), across the square and to the right as you exit the train station, and one at the Rathaus (☎130 920; Jesuitenplatz 2, Rathaus; ⊙9am-6pm Mon-Fri, 10am-4pm Sat & Sun).

❶ Getting There & Away

Koblenz has two train stations, the main Hauptbahnhof on the Rhine's left bank about 1km south of the city centre, and Koblenz-Ehrenbreitstein on the right bank (right below Festung Ehrenbreitstein).

THE MOSELLE VALLEY

While plenty of places in Germany demand that you hustle, the Moselle (in German, Mosel) gently suggests that you should, well...just mosey. The German section of the river, which rises in France and then traverses Luxembourg, runs for 195km from Trier to Koblenz on a slow, serpentine course, revealing new scenery

at every bend. Unlike the Romantic Rhine, it's spanned by plenty of bridges.

❶ Getting There & Around

Driving is the easiest way to see the Moselle. If you're coming from Koblenz, the B49 and then, after Bullay, the B53 follow the river all the way to Trier, crossing it several times.

The rail line linking Koblenz with Trier (€19.20, 1½ to two hours, at least hourly) – most people begin their visit to the area in one of these cities – follows the Moselle (and stops at its villages) only as far upriver as Bullay (€11.10, 49 to 65 minutes from Koblenz, 38 to 53 minutes from Trier). From there, hourly shuttle trains head upriver to Traben-Trarbach (€3.40, 20 minutes, hourly). The villages between Traben-Trarbach and Trier, including Kröv, Ürzig and Bernkastel-Kues, are served by bicycle-carrying bus 333 (six times daily Monday to Friday, three times daily Saturday and Sunday), run by Moselbahn buses (www.moselbahn.de)

Burg Eltz

Victor Hugo thought this fairy-tale castle, hidden away in the forest above the left bank of the Moselle, was 'tall, terrific, strange and dark'. Indeed, 850-year-old fairy-tale **Burg Eltz** (www.burg-eltz.de; tour adult/student/family €8/5.50/24; ⊙9.30am-5.30pm Apr-Oct), owned by the same family for more than 30 generations, has a forbidding exterior somewhat softened by the turrets that crown it like candles on a birthday cake. The **treasury** features a rich collection of jewellery, porcelain and weapons.

By car, you can reach Burg Eltz – which has never been destroyed – via the village of Münstermaifeld.

Beilstein

☎ 02673 / POP 140

On the right bank of the Moselle about 50km upriver from Koblenz, Beilstein (www.beilstein-stadtfuehrung.de) is a pint-sized village right out of the world of fairy tales. Little more than a cluster of houses surrounded by steep vineyards, its historic highlights include the **Marktplatz** and, down an alleyway, a centuries-old stone **synagogue** (Weingasse 13), now occupied by an art shop called Galerie 13. Above town looms **Burg Metternich,** a hilltop castle reached via a staircase.

Traben-Trarbach

 06541 / POP 5850

Traben-Trarbach is perfect for a relaxing, turn-of-the-20th-century-style river-town holiday – and makes an excellent base for exploring the valley by bike or car. A major centre of the wine trade a century ago, the town's winemakers still welcome visitors for tasting and sales.

Traben lost its medieval look to three major fires but was well compensated with beautiful Jugendstil (art nouveau) villas – and lots of wisteria. It united with Trarbach, across the river, in 1904.

Sights

HOTEL BELLEVUE   Hotel

(Am Moselufer 11, Traben) Of Traben's sinuous **art-nouveau villas**, the most seductive – and the only one open to the public – is the riverfront Hotel Bellevue, built in 1903 and easily recognised by its Champagne-bottle-shaped slate turret. Hotel reception sells an illustrated brochure about local Jugendstil buildings (€3).

🛏 Sleeping & Eating

HOTEL BELLEVUE

Historic Hotel €€€

(☏7030; www.bellevue-hotel.de; Am Moselufer 11, Traben; d €150-190; @ 🛜 ☒) Classy, romantic and historic, this exquisite Jugendstil (art nouveau) hotel, facing the river, offers perks that include bike and canoe hire, pool and sauna. The elegant gourmet **restaurant** (mains €19 to €27), adorned with exquisite stained glass, serves regional and Mediterranean-inspired cuisine.

WEINGUT CASPARI   German €€

(☏5778; www.weingut-caspari.de; Weiherstrasse 18, Trarbach; mains €6.50-16.90) Six short blocks inland from the bridge, this rustic, old-time *Strausswirtschaft* (winery-cum-eatery) serves hearty local pork speciali-ties, such as *Feiner Grillschinken Moselart* (boiled ham with potato puree and sauer-kraut), and their own delicious rieslings.

ℹ Information

Tourist office (☏839 80; www.traben-trarbach .de; Am Bahnhof 5, Traben; ⏱10am-5pm Mon-Fri May-Aug, to 6pm Sep & Oct, to 4pm Nov-Apr, 11am-3pm Sat May-Oct; 🛜)

Bernkastel-Kues

 06531 / POP 6500

This charming twin town, some 50km downriver from Trier, is the hub of the 'Middle Moselle' region. Bernkastel, on the right bank, is a symphony in half-timber, stone and slate and teems with wine taverns – and tour groups. Kues, the birthplace of theologian Nicolaus Cusanus (1401-64), has little fairy-tale flair but

Burg Eltz in the Moselle Valley
IAIN MASTERTON/GETTY IMAGES ©

Left: Fountain of St Peter and the Four Virtues, Trier; **Right:** Beilstein (p220)

(BELOW) ADAM WOOLFITT/CORBIS ©; (RIGHT) HANS-PETER MERTEN/GETTY IMAGES ©

is home to the town's most important historical sights.

Sights

MARKTPLATZ Square

(Bernkastel) Bernkastel's pretty Marktplatz, a block inland from the bridge, is enclosed by a romantic ensemble of half-timbered houses with beautifully decorated gables. Note the medieval iron handcuffs, to which criminals were attached, on the facade of the old **Rathaus.**

On Karlstrasse, the alley to the right as you face the Rathaus, the tiny **Spitzhäuschen** resembles a giant bird's house, its narrow base topped by a much larger, precariously leaning, upper floor. More such crooked gems line **Römerstrasse** and its side streets.

FREE **ST-NIKOLAUS-HOSPITAL** Historic Building
(Cusanusstrasse 2, Kues; guided tour €5; ⊙9am-6pm Sun-Fri, 9am-3pm Sat, guided tour 10.30am Tue & 3pm Fri Apr-Oct) Most of Kues' sights are conveniently grouped near the bridge in the late-Gothic St-Nikolaus-Hospital, an old-age home founded by Cusanus in 1458 for 33 men (one for every year of Jesus' life). You're free to explore the cloister and Gothic *Kapelle* (chapel) at leisure, but the treasure-filled library can only be seen on a **guided tour**.

MOSEL-WEINMUSEUM Museum
(www.moselweinmuseum.de; Cusanusstrasse 2, Kues; adult/13-18yr €5/3; ⊙10am-6pm Apr-Oct, 11am-5pm Nov, Dec, Feb & Mar) Part of the St-Nikolaus-Hospital complex, the multimedia Moselle Wine Museum has interactive terminals (in German, English and Dutch) and attractions such as an Aromabar (you have to guess what you're smelling). In the nearby **Vinothek**

(www.moselvinothek.de), you can sample 10 Moselle wines by the glass (about €2) or, in the cellar, indulge in an 'all you can drink' wine tasting (€15) with about 150 vintages to choose from.

Sleeping & Eating

HOTEL MOSELBLÜMCHEN   Hotel €€
(☎2335; www.hotel-moselbluemchen.de; Schwanenstrasse 10, Bernkastel; s €42-79, d €69-129; P@🛜) This traditional, family-run hotel is situated on a narrow alley behind the tourist office. It has 20 tasteful rooms and a small sauna, and can arrange bike rental. In the **restaurant**, German and local specialities include sauerkraut and homemade wurst.

 Information

Tourist office (☎500 190; www.bernkastel.de; Am Gestade 6, Bernkastel; ⏰9 or 10am-4 or 5pm Mon-Fri year-round, also open 10am-5pm Sat & 10am-1pm Sun May-Oct)

Trier
☎0651 / POP 105,250

A Unesco World Heritage Site since 1986, the handsome, leafy university city of Trier is home to Germany's finest ensemble of Roman monuments – including several elaborate thermal baths – as well as architectural gems from later ages.

Sights & Activities

HAUPTMARKT   Square
Anchored by a festive **fountain** (1595) dedicated to St Peter and the Four Virtues, Trier's central market square is surrounded by medieval and Renaissance architectural treasures such as the **Rotes Haus** (Red House) and the **Steipe,** which now house an attractive cafe and the **Spielzeugmuseum** (Toy Museum; www .spielzeugmuseum-trier.de; Dietrichstrasse 51, 2nd fl; adult/child/family €4.50/2.50/12; ⏰11am-6pm Tue-Sun Apr-Oct, to 5pm Nov-Mar) chock full of miniature trains, dolls and other childhood delights.

On the south side, **St-Gangolf-Kirche** (⏰8 or 9am-6.30pm), a Gothic church built in the 14th and 15th centuries, is reached via an angel-bedecked, 18th-century baroque portal.

PORTA NIGRA   Roman Gate
(adult/student €3/2.10, incl Stadtmuseum Simeonstift €7.20/5.80; ⏰9am-6pm Apr-Sep, to 5pm Mar & Oct, to 4pm Nov-Feb) Top billing among Trier's Roman monuments goes to the Porta Nigra, a brooding 2nd-century city gate that's been blackened by time (hence the name, Latin for 'black gate'). A marvel of engineering and ingenuity, it's held together by nothing but gravity and iron rods. In the 11th century, Archbishop Poppo converted the structure into St Simeonkirche, a church named in honour of a Greek hermit who spent a stint holed up in its east tower.

DOM   Church
(www.dominformation.de; Liebfrauenstrasse 12; ⏰10am-5pm Mon-Sat, 12.30-5pm Sun, shorter hrs Nov-Mar; ♿) Built above the palace of Constantine the Great's mother, Helena, this fortress-like cathedral is mostly Romanesque, with some soaring Gothic and eye-popping baroque embellishments.

To see some dazzling ecclesiastical equipment and peer into early Christian history, head upstairs to the **Domschatz** (cathedral treasury; adult/child €1.50/0.50; ⏰10am-5pm Mon-Sat, 12.30-5pm Sun Apr-Oct, 11am-4pm Tue-Sat, 12.30-4pm Sun & Mon Nov-Mar) or go around the corner to the **Bischöfliches Dom-und Diözesanmuseum** (📞710 5255; www.bistum-trier.de/museum; Windstrasse 6-8; adult/student €3.50/2; ⏰9am-5pm Tue-Sat, 1-5pm Sun).

LIEBFRAUENBASILIKA   Church
(Liebfrauenstrasse; ⏰8am-7pm Mon-Sat, to 6pm Sun Apr-Oct, 8am-5pm Nov-Mar) One of Germany's earliest Gothic churches. The cruciform structure is supported by a dozen pillars symbolising the 12 Apostles and, despite its strict symmetry, has a light, mystical quality.

KONSTANTIN BASILIKA   Church
(www.konstantin-basilika.de; Konstantinplatz; ⏰10am-6pm Apr-Oct, 10 or 11am-noon and 2 or 3pm-4pm Tue-Sat, noon-1pm Sun Nov-Mar) Constructed around AD 310 as Constantine's throne hall, the brick-built Konstantin Basilika (Aula Palatina) is now a typically austere Protestant church. Its dimensions (67m long and 36m high) are truly mind-blowing considering that it was built by the Romans.

KAISERTHERMEN   Roman Site
(Imperial Baths; Palastgarten; adult/student €3/2.10) On the southern edge of the Palastgarten, the Kaiserthermen is a vast thermal bathing complex created by Constantine.

AMPHITHEATER   Roman Site
(Olewiger Strasse; adult/child €3/2.10; ⏰9am-6pm Apr-Sep, to 5pm Mar & Oct, to 4pm Nov-Feb) Trier's Roman Amphitheater, built in the late 2nd century AD, was once capable of holding 20,000 spectators during gladiator tournaments and animal fights – or when Constantine the Great crowned his battlefield victories by feeding his enemies to voracious animals.

Tours

CITY WALKING TOUR   Walking Tour
(adult/6-14yr €8.50/5; ⏰1.30pm Sat Apr-Oct) Two-hour tours in English begin at the tourist office.

Sleeping & Eating

Hotel prices rise on Friday and Saturday.

HOTEL RÖMISCHER
KAISER   Hotel €€
(📞977 00; www.friedrich-hotels.de; Porta-Nigra-Platz 6; s/d from €73.50/111; 📶) Built in 1894, this hotel – convenient to the train station and the old city – offers 43 bright, comfortable rooms with solid wood furnishings, parquet floors and spacious bathrooms.

ZUM DOMSTEIN   Roman €€
(www.domstein.de; Hauptmarkt 5; mains €8.90-18.50, Roman dinner €17-35) A German-style bistro where you can either dine like an ancient Roman or feast on more conventional German and international fare.

THOMAS WINZ/GETTY IMAGES ©

Roman dishes are based on the recipes of Marcus Gavius Apicius (1st century AD).

ℹ️ Information

Tourist office (📞 978 080; www.trier-info.de; just inside Porta Nigra; 🕘9 or 10am-5 or 6pm Mon-Sat, 9 or 10am-1pm or later Sun)

COLOGNE & NORTHERN RHINELAND

Cologne

📞 0221 / POP 1 MILLION

Cologne (Köln) offers seemingly endless attractions, led by its famous cathedral whose filigree twin spires dominate the skyline. The city's museum landscape is especially strong when it comes to art but also has something in store for fans of chocolate, sports and even Roman history.

Cologne is also like a 3-D textbook on history and architecture. Drifting about town you'll stumble upon an ancient Roman wall, medieval churches galore, nondescript postwar buildings, avant-garde structures and even a new postmodern quarter right on the Rhine.

Sights

RÖMISCH-GERMANISCHES MUSEUM
Museum

(Roman Germanic Museum; 📞 2212 2304; www.museenkoeln.de; Roncalliplatz 4; adult/child €8/4; 🕙10am-5pm Tue-Sun) Highlights include the giant **Poblicius tomb** (AD 30–40), the magnificent 3rd-century **Dionysus mosaic** around which the museum was built, and astonishingly well preserved glass items. Insight into daily Roman life is gained from such items as toys, tweezers, lamps and jewellery, the designs of which have changed surprisingly little since Roman times.

MUSEUM LUDWIG
Museum

(📞 2212 6165; www.museenkoeln.de; Bischofs-gartenstrasse 1; adult/child €10/7; 🕙10am-6pm Tue-Sun) Considered a mecca of post-modern art, Museum Ludwig presents a survey of all major 20th-century genres. There's plenty of American pop art, including Andy Warhol's *Brillo Boxes*, alongside a comprehensive Picasso collection and plenty of works by Sigmar Polke.

Cologne

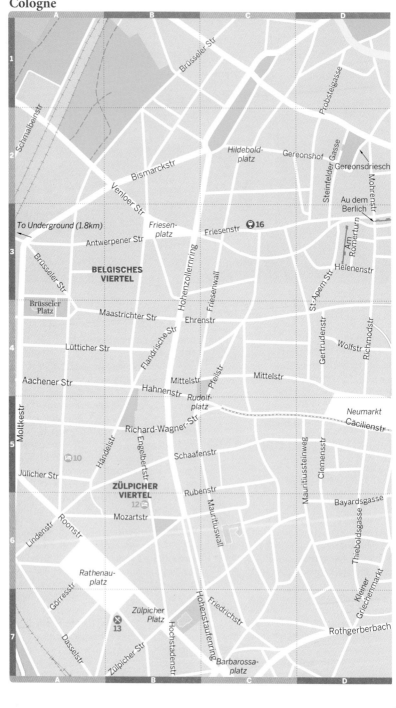

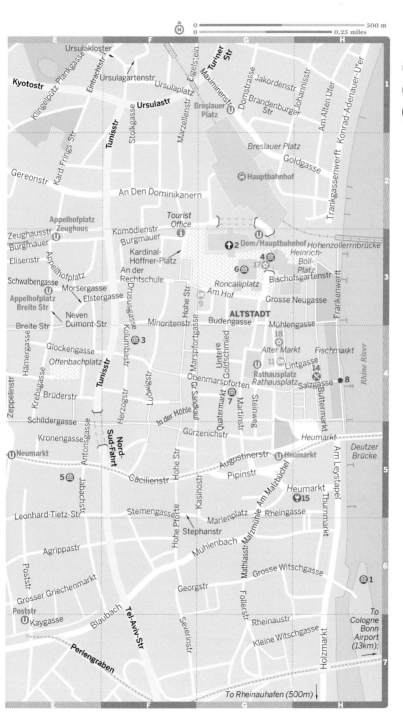

0   500 m
0   0.25 miles

Kyotostr

Ursulakloster
Eintrachtstr
Plankgasse
Ursulagartenstr
Ursulaplatz
Ursulastr
Stolkgasse
Marzellenstr
Eigelstein
Turiner Str
Maximinenstr
Breslauer Platz
Domstrasse
Jakordenstr
Brandenburger Str
Johannisstr
Am Alten Ufer
Konrad-Adenauer-Ufer

Klingelputz
Kard-Frings-Str
Tunisstr
Gereonstr
An Den Dominikanern

Breslauer Platz
Goldgasse
Trankgassenwerft

Hauptbahnhof

Appelhofplatz
Zeughaus
Zeughausstr
Burgmauer
Elisenstr
Appelhofplatz
Schwalbengasse
Appelhofplatz
Breite Str
Morsergasse
Elstergasse
Neven
Dumont-Str
Breite Str

Komödienstr
Burgmauer
Kardinal-
Höffner-Platz
An der
Rechtschule
Drususgasse
Tourist
Office

2 Dom/Hauptbahnhof
Hohenzollernbrücke
4
17
6
Heinrich-
Böll-
Platz
Bischofsgartenstr

Roncalliplatz
Am Hof
Grosse Neugasse
Frankenwerft

Hämergasse
Glockengasse
Offenbachplatz
Tunisstr
Kolumbastr
Herzogstr
Ludwigstr
Zeppelinstr
Krebsgasse
Brüderstr
Schildergasse
Kronengasse
Nord-
Süd-
Fahrt
Neumarkt

9
Hohe Str
Minoritenstr
Budengasse
Marspfortgasse
ALTSTADT
Mühlengasse
18
Alter Markt
11
Lintgasse
14
Fischmarkt
Rhine River

3
Obenmarspforten
Untere
Goldschmied
Gr. Sandkaul
Quatermarkt
7
Martinstr
Steinweg
In der Höhle
Gürzenichstr
Rathausplatz
Rathausplatz
Salzgasse
8
Buttermarkt

Heumarkt
Heumarkt
Augustinerstr
Pipinstr
Am Leystapel
Deutzer
Brücke

5
Jabachstr
Cäcilienstr
Hohe Str
Kasinostr
Antonsgasse
Leonhard-Tietz-Str
Stemengasse
Hohe Pforte
Stephanstr
Marienplatz
Mühlenbach
Mathiasstr
Malzmühle
Am Malzbüchel
Rheingasse
15
Thurnmarkt

Agrippastr
Poststr
Grosser Griechenmarkt
Poststr
Kaygasse
Blaubach
Tel-Aviv-Str
Georgstr
Follerstr
Grosse Witschgasse
1
Severinstr
Rheinaustr
Kleine Witschgasse
Holzmarkt
To
Cologne
Bonn
Airport
(13km);

Perlengraben

To Rheinauhafen (500m)

Cologne

MUSEUM SCHNÜTGEN Museum
(☎ 2212 3620; www.museenkoeln.de; Cäcilienstrasse 29; adult/child €5/3; ⊙10am-6pm Tue-Sun, to 8pm Thu) East of the Neumarkt, the Cultural Quarter encompasses the Museum Schnütgen, a repository of medieval religious art and sculpture. Part of the exhibit shows the beautiful setting of the Romanesque Cäcilienkirche (Cecily Church). Also part of the atrium complex is the **Rautenstrauch-Joest-Museum**.

WALLRAF-RICHARTZ-MUSEUM & FONDATION CORBOUD Museum
(☎ 2212 1119; www.museenkoeln.de; Obenmarspforten; adult/child €9/6; ⊙10am-6pm Tue-Sun, to 9pm Thu) A famous collection of paintings from the 13th to the 19th centuries, the Wallraf-Richartz-Museum occupies a postmodern cube designed by the late OM Ungers. Standouts include brilliant examples from the Cologne School, known for its distinctive use of colour. Upstairs are Dutch and Flemish artists, including Rembrandt and Rubens, Italians such as Canaletto and Spaniards such as Murillo.

KOLUMBA Museum
(☎ 933 1930; www.kolumba.de; Kolumbastrasse 4; adult/child €5/free; ⊙noon-5pm Wed-Mon, to 7pm Thu) Art, history, architecture and spirituality form a harmonious tapestry in this spectacular collection of religious treasures of the Archdiocese of Cologne. Coptic textiles, Gothic reliquary and medieval painting are juxtaposed with works by Bauhaus legend Andor Weiniger and edgy room installations.

CHOCOLATE MUSEUM Museum
(Schokoladen Museum; ☎ 931 8880; www .schokoladenmuseum.de; Am Schokoladenmuseum 1a; adult/concession €8.50/6; ⊙10am-6pm Tue-Fri, 11am-7pm Sat & Sun) At this high-tech temple to the art of chocolate-making, exhibits on the origin of the 'elixir of the gods', as the Aztecs called it, and the cocoa-growing process are followed by a live-production factory tour and a stop at a chocolate fountain for a sample.

 Tours

KD RIVER CRUISES Boat Tour
(☎ 258 3011; www.k-d.com; Frankenwerft 35; tour €10; ⊙10.30am-5pm) One of several companies offering one-hour spins taking in the splendid Altstadt panorama; other options include sunset cruises.

 Sleeping

HOTEL HOPPER ET CETERA Hotel €€
(☎ 924 400; www.hopper.de; Brüsseler Strasse 26; s €95-120, d €135-180; P @ ☎) A waxen monk welcomes you to this former mon-

STEVE VIDLER/ALAMY ©

Don't Miss Kölner Dom

Cologne's geographical and spiritual heart – and its single-biggest tourist draw – is the magnificent Kölner Dom. With its soaring twin spires, this is the Mt Everest of cathedrals, jam-packed with art and treasures.

The Dom is Germany's largest cathedral and must be circled to truly appreciate its dimensions. Note how its lacy spires and flying buttresses create a sensation of lightness and fragility despite its mass and height. Soft light filters through the dazzling **stained-glass windows**, including the spectacular new one by Gerhard Richter in the transept – a kaleidoscope of 11,500 squares in 72 colours. Among the cathedral's numerous treasures, the *pièce de résistance* is the **Shrine of the Three Kings** behind the main altar, a richly bejewelled and gilded sarcophagus said to hold the remains of the kings who followed the star to the stable in Bethlehem where Jesus was born.

Other highlights include the **Gero Crucifix** (970), notable for its monumental size and an emotional intensity rarely achieved in those early medieval days; the **choir stalls** from 1310, richly carved from oak; and the **altar painting** by local artist Stephan Lochner from around 1450.

For an exercise fix, climb the 509 steps up the Dom's **south tower** (adult/child €3/1.50; 9am-4pm Nov-Feb, to 5pm Mar-Apr & Oct, to 6pm May-Sep) to the base of the steeple that dwarfed all buildings in Europe until Gustave Eiffel built a certain tower in Paris.

NEED TO KNOW

Cologne Cathedral; 1794 0200; www.koelner-dom.de; 6am-10pm May-Oct, to 7.30pm Nov-Apr, south tower 9am-6pm May-Sep, to 5pm Mar-Apr & Oct, to 4pm Nov-Feb

astery whose 49 rooms sport eucalyptus floors, cherry furniture and marble baths along with lots of little pampering touches like iPod docks.

DOM HOTEL Luxury Hotel **€€€**
(20240; www.starwoodhotels.com; Domkloster 2a; s/d from €170/195;) This temple to overnight stays is right on the

plaza with Cologne's iconic cathedral. Built in 1857, and renovated and rebuilt innumerable times since, the 120 rooms drip with traditional luxury and most have views of the namesake Dom.

LINT HOTEL
Hotel €€

(☎920 550; www.lint-hotel.de; Lintgasse 7; s €60-90, d €90-130; 🛜) Cute, contemporary and eco-conscious (solar-panelled roof) hotel in the heart of the Altstadt. The 18 rooms have hardwood floors and the breakfast buffet (included) has organic foods.

MEININGER CITY HOSTEL & HOTEL
Hostel €

(☎355 332 014; www.meininger-hostels.com; Engelbertstrasse 33-35; dm €18-24, s/d from €48/70; @🛜) In a former hotel, this charming hostel in the cool Zülpicher Viertel is loaded with retro appeal coupled with modern rooms featuring lockers, reading lamps, a small TV and private bathrooms.

Eating & Drinking

FEYNSINN
International €€

(☎240 9210; www.cafe-feynsinn.de; Rathenauplatz 7; mains €7-18) What used to be a small cafe famous for its eccentric glass-shard chandelier has morphed into a well-respected restaurant where organic ingredients are woven into sharp-flavoured dishes. The owners raise their own meat.

SÜNNER IM WALFISCH
German €€€

(www.walfisch.net; Salzgasse 13; mains €13-20) In a building that can trace its foundation back to at least 1626, this trad German restaurant does a fine job with all the classics and is a cut above the often humdrum Altstadt tourist experience.

PÄFFGEN
Beer Hall

(www.paeffgen-koelsch.de; Friesenstrasse 64-66) Busy, loud and boisterous, Päffgen has been pouring *Kölsch* since 1883 and hasn't lost a step since. In summer you can enjoy the refreshing brew and other local specialities beneath starry skies

in the beer garden. Potato pancakes are served on Fridays.

MALZMÜHLE
Beer Hall

(☎210 117; www.muehlenkoelsch.de; Heumarkt 6; mains €6-15; ⏰10am-midnight) Expect plenty of local colour at this convivial beer hall off the beaten tourist track. It brews *Kölsch* with organic ingredients and is also known for its lighter *Malzbier* (malt beer, 2% alcohol).

Entertainment

PAPA JOE'S KLIMPERKASTEN
Piano Bar

(☎258 2132; www.papajoes.de; Alter Markt 50) A piano player tickles the ivories nightly in this museum-like place where the smoky brown walls are strewn with yesteryear's photographs.

KÖLNER PHILHARMONIE
Classical Music

(☎280 280; www.koelner-philharmonie.de; Bischofsgartenstrasse 1) The famous Kölner Philharmoniker is the 'house band' in this grand, modern concert hall below the Museum Ludwig.

ℹ️ Information

Tourist office (☎0221 2213 0400; www.koelntourismus.de; Kardinal-Höffner-Platz 1; ⏰9am-8pm Mon-Sat, 10am-5pm Sun)

ℹ️ Getting There & Away

Air

About 18km southeast of the city centre, Cologne Bonn Airport (CGN; www.airport-cgn.de) has direct flights to 130 cities and is served by numerous airlines, with destinations across Europe. The S13 train connects the airport and the Hauptbahnhof every 20 minutes (€2.80, 15 minutes). Taxis charge about €30.

Train

Services are fast and frequent in all directions. A sampling: Berlin (€113, 4¼ hours), Frankfurt (€67, 1¼ hours) and Munich (€134, 4½ hours).

Düsseldorf

📋 0211 / POP 589,000

Düsseldorf dazzles with boundary-pushing architecture, zinging nightlife and an art scene to rival many higher-profile cities. It's a posh and modern city that seems all buttoned-up business at first glance: banking, advertising, fashion and telecommunications are among the fields that have made North Rhine–Westphalia's capital one of Germany's wealthiest cities.

Yet all it takes is a few hours of bar-hopping around the Altstadt, the historical quarter along the Rhine, to realise that locals have no problem letting their hair down once they shed those Armani jackets.

The Altstadt may claim to be the 'longest bar in the world' but some attention has strayed to Medienhafen, a redeveloped harbour area and a feast of international avant-garde architecture.

Düsseldorf has long had a love affair with art, dating back to Jan Wellem's generous patronage, and the city has several high-calibre museums to prove it.

◉ Sights

MARKTPLATZ   Square
The historic Marktplatz, framed by the Renaissance **Rathaus** (town hall; 1573) and accented by an equestrian **statue of Jan Wellem**.

The art-loving elector lies buried nearby in the early baroque **Andreaskirche** (www.dominikaner-duesseldorf.de; Andreasstrasse 27; ⊙8am-6.30pm), which is drenched in fanciful white stucco.

RHEINUFERPROMENADE   Promenade
(Rhine River Walk) Burgplatz marks the beginning of the Rheinuferpromenade, whose cafes and benches fill with people in fine weather, creating an almost Mediterranean flair.

RHEINTURM   Tower
(Stromstrasse 20; adult/child €4/2.50; ⊙10am-11.30pm) Spearing the sky at the southern end of the Rhine promenade, the Rheinturm has an observation deck at the 168m level of its overall height of 240m.

View of the Rheinturm in the background, Düsseldorf

ARCHITECT: FRANK GEHRY; PHOTOGRAPHY: DAVID CLAPP/GETTY IMAGES ©

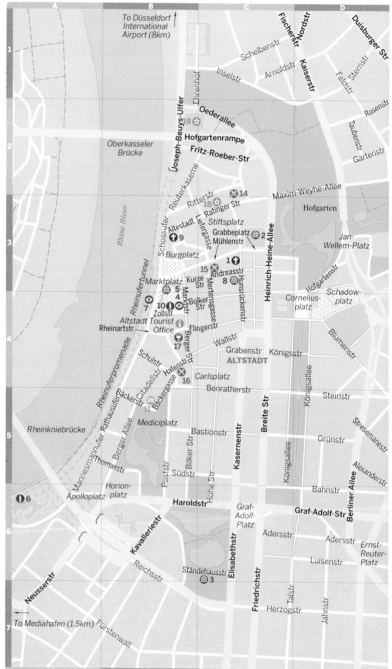

To Düsseldorf
International
Airport (8km)

Scheibenstr

Fischerstr

Nordstr

Duisburger Str

Inselstr

Arnoldstr

Kaiserstr

Feldstr

Sternstr

Rosenstr

Oberkasseler
Brücke

Oederallee

Hofgartenrampe

Fritz-Roeber-Str

Taubenstr

Gartenstr

Rhine River

Reuterkaseme

Schossufer

Ritterstr

14

18

Ratinger Str

Maxim-Weyhe-Allee

Hofgarten

Jan-
Wellem-Platz

Stiftsplatz

9

Altestadt

Liefergasse

Grabbeplatz

Mühlenstr

2

Burgplatz

1

15

Andreasstr

8

Heinrich-Heine-Allee

Cornelius-
platz

Hofgartenstr

Schadow-
platz

Marktplatz

5

Kurze
Str

Mertensgasse

Rheinufertunnel

7

10

4

Markstr

Bolker
Str

Hunstückenstr

Zollstr

Altstadt Tourist
Office

Rheinartstr

Flingerstr

17

Berger-Str

Wallstr

Grabenstr

Königsstr

ALTSTADT

Blumenstr

Schulstr

Hafenstr

16

Carlsplatz

Benratherstr

Königsallee

Steinstr

Stresemanestr

Rheinuferpromenade

Citadelstr

Bäckerstr

Bäckergasse

11

Mediciplatz

Bastionstr

Bilker Str

Südstr

Hohe Str

Kasernenstr

Breite Str

Königsallee

Grünstr

Bahnstr

Berliner Allee

Alexanderstr

Rheinkniebrücke

Berger Allee

Thomasstr

Mannesmannufer

Rathausufer

Poststr

6

Horion-
platz

Apolloplatz

Haroldstr

Graf-
Adolf-
Platz

Graf-Adolf-Str

Adersstr

Aderssr

Ernst-
Reuter-
Platz

Kavalleriestr

Reichsstr

Ständehausstr

3

Elisabethstr

Friedrichstr

Luisenstr

Neusserstr

Fürstenwall

To Mediahafen (1.5km)

Herzogstr

Talstr

Jahnstr

Düsseldorf

ST LAMBERTUSKIRCHE   Church
(Church of St Lambert; www.lambertuskirche.de;
Stiftsplatz; ⊙8am-5pm) The twisted tower
of the 14th-century St Lambertuskirche
shadows treasures that span several
centuries. Look for the Gothic tabernacle,
the Renaissance marble tombs, baroque
altars and modern windows.

MEDIENHAFEN   Architecture
South of the Altstadt, the Medienhafen
(Media Harbour) is an office quarter
that's been wrought from the remains of
the old city harbour. Despite a few trendy
restaurants and design shops, there's a
paucity of life in the streets as yet. Modern
architecture fans, however, will want to
head right down. The most eye-catching
structure is clearly the warped Neuer
Zollhof, a typically sculptural design by
Frank Gehry. A new pedestrian bridge links
to another quay dominated by William
Alsop's **Colorium**, easily recognised by its
kaleidoscopic glass facade. New additions
include **Hafen** by Helmut Jahn while the
huge **Casa Stupenda** by Renzo Piano
remains in a holding pattern.

233

ARCHITECTS: KIESSLER + PARTNER; PHOTOGRAPHY: IMAGEBROKER/ALAMY

Don't Miss Kunstsammlung Nordrhein-Westfalen

The regional art museum is spread over three separate buildings. Its diversity and richness reflect the high importance art has in local life. During opening hours, a shuttle bus runs every 20 minutes between K20 and K21.

K20 Grabbeplatz (☎ 838 1130; Grabbeplatz 5; adult/child €12/9.50) A collection that spans the arc of 20th-century artistic vision gives the K20 an enviable edge in the art world. Paul Klee is well represented but walls are also graced by plenty of other Western European and American big-shots, including Picasso, Matisse, Robert Rauschenberg, Jasper Johns and Düsseldorf's own Joseph Beuys. A recent revamp has made things even more impressive.

K21 Ständehaus (☎ 838 1630; Ständehausstrasse 1; adult/child €10/2.50) A stately 19th-century parliament building forms the incongruous setting of the cutting-edge K21, which brims with canvases, photographs, installations and video art created after 1980 by an international cast of artists. Look for works by Andreas Gursky, Candida Höfer, Bill Viola and the late Nam June Paik.

NEED TO KNOW

Art Collection of North Rhine Westphalia; www.kunstsammlung.de; Combined ticket for 3 museums adult/child €20/5; ⊙10am-6pm Tue-Fri, 11am-6pm Sat & Sun

 Tours

HOP ON HOP OFF
CITY TOUR　　　　　　　　Bus Tour
(www.duesseldorf-tourismus.de; Immermannstrasse 65; adult child from €12/5) The city's tourist office operates a daytime bus tour of the city that's a good way to get a handle on the sprawl that is Düsseldorf in 90 minutes.

 **Sleeping**

SIR & LADY ASTOR　　　　　Hotel €€
(☎ 173 370; www.sir-astor.de; Kurfürstenstrasse 18 & 23; s €85-170, d €95-250; @ 🛜) Never

mind the ho-hum setting on a residential street near the Hauptbahnhof: this unique twin boutique hotel brims with class, originality and charm. Check-in is at Sir Astor, furnished in 'Scotland-meets-Africa' style, while Lady Astor across the street goes more for French floral sumptuousness.

MAX HOTEL GARNI
Hotel €€

(☏ 386 800; www.max-hotelgarni.de; Adersstrasse 65; s/d from €70/85; @ 🛜) Upbeat, contemporary and run with personal flair, this charmer is a Düsseldorf favourite. The 11 rooms are good-sized and decked out in bright hues and warm woods. The reception isn't always staffed, so call ahead to arrange an arrival time.

HOTEL ORANGERIE
Hotel €€€

(☏ 866 800; www.hotel-orangerie-mcs.de; Bäckergasse 1; s €110-165, d €130-210; 🛜) Ensconced in a neoclassical mansion in a quiet corner of the Altstadt, this place puts you within staggering distance of pubs, the river and museums, yet offers a quiet and stylish refuge to retire to.

 ## Eating

BRAUEREI IM FÜCHSCHEN
German €€

(☏ 137 470; www.fuechschen.de; Ratinger Strasse 28; mains €5-15; ⏱ 9am-1am) Boisterous, packed and drenched with local colour – the 'Little Fox' in the Altstadt is all you expect a Rhenish beer hall to be. The kitchen makes a mean *Schweinshaxe* (roast pork leg). This is one of the best *Altbier* breweries.

ZUM SCHIFFCHEN
German €€

(☏ 132 421; www.brauerei-zum-schiffchen.de; Hafenstrasse 5; mains €7-20) History pours from every nook and cranny in this almost ridiculously cosy Altstadt restaurant specialising in hearty German and Rhenish meals. Were portions as huge when Napoléon dropped by a couple of centuries ago? Reservations recommended (he didn't need any); slightly more restrained than some of the other trad joints.

WEINHAUS TANTE ANNA
Modern European €€€

(www.tanteanna.de; Andreasstrasse 2; mains/menus from €25/45) This is like your aunt's place if she was a baroness; silver serving plates, subdued carved-wood interior, wines decanted and poured properly, the details do go on. The menu changes constantly and shows the range of the kitchen, whether it is boar piglet loin with celery and potato gnocchi or a simply superb springtime asparagus special.

 ## Drinking

ZUM UERIGE
Beer Hall

(☏ 866 990; www.uerige.de; Berger Strasse 1) This cavernous beer hall is the best place to soak it all up. The suds flow so quickly from giant copper vats that the waiters – called *Köbes* – simply carry huge trays of brew and plonk down a glass whenever they spy an empty.

 ## Entertainment

TONHALLE
Classical Music

(☏ 899 6123; www.tonhalle-duesseldorf.de; Ehrenhof 1) The imposing domed Tonhalle, in a converted 1920s planetarium, is the home base of the Düsseldorfer Symphoniker (Düsseldorf Symphony Orchestra).

STONE IM RATINGER HOF
Club

(☏ 210 7828; www.stone-club.de; Ratinger Strasse 10; cover varies; ⏱ Wed, Fri & Sat) The venerable Ratinger Hof has returned to its rock roots and is now the 'it' place for lovers of indie and alt-sounds.

ℹ Information

Düsseldorf Tourist Information (www .duesseldorf-tourismus.de) has two offices: **Altstadt tourist office** (Marktstrasse/Ecke Rheinstrasse; ⏱ 10am-6pm) and **Hauptbahnhof tourist office** (Immermannstrasse 65b; ⏱ 9.30am-7pm Mon-Fri, to 5pm Sat)

ℹ Getting There & Away

Air

Düsseldorf International Airport (DUS; www.dus -int.de) has three terminals and is served by a wide range of airlines.

Train

Düsseldorf is part of a dense S-Bahn and regional train network in the Rhine-Ruhr region, including Cologne (€12, 30 minutes). ICE/IC train links include Berlin (€107, 4¼ hours), Hamburg (€78, 3¾ hours) and Frankfurt (€78, 1¾ hours).

Bonn

📞 0228 / POP 324,900

When this friendly, relaxed city on the Rhine became West Germany's 'temporary' capital in 1949 it surprised many, including its own residents. When in 1991 a reunited German government decided to move to Berlin, it shocked many, *especially* its own residents.

A generation later, Bonn is doing just fine, thank you. It has a healthy economy and lively urban vibe. For visitors, the birthplace of Ludwig van Beethoven has plenty in store, not least the great composer's birth house, a string of top-rated museums, a lovely riverside setting and the nostalgic flair of the old government quarter.

◉ Sights

Bonn can be seen on an easy day trip from Cologne or as a stop on the busy Rhine railway line. There is a concentration of sights in the Altstadt but others are rather removed from the centre.

Altstadt

MÜNSTER BASILICA — Church
(📞 985 880; www.bonner-muenster.de; Münsterplatz; ⏱ 7am-7pm) A good place to start exploring Bonn's historic centre is on Münsterplatz, where the landmark Münster Basilica was built on the graves of the two martyred Roman soldiers who later got promoted to be the city's patron saints. It got its Gothic look in the 13th century but the Romanesque origins survive beautifully in the ageing cloister (open till 5pm).

BEETHOVEN-HAUS — Museum
(📞 981 7525; www.beethoven-haus-bonn.de; Bonngasse 24-26; adult/child €5/4; ⏱ 10am-6pm Mon-Sat, 11am-6pm Sun Apr-Oct, to 5pm Nov-Mar) The famous composer first saw the light of day in 1770 in the rather plain Beethoven Haus. It's now the repository of a pretty static array of letters, musical scores, instruments and paintings.

Tickets are also good for the **Digitales Beethoven-Haus** next door, where you can experience the composer's genius during a spacey, interactive 3-D multimedia show or deepen your knowledge in the digital archive.

Bundesviertel & Museumsmeile

From 1949 to 1999, the nerve centre of West German political power lay about 1.5km southeast of the Altstadt along Adenauerallee. A good way to explore the district is by following the **Weg der Demokratie** (Path of Democracy; www.wegder demokratie.de), a self-guided walking tour taking in 18 key historic sites. It starts at the Haus der Geschichte der Bundesrepublik Deutschland.

Bonn's Museum Mile sits opposite the government quarter, on the western side of the B9.

HAUS DER GESCHICHTE DER BUNDESREPUBLIK DEUTSCHLAND — Museum
(FRG History Museum; 📞 916 50; www.hdg. de; Willy-Brandt-Allee 14; ⏱ 9am-7pm Tue-Fri, 10am-6pm Sat & Sun) The Haus der Geschichte der Bundesrepublik Deutschland presents a highly engaging and intelligent romp through recent German history, starting when the final bullet was fired in WWII. Walk through the fuselage of a Berlin Airlift 'Rosinenbomber', watch classic clips in a 1950s movie theatre, examine Erich Honecker's arrest warrant, stand in front of a piece of the Berlin Wall or see John F Kennedy's famous 'Ich bin ein Berliner' speech.

KUNSTMUSEUM BONN   Museum

(☎ 776 260; www.kunstmuseum-bonn.de; Friedrich-Ebert-Allee 2; adult/concession €7/3.50; ⏰ 11am-6pm Tue & Thu-Sun, to 9pm Wed) Beyond the dramatic foyer, get your fix of August Macke and other Rhenish expressionists, as well as such avant-gardists as Beuys, Baselitz and Kiefer.

Tours

Beethoven fans can follow in his foot-steps, either via a free **Beethoven Walk** pamphlet or an **iTour** audio guide (rental €7.50), both available at the tourist office.

BIG CITY TOUR   Tour

(www.bonn.de; Bonn Information, Windeck-strasse 1; adult/concession €16/8; ⏰ 2pm daily Apr-Nov, Sat Dec-Mar) A combination bus and walking tour run by the tourist office, this 2½-hour tour takes in almost everything.

Sleeping

HOTEL PASTIS   Pension €€

(☎ 969 4270; www.hotel-pastis.de; Hatschier-gasse 8; s/d from €60/95) This little hotel-restaurant combo is so fantastically French, you'll feel like donning a beret and affecting a silly accent. After dining on unfussy gourmet cui-sine – paired with great wines, *bien sûr* – you'll sleep soundly in the basic comfortable rooms.

AMERON HOTEL KÖNIGSHOF

    Hotel €€€

(☎ 260 10; www.hotel-koenigshof-bonn.de; Adenauerallee 9; r €100-250; P ❄ @ 🛜) Sit back on the leafy terrace and enjoy sweeping views of the Rhine from this luxuri-ous understated hotel that

dates to the 1950s. Rooms have some bold colour combinations. The stylish restaurant, Oliveto, is known for its Med-influenced fare.

Eating & Drinking

WEINKOMMISSAR   Wine Bar

(www.weinkommissar.de; Friedrichstrasse 20; wines from €5; ⏰ noon-11pm Mon-Sat) In the heart of the Altstadt, pause from your stroll, stop humming Beethoven's 5th and sit back and enjoy one of many wines sold by the glass at this simple little spot that opens to the street. There are little tasty nibbles to wash down.

BRAUHAUS BÖNNSCH   Brewery €€

(☎ 650 610; www.boennsch.de; Sterntorbrücke 4; mains €7-15; ⏰ 11am-1am) The unfiltered ale is a must at this congenial brew-pub adorned with photographs of famous politicians: Willy Brandt to, yes, Arnold Schwarzenegger. Schnitzel, various pork cuts and sausage dominate the menu, but the *Flammkuchen* is always a crowd-pleaser.

Beethoven-Haus, Bonn
ATLANTIDE S.N.C./GETTY IMAGES ©

ZUM GEQUETSCHTEN German €€
(638 104; Sternstrasse 78; mains €9-18; ⏲noon-1am, kitchen to 11am) This traditional restaurant-pub is festooned with eye-catching blue tiles and is one of the most storied inns in town. The menu is mostly back-to-basics German, although some salads that *don't* contain sausage and some sandwiches make appearances.

 Information

Bonn Information (775 000; www.bonn.de; Windeckstrasse 1; ⏲10am-6pm Mon-Fri, to 4pm Sat, to 2pm Sun) Has excellent free information and tours in English.

 Getting There & Away

Cologne Bonn Airport (CGN; www.airport-cgn.de) has flights across Europe. Express bus SB60 makes the trip between the airport and Hauptbahnhof every 20 or 30 minutes between 4.45am and 12.30am (€7.10, 26 minutes). For a taxi to/from the airport budget between €35 and €40.

Bonn is linked by train to Cologne many times hourly by U-Bahn lines U16 and U18, regional trains (€7, 30 minutes) and even ICs.

Aachen

📞0241 / POP 258,700

The Romans nursed their war wounds and stiff joints in the steaming waters of Aachen's mineral springs, but it was Charlemagne who put the city firmly on the European map. Charlemagne's legacy lives on in the stunning Dom, which in 1978 became Germany's first Unesco World Heritage Site.

◉ Sights

RATHAUS Historic Building
(Markt; adult/concession €5/3; ⏲10am-6pm) The Dom gazes serenely over Aachen's Rathaus, a splendid Gothic pile festooned with 50 life-size statues of German rulers, including the 30 kings crowned in town. Inside, the undisputed highlights are the **Kaisersaal** with its epic 19th-century **frescoes** by Alfred Rethel and the replicas of the **imperial insignia**: a crown, orb and sword (the originals are in Vienna).

DOMSCHATZKAMMER Museum
(Cathedral Treasury; 4770 9127; adult/child €6.50/5.50; ⏲10am-1pm Mon, to 5pm Tue-Sun Jan-Mar, 10am-1pm Mon, to 6pm Tue, Wed & Fri-Sun, to 9pm Thu Apr-Dec) The cathedral treasury is a veritable mother lode of gold, silver and jewels. Focus your attention on the **Lotharkreuz**, a 10th-century processional cross, and the **marble sarcophagus** that held Charlemagne's bones until his canonisation; the relief shows the rape of Persephone.

Rathaus, Aachen

EURASIA/GETTY IMAGES ©

Don't Miss Aachen's Dom

It's impossible to overestimate the significance of Aachen's magnificent cathedral. The burial place of Charlemagne, it's where more than 30 German kings were crowned and where pilgrims have flocked since the 12th century.

The oldest and most impressive section is Charlemagne's palace chapel, the **Pfalzkapelle**, an outstanding example of Carolingian architecture. Completed in 800, the year of the emperor's coronation, it's an octagonal dome encircled by a 16-sided ambulatory supported by antique Italian pillars. The colossal brass **chandelier** was a gift from Emperor Friedrich Barbarossa during whose reign Charlemagne was canonised in 1165.

To accommodate the floods of the faithful, a Gothic **choir** was docked to the chapel in 1414 and filled with such priceless treasures as the **pala d'oro**, a gold-plated altar-front depicting Christ's Passion, and the jewel-encrusted gilded copper **pulpit**, both fashioned in the 11th century. At the far end is the gilded **shrine of Charlemagne** that has held the emperor's remains since 1215. In front, the equally fanciful **shrine of St Mary** shelters the cathedral's four prized relics.

Unless you join a **guided tour** (adult/child €5/4; ⊙11am-4.30pm Mon-Fri, 1-4pm Sat & Sun, tours in English 2pm), you'll barely catch a glimpse of Charlemagne's white marble **imperial throne** in the upstairs gallery.

NEED TO KNOW

www.aachendom.de; ⊙10am-7pm Apr-Dec, to 6pm Jan-Mar

SUERMONDT LUDWIG MUSEUM   Museum

(✆479 800; www.suermondt-ludwig-museum.de; Wilhelmstrasse 18; adult/child €5/3; ⊙noon-6pm Tue, Thu & Fri, noon-8pm Wed, 10am-6pm Sat & Sun) Of Aachen's two art museums, the Suermondt Ludwig Museum is especially proud of its medieval sculpture but also has fine works by Cranach, Dürer, Macke, Dix and other masters.

LUDWIG FORUM FÜR INTERNATIONALE KUNST   Museum

(Ludwig Forum for International Art; ☎180 7104; www.ludwigforum.de; Jülicherstrasse 97-109; adult/child €5/3; ⏱noon-6pm Tue, Wed & Fri, noon-8pm Thu, 11am-6pm Sat & Sun) Aachen's contemporary art museum counts works by Warhol, Immendorf, Holzer, Penck, Haring and others among its permanent collection, and also stages progressive changing exhibits.

 Tours

OLD TOWN GUIDED TOUR   Walking Tour

(adult/child €8/4; ⏱11am Sat Apr-Dec) The tourist office runs 90-minute English-language walking tours.

 Sleeping

HOTEL DREI KÖNIGE   Hotel €€

(☎483 93; www.h3k-aachen.de; Büchel 5; s €90-130, d €120-180, apt €140-240; ☎) The radiant Mediterranean decor is an instant mood enhancer at this family-run favourite with its doesn't-get-more-central location.

Some rooms are a tad twee but the two-room apartment sleeps up to four. Breakfast (included) on the 4th floor comes with dreamy views over the rooftops and the cathedral.

AQUIS GRANA CITY HOTEL   Hotel €€

(☎4430; www.hotel-aquis-grana.de; Büchel 32; r from €100/150; P ☎) The best quarters at this gracious hotel have terrace and balcony views of the Rathaus. But even in the most modest of the 98 rooms, you couldn't be any closer to the heart of town. The hotel offers a full range of services.

 Eating & Drinking

Aachen is the birthplace of the famous *Printen*, crunchy spiced cookies spiked with herbs or nuts and drenched in chocolate or frosting. You'll find them sold in bakeries across town.

LEO VAN DEN DAELE   Cafe €

(www.van-den-daele.de; Büchel 18; treats from €3) Leather-covered walls, tiled stoves and antiques forge the yesteryear flair of this

Schloss Augustusburg, Brühl

HANS GEORG EIBEN/GETTY IMAGES ©

Detour: Brühl

Brühl wraps an astonishing number of riches into a pint-size package. The town, halfway between Cologne and Bonn, languished in relative obscurity until the 18th century, when archbishop-elector Clemens August (1723–61) – friend of Casanova and himself a lover of women, parties and palaces – made it his residence. His two made-to-impress rococo palaces, at opposite ends of the elegant **Schlosspark**, landed on Unesco's list of World Heritage Sites in 1984.

The larger and flashier of the two palaces, **Schloss Augustusburg** (✆440 00; Max-Ernst-Allee; adult/child €5/4.50) is a little jewel box inside a moat. It was designed by François Cuvilliés. On guided tours you'll learn fascinating titbits about hygiene, dating and other aspects of daily life at court. The architectural highlight is a ceremonial staircase by Balthasar Neumann, a dizzying symphony in stucco, sculpture and faux marble.

Cuvilliés also dreamed up **Jagdschloss Falkenlust** (Otto-Weis-Strasse; adult/child €3.50/3), a hunting lodge where Clemens August liked to indulge his fancy for falconry. A particular gem is the chapel, awash in shells, minerals and crystals.

The two palaces are a wonderful 30-minute stroll apart on a wide 2.5km promenade through the Schlosspark.

Brühl is regularly served by regional trains from Cologne (€3.30, 15 minutes) and Bonn (€4.20, 10 minutes).

rambling cafe institution. Come for all-day breakfast, a light lunch or divine cakes (the strudel and the Belgian Reisfladen, made with rice, are specialities), which are shown off in the front window.

AM KNIPP German €€
(✆331 68; www.amknipp.de; Bergdriesch 3; mains €8-18; ◷dinner Wed-Mon) Hungry grazers have stopped by this traditional inn since 1698, and you too will have a fine time enjoying hearty German cuisine served amid a flea market's worth of twee knick-knacks. A vast, lovely beer garden as well.

**GASTSTÄTTE
POSTWAGEN** German €€
(✆350 01; www.postwagen-aachen.de; Krämer-strasse 2; mains €10-20) This oh-so-evocative old place, tacked onto the Rathaus, oozes olde-worlde flair from every nook and cranny and is a good place for classic German meals. The downstairs is made to look like an 18th-century postal coach (hence the name).

NOBLIS Bakery €
(Münsterplatz; snacks from €3; ◷8am-7pm) This gorgeous bakery is right across from the Dom. It has a stunning array of sand-wiches and other goods ready to eat at tables on the square or as a picnic in the nearby parks. Get your *Printen* here.

ℹ Information

Tourist office (✆0241 180 2961, 0241 180 2960; www.aachen-tourist.de; Friedrich-Wilhelm-Platz; ◷9am-6pm Mon-Fri, to 2pm Sat, also 10am-2pm Sun Easter-Dec)

ℹ Getting There & Away

Regional **trains** to Cologne (€16, one hour) run twice hourly, with some proceeding beyond.

Berlin

Berlin is a bon vivant, passionately feasting on the smorgasbord of life. It's a scene-stealing combo of glamour and grit that will fascinate anyone keen on history and culture, art and architecture, restaurants and nightlife. A contagious energy permeates its cafes, bars, clubs and classic cabarets. Indie boutiques and progressive restaurants compete for your time with world-class museums and striking landmarks.

Explore this virtual 3-D textbook, where you'll find history staring you in the face at every turn. While Schloss Charlottenburg and Unter den Linden take you back to the Prussian era, the dark age of the Third Reich reverberates through the Scheunenviertel, the old Jewish quarter. Checkpoint Charlie and the East Side Gallery reflect the tense times of the Cold War. Potsdamer Platz and the new government quarter, meanwhile, stand representative of a forward-looking, post-reunification Berlin.

Must-sees or aimless explorations – Berlin delivers it all in one exciting and memorable package.

Brandenburger Tor (p254)

Berlin

2 km
1 miles

Bornholmer Str

Berliner Str

Bornholmer Str   Wisbyer Str   B109

Schivelbeiner Str

Gesundbrunnen

Eberswalder Strasse

Schönhauser Allee   B96a

PRENZLAUER BERG

Berliner Allee

Volkspark Humboldthain

Hussitenstr

Humboldthain

See Prenzlauer Berg Map (p268)

Voltastr

Bernauer Str

Kastanienallee

Pappelallee

Prenzlauer Allee

Wichertstr

Greifswalder Str

Michelangelostr

Bernauer Str

Ernst-Thälmann-Park

Danziger Str

Greifswalder Str

B2   B96a

Kniprodestr

Volkspark Prenzlauer Berg

①

SCHEUNENVIERTEL

Senefelderplatz

Rosenthaler Platz

Rosa Luxemburg Platz   Torstr

④

Weinmeisterstr

Friedenstr

Volkspark Friedrichshain

Landsberger Allee

Landsberger Allee

Otto-Braun-Str

Mollstr

Petersburger Str

Thaerstr

Friedrichstr

②

Schillingstr

Strausberger Platz

Frankfurter Tor

Frankfurter Allee

Unter den Linden

Werderscher Markt

Grunerstr

Jannowitzbrücke

Weberwiese

Frankfurter Tor

Leipziger Str   B1

Märkisches Museum

Spittelmarkt

Stralauer Platz

FRIEDRICHSHAIN

Ostbahnhof   B96a

Boxhagener Str

Wühlischstr

Spree River

B96a

Warschauer Str

Warschauer Str

Ostkreuz

Wilhelmstr

Kochstr

Lindenstr

Oranienstr

Ritterstr

See Mitte Map (p256)

Mühlenstr

Stralauer Allee

KREUZBERG

Moritzplatz

Görlitzer Bahnhof

Skalitzerstr

Schlesisches Tor

Prinzenstr

Kottbusser Tor

Böckler Park

Wiener Str

Görlitzer Park

Vor dem Schlesischen Tor

ehringdamm

Reichenberger Str   B178

Gneisenaustr

Schönleinstr

See Kreuzberg & Friedrichshain Map (p264)

Yorckstr

Urbanstr

Pannierstr

NEUKÖLLN

Eisenstr

Treptower Park

Bergmannstr

ktoriapark

Südstern

Friedhöfe an der Bergmannstrasse

Hermannplatz

Sonnenallee

Platz der Luftbrücke

Columbiadamm

Volkspark Hasenheide

B96

Karl-Marx-Str

Paradestr

Boddinstr

Rathaus Neukölln

Tempelhofer Park

Leinestr

Tempelhofer Damm

TEMPELHOF

A100

BRITZ

① Berlin Wall

② Museumsinsel

③ Reichstag

④ Scheunenviertel

⑤ Potsdam

⑥ Brandenburger Tor

Berlin's Highlights

①

Confront the Cold War at the Berlin Wall

It's been almost 25 years since the Berlin Wall collapsed, but you can still sense the ghosts of the Cold War when standing in the shadow of a surviving section of this grim and grey divider of humanity. Above: Berlin Wall section, Mauerpark; Top Right: Checkpoint Charlie; Bottom Right: Gedenkstätte Berliner Mauer

Need to Know

TOUR Berlin on Bike runs Wall tours in English. **MUSEUMS** For more Wall history, visit Mauermuseum (p255). **For further details, see p258**

Berlin Wall Don't Miss List

BY MARTIN 'WOLLO' WOLLENBERG, BICYCLE TOUR OPERATOR AND WALL EXPERT

1 MAUERPARK

This park was built right on top of the Berlin Wall and is hugely popular, especially on Sundays when there's a great flea market (p277) and outdoor karaoke (p263).

2 GEDENKSTÄTTE BERLINER MAUER

This is the only site (p258) where you can still see all the elements of the Wall and the death strip: a section of original wall with its rounded top to make it harder to climb over; the sand strip patrolled by motorised guards; the lamps that bathed the strip in fierce light at night; and even an original guard tower. The Documentation Centre has lots of interesting background information.

3 GEDENKSTÄTTE GÜNTER LITFIN

Günter Litfin was the first person shot dead by GDR border guards as he tried to flee to West Berlin a few days after the Wall was built. His brother Jürgen keeps alive his legacy with a small **exhibit** (☎ 0163 379 7290; www .gedenkstaetteguenterlitfin.de; Kieler Strasse 2; tours half-hourly ⏰ 11.30am-1.30pm Sun-Thu Mar-Oct) in an authentic GDR watchtower. It's the only such tower accessible and open on a regular basis.

4 CHECKPOINT CHARLIE

Internationally, Checkpoint Charlie (p255) is the best-known border crossing. Berliners were not allowed to use it; it was only for foreigners and diplomats. This was the only place during the entire Cold War where there was a direct confrontation between the US and the Soviets when tanks faced off shortly after the Wall went up.

5 BORDER CROSSING BORNHOLMER STRASSE

The Bornholmer Brücke steel bridge was the first border crossing to open on 9 November, 1989. Masses of East Berliners headed here on that night, completely overwhelming the border guards who had no choice but to open the gates.

Marvel at the Museumsinsel Treasures

At Museumsinsel (Museum Island; p259) you can walk through ancient Babylon, meet an Egyptian queen, clamber up a Greek altar or be mesmerised by Monet's water lilies. It's one of Germany's most important treasure troves, with 6000 years of art, artefacts, sculpture and architecture spread across five museums. It's been a Unesco World Heritage Site since 1999. Pergamonmuseum (p262)

2

3 Ride to the Top of the Reichstag

This famous Berlin landmark (p254) has been set on fire, bombed, left to crumble and wrapped in fabric before emerging as the proud home of the German parliament, the Bundestag, in 1999. The plenary hall can only be seen on guided tours, but – with a prior reservation – you can catch the lift to the sparkling rooftop glass dome for free.

Shop Till you Drop in the Scheunenviertel 4

The Scheunenviertel is among Berlin's most charismatic quarters. You'll find surprises in this village-like labyrinth: an intriguing public sculpture, a bleeding-edge gallery, a cosy watering hole, a 19th-century ballroom and flower-festooned hidden courtyards. With plenty of local and international designer boutiques, it's a fashionista haven to boot.

Hackesche Höfe courtyard complex (p257)

5 Go Palace-Hopping in Potsdam

A quick train ride from Berlin, pretty Potsdam wows with abundant lakes, romantic parks, remarkable art and, above all, the Unesco-listed park and palace ensemble of Sanssouci (p279), whose jewel is the eponymous rococo palace. In the 20th century, Potsdam made history when the Allied leaders convened at Schloss Cecilienhof (p282) to hammer out Germany's post-WWII fate. Schloss Sanssouci

6 Brandenburger Tor

Prussian emperors, Napoléon and Hitler have all marched through this neoclassical royal city gate (p254) that was once trapped east of the Berlin Wall. It was in front of this landmark where US President Ronald Reagan said the now famous words back in 1987: 'Mr Gorbachev, tear down this wall!' Two years later, the wall was history.

Berlin's Best...

Capital Views

○ **Reichstag dome** (p254)
Pinpoint landmarks while
standing atop the German
parliament building

○ **Solar** (p273) Steer
towards this snazzy lounge
for cocktails with a view

○ **Fernsehturm** (p260)
(TV Tower) Get high on
Germany's tallest building

Freebies

○ **East Side Gallery** (p263)
Explore the longest surviving
stretch of the Berlin Wall

○ **Holocaust Memorial**
(p255) Reflect upon the
unspeakable horrors of the
WWII Jewish genocide

○ **Reichstag** (p254) Book
ahead for close-ups of
Foster's fantastic glass dome

○ **Topographie des Terrors**
(p261) Learn about the inner
workings of the Nazi state's
most feared organisations

○ **Unter den Linden** (p254)
Wander along this boulevard
of historic beauties

Riverside Pleasures

○ **Boat Cruises** (p266) Drift
past the sights of the historic
centre and beyond

○ **Beach Bars** (p273) Enjoy
the sunshine, cocktail in
hand, toes in the sand

○ **Riverside Promenade**
(p266) Jog, stroll, blade or
bike through the government
district

Need to Know

Bold Architecture

o **Jüdisches Museum**
(p263) Lightning bolt-shaped Daniel Libeskind marvel

o **Neues Museum**
(p259) Architectural alchemy courtesy of David Chipperfield

o **Deutsches Historisches Museum** (p255) IM Pei's glass-spiral-fronted museum by the 'Mandarin of Modernism'

o **Two to three months**
Book tickets for the Berliner Philharmonie, the Unter den Linden @ Schillertheater, Sammlung Boros and top-flight events.

o **One month before**
Make online reservations for access to the Reichstag dome.

o **One week before**
Book a table at trendy and Michelin-starred restaurants and get online tickets for the Neues Museum and the Pergamonmuseum.

RESOURCES

o **Visit Berlin** (www .visitberlin.de) Official tourist authority information.

o **Museumsportal Berlin** (www.museumsportal-berlin .de) Gateway to the city's museums.

o **Exberliner** (www. exberliner.de) Online version of monthly English-language city mag.

o **Berlin Unlike** (http:// berlin-unlike.net) Hip guide with reviews, happenings and a free newsletter.

GETTING AROUND

o **U-Bahn** (subway, underground) The most efficient way to get around.

o **S-Bahn** (light rail) Fewer stops than U-Bahn and not as frequent.

o **Bus** Slow but good for sightseeing.

o **Bicycle** Rental stations abound eg **Fahrradstation** (✆central reservations 0180 510 8000; www.fahrradstation .de), with six central locations.

o **Taxi** Plentiful and fairly inexpensive; ride 2km for €4 with the *Kurzstreckentarif*.

BE FOREWARNED

o **Opening times** Most palaces in Potsdam's Park Sanssouci are closed on Monday; some open only at weekends in the off-season.

o **Party** Some clubs only kick into high gear around 4am at weekends.

o **Shopping** Most stores, especially smaller ones, don't accept credit cards. Many boutiques open around noon.

Left: Stelae at the Holocaust Memorial;
Above: Jüdisches Museum

T) DESIGNER: PETER EISENMAN; PHOTOGRAPHER: PAOLO CORDELLI/ GETTY IMAGES; © (ABOVE) ARCHITECT: DANIEL LIBESKIND; PHOTOGRAPHER: ROBERT WALLIS/CORBIS ©

Berlin Walking Tour

This walk checks off Berlin's blockbuster landmarks as it cuts through the historic city centre, Mitte (literally 'Middle'). This is the birthplace and glamorous heart of Berlin, a high-octane cocktail of culture, architecture and commerce.

WALK FACTS
- **Start** Reichstag
- **Finish** Hackescher Markt
- **Distance** 4.5km
- **Duration** 1½ to 2 hours

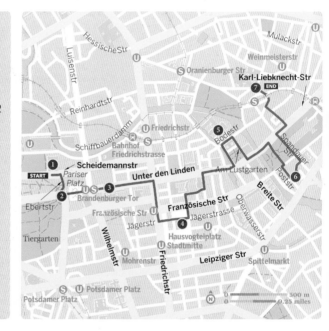

❶ Reichstag

The 1894 Reichstag is the historic anchor of Berlin's federal government quarter and home of the German parliament. The sparkling glass dome, added during the building's 1990s revamp, has become a shining beacon of unified Berlin.

❷ Brandenburg Gate

The only remaining gate of Berlin's 18th-century town wall, the Brandenburg Gate became an involuntary neighbour of the Berlin Wall during the Cold War and the backdrop to Ronald Reagan's 1987 'tear down this wall' speech. It's now a cheery symbol of German reunification.

❸ Unter den Linden

Originally a riding path linking the city palace with the royal hunting grounds in Tiergarten, Unter den Linden has been Berlin's most elegant showpiece road since the 18th century. Grand old buildings line up like Prussian soldiers for inspection, including the city's oldest university, the state opera and the royal armoury. Cafe Einstein at No 42 makes for an arty pit stop.

❹ Gendarmenmarkt

Berlin's most beautiful square, Gendarmenmarkt is bookended by the domed German and French cathedrals with the famous Konzerthaus Berlin (Concert Hall) in between. This is the city at its ritziest, where streets are lined with elegant hotels, upmarket restaurants and fancy cocktail bars.

 Museumsinsel

The sculpture-studded Palace Bridge leads to the twee Spree island where Berlin's settlement began in the 13th century. Its northern half, Museum Island, is Berlin's richest treasure chest of art, sculpture and objects spread across five grand museums that collectively became a Unesco World Heritage Site in 1999.

6 Nikolaiviertel

With its cobbled lanes and higgledy-piggledy houses, the pint-sized Nikolai Quarter may look medieval, but don't be fooled: like leg warmers and leotards it's a product of the 1980s, built by the GDR government to celebrate Berlin's 750th birthday. A stand-out among the few original buildings around here is the twin-spired Nikolaikirche (Church of St Nicholas), now a museum. If you need a break, pop by Brauhaus Georgbräu by the river.

7 Scheunenviertel

Berlin's historic Jewish quarter, the Scheunenviertel languished in GDR days but, since reunification, has been rebooted as a charismatic shopping, eating and partying zone. Fuel up on coffee at the Hackesche Höfe courtyard complex, then schlep to the quarter's many indie boutiques for local fashion, edgy art and clever knick-knacks.

Berlin in...

ONE DAY

Book ahead for an early lift ride up to the **Reichstag**, then swing by the **Brandenburg Gate** before exploring the maze of the **Holocaust Memorial** and admiring the architecture of **Potsdamer Platz**. Ponder Nazi horrors at the **Topographie des Terrors** and Cold War madness at **Checkpoint Charlie**.

Next, pop into the **Friedrichstadt-passagen** for a dose of retail therapy before making your way to Museumsinsel via **Gendarmenmarkt**. Spend at least an hour marvelling at the antique treasures at the **Pergamonmuseum**, then take a leisurely meander around the **Scheunenviertel** and have dinner there.

TWO DAYS

Come to grips with what life in divided Berlin was like at the **Gedenkstätte Berliner Mauer**, as well as on a walk along the **East Side Gallery** and a spin around the **DDR Museum**. Digest your impressions on a river cruise around **Museumsinsel**, then report for your audience with Queen Nefertiti at the **Neues Museum**. After dinner, travel back to the Golden Twenties at the cosy-glam **Chamäleon Varieté**.

Beer garden, Brauhaus Georgbräu, Nikolaiviertel
MARK DAFFEY/GETTY IMAGES ©

Discover Berlin

Neue Wache
JOHN FREEMAN/GETTY IMAGES ©

BERLIN
030 / POP 3.5 MILLION

◉ Sights

Reichstag & Unter den Linden

REICHSTAG *Historic Building*
(Map p256; www.bundestag.de; Platz der Republik 1; ☺lift ride 8am-midnight, last entry 11pm; 🚌100, Ⓢ Bundestag, 🚇Brandenburger Tor)
One of Berlin's most iconic buildings, the Reichs-tag has been burned, bombed, rebuilt, buttressed by the Berlin Wall, wrapped in fabric and eventually turned into the modern home of Germany's parliament, the Bundestag. The grand old structure was designed by Paul Wallot in 1894 and given a total post-reunification make-over by Lord Norman Foster. The famous architect preserved only its historical shell while adding the glistening glass dome, which can be reached by lift (reservations mandatory; see the website).

BRANDENBURGER TOR & PARISER PLATZ
Historic Site
(Map p256; Ⓢ Brandenburger Tor, 🚇Brandenburger Tor) A symbol of division during the Cold War, the landmark Branden-burg Gate now epitomises German reunification and often serves as a photogenic backdrop for festivals, concerts and New Year's Eve parties. Carl Gotthard Langhans found inspiration in the Acropolis in Athens for the elegant triumphal arch, completed in 1791 as the royal city gate. Brandenburger Tor stands sentinel over Pariser Platz, a harmonious-ly proportioned square once again framed by banks as well as the US, British and French embassies, just as it was during its early 19th-century heyday.

HOLOCAUST MEMORIAL
Memorial

(Map p256; ☏ 2639 4336; www.stiftung-denkmal.de; Cora-Berliner-Strasse 1; admission free, audioguide €3; ⊙ field 24hr, information centre 10am-8pm Tue-Sun, last entry 7.15pm Apr-Sep, 6.15pm Oct-Mar; Ⓢ Brandenburger Tor, Ⓡ Brandenburger Tor) The football-field-sized Memorial to the Murdered European Jews (colloquially known as the Holocaust Memorial) by American architect Peter Eisenman consists of 2711 sarcophagi-like concrete columns rising in sombre silence from undulating ground. For context, visit the subterranean **Ort der Information** (information centre), with exhibits that will leave no heart untouched.

FREE HITLER'S BUNKER
Historic Site

(Map p256; cnr In den Ministergärten & Gertrud-Kolmar-Strasse; ⊙ 24hr; Ⓢ Brandenburger Tor, Ⓡ Brandenburger Tor) Berlin was burning and Soviet tanks were advancing relentlessly when Adolf Hitler committed suicide on 30 April 1945 alongside Eva Braun, his long-time companion, hours after their marriage. Today, a parking lot covers the site, revealing its dark history only via an information panel with a diagram of the vast bunker network, technical data on its construction and information on its post-WWII history.

BEBELPLATZ
Memorial

(Map p256; Bebel Square; 🚌 100, 200, Ⓢ Französische Strasse, Hausvogteiplatz) On this tree-less square, books by Brecht, Mann, Marx and other 'subversives' went up in flames during the first full-blown public book burning, staged by the Nazi German Student League in 1933. Michael Ullmann's underground installation, **Empty Library**, beneath a glass pane at the square's centre, poignantly commemorates the event. Surrounding the square is a trio of hand-some 18th-century buildings constructed under King Frederick the Great: the **Alte Königliche Bibliothek** (Old Royal Library; 1780); the **Staatsoper Unter den Linden** (State Opera; 1743); and the copper-domed **St Hedwigskirche** (1783). The palatial building opposite Bebelplatz is the 1810 **Humboldt Universität**, where Marx and Engels studied and the Brothers Grimm and Albert Einstein taught. In

2012 it became one of Germany's 11 'elite universities'. A mighty **equestrian statue of King Frederick the Great** stands in the median strip of Unter den Linden.

DEUTSCHES HISTORISCHES MUSEUM
Museum

(Map p256; ☏ 203 040; www.dhm.de; Unter den Linden 2; adult/concession €8/4; ⊙ 10am-6pm; 🚌 100, 200, Ⓡ Alexanderplatz, Hackescher Markt) This engaging museum zeroes in on two millennia of German history in all its gore and glory; not in a nutshell but on two floors of a Prussian-era armoury. Check out the Nazi globe, the pain-wracked faces of dying warrior sculptures in the courtyard, and the temporary exhibits in the boldly modern annex designed by IM Pei.

FREE NEUE WACHE
Memorial

(Map p256; Unter den Linden 4; ⊙ 10am-6pm; 🚌 100, 200, Ⓢ Hausvogteiplatz) This neoclassical Schinkel structure from 1818 was originally a Prussian royal guardhouse and is now an antiwar memorial with an austere interior dominated by Käthe Kollwitz's emotional sculpture of a mother cradling her dead soldier son.

Friedrichstrasse

FREE CHECKPOINT CHARLIE
Historic Site

(Map p256; cnr Zimmerstrasse & Friedrichstrasse; ⊙ 24hr; Ⓢ Kochstrasse, Stadtmitte) Check-point Charlie was the principal gateway for foreigners and diplomats between the two Berlins from 1961 to 1990. A free open-air exhibit that illustrates milestones in post-WWII history is one redeeming aspect and the Berlin Wall Panorama, a monumental 360-degree painting depicting Berlin during its division, should also have opened by the time you read this.

MAUERMUSEUM
Museum

(Haus am Checkpoint Charlie; Map p256; ☏ 253 7250; www.mauermuseum.de; Friedrichstrasse 43-45; adult/concession €12.50/9.50; ⊙ 9am-10pm; ♿; Ⓢ Kochstrasse, Stadtmitte) The Cold War years, especially the history and horror of the Berlin Wall, are engagingly documented in this privately run tourist magnet at Checkpoint Charlie. The best bits are about ingenious escapes

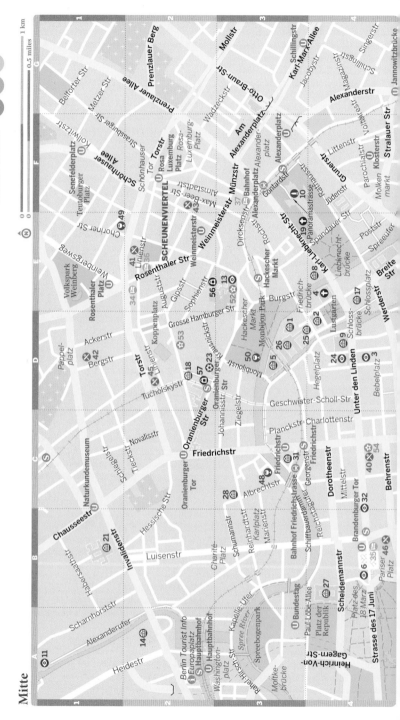

Mitte

0 km
0 miles

0.5 miles
1 km

to the West in hot-air balloons, tunnels, concealed car compartments and even a one-man submarine.

GENDARMENMARKT Square
(Map p256; ⊘24hr; **S** Französische Strasse, Stadtmitte) Berlin's most graceful square is bookended by the domed German and French cathedrals and punctuated by the grandly porticoed **Konzerthaus Berlin** (Map p256; ✒tickets 203 092 101; www .konzerthaus.de; Gendarmenmarkt 2; **S** Stadt-mitte, Französische Strasse).

Scheunenviertel

FREE HACKESCHE HÖFE Historic Site
(Map p256; ✒2809 8010; www.hackesche-hoefe .com; Rosenthaler Strasse 40/41, Sophienstrasse 6; 🚊M1, 🚉Hackescher Markt) The Hacke-sche Höfe is the largest and most famous of the interlinked courtyard complexes peppered throughout the Scheunenvier-tel. Take your sweet time pottering around this tangle of cafes, galleries, boutiques and entertainment venues.

NEUE SYNAGOGE Synagogue
(Map p256; ✒8802 8300; www.cjudaicum.de; Oranienburger Strasse 28-30; adult/concession €3/2; ⊘10am-8pm Sun & Mon, to 6pm Tue-Thu, to 5pm Fri, reduced hr Nov-Apr; **S** Oranienburger Tor, 🚉Oranienburger Strasse) The sparkling gilded dome of the New Synagogue is the most visible symbol of Berlin's revitalised Jewish community. The 1866 original was Germany's largest synagogue but its modern incarnation is not so much a house of worship as a place of remem-brance called **Centrum Judaicum**.

FREE JÜDISCHE
MÄDCHENSCHULE Historic Building
(Map p256; www.maedchenschule.org; Auguststrasse 11-13; ⊘vary; **S** Oranienburger Tor, 🚊M1, 🚉Oranienburger Strasse) After languishing for years, the grand 1920s former Jewish girls' school reopened in early 2012 as the new home of three renowned Berlin **galleries** – Eigen+Art, Camera Work and Michael Fuchs – and three **eateries**, including a deli, a kosher restaurant and the elegant Pauly Saal. Camera Work also operates **Museum The Kennedys** on the 2nd floor.

BERLIN SIGHTS

Mitte

BERLIN SIGHTS

FREE GEDENKSTÄTTE
BERLINER MAUER   Memorial
(Map p268; ☎467 986 666; www.berliner
-mauer-gedenkstaette.de; Bernauer Strasse btwn
Gartenstrasse & Brunnenstrasse ; ⊙9.30am-7pm
Apr-Oct, to 6pm Nov-Mar, open-air exhibit 24hr;
🚉Nordbahnhof) The Berlin Wall Memorial is
the central memorial site of German division. It incorporates a stretch of the original wall, along with vestiges of the border
installations, escape tunnels, a chapel
and a monument. This is the only place

where you can see how all the elements
of the wall and the death strip fit together
and how the border was enlarged and
perfected over time.

MUSEUM FÜR NATURKUNDE   Museum
(Museum of Natural History; Map p256; ☎2093
8591; www.naturkundemuseum-berlin.de; Invalidenstrasse 43; adult/concession incl audioguide
€6/3.50; ⊙9.30am-6pm Tue-Fri, 10am-6pm
Sat & Sun; ⓈNaturkundemuseum) Fossils and
minerals don't quicken your pulse? Well,

how about the world's largest mounted dino? The 12m-high *Brachiosaurus branchai* is joined by a dozen other Jurassic buddies, an ultrarare *Archaeopteryx* and, soon, the world's most famous dead polar bear, Knut, ex-resident of the Berlin Zoo.

Museuminsel

NEUES MUSEUM
Museum

(New Museum; Map p256; 266 424 242; www.smb.museum; adult/concession €10/5; 10am-6pm Sun-Wed, to 8pm Thu-Sat; 100, 200, Hackescher Markt) David Chipperfield's reconstruction of the bombed-out New Museum is the new home of the show-stopping **Ägyptisches Museum** (Egyptian Museum) and the equally enthralling **Museum für Vor- und Frühgeschichtliche** (Museum of Pre- and Early History). This is where you come to marvel at such unique treasures as the famous bust of 3330-year-old – yet timelessly beautiful – Queen Nefertiti; the magical Berlin Gold Hat, a tall cone elaborately swathed in bands of astrological symbols; and jewellery, weapons and silver and gold from ancient Troy. To ensure admission and cut waiting times, get advance tickets online.

ALTES MUSEUM
Museum

(Old Museum; Map p256; 266 424 242; www.smb.museum; Am Lustgarten; adult/concession €8/4; 10am-6pm Fri-Wed, to 8pm Thu; 100, 200, Friedrichstrasse) A curtain of fluted columns gives way to the Pantheon-inspired rotunda of the grand, neoclassical Old Museum, which harbours a prized antiquities collection. Top draws include the *Praying Boy* bronze sculpture, Roman silver vessels and portraits of Caesar and Cleopatra.

ALTE NATIONALGALERIE
Museum

(Old National Gallery; Map p256; 266 424 242; www.smb.museum; Bodestrasse 1-3; adult/concession €8/4; 10am-6pm Fri-Wed, to 10pm Thu; 100, 200, Hackescher Markt) The Greek temple–style Old National Gallery is a three-storey showcase of top-notch 19th-century European art. To get a sense of the period's virtuosity, pay special attention to Franz Krüger and Adolf Menzel's canvases glorifying Prussia and to the moody landscapes by Romantic heart-throb, Caspar David Friedrich.

BODEMUSEUM
Museum

(Map p256; 266 424 242; www.smb.museum; Monbijoubrücke; adult/concession €8/4; 10am-6pm Tue, Wed & Fri-Sun, to 10pm Thu; Hackescher Markt) On the northern tip of Museumsinsel, this palatial edifice by Ernst von Ihne houses European sculpture from the Middle Ages to the 18th century, including key works by Tilmann Riemenschneider, Donatello, Giovanni Pisano and Ignaz Günther.

BERLINER DOM
Church

(Berlin Cathedral; Map p256; 2026 9110; www.berlinerdom.de; Am Lustgarten; adult/concession €7/4; 9am-8pm Mon-Sat, noon-8pm Sun Apr-Sep, to 7pm Oct-Mar; 100, 200, Hackescher Markt) Pompous yet majestic, the Italian Renaissance–style former royal court church (1905) does triple duty as house of worship, museum and concert hall.

Bodemuseum

HUMBOLDT-BOX
Museum

(Map p256; ☎0180 503 0707; www.humboldt
-box.com; Schlossplatz; adult/concession
€4/2.50; ☺10am-8pm; 🚌100, 200, 🚊Alex-
anderplatz, Hackescher Markt) This oddly
shaped structure offers a sneak preview
of the planned reconstruction of the
Berlin City Palace, to be known as Hum-
boldtforum. On display are teasers from
each future resident – the Ethnological
Museum, the Museum of Asian Art and
the Central Library – along with a fantastically detailed model of the historic city
centre. Catch the great views from the
upstairs cafe terrace.

Alexanderplatz

FERNSEHTURM
Tower

(TV Tower; Map p256; ☎2063 0990; Panorama-
strasse 1a; admission €1; ☺11am-3am) The
tallest structure in Germany, the 368m-
high TV Tower is as iconic to Berlin as the
Eiffel Tower is to Paris. Come early to beat
the queue for the lift to the panorama level
at 203m, where views are unbeatable on
clear days.

DDR MUSEUM
Museum

(GDR Museum; Map p256; ☎847 123 731; www
.ddr-museum.de; Karl-Liebknecht-Strasse 1;
adult/concession €6/4; ☺10am-8pm Sun-Fri, to
10pm Sat; 🚼; 🚌100, 200, 🚊Hackescher Markt)
The touchy-feely GDR Museum does a
delightful job at pulling back the iron curtain on an extinct society. You'll learn that
in East Germany, kids were put through
collective potty training, engineers earned
little more than farmers and everyone, it
seems, went on nudist holidays.

MARIENKIRCHE
Church

(Map p256; www.marienkirche-berlin.de; Karl-
Liebknecht-Strasse 8; ☺10am-6pm; 🚌100,
200, 🚊Hackescher Markt, Alexanderplatz) This
13th-century Gothic brick gem is one of
Berlin's oldest surviving churches.

Potsdamer Platz & Tiergarten

This new quarter, forged from ground once
bisected by the Berlin Wall is a showcase
of fabulous contemporary architecture. Art
lovers should not skip the nearby Kulturforum museums, especially the Gemäldegalerie and the Neue Nationalgalerie,

Left: Altes Museum (p259); **Below:** Topographie des Terrors

both neighbours of the world-class Berliner Philharmonie. The leafy Tiergarten, with its rambling paths and hidden beer gardens, makes for a perfect sightseeing break.

GEMÄLDEGALERIE Gallery
(Map p264; ☎ 266 424 242; www.smb.museum/gg; Matthäikirchplatz 8; adult/concession €8/4; ⏰10am-6pm Tue, Wed & Fri-Sun, to 10pm Thu; 🚍M29, M41, 200, Ⓢ Potsdamer Platz, Ⓡ Potsdamer Platz) The principal Kulturforum museum boasts one of the world's finest and most comprehensive collections of European art from the 13th to the 18th centuries. A walk past masterpieces by Rembrandt, Dürer, Hals, Vermeer, Gainsborough and many more Old Masters covers almost 2km.

NEUE NATIONALGALERIE Gallery
(Map p256; ☎ 266 2951; www.neue-nationalgalerie.de; Potsdamer Strasse 50; adult/concession €10/5; ⏰10am-6pm Tue, Wed & Fri, to 10pm Thu, 11am-6pm Sat & Sun; Ⓢ Potzdamer Platz, Ⓡ Potsdamer Platz) This light-flooded glass temple by Ludwig Mies van der Rohe presents international 20th-century art until 1960 in changing configurations. Expect all the usual suspects from Picasso to Dalí, plus an outstanding collection of German expressionists such as George Grosz and Ernst Ludwig Kirchner.

TOPOGRAPHIE DES TERRORS Memorial
(Topography of Terror; Map p256; ☎ 2548 6703; www.topographie.de; Niederkirchner Strasse 8; ⏰10am-8pm May-Sep, to dusk Oct-Apr; ♿; Ⓢ Potsdamer Platz, Ⓡ Potsdamer Platz) In the same spot where once stood the most feared institutions of Nazi Germany (including the Gestapo headquarters and the SS central command), this compelling exhibit dissects the anatomy of the Nazi state. By chronicling the stages of terror and persecution, it puts a face on the perpetrators and details the impact these brutal institutions had on all of Europe. A short stretch of the Berlin Wall runs along Niederkirchner Strasse.

261

PAOLO CORDELLI/GETTY IMAGES ©

Don't Miss **Pergamonmuseum**

An Aladdin's cave of treasures, the Pergamon opens a fascinating window onto the ancient world and is the one museum in Berlin that should not be missed. The Pergamon unites three major collections, each with their own signature sights. The undisputed highlight of the **Antikensammlung** (Collection of Classical Antiquities) is the museum's namesake, the **Pergamon Altar** (165 BC), which cuts a commanding presence in the first hall. This massive marble shrine hails from the Greek metropolis of Pergamon (now Bergama in Turkey) and centres on a steep and wide staircase. A small door to the right of the altar opens to another key exhibit: the giant **Market Gate of Miletus** (2nd century AD). Merchants and customers once flooded through here onto the market square of this Roman trading town (also in today's Turkey) that functioned as a link between Asia and Europe.

Step through the gate and travel back 800 years to yet another culture and civilisation: Babylon during the reign of King Nebuchadnezzar II. You're now in the **Vorderasiatisches Museum** (Museum of Near Eastern Antiquities), where it's impossible not to be awed by the reconstructed **Ishtar Gate**, the **Processional Way** leading up to it and the facade of the king's **throne hall**. All are sheathed in glazed bricks glistening in radiant blue and ochre.

Upstairs is the Pergamon's third collection, the **Museum für Islamische Kunst** (Museum of Islamic Art). Standouts here include the fortress-like, 8th-century **caliph's palace** from Mshatta in the desert of what today is Jordan, and the 17th-century **Aleppo Room** from the house of a Christian merchant in Syria, with its richly painted, wood-panelled walls.

NEED TO KNOW

Map p256; ☏266 424 242; www.smb.museum; Am Kupfergraben 5; adult/concession €8/4; ⏱10am-6pm Fri-Wed, to 9pm Thu; ☒Hackescher Markt, Friedrichstrasse, ▣100

BAUHAUS ARCHIV
Museum

(Map p275; ☏254 0020; www.bauhaus.de; Klingelhöferstrasse 14; adult/concession Sat-Mon €7/4, Wed-Fri €6/3; ☻10am-5pm Wed-Mon; ⑤Nollendorfplatz) At this treasure trove of all things Bauhaus, curators use study notes, workshop pieces, photographs, blueprints, models and other objects and documents to mount changing exhibits illustrating the Bauhaus theories.

FREE TIERGARTEN
Park

(Map p275; ☐200, ☐Potsdamer Platz) Berlin's rulers used to hunt boar and pheasants in the rambling Tiergarten until Peter Lenné landscaped the grounds in the 18th century. Tiergarten is bisected by Strasse des 17 Juni, home to a **Soviet WWII memorial** and a weekend **flea market**. Big festivals and parades are staged along here and around the landmark **Siegessäule** (Victory Column; Map p275; Grosser Stern; ☐100, 200), a paean to 19th-century Prussian military triumphs.

Kreuzberg

Kreuzberg gets its street cred from being delightfully edgy, bipolar, wacky and, most of all, unpredictable. While the western half around Bergmannstrasse has an upmarket, genteel air, eastern Kreuzberg (still nicknamed SO36 after its pre-reunification postal code) is a multi-cultural mosaic, a bubbly hodgepodge of tousled students, aspiring creatives, shisha-smoking Turks and Arabs and international life artists.

JÜDISCHES MUSEUM
Museum

(Jewish Museum; Map p264; ☏2599 3300; www.jmberlin.de; Lindenstrasse 9-14; adult/concession €5/2.50; ☻10am-10pm Mon, to 8pm Tue-Sun, last admission 1hr before closing; ⑤Hallesches Tor, Kochstrasse) In a landmark building by American-Polish architect Daniel Libeskind, this engaging museum offers a chronicle of the trials and triumphs in 2000 years of Jewish history in Germany. Learn about Jewish cultural contributions, holiday traditions, the difficult road to emancipation and outstanding individuals such as the philosopher Moses Mendelssohn, blue jeans inventor Levi Strauss and the painter Felix Nussbaum.

DEUTSCHES TECHNIKMUSEUM
Museum

(German Museum of Technology; Map p264; ☏902 540; www.dtmb.de; Trebbiner Strasse 9; adult/concession €6/3, after 3pm if under 18 free, audioguide €2/1; ☻9am-5.30pm Tue-Fri, 10am-6pm Sat & Sun; ⊕; ⑤Gleisdreieck) Fantastic for kids, this giant shrine to technology counts the world's first computer, an entire hall of vintage locomotives and extensive exhibits on aviation and navigation among its top attractions. At the adjacent **Spectrum Science Centre**, kids can participate in around 250 experiments.

Friedrichshain

There are few standout sights, but the web of boutique- and cafe-lined streets around Boxhagener Platz will happily repay those who simply wander and soak up the district's unique character. After dark, Friedrichshain morphs into a hugely popular bar-stumbling and high-energy party zone.

EAST SIDE GALLERY
Historic Site

(Map p264; www.eastsidegallery-berlin.de; Mühlenstrasse btwn Oberbaumbrücke & Ostbahnhof; ☻24hr; ⑤Warschauer Strasse, ☐Ostbahnhof, Warschauer Strasse) The year was 1989. After 28 years the Berlin Wall, that grim and grey divider of humanity, finally met its maker. Most of it was quickly dismantled, but along Mühlenstrasse, paralleling the Spree River, a 1.3km stretch became the East Side Gallery, the world's largest open-air mural collection.

Prenzlauer Berg

Prenzlauer Berg went from rags to riches after reunification to emerge as one of Berlin's most desirable residential neighbourhoods. Its ample charms are best experienced on a leisurely meander.

FREE MAUERPARK
Park

(Map p268; www.mauerpark.info; btwn Bernauer Strasse, Schwedter Strasse & Gleimstrasse; ⑤Eberswalder Strasse, ☐M1) Long-time locals, neo-Berliners and global visitors – everyone flocks to Mauerpark, especially on Sundays. It's a wild and wacky urban tapestry where a flea market, outdoor karaoke, artists and bands provide entertainment and people gather for barbecues, basketball, badminton and boules.

Kreuzberg & Friedrichshain

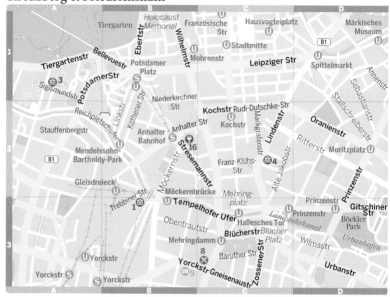

Kreuzberg & Friedrichshain

A graffiti-covered section of the Berlin Wall, which once bisected the park, quietly looms above it all.

Charlottenburg

The glittering heart of West Berlin during the Cold War, Charlottenburg has been eclipsed by historic Mitte and other eastern districts since reunification, but is now trying hard to stage a comeback with major construction and redevelopment around Zoo station. Its main artery is the 3.5km-long Kurfürstendamm (Ku'damm for short), Berlin's busiest shopping strip.

SCHLOSS CHARLOTTENBURG Palace
(Map p275; ☎ 320 911; www.spsg.de; Spandauer Damm 20-24; day pass adult/concession €15/11; ☐145, 309, Ⓢ Richard-Wagner-Platz, Sophie-Charlotte-Platz) The grandest of Berlin's surviving nine former royal pads consists of the main palace and two outbuildings

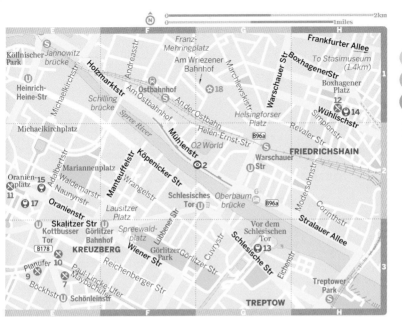

in the lovely **Schlossgarten** (palace park).
Visit Wednesday to Sunday, when all
palace buildings are open. The Schloss
was built as the summer residence of
Sophie Charlotte, wife of King Friedrich I.
The couple's baroque living quarters in the
palace's oldest section, the **Altes Schloss**
(Map p275; 📞 320 911; www.spsg.de; Spandauer
Damm; adult/concession €12/8; ⏰10am-6pm
Tue-Sun Apr-Oct, to 5pm Tue-Sun Nov-Mar; 🚌145,
309, S Richard-Wagner-Platz, Sophie-Charlotte-
Platz), are an extravaganza in stucco,
brocade and overall opulence. Highlights
include the Oak Gallery, a wood-panelled
festival hall draped in family portraits; the
lovely Oval Hall overlooking the park;
and the dazzling Porcelain Chamber,
smothered in nearly 3000 pieces of
Chinese and Japanese blueware. The most
beautiful rooms, though, are the flamboyant private chambers of Frederick the
Great in the **Neuer Flügel** (New Wing; Map
p275; 📞 320 911; www.spsg.de; Spandauer Damm
20-24; adult/concession incl audioguide €6/5;
⏰10am-6pm Wed-Mon Apr-Oct, to 5pm Wed-Mon
Nov-Mar; 🚌M45, 309, S Richard-Wagner-Platz,
Sophie-Charlotte-Platz), designed by star
architect du jour Georg Wenzeslaus von
Knobelsdorff in 1746.

**KAISER-WILHELM-
GEDÄCHTNISKIRCHE** Church
(Kaiser Wilhelm Memorial Church; Map p275;
📞 218 5023; www.gedaechtniskirche.com;
Breitscheidplatz; ⏰9am-7pm; S Zoologischer
Garten, Kurfürstendamm, 🚇Zoologischer Garten)
The bombed-out tower of this landmark
church serves as an antiwar memorial,
standing quiet and dignified amid the
roaring traffic. The adjacent octagonal hall
of worship, added in 1961, has amazing
midnight-blue glass walls and a giant
Jesus 'floating' above the altar.

BERLIN ZOO Zoo
(Map p275; 📞 254 010; www.zoo-berlin.de;
Hardenbergplatz 8; adult/child €13/6.50, with
aquarium €20/10; ⏰9am-7pm Apr-mid–Oct,
9am-5pm mid-Oct–Mar; S Zoologischer Garten,
🚇Zoologischer Garten) Germany's oldest
animal park opened in 1844 with furry
and feathered critters from the royal
family's private reserve. Today some
16,000 animals from all continents,
1500 species in total, make their home
here. Cheeky orang-utans, cuddly koalas,
endangered rhinos, playful penguins and
Bao Bao, a rare giant panda, are among
the top drawcards.

STORY OF BERLIN
Museum

(Map p275; 8872 0100; www.story-of-berlin.de; Kurfürstendamm 207-208, enter via Ku'damm Karree mall; adult/concession €10/8; ⏱10am-8pm, last admission 6pm; [S]Uhlandstrasse) This multimedia museum breaks down 800 years of Berlin history into bite-sized chunks that are easy to swallow but substantial enough to be satisfying. Don't miss the guided tour of a fully functional Cold War–era atomic bunker beneath the building.

Tours

Walking & Cycling

BERLIN WALKS
Walking Tour

(☎301 9194; www.berlinwalks.de; tours €12-15, concession €9-12) Get under the city's historical skin with the local expert guides of Berlin's longest-running English-language walking-tour company.

BERLIN ON BIKE
Bicycle Tour

(Map p268; ☎4373 9999; www.berlinonbike.de; Knaackstrasse 97; tours incl bike €19, concession €17; ⏱Mar-Oct; [S]Eberswalder Strasse) Wellestablished company with an intriguing

repertoire far beyond the blockbuster sights, with excursions heading deep behind the former Iron Curtain, along the Berlin Wall, into alt-flavoured Kreuzberg or to Berlin's hidden oases.

Boat

Tours range from one-hour spins around the historic centre (from €11) to longer trips to Schloss Charlottenburg and beyond (from €15). Most offer live commentary in English and German.

Sleeping

Mitte

CIRCUS HOTEL
Hotel €€

(Map p256; ☎2000 3939; www.circus-berlin.de; Rosenthaler Strasse 1; d €80-110; @ ⏶; [S]Rosenthaler Platz) Our favourite budget boutique hotel. Rooms come with upbeat colours, thoughtful design details, sleek oak floors and quality beds. Unexpected perks include a well-stocked library and free iPod, netbook and DVD player rentals. Fabulous breakfast buffet to boot.

HOTEL AMANO
Hotel €€

(Map p256; ☎809 4150; www.amanogroup.de; Auguststrasse 43; d €80-160; [P] ❄ @ ⏶; [S]Rosenthaler Platz) An instant hit with style-minded wallet-watchers, Amano has inviting public areas dressed in brushed-copper walls and cocoa-hued banquettes. In rooms, white furniture teams up with oak floors and natural-toned fabrics to create crisp cosiness. The standard rooms are a case study in efficiency, so get an apartment for more elbow room.

MOTEL ONE BERLIN-ALEXANDERPLATZ
Hotel €

(Map p256; ☎2005 4080; www.motel-one.de; Dircksenstrasse 36; d from €69; [P] ❄ @ ⏶; [S]Alexanderplatz, [R]Alexanderplatz) If you value location over

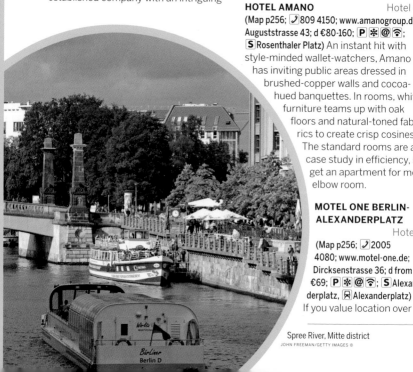

Spree River, Mitte district

luxury, this fast-growing budget designer chain makes for an excellent crash pad. Smallish rooms come with up-to-the-minute touches (Loewe flat-screen TVs, granite counters, massage shower heads, air-con) that are normally the staple of posher players. This is the most central of seven Motel One properties around town, including one at Zoo station and another at Hauptbahnhof.

ADINA APARTMENT HOTEL BERLIN CHECKPOINT

CHARLIE Apartment €€

(Map p256; ☎ 200 7670; www.adina.eu; Krausenstrasse 35-36; d €110-160, 1-bedroom apt from €140; P ※ @ ☎ ☰; S Stadtmitte, Spittelmarkt) Adina's contemporary and roomy one- and two-bedroom apartments with full kitchens are tailor-made for cost-conscious families, anyone in need of elbow room and self-caterers (a supermarket is a minute away). See the website for details about other Adina properties in town.

HOTEL ADLON

KEMPINSKI Luxury Hotel €€€

(Map p256; ☎ 226 10; www.kempinski.com; Pariser Platz, Unter den Linden 77; r from €250; ※ @ ☎ ☰; S Brandenburger Tor, ☒ Brandenburger Tor) Opposite Brandenburger Tor, the Adlon has been Berlin's most high-profile defender of the grand tradition since 1907. The striking lobby is a mere overture to the full symphony of luxury awaiting in spacious, amenity-laden rooms and suites where the decor is old-fashioned in a regal sort of way.

Potsdamer Platz & Tiergarten

MANDALA HOTEL Luxury Hotel €€€

(Map p256; ☎ 590 050 000; www.themandala.de; Potsdamer Strasse 3; ste €145-360; P ※ @ ☎; S Potsdamer Platz, ☒ Potsdamer Platz) How 'suite' it is to be staying at this swank cocoon of effortless sophistication and unfussy ambience. Suites come in six sizes (40 to 101 sq metres) and are equipped with a kitchenette, walk-in closets and spacious desks in case you're here to ink that deal.

If You Like…
Red Berlin

If the DDR Museum (p260), the Gedenkstätte Berliner Mauer (p258) and the East Side Gallery (p263) have piqued your interest in life under socialism, deepen your knowledge at these historic sites.

1 STASIMUSEUM

(☎ 553 6854; www.stasimuseum.de; Haus 1, Ruschestrasse 103; adult/concession €5/4; ⊙ 11am-6pm Mon-Fri, noon-6pm Sat & Sun; S Magdalenenstrasse) The former head office of the Ministry of State Security is now the Stasimuseum, where you can marvel at cunningly low-tech surveillance devices (hidden in watering cans, rocks, even neckties), a prisoner transport van with teensy, lightless cells and the obsessively neat offices of Stasi chief Erich Mielke.

2 STASI PRISON

(☎ 9860 8230; www.stiftung-hsh.de; Genslerstrasse 66; tour adult/concession €5/2.50; ⊙ tours hourly 11am-3pm Mon-Fri, 10am-4pm Sat & Sun, English tour 2.30pm daily; ☐ M5 to Freienwalder Strasse, then 1km walk via Freienwalder Strasse) Victims of Stasi persecution often ended up in the grim Stasi Prison, now a memorial site officially called Gedenkstätte Hohenschönhausen. Tours reveal the full extent of the terror and cruelty perpetrated upon thousands of suspected regime opponents, many utterly innocent.

3 TRÄNENPALAST

(Map p256; ☎ 4677 7790; www.hdg.de; Reichstagsufer 17; ⊙ 9am-7pm Tue-Fri, 10am-6pm Sat & Sun; S Friedrichstrasse, ☒ 100) This exhibit uses original objects (including the claustrophobic passport-control booths and a weapons auto-firing system), photographs and historical footage to document the division's social impact on the daily lives of Germans on both sides of the border.

RITZ-CARLTON BERLIN

Luxury Hotel €€€

(Map p256; ☎ 337 777; www.ritzcarlton.com; Potsdamer Platz 3; d €176-455; P ※ @ ☎ ☰; S Potsdamer Platz, ☒ Potsdamer Platz) At one of Berlin's most popular full-on luxury addresses, rooms and suites are done up in soothing natural hues and classical dark-wood furniture, enhanced by original watercolours by German contemporary artist Markus Lüpertz. Expect all the trappings of a big-league player, including a high-end restaurant, bar and spa.

Kreuzberg & Friedrichshain

HOTEL RIEHMERS HOFGARTEN
Hotel €€

(Map p264; ☎7809 8800; www.riehmers -hofgarten.de; Yorckstrasse 83; d €126-143; 🛜; Ⓢ Mehringdamm) Take a romantic 19th-century building, add contemporary art, stir in a few zeitgeist touches such as iPod docking stations and you'll get one winning cocktail of a hotel. Riehmers' high-ceilinged rooms are modern but not stark; if you're noise-sensitive, get a courtyard-facing one.

NHOW
Hotel €€

(Map p264; ☎290 2990; www.nhow-hotels.com; Stralauer Allee 3; d €115-275; Ⓟ🛜; Ⓢ Warschauer Strasse, Ⓡ Warschauer Strasse) Nhow bills itself as a 'music and lifestyle hotel' and underscores the point by having its own on-site recording studios.

The look of the place is certainly dynamic, what with a sideways tower jutting out over the Spree and Karim Rashid's vibrant digi-pop design that would make Barbie proud. Rooms are more subdued, despite the pink, blue and black colour scheme.

Prenzlauer Berg

EASTSEVEN BERLIN HOSTEL
Hostel €

(Map p268; ☎9362 2240; www.eastseven.de; Schwedter Strasse 7; dm €17-19, d €50; @ 🛜; Ⓢ Senefelderplatz) Friendly and fun, this top-rated small hostel fires on all cylinders and is within a whisker of hip hang-outs and public transport. Cultural and language barriers melt quickly over a barbecue in the idyllic back garden, dinner in the modern kitchen (with dishwasher!) or chilling in the retro lounge.

🌿 HOTEL KASTANIENHOF
Hotel €€

(Map p268; ☎443 050; www.kastanienhof.biz; Kastanienallee 65; d €105-140; Ⓟ @ 🛜; Ⓢ Rosenthaler Platz, 🚃 M1 to Zionskirchstrasse, Ⓢ Senefelderplatz) This charmer puts you right onto Kastanienallee, with its many cafes and restaurants, although the hotel design itself has more of a traditional

Prenzlauer Berg

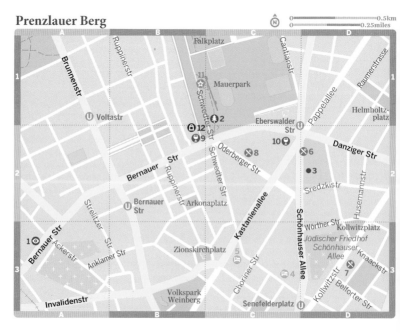

bent. Family owned and with fall-over-backwards staff, it has 35 rooms, including themed ones decorated with historical photos, paintings and information about Berlin landmarks.

Charlottenburg

HOTEL CONCORDE BERLIN Hotel €€€

(Map p275; ☏800 9990; www.concorde-hotels .com/concordeberlin; Augsburger Strasse 41; d €150-300; P ❄ @ ☎; S Kurfürstendamm) If you like edgy design combined with the amenities of a big-city property, the Concorde should fit the bill. The 311 rooms and suites are supersized, warmly furnished and accented with quality prints by contemporary German artists.

HOTEL ASKANISCHER HOF Hotel €€

(Map p275; ☏881 8033; www.askanischer-hof.de; Kurfürstendamm 53; d €120-180; ☎; S Adenauerplatz) If you're after character and retro flair, you'll find heaps of both at this 17-room jewel with a Roaring Twenties' pedigree. An ornate oak door leads to a quiet oasis where no two rooms are alike but all are filled with antiques, lace curtains, frilly chandeliers and time-worn oriental rugs.

 Eating

Mitte

KATZ ORANGE International €€€

(Map p256; ☏983 208 430; www.katzorange .com; Bergstrasse 22; mains €13-22; ☺dinner Tue-Sat year-round, lunch May-Sep; S Rosenthaler Platz) With its gourmet organic farm-to-table menu, feel-good country styling and swift and smiling servers, the Orange Cat hits a purr-fect gastro grand slam. The setting in a historic brewery with fairy-tale flourishes is stunning, especially in summer when the patio opens. Fabulous cocktails, too.

HARTWEIZEN Italian €€

(Map p256; ☏2849 3877; www.hartweizen.com; Torstrasse 96; mains €11-24; ☺dinner Mon-Sat; S Rosenthaler Platz) With its simple wooden tables, panorama windows and bright bulbs, Hartweizen is eons away from Chianti-bottle kitsch and is, quite simply, a top Italian restaurant focused on the feisty flavours of the Puglia region.

SCHWARZWALDSTUBEN German €€

(Map p256; ☏2809 8084; Tucholskystrasse 48; dishes €7-14; ⋒Oranienburger Strasse) In the mood for a *Hansel and Gretel* moment? Then join the other 'lost kids' in this send up of the Black Forest, complete with plastic pines and baseball-capped Bambi heads. We can't get enough of the *geschmelzte Maultaschen* (sautéed ravioli-like pasta) and the giant schnitzels, which are perfect foils for the Rothaus Tannenzäpfle beer.

UMA Asian €€€

(Map p256; ☏301 117 324; www.uma-restaurant .de; Behrenstrasse 72; mains €16-55; ☺dinner Mon-Sat; ⋒100, S Brandenburger Tor, ⋒Brandenburger Tor) Japanese for horse, Uma raises the bar for luxury with its exquisite decor, eye-catching artwork and Euro-inflected Asian dishes that weave flavours together like fine tapestries. Aside from sushi and sashimi, there are meaty mains from the robata (charcoal) grill and such tasty morsels as Korean fried octopus and wasabi-infused soft-shell crab meant for sharing.

BERLIN EATING

The Berlin Wall

For 28 years the Berlin Wall, the most potent symbol of the Cold War, divided not only a city but the world. Shortly after midnight on 13 August 1961 East German soldiers and police began rolling out miles of barbed wire that would soon be replaced with prefab concrete slabs. The wall was a desperate measure taken by the German Democratic Republic (GDR) government to stop the sustained brain and brawn drain it had experienced since its 1949 founding. Around 3.6 million people had already left for the West, putting the GDR on the verge of economic and political collapse.

The Wall's demise in 1989 came as unexpectedly as its construction. Once again the GDR was losing its people in droves, this time via Hungary, which had opened its borders with Austria. Something had to give. It did on 9 November 1989 when a GDR spokesperson (mistakenly, it later turned out) announced during a press conference that all travel restrictions to the West would be lifted. Immediately. Amid scenes of wild partying, the two Berlins came together again.

MONSIEUR VUONG   Asian €€
(Map p256; ☎9929 6924; www.monsieurvuong
.de; Alte Schönhauser Strasse 46; mains around
€8; ⊙noon-midnight; Ⓢ Weinmeisterstrasse,
Rosa-Luxemburg-Platz) Berlin's godfather of
upbeat Indochina nosh-stops, Monsieur
has been copied many times – the
concept is just that good. Pick from a
compact menu of flavour-packed soups
and two or three oft-changing mains, then
sit back and enjoy your leftover money.

**AUGUSTINER AM
GENDARMENMARKT**   German €€
(Map p256; ☎2045 4020; www.augustiner-braeu
-berlin.de; Charlottenstrasse 55; mains €6-19;
⊙10am-1am; Ⓢ Französische Strasse) Tourists,
concert-goers and hearty food-lovers rub
shoulders at rustic tables in Berlin's first
authentic Bavarian beer hall. Sausages,
roast pork and pretzels provide rib-
sticking sustenance, but there's also
plenty of lighter (even meat-free) fare
and great lunch specials.

COOKIES CREAM   Vegetarian €€€
(Map p256; ☎2749 2940; www.cookiescream
.com; Behrenstrasse 55; mains €20, 3-course
menu €36; ⊙dinner Tue-Sat; ☑; Ⓢ Französische Strasse) Kudos if you can locate this
hip herbivore haven right away. Hint:
the entrance is in the service alley of the
Westin Grand Hotel. Ring the bell to enter

an elegantly industrial loft for flesh-free,
flavour-packed dishes from current-
harvest ingredients. This grand culinary
journey also gets you free admission to
the eponymous nightclub (p23).

Potsdamer Platz & Tiergarten

QIU   International €€
(Map p256; ☎590 051 230; www.qiu.de; Mandala
Hotel, Potsdamer Strasse 3; 2-course lunch €14;
⊙lunch Mon-Fri; ☐200, Ⓢ Potsdamer Platz,
Ⓡ Potsdamer Platz) The two-course business lunch at this stylish lounge in the
Mandala Hotel is a virtual steal, while at
night the sensuous setting amid mood-lit
fringe lamps and golden mosaic waterfall
is great for pre-dinner or post-show
cocktails.

VAPIANO   Italian €€
(Map p256; ☎2300 5005; www.vapiano.de;
Potsdamer Platz 5; mains €5.50-9; ⊙11am-mid-
night Mon-Sat, to 11pm Sun; ☐200, Ⓢ Potsdamer Platz, Ⓡ Potsdamer Platz) Mix-and-match
pastas, creative salads and crusty pizzas
are all prepared right before your eyes
amid jazzy decor by Matteo Thun at this
stylish self-service canteen. Nice touch:
a condiment basket with fragrant fresh
basil and quality oil and balsamico. Your
order is recorded on a chip card and paid
for on leaving.

Kreuzberg & Northern Neukölln

CAFE JACQUES — International €€
(Map p264; ☎694 1048; Maybachufer 8; mains €12-20; ☺dinner; S Schönleinstrasse) A favourite with off-duty chefs and food-savvy locals, Jacques infallibly charms with flattering candlelight, warm decor and fantastic wine. It's the perfect date spot but, quite frankly, you only have to be in love with good food to appreciate the French- and North African–inspired blackboard menu.

HORVÁTH — Austrian €€€
(Map p264; ☎6128 9992; www.restaurant -horvath.de; Paul-Lincke-Ufer 44a; 3-/7-course menu €40-76; ☺dinner Tue-Sun; S Kottbusser Tor) At his canalside bistro, newly minted Michelin chef Sebastian Frank performs culinary alchemy with Austrian classics, fearlessly combining textures, flavours and ingredients. Despite the fanciful cuisine, the ambience in the elegantly rustic dining room remains relaxed.

DEFNE — Turkish €€
(Map p264; ☎8179 7111; www.defne-restaurant.de; Planufer 92c; mains €7.50-16; ☺dinner; S Kottbusser Tor, S Schönleinstrasse) If you thought Turkish cuisine stopped at the doner kebab, Defne will teach you otherwise. The appetiser platter alone elicits intense food cravings (fabulous walnut-chilli paste!), but inventive mains such as *ali nacik* (sliced lamb with pureed eggplant and yoghurt) also warrant repeat visits.

MAX UND MORITZ — German €€
(Map p264; ☎6951 5911; www.maxund moritzberlin.de; Oranienstrasse 162; mains €9-15; ☺dinner; S Moritzplatz) The patina of yesteryear hangs over this ode-to-old-school brewpub named for the cheeky Wilhelm Busch cartoon characters. Since 1902 it has lured hungry eaters with sudsy home brews and granny-style Berlin fare.

CURRY 36 — German €
(Map p264; www.curry36.de; Mehringdamm 36; snacks €2-6; ☺9am-4pm Mon-Sat, to 3pm Sun; S Mehringdamm) Top-ranked *Currywurst* purveyor that's been frying 'em up since the days when Madonna was singing about virgins.

SPÄTZLE & KNÖDEL — German €€
(Map p264; ☎2757 1151; Wühlischstrasse 20; mains €8-15; ☺dinner; S Samariterstrasse) Great gastropub where you can get your southern German comfort-food fix with waist-expanding portions of roast pork,

Uma (p269), Mitte district

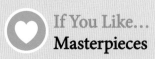

If You Like...
Masterpieces

If you didn't get your fill of fabulous paintings at the Gemäldegalerie (p261), the Alte Nationalgalerie (p259) or the Neue Nationalgalerie (p261), make a beeline to these great galleries for another art fix.

1 HAMBURGER BAHNHOF – MUSEUM FÜR GEGENWART

(Map p256; ☎ 266 424 242; www.hamburgerbahnhof.de; Invalidenstrasse 50-51; adult/concession €8/4; ⏰10am-6pm Tue-Fri, 11am-8pm Sat, 11am-6pm Sun; ⓢHauptbahnhof, ⓡHauptbahnhof) Berlin's main contemporary-art museum opened in 1996 in an old railway station, where the loft and grandeur are a great backdrop for the Aladdin's cave of paintings, installations, sculptures and video art. Exhibits span the arc of post-1950 artistic endeavours – conceptual art, pop art, minimal art, fluxus – and include seminal works by key players like Andy Warhol, Cy Twombly, Joseph Beuys and Robert Rauschenberg.

2 MUSEUM BERGGRUEN

(Map p275; ☎ 266 424 242; www.smb.museum/mb; Schlossstrasse 1; ☐145, 309, ⓢRichard-Wagner-Platz, Sophie-Charlotte-Platz) Fans of classical modern art will be in their element at this classy museum with a special focus on Picasso, Klee, Matisse and Giacometti. It was closed for renovation at the time of writing, but a new extension should have opened by the time you read this. See the website for updates.

3 SAMMLUNG BOROS

(Map p256; ☎ 2759 4065; www.sammlung-boros.de; Reinhardtstrasse 20; adult/concession €10/6; ⏰2-6pm Fri, 10am-6pm Sat & Sun; ⓢOranienburger Tor, Friedrichstrasse, ☐M1, ⓡFriedrichstrasse) This Nazi-era bunker turned shining beacon of art thanks to a stellar private collection of artists – Olafur Eliasson, Damien Hirst, Sarah Lucas and Wolfgang Tilmans among them. Entry is by guided tour (also in English) only. Book online as early as possible.

4 SAMMLUNG SCHARF-GERSTENBERG

(Map p275; ☎ 266 424 242; www.smb.museum/ssg; Schlossstrasse 70; adult/concession €6/3; ⏰10am-6pm Tue-Sun; ⓢSophie-Charlotte-Platz, then bus 309, ⓢRichard-Wagner-Platz, then bus 145) This stellar gallery trains the spotlight on surrealism, with large bodies of work by Magritte, Max Ernst, Dalí, Dubuffet and their 18th-century precursors such as Goya and Piranesi.

goulash and, of course, the eponymous *Spätzle* (German mac 'n cheese) and *Knödel* (dumplings).

Prenzlauer Berg

LUCKY LEEK Vegan €€
(Map p268; ☎ 6640 8710; www.lucky-leek.de; Kollwitzstrasse 46; mains around €12; ⏰dinner Tue & Thu-Sun; ✍; ⓢSenefelderplatz) This sprightly vegan joint crushes the competition by leagues, thanks to quality ingredients, inspired flavour combinations, creative and colourful presentation and enthusiastic staff.

KONNOPKE'S IMBISS Sausages €
(Map p268; Schönhauser Allee 44a; sausages €1.30-1.70; ⏰10am-8pm Mon-Fri, noon-8pm Sat; ⓢEberswalder Strasse) Brave the inevitable queue for legendary *Currywurst* from one of the city's cult sausage kitchens, now in shiny new glass digs but in the same historic spot since 1930.

ODERQUELLE German €€
(Map p268; ☎ 4400 8080; Oderberger Strasse 27; mains €8-16; ⏰dinner; ⓢEberswalder Strasse) It's always fun to pop by this woodsy resto and see what's inspired the chef this day. Most likely it'll be a delicious, well-crafted German meal, perhaps with a slight Mediterranean nuance.

Charlottenburg

GOOD FRIENDS Chinese €€
(Map p275; ☎ 313 2659; www.goodfriends-berlin.de; Kantstrasse 30; mains €10-20; ⏰noon-2am; ⓡSavignyplatz) Sinophiles tired of the Kung Pao school of Chinese cooking will appreciate the real thing at this well-established Cantonese restaurant.

OSTERIA CENTRALE Italian €€
(Map p275; ☎ 3101 3263; Bleibtreustrasse 51; mains €10-20; ⏰dinner Mon-Sat; ⓡSavignyplatz) This neighbourhood Italian fits like a well-worn shoe and lets you dip into a pool of pleasurable classics from around the boot.

CAFÉ-RESTAURANT WINTERGARTEN IM LITERATURHAUS
International €€

(Map p275; ☑ 882 5414; www.literaturhaus-berlin.de; Fasanenstrasse 23; mains €8-16; ⏰ 9.30am-1am; Ⓢ Uhlandstrasse) Tuck into seasonal bistro cuisine amid graceful Old Berlin flair or, if weather permits, in the idyllic garden. Breakfast is served until 2pm.

Drinking

Mitte

BERLINER REPUBLIK
Pub

(Map p256; www.die-berliner-republik.de; Schiffbauer-damm 8; ⏰ 10am-6am; Ⓢ Friedrichstrasse, Ⓡ Friedrichstrasse) Just as in a mini–stock exchange, the cost of drinks fluctuates with demand at this raucous riverside pub. It all goes Pavlovian when a heavy brass bell rings, signalling rock-bottom prices.

NEUE ODESSA BAR
Bar

(Map p256; Torstrasse 89; Ⓢ Rosenthaler Platz) Rub shoulders with a global mix of grown-ups with a hot fashion sense at this comfy-chic and always busy Torstrasse staple. Smoking allowed.

STRANDBAR MITTE
Bar

(Map p256; ☑ 2838 5588; www.strandbar-mitte.de; Monbijoustrasse 1-3; ⏰ from 10am May-Sep; Ⓣ M1, Ⓡ Oranienburger Strasse) With a full-on view of the Bodemuseum, palm trees and relaxed ambience, this riverside playground is great for balancing a surfeit of sightseeing stimulus with a revivifying drink.

Potsdamer Platz & Tiergarten

CAFÉ AM NEUEN SEE
Bar

(Map p275; ☑ 254 4930; www.cafe-am-neuen-see.de; Lichtensteinallee 2; ⏰ 9am-11pm; Ⓣ 100, 200) This lakeside Tiergarten restaurant serves pizza (€11) and German fare (mains €10 to €26) year-round, but the time to visit is during beer-garden season when long wooden tables brim with tourists and locals in search of a micro-vacation from the city bustle.

SOLAR
Bar

(Map p264; ☑ 0163 765 2700; www.solar-berlin.de; Stresemannstrasse 76; ⏰ 6pm-2am Sun-Thu, to 4am Fri & Sat; Ⓡ Anhalter Bahnhof) Views of the skyline are truly impressive at this chic 17th-floor sky lounge with dim lighting and soft black-leather couches. Enter via the chunky high-rise behind the Pit Stop auto shop.

Kreuzberg & Friedrichshain

WÜRGEENGEL
Bar

(Map p264; www.wuergeengel.de; Dresdner Strasse 122; ⏰ from 7pm; Ⓢ Kottbusser Tor) For a swish night out, point the compass to this '50s-style cocktail cave complete with glass ceiling, chandeliers and shiny black tables. Smoking allowed.

FREISCHWIMMER
Beer Garden

(Map p264; ☑ 6107 4309; www.freischwimmer-berlin.de; Vor dem Schlesischen Tor 2a; ⏰ from 4pm Tue-Fri, 10am Sat & Sun; Ⓢ Schlesisches

Strandbar Mitte
LOOK DIE BILDAGENTUR DER FOTOGRAFEN GMBH/ALAMY ©

Gay & Lesbian Berlin

Berlin's legendary liberalism has spawned one of the world's biggest, most divine and diverse GLBT playgrounds. The closest that Berlin comes to a 'gay village' is Schöneberg (Motzstrasse and Fuggerstrasse especially), where the rainbow flag has proudly flown since the 1920s. There's still plenty of (old-school) partying going on here, but anyone under 35 will likely feel more comfortable elsewhere. Current hipster central is Kreuzberg, which teems with party pens along Mehringdamm and Oranienstrasse. Across the river, Friedrichshain has such key clubs as Berghain and the hard-core Lab.oratory.

Mann-O-Meter (☎ 216 8008; www.mann-o-meter.de; Bülowstrasse 106; ⏰ 5-10pm Tue-Fri, 4-8pm Sat & Sun; S Nollendorfplatz) One-stop information centre that also operates a hotline to report attacks on gays.

Siegessäule (www.siegesaeule.de) Weekly freebie mag is the bible for all things gay and lesbian in Berlin.

Tor) In summer, few places are more idyllic than this rustic ex-boathouse turned all-day, canal-side chill zone. Snacks and light meals (mains €7 to €15) are served, but they're more of an afterthought. It's sometimes open in winter, but it's not the same – call ahead for hours.

LUZIA
Bar

(Map p264; ☎ 8179 9958; Oranienstrasse 34; ⏰ from noon till late; S Kottbusser Tor) Tarted up nicely with vintage furniture, baroque wallpaper and whimsical wall art by Chin Chin, Luzia draws its crowd from SO36's more sophisticated urban dwellers. Smoker's lounge.

HOPS & BARLEY
Pub

(Map p264; ☎ 2936 7534; Wühlischstrasse 40; S Warschauer Strasse, R Warschauer Strasse) Conversation flows as freely as the unfiltered Pilsner, malty *dunkel* (dark), fruity *weizen* (wheat) and potent cider produced right at this congenial microbrewery inside a former butcher's shop.

Prenzlauer Berg

PRATER
Beer Garden

(Map p268; ☎ 448 5688; www.pratergarten.de; Kastanienallee 7-9; ⏰ from noon Apr-Sep in good weather; S Eberswalder Strasse) Berlin's oldest beer garden (since 1837) has kept much of its traditional charm and is a fantastic place to hang and guzzle a cold one beneath the ancient chestnut trees (self-service).

Charlottenburg

PURO SKYLOUNGE
Bar, Club

(Map p275; ☎ 2636 7875; www.puro-berlin.de; Tauentzienstrasse 11; ⏰ Tue-Sat; S Kurfürstendamm) Puro has quite literally raised the bar in Charlottenburg – by moving it to the 20th floor of the Europa Center, that is. Trade Berlin funky-trash for sleek decor, fabulous views and high-heeled hotties.

 Entertainment

CHAMÄLEON VARIETÉ
Cabaret

(Map p256; ☎ 400 0590; www.chamaeleonberlin.com; Rosenthaler Strasse 40/41; 🚋 M1, R Hackescher Markt) A marriage of art nouveau charms and high-tech theatre trappings, this intimate 1920s-style cabaret in an old ballroom presents classy variety shows – comedy, juggling acts and singing – often in sassy, sexy and unconventional fashion.

BERLINER PHILHARMONIE
Classical Music

(Map p256; ☎ 2548 8999; www.berliner-philharmoniker.de; Herbert-von-Karajan-Strasse 1; 🚌 200, S Potsdamer Platz, R Potsdamer Platz) This landmark concert hall has supreme acoustics and, thanks to Hans Scharoun's clever terraced vineyard design, not a bad seat in the house. It's the home base of the world-famous Berliner Philharmoniker, currently led by Sir Simon Rattle.

Charlottenburg

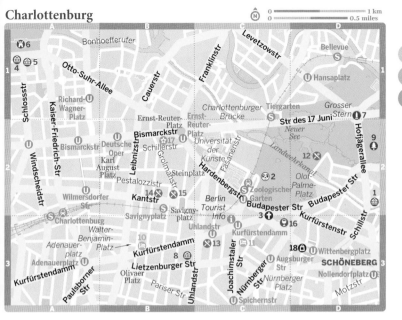

Charlottenburg

STAATSOPER UNTER DEN LINDEN @ SCHILLERTHEATER Opera
(Map p275; ☎ information 203 540, tickets 2035 4555; www.staatsoper-berlin.de; Bismarckstrasse 110 ; Ⓢ Ernst-Reuter-Platz) Point your highbrow compass towards the Daniel Barenboim–led Staatsoper, Berlin's top opera company. While its historic digs on Unter den Linden are getting a facelift (probably until 2014), the high-calibre productions are staged at the Schiller Theater in Charlottenburg.

CLÄRCHENS BALLHAUS Club
(Map p256; ☎ 282 9295; www.ballhaus.de; Auguststrasse 24; ⏱ restaurant 12.30-11.30pm, dancing nightly; 🚋 M1, 🚆 Oranienburger Strasse) Yesteryear is now at this late, great 19th-

Left: Flohmarkt am Mauerpark; **Right:** Fassbender & Rausch
(BELOW) MICHAEL TAYLOR/GETTY IMAGES ©; (RIGHT) DAVID PEEVERS/GETTY IMAGES ©

century dance hall where groovers and grannies hoof it across the parquet without even a touch of irony. There are different sounds nightly – salsa to swing, tango to disco – and a live band on Saturdays.

COOKIES Club
(Map p256; www.cookies.ch; cnr Friedrichstrasse & Unter den Linden; ⊘from midnight Tue, Thu & Sat; S Französische Strasse) Upstairs, top electro DJs heat up the swank crowd on the mosaic dance floor that segues smoothly into the **Drayton Bar** (Map p256; ☎280 8806; www.draytonberlin.com; Behrensstrasse 55; ⊘Tue-Sat; S Französische Strasse).

BERGHAIN/PANORAMA BAR Club
(Map p264; www.berghain.de; Am Wriezener Bahnhof; ⊘Sat; ⊠Ostbahnhof) Only world-class spinmasters heat up this hedonistic bass junkie hellhole inside a labyrinthine ex-power plant. One floor up, Panorama Bar pulsates with house and electro, while the big factory floor below is gay-leaning and hard techno. Best time: after 4am. Strict door, no cameras.

 Shopping

KADEWE Department Store
(Map p275; www.kadewe.de; Tauentzienstrasse 21-24; ⊘10am-8pm Mon-Thu, to 9pm Fri, 9.30am-8pm Sat; S Wittenbergplatz) Just past the centennial mark, this venerable department store has an assortment so vast that a pirate-style campaign is the best way to plunder its bounty. Even if you're pushed for time, don't miss the legendary 6th-floor gourmet food hall.

FASSBENDER & RAUSCH Food
(Map p256; ☎2045 8443; www.fassbender-rausch.com; Charlottenstrasse 60; ⊘10am-8pm Mon-Sat, 11am-8pm Sun; S Stadtmitte) If the Aztecs thought of chocolate as the elixir of the gods, then this emporium of truffles and pralines must be heaven. Bonus: the chocolate volcano and giant replicas of Berlin landmarks.

FRIEDRICHSTADTPASSAGEN
Shopping Centre
(Map p256; Friedrichstrasse btwn Französische
Strasse & Mohrenstrasse; ⏱10am-8pm Mon-Sat;
Ⓢ Französische Strasse, Stadtmitte) Even if
you're not part of the Gucci and Prada brigade, the wow factor of this trio of shopping complexes (called *Quartiere*) linked
by a subterranean passageway is
undeniable.

AMPELMANN GALERIE Souvenirs
(Map p256; ☎4472 6438; www.ampelmann.de;
Court V, Hackesche Höfe, Rosenthaler Strasse
40-41; ⏱9.30am-10pm Mon-Sat, 10am-7pm Sun;
Ⓜ M1, Ⓡ Hackescher Markt) It took a vocifer-
ous grass-roots campaign to save the little
Ampelmann, the endearing East German
traffic-light man. Now the beloved cult
figure and global brand graces an entire
store's worth of T-shirts, towels, key rings,
cookie cutters and other knick-knacks.

BONBONMACHEREI Food
(Map p256; ☎4405 5243; www.bonbonmacherei
.de; Oranienburger Strasse 32, Heckmann
Höfe; ⏱noon-8pm Wed-Sat Sep-Jun; Ⓜ M1,

Ⓡ Oranienburger Strasse) The aroma of pep-
permint and liquorice wafts through this
old-fashioned basement candy kitchen,
where the owners use antique equipment
and time-tested recipes to churn out such
tasty treats as their signature leaf-shaped
Berliner Maiblätter.

**FLOHMARKT AM
MAUERPARK** Flea Market
(Map p268; www.mauerparkmarkt.de; Bernauer
Strasse 63-64; ⏱10am-5pm Sun; Ⓢ Eberwalder
Strasse) Join the throngs of thrifty trinket
hunters, bleary-eyed clubbers and excited
tourists sifting for treasure at this always
busy flea market right where the Berlin
Wall once ran. Source new faves among
retro threads, local-designer T-shirts,
vintage vinyl and offbeat stuff. Ethnic
food stands and beer gardens, including **Mauersegler** (Map p268; ☎9788 0904;
www.mauersegler-berlin.de; Bernauer Strasse
63; ⏱11am-2am May-Oct, 9am-7pm Sun year-
round; 🛜; Ⓢ Eberswalder Strasse), provide
sustenance.

ℹ Information

Tourist Information

The city tourist board, **Visit Berlin** (🗷2500 2333; www.visitberlin.de), operates four offices and a call centre with multilingual staff who field general questions and can make hotel and ticket bookings.

Brandenburger Tor (South Wing, Pariser Platz; ⏱10am-7pm; **S** Brandenburger Tor, **R** Brandenburger Tor) Extended hours April to October.

Hauptbahnhof (Hauptbahnhof, ground fl, Europaplatz north entrance; ⏱8am-10pm; **S** Hauptbahnhof, **R** Hauptbahnhof)

Neues Kranzler Eck (Neues Kranzler Eck, Kurfürstendamm 22; ⏱9.30am-8pm Mon-Sat, to 6pm Sun; **S** Kurfürstendamm) Extended hours April to October.

ℹ Getting There & Away

Air

Berlin's brand-new Berlin Brandenburg Airport (BBI; www.berlin-airport.de) has been taking shape next to Schönefeld Airport, about 24km southeast of the city centre, since 2006. At the time of writing, construction problems and safety concerns had delayed the original June 2012 opening to autumn 2013, although further delays are possible. In the meantime, most major international airlines, as well as many discount carriers, including Ryanair, easyJet, Air Berlin and Germanwings, continue to fly into Berlin's two other airports.

Tegel Airport (TXL; 🗷0180 5000 186; www.berlin-airport.de) About 8km northwest of the city centre.

Schönefeld Airport (SXF; 🗷0180 5000 186; www.berlin-airport.de) About 22km southeast. Is being expanded into Berlin Brandenburg Airport.

Train

Berlin is well connected by train to other German cities, as well as to popular European destinations, including Prague, Warsaw and Amsterdam. While all long-distance trains converge at the Hauptbahnhof, some also stop at other stations such as Spandau, Ostbahnhof, Gesundbrunnen and Südkreuz.

ℹ Getting Around

To/From the Airports

TEGEL The **TXL bus** connects Tegel with Alexanderplatz (40 minutes) every 10 minutes. For Kurfürstendamm and Zoo Station, take bus X9 (20 minutes). Each of these trips costs €2.40. Taxi rides cost about €20 to Zoologischer Garten and €23 to Alexanderplatz and should take between 30 and 45 minutes.

SCHÖNEFELD The **Airport-Express** trains make the 30-minute trip to central Berlin twice hourly. Note: these are regular regional trains, identified as RE7 and RB14 in timetables. You need a transport ticket covering zones ABC (€3.10). Taxi rides average €40 and take 35 minutes to an hour.

Schloss Cecilienhof (p282), Potsdam
RICK GERHARTER/GETTY IMAGES ©

BERLIN BRANDENBURG Once the new airport is up and running, Airport-Express trains are expected to depart for central Berlin from the new airport's own station every 15 minutes. The trip will be covered by ABC tickets (€3.10).

Public Transport

One ticket is good on all forms of public transport. Most trips within Berlin require an AB ticket (€2.40), valid for two hours (interruptions and transfers allowed, round trips not).

One-day travel passes (Tageskarte) are valid for unlimited travel on all forms of public transport until 3am the following day. The cost for the AB zone is €6.50. Group day passes (Kleingruppenkarte) are valid for up to five people travelling together and cost €15.50.

Buy tickets from vending machines in U-Bahn or S-Bahn stations and aboard trams, from bus drivers and at station offices and news kiosks sporting the yellow BVG logo.

All tickets, except those bought from bus drivers and on trams, must be stamped before boarding. Anyone caught without a validated ticket escapes only with a red face and a €40 fine, payable on the spot.

U-Bahn

U-Bahn lines (underground, subway) are best for getting around Berlin quickly. Trains operate from 4am until about 12.30am and throughout the night on Friday, Saturday and public holidays (all lines except U4 and U55).

S-Bahn

The S-Bahn (suburban trains) don't run as frequently as U-Bahns but make fewer stops and thus are useful for covering longer distances.

Bus & Tram

Buses are slow but useful for city sightseeing on the cheap. They run frequently between 4.30am and 12.30am. Trams only operate in the eastern districts.

Taxi

You can order a taxi (⚡44 33 11, 20 20 20) by phone, flag one down or pick one up at a rank. Flag fall is €3.20, then it's €1.65 per kilometre up to 7km and €1.28 for each kilometre after that.

AROUND BERLIN
Potsdam

⚡ 0331 / POP 152,000

Potsdam, on the Havel River just southwest of Berlin, is the capital and crown jewel of the federal state of Brandenburg. Scores of visitors are drawn to the stunning architecture of this former Prussian royal seat and to soak up the air of history that hangs over its elegant parks.

Headlining the roll call of palaces is Schloss Sanssouci, the private retreat of King Friedrich II (Frederick the Great), who was also the visionary behind many of Potsdam's other fabulous pads and parks, which miraculously survived WWII with nary a shrapnel wound. When the shooting stopped, the Allies chose Schloss Cecilienhof for the Potsdam Conference of August 1945 to lay the groundwork for Germany's postwar fate.

 Sights

Schloss & Park Sanssouci

ORANGERIESCHLOSS Palace

The dominant building in the centre of Park Sanssouci is the Orangery Palace, a 300m-long Italian Renaissance–style palace that was Friedrich Wilhelm IV's favourite building project. Tours take in the **Raphaelsaal**, with its 19th-century copies of the famous painter's masterpieces. The **tower** (€2) delivers sweeping park views.

CHINESISCHES HAUS Historic Building

(Am Grünen Gitter; admission €2; ⊙10am-6pm Tue-Sun May-Oct; 🚌605 to Schloss Charlottenhof, 606 or 695 to Schloss Sanssouci, 🚊91 to Schloss Charlottenhof) The cloverleaf-shaped shutterbug favourite sports an enchanting exterior of exotically garbed and gilded figures sipping tea, dancing and playing musical instruments amid palm-shaped pillars. Inside is a precious collection of Chinese and Meissen porcelain.

NEUES PALAIS Palace

(New Palace; ⚡969 4200; Am Neuen Palais; adult/concession €6/5; ⊙10am-6pm Wed-Mon Apr-Oct, to 5pm Nov-Mar; 🚌695 or 605 to Neues

279

Potsdam

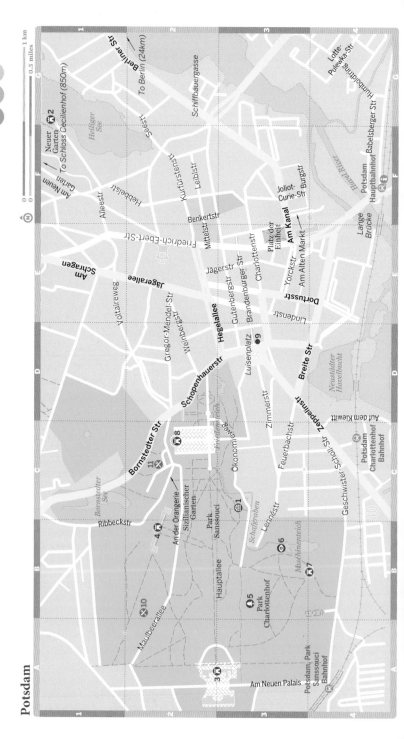

Potsdam

Palais, 🚊 to Potsdam, Park Sanssouci Bahnhof) At the far western end of the park, the New Palace has made-to-impress dimensions, a central dome and a lavish exterior capped with a parade of sandstone figures.

The interior attests to the high level of artistry and craftsmanship of the time. Memorable rooms include the **Grottensaal** (grotto hall), a rococo delight with shells, fossils and baubles set into the walls and ceilings; the **Marmorsaal**, a large banquet hall of Carrara marble with a wonderful ceiling fresco; and the **Jagdkammer** (hunting chamber), with lots of dead furry things and fine gold tracery on the walls.

PARK CHARLOTTENHOF   Park
Laid out by Peter Lenné for Friedrich Wilhelm IV, Park Charlottenhof segues imperceptibly from Park Sanssouci but gets a lot fewer visitors. Buildings here reflect the king's passion for Italy. The small neoclassical **Schloss Charlottenhof** (tour adult/concession €4/3; ⊙10am-6pm Tue-Sun May-Oct), for instance, was modelled after a Roman villa and features a Doric portico and bronze fountain. It was designed by Karl Friedrich Schinkel who, aided by his student Ludwig Persius, also dreamed up the nearby **Römische Bäder** (Roman Baths; adult/concession €3/2.50; ⊙10am-6pm Tue-Sun May-Oct), a picturesque ensemble of an Italian country villa. A same-day combination ticket is €5 (concession €4).

SCHLOSS SANSSOUCI   Palace
(www.spsg.de; adult/concession incl audioguide Apr-Oct €12/8, Nov-Mar €8/5 ; ⊙10am-6pm Tue-Sun Apr-Oct, to 5pm Nov-Mar; 🚌 695, 606) The biggest stunner, and what everyone comes to see, is Schloss Sanssouci, the celebrated rococo palace designed by

Georg Wenzeslaus von Knobelsdorff for King Frederick the Great in 1747. Admission is by timed ticket only; come early, preferably at opening and – if possible – avoid weekends and holidays. Otherwise, only city tours booked through the Potsdam tourist office guarantee admission.

Standouts on the audio guided tours include the **Konzertsaal** (concert hall), whimsically decorated with vines, grapes and even a cobweb where spiders frolic. King Frederick himself gave flute recitals here. Also note the intimate **Bibliothek** (library), lidded by a gilded sunburst ceiling, where the king would seek solace amid 2000 leather-bound tomes ranging from Greek poetry to the latest releases by his friend Voltaire. Another highlight is the **Marmorsaal** (marble room), an elegant white Carrara marble symphony modelled after the Pantheon in Rome.

Altstadt

Although Potsdam's historic town centre fell victim to WWII bombing and socialist town planning, it's still worth a leisurely stroll. Coming from Park Sanssouci, you'll pass by the baroque **Brandenburger Tor** (Brandenburg Gate), a triumphal arch built to commemorate Frederick the Great's 1770 victory in the Seven Years War. It's the gateway to pedestrianised Brandenburger Strasse, the main commercial drag, which takes you straight to the **Holländisches Viertel** (Dutch Quarter).

Neuer Garten & Around

North of the Potsdam old town, the winding lakeside Neuer Garten (New Garden), laid out in natural English style on the

Gilded statues, Park Sanssouci (p279)

DAVID PEEVERS/GETTY IMAGES ©

western shore of the Heiliger See, is another fine park in which to relax.

SCHLOSS CECILIENHOF Palace

(☏ 969 4244; www.spsg.de; Im Neuen Garten 11; tours adult/concession €6/5; ⊙ 10am-6pm Tue-Sun Apr-Oct, to 5pm Nov-Mar; 🚌 603) This rustic English-style country palace was completed in 1917 for Crown Prince Wilhelm and his wife Cecilie, but is really more famous for hosting the 1945 Potsdam Conference where Stalin, Truman and Churchill hammered out Germany's postwar fate. The conference room, with its giant round table, looks as though the delegates just left.

MARMORPALAIS Palace

(☏ 969 4550; www.spsg.de; Im Neuen Garten 10; tour adult/concession €5/4; ⊙ 10am-6pm Tue-Sun May-Oct, 10am-4pm Sat & Sun Nov-Mar, 10am-6pm Sat & Sun Apr; 🚌 603) The neoclassical Marble Palace was built in 1792 as a summer residence for Friedrich Wilhelm II by Carl Gotthard Langhans (of Berlin's Brandenburg Gate fame) and has a stunning interior marked by a grand central staircase, marble fireplaces, stucco ceilings and lots of precious Wedgwood porcelain.

 Tours

POTSDAM SANSSOUCI TOUR Guided Tour

(tours with/without Sanssouci Palace €27/16; ⊙ Tue-Sun Apr-Oct) The local tourist office runs the 3½-hour Potsdam Sanssouci Tour, which checks off the highlights and guarantees admission to Schloss Sanssouci. Tours are in English and German and leave at 11am from Luisenplatz and at 11.10am from the tourist office at the Hauptbahnhof.

 Eating & Drinking

DRACHENHAUS German €€

(☏ 505 3808; www.drachenhaus.de; Maulbeerallee 4a; mains €7.50-25; ⊙ 11am-7pm or later Apr-Oct, 11am-6pm Tue-Sun Nov-Feb) Right in Park Sanssouci, the exotic Dragon House is a Chinese miniature palace inspired by the Ta-Ho pagoda in Canton. It now houses a pleasant cafe-restaurant serving coffee, homemade cakes and regional cuisine, in summer beneath a tree canopy.

POTSDAM HISTORISCHE MÜHLE International €€

(☏ 281 493; www.moevenpick-restaurants.com; Zur Historischen Mühle 2; mains €10-18; ⊙8am-11pm) This vast restaurant, part of the Mövenpick chain, lures punters with international favourites, a beer garden and a children's playground.

 Information

Tourist office (☏ 2755 8899; www.potsdam-tourism.com; Babelsberger Strasse 16, inside the Hauptbahnhof, next to platform 6; ⊙9.30am-8pm Mon-Sat May-Oct, to 6pm Mon-Sat Nov-Apr, 10am-4pm Sun year-round) There's another office at Brandenburger Tor.

ⓘ Getting There & Away

Regional trains leaving from Berlin-Hauptbahnhof and Zoologischer Garten take about half an hour to reach Potsdam Hauptbahnhof. The S7 from central Berlin makes the trip in about 40 minutes. You need a ticket covering zones A, B and C (€3.10) for either service.

Sachsenhausen Concentration Camp

Built by prisoners brought here from another concentration camp, Sachsenhausen opened in 1936 as a model for other camps. Tens of thousands died here from hunger, exhaustion, illness, exposure, medical experiments and executions. Thousands more succumbed during the death march of April 1945, when the Nazis evacuated the camp in advance of the Red Army. Updated many times since, today's memorial delivers a predictably sobering experience.

Sights

FREE **GEDENKSTÄTTE UND MUSEUM SACHSENHAUSEN** Memorial

(☏ 2000; www.stiftung-bg.de; Strasse der Nationen 22; ⊙8.30am-6pm mid-Mar–mid-Oct, to 4.30pm mid-Oct–mid-Mar, most exhibits closed Mon) Unless you're on a guided tour, pick up a leaflet (€0.50) or, better yet, an audioguide (€3, including leaflet) at the visitor centre to get a better grasp of this huge site.

Proceed to **Tower A**, the entrance gate, cynically labelled, as at Auschwitz, *Arbeit Macht Frei* (Work Sets You Free). Beyond here is the roll-call area, with barracks and other buildings fanning out beyond. Off to the right, two restored barracks illustrate the abysmal living conditions prisoners endured.

Further on, the **Prisoners' Kitchen** zeroes in on key moments in the camp's history during its various phases. Exhibits include instruments of torture, the original gallows and, in the cellar, heart-wrenching artwork scratched into the wall by prisoners.

The most sickening displays, though, deal with the extermination area called **Station Z**, which consisted of an execution trench, a crematorium and a gas chamber.

ⓘ Getting There & Away

The S1 makes the trip thrice hourly from central Berlin (eg Friedrichstrasse station) to Oranienburg (€3, 45 minutes). Hourly regional RE5 and RB12 trains leaving from Hauptbahnhof are faster (€3.10, 25 minutes). From the station it's a 2km signposted walk to the camp entrance.

Dresden & the East

Saxony has everything you could want in a holiday. Expect to be captivated by story-book castles peering down from craggy mountaintops, cobbled marketplaces serenaded by mighty churches, exuberant palaces, nostalgic steam trains and folk traditions by the indigenous Sorb minority. And through it all courses the broad-shouldered Elbe in its steady eternal flow out to the North Sea past vineyards, sandstone cliffs and villa-studded hillsides.

Many heavyweights have shaped Saxony's cultural landscape: Bach, Canaletto, Goethe and Wagner among them. Dresden's Semperoper and the Gewandhausorchester in Leipzig have for centuries been among the world's finest musical venues.

The two cities naturally also grab top historical billing. The former became synonymous with the devastation of WWII, but has since resurrected its baroque heritage. And it was Leipzig that sparked the 'peaceful revolution' of 1989 that brought down the Berlin Wall, which led to the reunification of Germany.

Dresden and the Elbe River (p296)

Dresden & the East

POLAND

Oder

Worta

Debno

Kostryzn

Frankfurt an der Oder

Eisenhüttenstadt

Oder

Szczecin

Pasewalk

Schwedt

Lower Oder Valley National Park

Lübben

MECKLENBURG-WESTERN POMERANIA

Neubrandenburg

Finow

Eberswalde

Müritz National Park

Neustrelitz

Sachsenhausen Concentration Camp

Oranienburg

Berlin

Teltow

Lake Müritz

Rheinsberg

Spandau

Potsdam

Brandenburg an der Havel

③ Lutherstadt Wittenberg

Dessau-Rosslau

Elbe River

LOWER SAXONY

Goslar

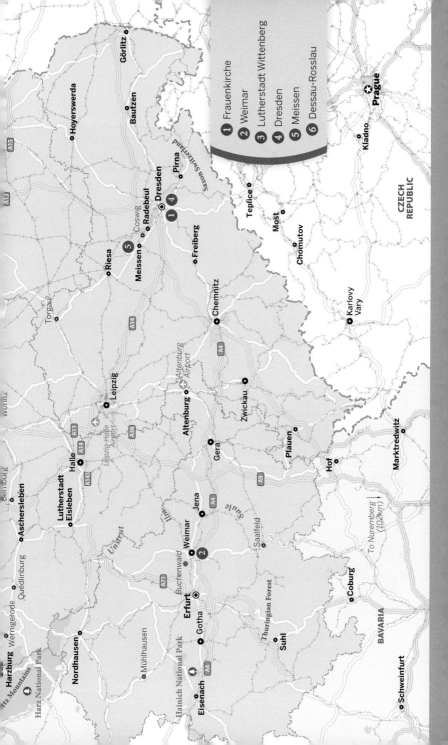

Dresden & the East's Highlights

1

Be Awed by the Frauenkirche

It's hard to fathom that Dresden's gorgeous landmark church was reconstructed from a massive pile of wartime rubble in the same spot where the baroque original welcomed worshippers from 1743 until 1945. Rebuilt with donations from around the world, it is once again the crowning glory of Dresden's sparkling skyline.

Need to Know

ENJOY a concert held year-round. **JOIN** a guided tour or rent an audioguide. **WATCH** the introductory film at the Frauenkirche visitors centre. **For further coverage, see p296**

Frauenkirche Don't Miss List

BY REVEREND SEBASTIAN FEYDT

1 DOME

The Frauenkirche dome is the most distinctive feature of Dresden's silhouette. It's the largest stone cupola north of the Alps and the only one that is shaped like a bell. You can also climb up to a viewing platform for superb views of the curving Elbe River.

2 SPIRE CROSS

When you first enter the church, it seems so new and intact, but take a closer look and you'll discover some remaining scars. For instance, the spire cross that once crowned the top of the Frauenkirche dome is displayed in exactly the same condition it was found in when discovered underneath a pile of rubble back in 1993.

3 ALTAR

The main altar is special in several ways: what you see has been reassembled from almost 2000 individual fragments, meaning that much of it is actually from the original altar. The scene that it depicts – Jesus in the Garden of Gethsemane – is rarely found on an altar.

4 VIEWS

There are several vantage points from which to admire the outline of the Frauenkirche. If you want to see it as part of the city panorama, head to the other Elbe bank for the glorious view that has inspired artists for centuries. To appreciate the facade with its new white and blackened original stones, take time to stroll around the church itself, right on Neumarkt. For a bird's-eye view of the massive 12,000-ton dome, head up the Hausmannsturm (tower) of the nearby Residenzschloss (p301).

5 SPIRITUAL SIDE

The Frauenkirche is not only a historical monument but also an active house of worship. If you're in town on a workday, a great time to visit is during the noontime German-language devotions that are accompanied by organ music and which begin with the ringing of the *Friedensglocke Jesaja* (the peace bell), which is the largest of the church's eight bells.

289

Mingle with Greatness in Weimar

Weimar (p308) experienced its heyday during the 18th-century Age of Enlightenment when it attracted a literal who's who of intellectual and cultural greats, from Goethe to Bach and, later, Kandinsky. You can still explore their old stomping grounds in an array of museums and sights, while the town's quaint streets, parks and gardens lend themselves to quiet contemplation. Monument to Johann Wolfgang von Goethe (left) and Friedrich Schiller, Weimar

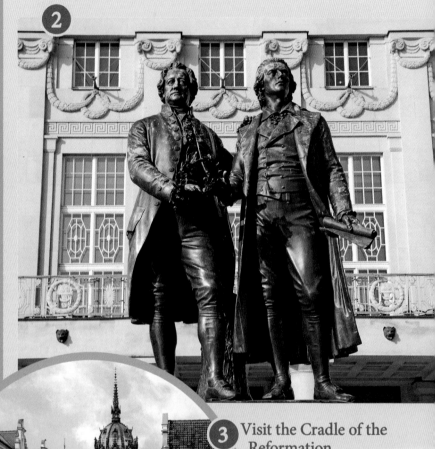

2

3 ## Visit the Cradle of the Reformation

Lutherstadt Wittenberg (p305) is the very crucible of the Reformation that culmina ed in the division of the Christian Church into Catholics and Protestants in the 16t century. This is the town where long-ter resident Martin Luther wrote his famous 95 theses challenging Catholic practices Exhibits at his former family home, the Lutherhaus, chart the development of his beliefs.

Be Dazzled by the Green Vault

Two mind-boggling treasure chambers inhabit Dresden's Residenzschloss. Stunners of the Neues Grünes Gewölbe (New Green Vault; p301) include gem-studded figurines and a cherry pit engraved with 185 faces. The Historisches Grünes Gewölbe (Historical Green Vault) showcases a further 3000 items in rooms recreated in lavish 18th-century style.

Marvel at Meissen Porcelain

Exquisite breakables from Meissen, the birthplace of European porcelain, have graced tables and display cases around the world since the early 18th century. A tour of the Erlebniswelt Haus Meissen (p301), next to the porcelain factory, includes demonstrations of the stunning artistry that goes into creating these fanciful plates, figures and teacups.

Behold the Bauhaus in Dessau-Rosslau

Chances are there's a little Bauhaus in your house, for this seminal early-20th-century architecture and design movement put the world on the path to modernism. Founded in 1919 in Weimar, it reached its peak in Dessau-Rosslau (p307) in 1925. Visit the legendary Bauhaus school once led by Walter Gropius and Mies van der Rohe, as well as their nearby private homes, the Meisterhäuser (Masters' Houses).

Dresden & the East's Best...

Historic Churches

○ **Frauenkirche** (p296)
Dresden's reconstructed landmark church

○ **Schlosskirche** (p306)
Onto whose door Luther nailed his 95 theses and where he's buried; in Lutherstadt Wittenberg

○ **Nikolaikirche** (p304)
Leipzig's ornate neoclassical church played a pivotal role in the downfall of East Germany

○ **Thomaskirche** (p303)
Johann Sebastian Bach's old stomping ground and burial place in Leipzig

GDR Museums

○ **Zeitgeschichtliches Forum** (p304) East German history in a nutshell; in Leipzig

○ **Stasi Museum** (p302)
Peels back the layers on the machinations of East Germany's secret police

○ **Zeitreise DDR Museum Radebeul** (p306) A glimpse into daily life behind the Iron Curtain

○ **DDR Museum Pirna** (p306) Thousands of objects transport you back to the days before the fall of the Wall

Famous Homes

○ **Goethe Nationalmuseum** (p309) Where Germany's literary lion penned seminal works; in Weimar

○ **Schiller Haus** (p309) The renowned dramatist lived in this fairly modest Weimar home

○ **Lutherhaus** (p306)
Luther raised his family in this former monastery in Lutherstadt Wittenberg

○ **Meisterhäuser** (p307)
Private homes of the leading lights of the Bauhaus School in Dessau-Rosslau

Unesco World Heritage Sites

○ **Dessau-Rosslau** (p307) The original Bauhaus school building and its main teachers' homes

○ **Lutherstadt Wittenberg** (p305) Key sites related to Luther and the Reformation

○ **Weimar** (p308) Homes, palaces and parks from its Enlightenment heyday

○ **Eisenach** (p312) Its Wartburg Castle played key moments in German history

t: Martin Luther's study at the Wartburg (p312);
Above: Goethe Nationalmuseum (p309)

Need to Know

ADVANCE PLANNING

○ **Three months before** Book tickets for concerts at Dresden's Semperoper or Leipzig's Gewandhausorchester.

○ **One month before** Get online tickets for Dresden's Historisches Grünes Gewölbe.

○ **One week before** Reserve a table at Leipzig's storied Auerbachs Keller or Erfurt's top-rated Alboth's.

RESOURCES

○ **Saxony. State of the Arts.** (www.saxonytourism .com) Saxony's official tourism site.

○ **Luther 2017** (www .luther2017.de) Dedicated to Martin Luther and the Reformation's 500th anniversary in 2017.

○ **Stiftung Bauhaus Dessau** (www.bauhaus -dessau.de) A primer about the Bauhaus movement.

○ **CyberSAX** (www .cybersax.de) Dresden's local listings online magazine.

GETTING AROUND

○ **Car** Key autobahns are the north–south A9 and A13 and the east–west A4.

○ **Train** Unless you venture into the countryside, the train is ideal for getting around. Save money with the **Sachsen-Ticket (€21 for one person, up to four additional people €3 each)**, valid for unlimited 2nd-class travel on any regional trains (RE, RB, S-Bahn) from 9am until 3am the following day (from midnight on Saturday and Sunday) throughout the region covered in this chapter.

BE FOREWARNED

○ **Dresden** Gets incredibly busy during the peak summer rush. If possible, schedule a visit here on a weekday and visit the most popular attractions (eg Green Vault) during lunchtime or late afternoon.

○ **Buchenwald Concentration Camp** Visits are not for the faint-of-heart. Plan for a little down time after your visit – your mind needs time to take it all in.

○ **Meissen** Long waits are common at the Erlebniswelt Haus Meissen. Plan extra time for your visit and take a stroll through the charming Altstadt (old town) while you wait for your time slot.

Dresden & the East Itineraries

From the Reformation to the invention of European porcelain and the collapse of Communism, on a tour of eastern Germany you visit places that witnessed historical milestones with worldwide implications.

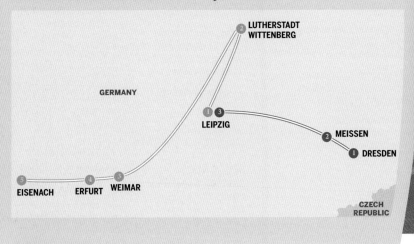

3 DAYS

DRESDEN TO LEIPZIG

Baroque, Porcelain & Freedom

Bookended by great cities, this quick trip lets you sample superb culture, character and architecture. It can easily be done by train. Kick-off is in pretty and evocative **(1) Dresden** that's literally risen from the ashes of WWII. Its lovely Elbe River setting lets it show off a stunning skyline dominated by the grand dome of the resurrected Frauenkirche. Book ahead for admission to the Historical Green Vault and perhaps a concert at the famous Semperoper.

The following day, enjoy a leisurely boat ride to **(2) Meissen**, where European porcelain was invented. Get the historical background in the museum at Albrechtsburg, then head to the Erlebniswelt Haus Meissen for the inside scoop on how this world-famous porcelain brand is made.

Spend the night in Meissen or continue straight on to **(3) Leipzig**. Note that most train connections require a change in Coswig. Leipzig is known as the City of Heroes for its key role in the fall of the Berlin Wall. Visit the Nikolaikirche, where weekly peace prayers are still held, learn about the history of East Germany at the Zeitgeschichtliches Forum and shudder at the sinister machinations of its secret police at the Stasi Museum.

Writers, Reformers & Composers

This region inspired some of the most famous writers, artists and composers of our time. It's also where the Reformation began. Start in **(1) Leipzig** and follow in the footsteps of Johann Sebastian Bach at the Thomaskirche and Bach-Museum, and of Robert Schumann at the coffee-house Zum Arabischen Coffe Baum. Wrap up with dinner at Auerbachs Keller, where sections of Goethe's Faust took place.

The next day, head north to **(2) Lutherstadt Wittenberg**, where protestant reformer Martin Luther lived, preached and published his 95 theses against church corruption. You'll come back to the Luther theme in a bit, but first steer towards **(3) Weimar** to walk in the footsteps of Goethe, Schiller and other thinkers and poets that lived and worked here during the town's 18th-century heyday.

Luther looms large again in **(4) Erfurt**, where the reformer studied philosophy between 1501 and 1505. Finish up in **(5) Eisenach**, on the edge of the Thuringian forest. It's home to another Bach museum, but really most famous for its medieval Wartburg castle, where Luther translated the Greek Bible into German.

Semperoper (p297), Dresden
EIBNER-PRESSEFOTO/DPA/CORBIS ©

Discover Dresden & the East

Zwinger, Dresden
MURAT TANER/GETTY IMAGES ©

DRESDEN

0351 / POP 512,000

There are few city silhouettes more striking than Dresden's. The classic view from the Elbe's northern bank takes in spires, towers and domes belonging to palaces, churches and stately buildings. Dresden's cultural heyday came under the 18th-century reign of Augustus the Strong (August der Starke) and his son Augustus III when the Saxon capital was known as the 'Florence of the north'. Their vision produced many of Dresden's iconic buildings, including the Zwinger and the Frauenkirche. The devastating bombing raids in 1945 levelled most of these treasures. But Dresden is a survivor and many of the most important landmarks have since been rebuilt, including the elegant Frauenkirche. Today, there's a constantly evolving arts and cultural scene and zinging pub and nightlife quarters, especially in the Outer Neustadt.

 Sights

FREE **FRAUENKIRCHE**
Church

(www.frauenkirche-dresden.de; Neumarkt; audioguide €2.50; usually 10am-noon & 1-6pm) The domed Frauenkirche – one of Dresden's most beloved symbols – has literally risen from the city's ashes. The original graced its skyline for two centuries before collapsing two days after the devastating February 1945 bombing. The East Germans left the rubble as a war memorial but after reunification a grassroots movement helped raise funds to rebuild the landmark. It was consecrated in November 2005.

ZWINGER
Museum

(☎ 4914 2000; www.skd.museum; Theaterplatz 1; adult/concession €10/7.50; ⊙10am-6pm Tue-Sun) The sprawling Zwinger is among the most ravishing baroque buildings in all of Germany. A collaboration between the architect Matthäus Pöppelmann and the sculptor Balthasar Permoser, it was primarily a party palace for royals, despite the odd name (which means dungeon). Ornate portals lead into the vast fountain-studded courtyard, which is framed by buildings lavishly festooned with evocative sculpture. Atop the western pavilion stands a tense-looking Atlas. Opposite him is a cutesy carillon of 40 Meissen porcelain bells, which emit a tinkle every 15 minutes.

Inside, the Zwinger's collections have gone through a bit of a roundabout in recent years, with several comings and goings. The most important permanent collection is the **Gemäldegalerie Alte Meister** (Old Masters Gallery), which features a roll call of Old Masters including Botticelli, Titian, Rubens, Vermeer and Dürer. A key work is the 500-year-old *Sistine Madonna* by Raphael.

Admission also gives you access to the **Porzellansammlung** (Porcelain Collection), a dazzling assortment of Meissen classics and East Asian treasures, and the **Mathematisch-Physikalischer Salon**, whose ancient scientific instruments, globes and timepieces should again be on view following massive restoration in early 2013.

ALBERTINUM
Gallery

(www.skd.museum; enter from Brühlsche Terrasse or Georg-Treu-Platz 2; adult/concession €8/6; ⊙10am-6pm; P) After massive renovations following severe 2002 flood damage, the Renaissance-era former arsenal is now the stunning home of the **Galerie Neue Meister** (New Masters Gallery), an ark of paintings by leading artistic lights since the Romantic period – Caspar David Friedrich to Claude Monet and Gerhard Richter – in gorgeous rooms orbiting a light-filled courtyard.

SEMPEROPER
Historic Building

(☎ 320 7360; www.semperoper-erleben.de; Theaterplatz 2; tour adult/concession €8/4; ⊙varies) One of Germany's most famous opera houses, the original Semperoper burned down a mere three decades after its 1841 inauguration. After reopening in 1878, the neo-Renaissance jewel entered its most dazzling period, hosting premieres of works by Richard Strauss, Carl Maria von Weber and Richard Wagner. Alas, WWII put an end to the fun and it wasn't until 1985 that music again filled the grand hall.

MILITÄRHISTORISCHES
MUSEUM DRESDEN
Museum

(☎ 823 2803; www.mhmbw.de; Olbrichtplatz 2; adult/concession €5/3; ⊙10am-6pm Tue-Sun, to 9pm Mon; 🚋7 or 8 to Stauffenbergallee) Even devout pacifists will be awed by this engaging museum that reopened in 2011 in a 19th-century arsenal bisected by a bold glass-and-steel wedge designed by Daniel Libeskind. Standouts among the countless intriguing objects are a 1975 Soyuz landing capsule, a V2 rocket and personal items of concentration camp victims.

FREE PFUNDS
MOLKEREI
Architecture

(☎ 808 080; www.pfunds.de; Bautzner Strasse 79; ⊙10am-6pm Mon-Sat, 10am-3pm Sun) The Guinness Book-certified 'world's most beautiful dairy shop' was founded in 1880 and is a riot of hand-painted tiles and enamelled sculpture, all handmade by Villeroy & Boch.

 Tours

GROSSE
STADTRUNDFAHRT
Bus Tour

(☎ 899 5650; www.stadtrundfahrt.com; day pass adult/concession €20/18; ⊙9.30am-5pm) This narrated hop-on, hop-off tour has 22 stops in the centre and the elegant outer villa districts along the Elbe. It includes short walking tours of the Zwinger, Fürstenzug, Frauenkirche and Pfunds Molkerei.

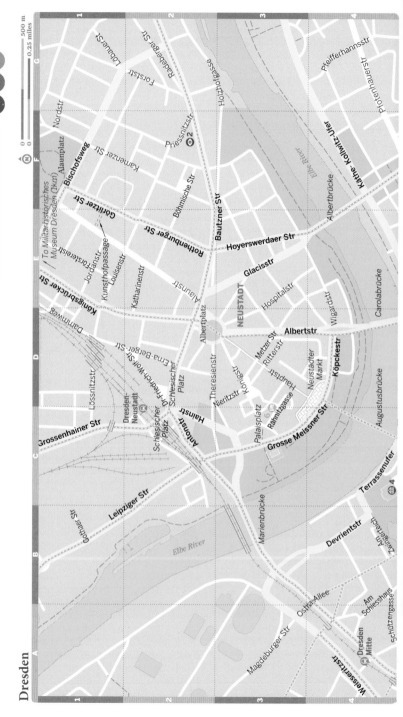

Dresden

DRESDEN & THE EAST DRESDEN

500 m
0.25 miles

Elbe River

NEUSTADT

To Militär-historisches
Museum Dresden (2km)

Lobauer Str
Radeberger Str
Forststr
Nordstr
Alaunplatz
Bischofsweg
Görlitzer Str
Kamenzer Str
Priessnitzstr
Böhmische Str
Bautzner Str
Käthe-Kollwitz-Ufer
Pfeifferhannsstr
Prießnitzstr
Holzhofgasse
Protenhauerstr
Albertbrücke

Rothenburger Str
Hoyerswerdaer Str
Glacisstr
Hospitalstr
Wigardstr
Carolabrücke

Königsbrücker Str
Förstereistr
Jordanstr
Kunsthofpassage
Louisenstr
Katharinenstr
Alaunstr
Albertplatz
Albertstr
Metzer Str
Ritterstr
Köpckestr

Dammweg
Lössnitzstr
Erna-Berger-Str
Friedrich-Wolf-Str
Schlesischer Platz
Theresienstr
Nieritzstr
Königstr
Hauptstr
Neustädter Markt
Augustusbrücke

Grossenhainer Str
Dresden
Neustadt
Schlesischer Platz
Antonstr
Hainstr
Palaisplatz
Rähnitzgasse
Grosse Meissner Str

Gothaer Str
Leipziger Str
Marienbrücke
Terrassenufer
Devrientstr
Altpieschen

Magdeburger Str
Ostra-Allee
Am Schiesshaus
Schützengasse
Dresden Mitte
Weisseritzstr

Elbe River

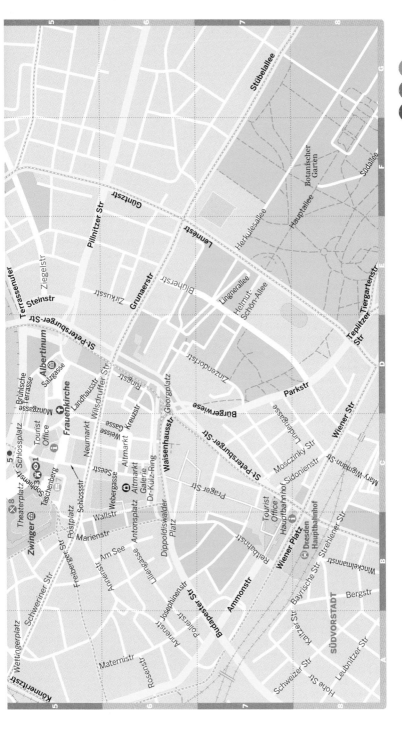

Stübelallee

Botanischer Garten

Hauptallee

Südallee

Herkulesallee

Lingnerallee

Helmut Schön-Allee

Güntzstr

Lennéstr

Pillnitzer Str

Ziegelstr

Zirkusstr

Grunaerstr

Blüherstr

Zinzendorfstr

Teplitzer Str

Tiergartenstr

Terrassenufer

Steinstr

St-Petersburger-Str

Albertinum

Brühlsche Terrasse

Salzgasse

Münzgasse

Frauenkirche

Landhausstr

Wildsruffer Str

Ringstr

Georgplatz

Parkstr

Wiener Str

Neumarkt

Weisse Gasse

Kreuzstr

Waisenhausstr

Bürgerwiese

St-Petersburger-Str

Lindengasse

Mosczinsky Str

Mary-Wiegmann-Str

Tourist Office

Schlossplatz

Theaterplatz

Sophienstr

Taschenberg

Zwinger

Seestr

Webergasse

Altmarkt

Galerie

Dr-Külz-Ring

Prager Str

Sidonienstr

Tourist Office

Hauptbahnhof

Wiener Platz

Dresden Hauptbahnhof

Postplatz

Wallstr

Antonsplatz

Reitbahnstr

Strehlener Str

Winckelmannstr

Marienstr

Dippoldiswalder Platz

Am See

Annenstr

Liliengasse

Josephinenstr

Pollastr

Budapester Str

Ammonstr

Bayrische Str

Kaitzer Str

SÜDVORSTADT

Bergstr

Hohe Str

Schweizer Str

Leubnitzer Str

Wettiner platz

Schweriner Str

Freiberger Str

Maternistr

Rosenstr

Könneritzstr

Dresden

Sleeping & Eating

HOTEL BÜLOW RESIDENZ   Hotel €€
(📞800 3291; www.buelow-residenz.de; Rähnitzgasse 19; d from €120, breakfast €18; P❄🛜)
This place occupies one of Dresden's oldest town houses and is a class act, from the
welcome drink to the spacious gold-and-
crimson-hued rooms baronially cloaked in
antiques, paintings and porcelain.

**HOTEL TASCHENBERGPALAIS
KEMPINSKI**   Hotel €€€
(📞491 20; www.kempinski-dresden.de; Taschenberg 3; r €170-230; ❄@🛜🏊) Checking in
here buys views over the Zwinger from
rakishly handsome rooms that beautifully
bridge the traditional and the contemporary with rich royal blue colour accents and
marble bathrooms with Bulgari toiletries.

CAFE ALTE MEISTER   International €€
(📞481 0426; www.altemeister.net; Theaterplatz
1a; mains €7-15; ⏱10am-1am) If you've worked
up an appetite from museum-hopping or
need a break from culture overload, retreat to this elegant filling station between
the Zwinger and the Semperoper for a
smoked-trout sandwich, light salad, lus-
cious cake or energy-restoring steak.

SOPHIENKELLER   Saxon €€
(📞497 260; www.sophienkeller-dresden.de;
Taschenberg 3; mains €7-14; ⏱11am-1am) The
1730s theme with waitstaff donned out
in period garb may be a bit overcooked
but the local specialities certainly aren't.
Great ambience amid vaulted ceilings in
the Taschenbergpalais building.

ℹ Information

Tourist office Frauenkirche (📞5016 0160;
www.dresden-tourist.de; Schlossstrasse 23;
⏱10am-7pm Mon-Fri, 10am-6pm Sat, 10am-3pm
Sun, reduced hours Jan-Mar)

Tourist office Hauptbahnhof (📞5016 0160; www
.dresden-tourist.de; Hauptbahnhof; ⏱9am-7pm)

ℹ Getting There & Away

Air

Dresden International (DRS; 📞881 3360; www
.dresden-airport.de) has flights to many German
cities and such destinations as Moscow, Vienna
and Zurich.

Train

Fast trains make the trip to Dresden from Berlin-
Hauptbahnhof in two hours (€38) and Leipzig
in 1¼ hours (€30). The S1 local train runs half-
hourly to Meissen (€5.60, 40 minutes).

Meissen
📞03521 / POP 29,000

Straddling the Elbe around 25km
upstream from Dresden, Meissen is the
cradle of European porcelain manufacturing and still hitches its tourism appeal
to the world-famous china first cooked
up in its imposing 1710 castle. Adjacent to
the soaring Gothic cathedral, it crowns a
ridge above the Altstadt whose meandering cobbled lanes offer an escape from
the porcelain pilgrims rolling in by tour
bus.

MATTHIAS HIEKEL/DPA/CORBIS ©

Don't Miss Residenzschloss

Dresden's fortress-like Renaissance city palace was home to the Saxon rulers from 1485 to 1918 and now shelters four precious collections, including the unmissable **Grünes Gewölbe** (Green Vault), a real-life 'Aladdin's Cave' spilling over with precious objects wrought from gold, ivory, silver, diamonds and jewels. There's so much of it, two separate 'treasure chambers' – the Historisches Grünes Gewölbe and the Neues Grünes Gewölbe – are needed to display everything.

Another important collection is the **Kupferstich-Kabinett**, which counts around half a million prints and drawings by 20,000 artists (including Dürer, Rembrandt and Michelangelo) in its possession.

In 2013, the historic weapons and armour of the **Rüstkammer** (armoury) normally displayed in the Zwinger will also move into the Residenzschloss. Here, they will join the exotic **Türckische Cammer** (Turkish Chamber), one of the richest collections of Ottoman art outside Turkey.

NEED TO KNOW
☏ 4914 2000; www.skd.museum; Schlossplatz; adult/concession €10/7.50; ⊙10am-6pm Wed-Mon

---

 Sights

**ERLEBNISWELT HAUS
MEISSEN** Museum
(☏ 468 208; www.meissen.com; Talstrasse 9; adult/child €9/4.50; ⊙9am-6pm May-Oct, 9am-5pm Nov-Apr) There's no 'quiet time' to arrive at the popular and unmissable porcelain museum where you can witness the astonishing artistry and craftsmanship that makes Meissen porcelain unique. Visits start with a 30-minute tour (with English audioguide) of the **Schauwerkstätten**, a series of four studios where you can observe live demonstrations of vase throwing, plate painting, figure moulding and the glazing process.

ALBRECHTSBURG — Castle, Museum

(☏470 70; www.albrechtsburg-meissen.de; Domplatz 1; adult/concession incl audioguide €8/4; ⏲10am-6pm Mar-Oct, 10am-5pm Nov-Feb) Lording it over Meissen, the 15th-century Albrechtsburg was the first German castle constructed for residential purposes but is more famous as the birthplace of European porcelain. Production began in the castle in 1710 and only moved to a custom-built factory in 1863. An exhibit on the second floor chronicles how it all began.

DOM — Church

(☏452 490; www.dom-zu-meissen.de; Domplatz 7; adult/concession €3.50/2.50; ⏲9am-6pm Sun-Fri, to 5pm Sat Apr-Oct, 10am-4pm Nov-Mar) Meissen's dome, a high-Gothic masterpiece begun in 1250, does not impress as much by its size as by the wealth of its interior decorations. Stained-glass windows showing scenes from the Old and New Testaments create an ethereal backdrop for the delicately carved statues in the choir, presumed to be the work of the famous Master of Naumburg.

❶ Information

Tourist office (☏419 40; www.touristinfo-meissen.de; Markt 3; ⏲10am-6pm Mon-Fri, 10am-4pm Sat & Sun Apr-Oct, 10am-5pm Mon-Fri, 10am-3pm Sat Nov, Dec, Feb & Mar)

❶ Getting There & Around

Boat

Steam boats operated by Sächsische Dampfschiffahrt (☏0331-452 139; www.saechsische-dampfschiffahrt.de; one-way/return €14/19.50; ⏲May-Sep) depart from the Terrassenufer in Dresden. Boats return upstream to Dresden at 2.45pm but take over three hours to make the trip. Many people opt to go one way by boat and the other by train.

Train

From Dresden, take the half-hourly S1 (€5.80, 40 minutes) to Meissen. For the porcelain factory, get off at Meissen-Triebischtal.

Leipzig

☏0341 / POP 532,000

Culture has been big in Leipzig for centuries. After all, Bach's one-time backyard was also where Wagner was born and Mendelssohn-Bartholdy ran a music academy. To this day, one of the world's top classical bands (the Gewandhausorchester) and oldest and finest boys choirs (the 800-year-old Thomanerchor) continue to delight audiences. Leipzig became known as the *Stadt der Helden* (City of Heroes) for its leading role in the 1989 'Peaceful Revolution'. Its residents organised protests against the communist regime in May of that year; by October, hundreds of thousands were taking to the streets and a few years later, the Cold War was history.

Sights

FREE STASI MUSEUM — Museum

(☏961 2443; www.runde-ecke-leipzig.de; Dittrichring 24; ⏲10am-6pm) In the GDR the walls had ears, as is chillingly documented in this exhibit in the former Leipzig headquarters of the East German secret police (the Stasi), a building known as the Runde Ecke (Round Corner). English-language audioguides aid in understanding the all-German displays on propaganda, preposterous disguises, cunning surveillance devices, recruitment (even among children), scent storage and other chilling machinations that reveal the GDR's all-out zeal when it came to controlling, manipulating and repressing its own people.

BACH-MUSEUM LEIPZIG — Museum

(☏913 7202; www.bach-leipzig.de; Thomaskirchhof 16; adult/concession €6/4, under 16 free; ⏲10am-6pm Tue-Sun) Completely updated, this interactive museum does more than tell you about the life and accomplishments of heavyweight musician Johann Sebastian Bach. Learn how to date a Bach manuscript, listen to baroque instruments or treat your ears to any composition he ever wrote.

Leipzig

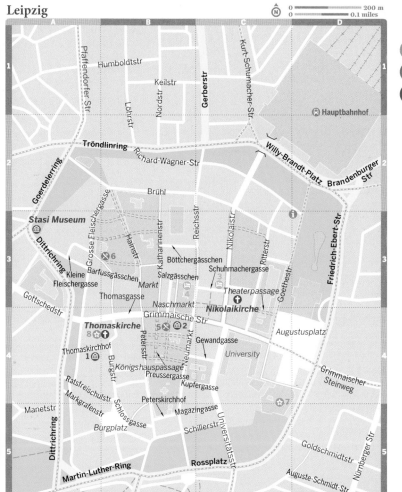

Leipzig

IMAGEBROKER/ALAMY ©

Don't Miss Nikolaikirche

Leipzig's Church of St Nicholas has Romanesque and Gothic roots but since 1797 has sported a striking neoclassical interior with palm-like pillars and cream-coloured pews. The church played a key role in the nonviolent movement that led to the downfall of the East German government. As early as 1982 it hosted 'peace prayers' every Monday at 5pm (still held today), which over time inspired and empowered local citizens to confront the injustices plaguing their country.

NEED TO KNOW
Church of St Nicholas; www.nikolaikirche-leipzig.de; Nikolaikirchhof 3; ⊙10am-6pm Mon-Sat & during services 9.30am, 11.15am & 5pm Sun

---

FREE **ZEITGESCHICHTLICHES FORUM** Museum
(Forum of Contemporary History; ☎222 00; www.hdg.de/leipzig; Grimmaische Strasse 6; ⊙9am-6pm Tue-Fri, 10am-6pm Sat & Sun) This fascinating exhibit tells the political history of the GDR from division and dictatorship to fall-of-the-Wall ecstasy and post-*Wende* blues.

FREE **THOMASKIRCHE** Church
(☎222 240; www.thomaskirche.org; Thomaskirch-hof 18; tower €2; ⊙church 9am-6pm, tower 1pm, 2pm & 4.30pm Sat, 2pm & 3pm Sun) The

composer Johann Sebastian Bach worked in the Thomaskirche as a cantor from 1723 until his death in 1750, and his remains lie buried beneath a bronze plate in front of the altar. The Thomanerchor (boys choir), once led by Bach, has been going strong since 1212 and now includes 100 boys aged eight to 18. You can climb the church tower.

 Tours

LEIPZIG ERLEBEN Walking, Bus
(☎71 04 230; www.leipzig-erleben.com; adult/concession €15/13) Runs two daily 2½-hour

combination walking/bus tours in German and English departing from the tourist office. If booked separately, the walking tour is €5, the bus tour €10.

 ## Sleeping & Eating

STEIGENBERGER GRANDHOTEL
HANDELSHOF Hotel €€€
(📞 350 5810; www.steigenberger.com/Leipzig; Salzgässchen 6; r from €160; ❄ @ 📶) Behind the imposing historic facade of a 1909 municipal trading hall, this luxe lodge outclasses most of Leipzig's hotels with its super-central location, charmingly efficient team and modern rooms dressed in crisp white-silver-purple colours. The stylish bi-level spa is the perfect bliss-out station.

MOTEL ONE Hotel €
(📞 337 4370; www.motel-one.de; Nikolaistrasse 23; d from €69, breakfast €7.50; P ❄ 📶) The Leipzig outpost of this fast-growing budget designer chain has a five-star location opposite the Nikolaikirche and also gets most other things right, from the Zeitgeist-capturing lobby-lounge to the snug but smartly designed rooms. No surprise it's often booked out.

AUERBACHS KELLER German €€€
(📞 216 100; www.auerbachs-keller-leipzig.de; Mädlerpassage; mains €14-22) Founded in 1525, Auerbachs Keller is one of Germany's best-known restaurants. It's cosy and touristy but the food's actually quite good and the setting memorable. In Goethe's *Faust - Part I,* Mephistopheles and Faust carouse here with students before riding off on a barrel. The scene is depicted on a carved tree trunk in what is now the Goethezimmer (Goethe Room), where the great writer allegedly came for 'inspiration'.

ZUM ARABISCHEN
COFFE BAUM Cafe, German €€
(📞 961 0060; www.coffe-baum.de; Kleine Fleischergasse 4; mains €8-16; ⏰ 11am-midnight) One of Europe's oldest coffee-houses, this rambling outpost has hosted poets, politicians, professors and everyone else since 1720. The warren of rooms, spread over several floors, is an atmospheric spot

to try a Leipziger Lerche (lark), a locally famous marzipan-filled shortcrust pastry. Other cakes, light meals and alcohol are also served. The small, free 'museum' has over 500 coffee-related objects.

 ## Entertainment

GEWANDHAUSORCHESTER
Classical Music
(📞 127 0280; www.gewandhaus.de; Augustusplatz 8; tours €4.50; ⏰ tours usually 12.30pm Thu) Led by Ricardo Chailly since 2005, the Gewandhaus is one of Europe's finest and oldest civic orchestras. Aside from giving concerts in the Neues Gewandhaus, it also performs with the Thomaner Boys' Choir in the Thomaskirche and with the Oper Leipzig.

THOMANERCHOR Classical Music
(📞 984 4211; www.thomaskirche.org; Thomaskirchhof 18; tickets €2) This famous boys' choir performs Bach motets and cantatas at 6pm on Friday and 3pm on Saturday and also sings during Sunday services at 9.30am and 6pm at the Thomaskirche. Performances are usually filled to capacity, so try to be there when doors open 45 minutes before concerts begin.

ℹ Information

Tourist office (📞 710 4255 room referral, 710 4260; www.ltm-leipzig.de; Katharinenstrasse 8; ⏰ 9.30am-6pm Mon-Fri, to 4pm Sat, to 3pm Sun, from 10am Nov-Mar)

ℹ Getting There & Away

Deutsche Bahn has frequent services to Frankfurt (€75, 3¾ hours), Dresden (€26, 1¼ hours) and Berlin (€45, 1¼ hours). Private Interconnex trains also go to Berlin twice daily (€19, 1¼ hours).

Lutherstadt Wittenberg
📞 03491 / POP 49,500

As its full name suggests, Wittenberg is first and foremost about Martin Luther (1483–1546), the monk who triggered the German Reformation by publishing his 95 theses against church corruption in 1517.

If You Like...
Peeking Behind the Iron Curtain

Not far from Dresden, in Radebeul and Pirna, two museums offer a fascinating glimpse into an extinct society. We're talking the GDR, the 'other' Germany that ceased to exist with reunification in 1990. Bafflingly eclectic collections of socialist-era flotsam and jetsam – including flags and posters, typewriters and radios, uniforms and furniture, dolls and detergents – have been assembled in these two privately managed 'time capsules'.

1 DDR MUSEUM PIRNA
(☏03501-774 842; www.ddr-museum-pirna.de; Rottwerndorferstrasse 45; adult/concession €5/4; ⏱10am-6pm Tue-Sun Apr-Oct, 10am-5pm Tue-Thu, Sat & Sun Nov-Mar) At the DDR Museum Pirna, in a former army barracks, you can snoop around a fully furnished apartment, sit in a classroom with GDR president Walter Ulbricht glowering at you, or find out how much a Junge Pioniere youth organisation uniform cost.

2 ZEITREISE DDR MUSEUM RADEBEUL
(☏0351-835 1780; www.ddr-museum-dresden.de; Wasastrasse 50; adult/concession €7.50/6; ⏱10am-6pm Tue-Sun) The Zeitreise DDR Museum Radebeul is large and well organised. Each of the four floors is dedicated to a particular theme, such as work, daily life and state institutions. This is rounded off by a fabulous collection of Trabi cars, Simson motorbikes and other vehicles. A timeline charts milestones in Cold War history and there's a restaurant serving GDR-era cuisine. The Zeitreise Museum is reached by taking tram 4 to Wasastrasse, eg from the Antonstrasse/Leipziger Strasse stop in Dresden-Neustadt (€3.80, 20 minutes).

Sometimes called the 'Rome of the Protestants', its many Reformation-related sites garnered it the World Heritage Site nod from Unesco in 1996.

◉ Sights

LUTHERHAUS Museum
(www.martinluther.de; Collegienstrasse 54; adult/concession €5/3; ⏱9am-6pm) Even those with no previous interest in the Reformation will likely be fascinated by the state-of-the-art exhibits in the Lutherhaus, the former monastery turned Luther family home. Through an engaging mix of accessible narrative (in German and English), spotlit artefacts (eg his lectern from the Stadtkirche, indulgences chests, Bibles, cloaks), famous oil paintings and interactive multimedia stations, you'll learn about the man, his times and his impact on world history.

FREE SCHLOSSKIRCHE Church
(Castle Church; Schlossplatz; ⏱10am-6pm Mon-Sat, 11.30am-6pm Sun) Did or didn't he nail those 95 theses to the door of the Schlosskirche? We'll never know for sure, for the original portal was destroyed by fire in 1760 and replaced in 1858 with a massive bronze version inscribed with the theses in Latin. Luther himself is buried inside below the pulpit, opposite his friend and fellow reformer Philipp Melanchthon.

FREE STADTKIRCHE ST MARIEN Church
(Jüdenstrasse 35; ⏱10am-6pm Mon-Sat, 11.30am-6pm Sun) This church was where Martin Luther's ecumenical revolution began, with the world's first Protestant worship services in 1521. The centrepiece is the large altar, designed jointly by Lucas Cranach the Elder and his son.

Sleeping & Eating

ALTE CANZLEY Hotel €€
(☏429 190; www.alte-canzley.de; Schlossplatz 3-5; s €70-125, d €85-139; P @ �?) The nicest place in town is in a 14th-century building opposite the Schlosskirche. Each of the eight spacious units are furnished in dark woods and natural hues, named for a

JULIE G WOODHOUSE/ALAMY ©

major historical figure and equipped with a kitchenette. The vaulted downstairs harbours Saxony-Anhalt's first certified organic restaurant (dishes €7 to €24).

IN VINO VERITAS
German, Mediterannean €€
(Mittelstrasse 3; dishes €6.90-18.50, antipasti €2.50-9; ☻dinner) Antipasti, tapas, salads or pasta dishes form the perfect accompaniment to the global wine menu at this upmarket modern bistro.

ⓘ Information

Tourist office (☎498 610; www.wittenberg.de; Schlossplatz 2; ☻9am-6pm Mon-Fri, 10am-4pm Sat & Sun)

ⓘ Getting There & Away

Wittenberg is on the main line to Halle and Leipzig (both €12.20, one hour). ICE (€30, 45 minutes) and RE trains (€21.50, 1¼ hours) travel to Berlin.

Dessau-Rosslau
☎0340 / POP 86,900

For Bauhaus junkies, Dessau represents the mother lode. Nowhere else in the world will you find a greater concentration of original 1920s Bauhaus structures than in this city on the Elbe River. Dessau was the home of the most influential design school of the 20th century during its most creative period from 1925 to 1932.

Sights

FREE BAUHAUSGEBÄUDE
Architecture
(Bauhaus Bldg; www.bauhaus-dessau.de; Gropius-allee 38; exhibition adult/concession €6/4, tours €4/3; ☻10am-6pm, tours 11am & 2pm daily, also noon & 4pm Sat & Sun) It's almost impossible to overstate the significance of the building, erected in 1925–26 as a school of Bauhaus art, design and architecture. Two key pioneers of modern architecture, Walter Gropius and Ludwig Mies van der Rohe, served as the school's directors. It was revolutionary, bringing industrial construction techniques such as curtain walling and wide spans into the public domain and presaging untold buildings worldwide.

MEISTERHÄUSER
Architecture
(Masters' Houses; www.meisterhaeuser.de; Ebertallee 63, 65-67 & 69-71, Masters' Houses; admission to all 3 houses adult/concession €7.50/5.50,

CARO/ALAMY ©

tours €11.50/8.50; ◷11am-6pm Tue-Sun, tours 12.30pm & 3.30pm daily, also 1.30pm Sat & Sun) The leading lights of the Bauhaus movement lived together as neighbours in these white cubist structures that exemplify the Bauhaus aim of 'design for living' in a modern industrial world.

Haus Feininger, former home of Lyonel Feininger, now pays homage to Dessau-born Kurt Weill, who later became playwright Bertolt Brecht's musical collaborator in Berlin, and composed *The Threepenny Opera* and its hit 'Mack the Knife', later immortalised by a rasping Louis Armstrong.

Haus Muche/Schlemmer (☎882 2138; Ebertallee 65/67), at No 65-67, it becomes poignant how the room proportions used and experiments, such as low balcony rails, don't really cut it in the modern world.

Haus Kandinsky/Klee (☎661 0934; Ebertallee 69/71) at No 69-71 is most notable for the varying pastel shades in which Wassily Kandinsky and Paul Klee painted their walls (recreated today).

❶ Information

Bauhaus Stiftung (Bauhaus Foundation; ☎650 8250; www.bauhaus-dessau.de; Gropiusallee 38;

◷10am-6pm) For info on, and tours of, Bauhaus buildings (also in English).

Tourist office (☎204 1442, accommodation 220 3003; www.dessau-rosslau-tourismus.de; Zerbster Strasse 2c; ◷10am-6pm Mon-Fri, to 1pm Sat)

❶ Getting There & Away

For Berlin (€36, 1½ hours), change in Lutherstadt Wittenberg (€7.50, 30 minutes). Direct regional services go to Leipzig (€11.10, 45 minutes), Halle (€11.10, 55 minutes) and Magdeburg (€11.10, 50 minutes).

Weimar

☎03643 / POP 65,500

Neither a monumental town nor a medieval one, Weimar appeals to those whose tastes run to cultural and intellectual pleasures. After all, this is the epicentre of the German Enlightenment, a symbol for all that is good and great in German culture. An entire pantheon of intellectual and creative giants lived and worked here: Goethe, Schiller, Bach, Cranach, Liszt, Nietzsche, Gropius, Herder, Feininger, Kandinsky, Klee...the list goes on (and on, and on).

Sights

GOETHE
NATIONALMUSEUM
Museum

(Frauenplan 1; combined ticket Goethe Haus & permanent museum exhibition adult/concession €10.50/8.50, permanent museum exhibition only adult/concession €6.50/5.50; 🕑9am-6pm Tue-Fri & Sun, to 7pm Sat) No other individual is as closely associated with Weimar as Johann Wolfgang von Goethe, who lived in this town from 1775 until his death in 1832, the last 50 years in what is now the **Goethe Haus** (📞545 401; Frauenplan 1; adult/concession €8.50/7; 🕑9am-6pm Tue-Fri & Sun, to 7pm Sat Apr-Sep, 9am-6pm Tue-Sun Oct, to 4pm Tue-Sun Nov-Mar). This is where he worked, studied, researched and penned Faust and other immortal works.

SCHILLER HAUS
Museum

(Schillerstrasse 12; adult/concession €5/4; 🕑9am-6pm Tue-Fri & Sun, to 7pm Sat) The dramatist Friedrich Schiller lived in Weimar from 1799 until his early death in 1805. Study up on the man, his family and life in Thuringia in a new permanent exhibit before plunging on to the private quarters, including the study with his deathbed and the desk where he wrote Wilhelm Tell and other famous works.

PARK AN DER ILM
Park

The sprawling Park an der Ilm, just east of the Altstadt, is as inspiring and romantic now as it was in Goethe's time. As well as providing a bucolic backdrop to the city, the park is home to several historic houses that can be visited separately. The highlights are **Goethes Gartenhaus** (Goethe's Garden House; adult/concession €4.50/3.50; 🕑10am-6pm Wed-Mon), where the writer lived from 1776 to 1782); **Römisches Haus** (Roman House; adult/concession €3.50/3; 🕑10am-6pm Wed-Mon), built under Goethe's supervision as the duke Carl August's summer retreat, with period rooms and an exhibit on the park; and the **Liszt-Haus** (Marienstrasse 17, Liszt House; adult/concession €4/3; 🕑10am-6pm Tue-Sun Apr-Sep, to 4pm Sat & Sun Oct-Mar), where the composer resided in 1848 and again from 1869 to 1886, and wrote the Faust Symphony. The park was created between 1778 and 1828.

Sleeping & Eating

HOTEL AMALIENHOF
Hotel €€

(📞5490; www.amalienhof-weimar.de; Amalienstrasse 2; s €67-75, d €97-105, ste €115-130; P 🛜) The charms of this hotel are manifold: classy antique furnishings, richly styled rooms that point to history without burying you in it, and a late breakfast buffet for those who take their holidays seriously. It's a splendid choice.

CASA DEI COLORI
Pension €€

(📞489 640; www.casa-colori.de; Eisfeld 1a; r €84-114; P 🛜) Possibly Weimar's most charming boutique Pension, the Casa

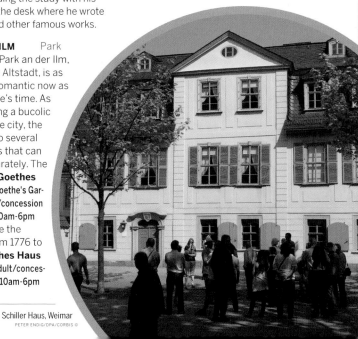

Schiller Haus, Weimar
PETER ENDIG/DPA/CORBIS ©

convincingly imports cheerfully exuberant Mediterranean flair to central Europe. The mostly good-sized rooms are dressed in bold colours and come with a small desk, a couple of comfy armchairs and a stylish bathroom.

GASTHAUS ZUM WEISSEN SCHWAN
German €€

(Frauentorstrasse 23; mains €11-22; ◷lunch & dinner Tue-Sat) At this venerable inn, you can fill your tummy with Goethe's favourite dish, which actually hails from his home town of Frankfurt (boiled beef with herb sauce, red beet salad and potatoes). The rest of the menu, though, is midrange Thuringian.

JO HANNS
German €€

(☎493 617; Scherfgasse 1; mains €11.50-17.50; ◷11am-midnight) The food is satisfying but it's the 130 wines from the Saale-Unstrut Region – many served by the glass – that give Jo Hanns a leg up on the competition. No matter whether you order the classic steak, or scallops and shrimp with mint-lime spaghetti, there's a bottle to suit.

❶ Information

Tourist office The central (☎7450; www.weimar.de; Markt 10, centre; ◷9.30am-7pm Mon-Sat, 3pm Sun) and Friedenstrasse (☎7450; Friedensstrasse 1; ◷10am-6pm Mon-Sat) tourist offices sell the WeimarCard (€14.50 for 48 hours) for free or discounted museum admissions and travel on city buses and other benefits.

❶ Getting There & Away

Direct IC trains run to Leipzig (€22, 1¼ hours, every two hours) and Dresden (€43, 2½ hours). There are a few direct services to Berlin (€54, 2¼ hours) but most require a change in Naumburg. Frequent regional and IC trains go to Erfurt (€8, 15 minutes) and Eisenach (€18, 45 minutes).

Buchenwald

The Buchenwald concentration camp **museum and memorial** (☎03643-4300; www.buchenwald.de; Ettersberg; ◷buildings & exhibits 10am-6pm Tue-Sun Apr-Oct, to 4pm Tue-Sun Nov-Mar, grounds open until sunset) are 10km northwest of Weimar. You first pass the memorial erected above the mass graves of some of the 56,500 victims from 18 nations that died here – including Jews, German antifascists, and Soviet and Polish prisoners of war. After the war, the Soviet victors established Special Camp No 2, in which 7000 so-called anticommunists and ex-Nazis were literally worked to death.

To get here, take bus 6 (direction Buchenwald) from Goetheplatz in Weimar. By car, head north on Ettersburger Strasse from Weimar train station and turn left onto Blutstrasse.

Buchenwald
DAVID PEEVERS/GETTY IMAGES ©

Erfurt

☎ 0361 / POP 205,000

Erfurt is a scene-stealing combo of sweeping squares, time-worn alleyways, perky church towers, idyllic river scenery, and vintage inns and taverns. In 1392 rich merchants founded the university, allowing students to study common law, rather than religious law. Its most famous graduate was Martin Luther, who studied philosophy here before becoming a monk at the local Augustinian monastery in 1505.

 Sights

MARIENDOM
Church

(St Mary's Cathedral; Domplatz; ⊙9am-6pm Mon-Sat, 1-6pm Sun) The Dom began life as a simple chapel founded in 742 by St Boniface, but the Gothic pile you see today has the hallmarks of the 14th century. Look for the superb stained-glass windows (1370–1420) featuring biblical scenes; the Wolfram (1160), a bronze candelabrum in the shape of a man; the Gloriosa bell (1497); a Romanesque stucco Madonna; and the 14th-century choir stalls.

SEVERIKIRCHE
Church

(Domplatz; ⊙9am-6pm Mon-Sat, 1-6pm Sun) The Severikirche, together with Erfurt's Dom forming the ensemble on Domplatz, is a five-aisled hall church (1280) with prized treasures that include a stone Madonna (1345), a 15m-high baptismal font (1467) and the sarcophagus of St Severus.

AUGUSTINERKLOSTER
Church

(Augustinian Monastery; Augustinerstrasse 10, enter on Comthurgasse; tours adult/concession €6/4; ⊙tours hourly 10am-noon & 2-5pm Mon-Sat, 11am & noon Sun) It's Luther lore galore at the Augustinerkloster. This is where the reformer lived from 1505 to 1511, and where he was ordained as a monk and read his first mass. Guided tours get you inside the monastery itself, including the cloister, a recreated Luther cell and an exhibit on the history of the Bible and Luther's life in Erfurt.

KRÄMERBRÜCKE
Bridge

Even if it could not claim to be the only bridge north of the Alps that's lined with houses on both sides, the medieval Merchant Bridge would still be a most charming spot. You can watch chocolate makers, potters, jewellers and other artisans at work in their teensy studios or enjoy a coffee or glass of wine in a cafe.

 Sleeping & Eating

HOTEL AM KAISERSAAL
Hotel €€

(☎658 560; www.bachmann-hotels.de; Futterstrasse 8; s/d €89/104; P �) Rooms are tip-top and appointed with all expected mod cons in this highly rated hotel. Request a room facing the yard, though, if street noise disturbs. Prices can be higher or lower according to day and demand. Take tram 1 or 5 to Futterstrasse.

OPERA HOSTEL
Hostel €

(☎6013 1360; www.opera-hostel.de; Walkmühlstrasse 13; dm €13-18, s/d/tr without bathroom €37/48/66, with bathroom €45/54/75, linen €2.50; @ �) Run with smiles and aplomb, this upmarket hostel in a historic building scores big with wallet-watching global nomads. Rooms are bright and spacious, many with an extra sofa for chilling, and you can make friends in the communal kitchen and on-site lounge-bar. Take bus 51 from Hauptbahnhof to Alte Oper.

ALBOTH'S
German €€€

(☎568 8207; www.alboths.de; Futterstrasse 15-16; 5-/7-course menu €67/87; ⊙dinner Tue-Sat, closed most of Feb & Aug) Alboth's rates consistently among the top restaurants in Thuringia. The choice of dishes is limited to a couple of menus, but you can order any main dish for €27, or any other course for €11. One menu has local specialities.

STEINHAUS
German €

(Allerheiligenstrasse 20-21; mains €4-8; ⊙from 11am-late, food till midnight) The ceiling beams may be ancient, but the crowd is intergenerational at this rambling gastro-pub-cum-beer-garden in the historic Engelsburg. Dips, baguettes, pasta and

Domplatz, Erfurt (p311)

MARTIN MOOS/GETTY IMAGES ©

gratins should keep your tummy filled and your brain balanced.

ℹ️ Information

Tourist office (www.erfurt-tourismus.de) The Benediktsplatz (📞664 00; Benediktsplatz 1; 🕐10am-7pm Mon-Fri, to 6pm Sat, to 4pm Sun) and Petersberg (📞601 5384; 🕐11am-6.30pm mid-Apr–Oct, to 4pm Nov & Dec, closed Jan–mid-Apr) branches of the tourist office sell the ErfurtCard (€12.90 per 48 hours), which includes a city tour, public transport and free or discounted admissions.

ℹ️ Getting There & Away

Car

Erfurt is just north of the A4 and is crossed by the B4 (Hamburg to Bamberg) and B7 (Kassel to Gera).

Train

Frequent IC/ICE connections with Berlin (€60, 2½ hours, change in Leipzig) and direct ICE connections with Dresden (€51, 2½ hours) and Frankfurt am Main (€54, 2¼ hours). Regional trains to Weimar (€5, 15 minutes) and Eisenach (€11.10, 45 minutes) run at least once hourly.

Eisenach

📞03691 / POP 42,750

Eisenach is a small town on the edge of the Thuringian forest whose modest appearance belies its association with two German heavyweights: Johann Sebastian Bach and Martin Luther.

◎ Sights

WARTBURG Castle
(www.wartburg-eisenach.de; tour adult/concession €9/5, museum & Luther study only €5/4; 🕐tours 8.30am-5pm, in English 1.30pm) This medieval castle is where Martin Luther went into hiding in 1521 under the assumed name of Junker Jörg after being excommunicated and placed under papal ban. During his 10-month stay, he translated the New Testament from Greek into German, contributing enormously to the development of the written German language.

BACHHAUS Museum
(www.bachhaus.de; Frauenplan 21; adult/concession €7.50/4; 🕐10am-6pm) Johann Sebastian Bach, who was born in

Eisenach in 1685, takes the spotlight in the revamped and enlarged Bachhaus, one of the best biographical museums in Germany. Exhibits are set up in the type of wattle-and-daub town house where the Bach family lived (the original was destroyed) and trace both his professional and private life through concise, intelligent and engaging bilingual panelling.

LUTHERHAUS Historic Building
(www.lutherhaus-eisenach.de; Lutherplatz 8; adult/concession €4.50/2.50; ⊙10am-5pm)
Displays in the house where the religious reformer Martin Luther lived when he was a schoolboy.

 ## Sleeping

HOTEL VILLA ANNA Boutique Hotel €€
(☏239 50; www.hotel-villa-anna.de; Fritz-Koch-Strasse 12; s €76, d €99-119; P⊙) This boutique hotel at the foot of the Wartburg has modern, good-sized rooms outfitted with ultracomfy beds and a big desk. Take bus 3, 10 or 11 to Prinzenteich.

HOTEL AUF DER WARTBURG Hotel €€€
(☏7970; http://wartburghotel.arcona.de; Auf der Wartburg; s €140-180, d €235-355; P) This hotel has subdued colours and furnishings to match the location on the historic Wartburg. For serious opulence, book one in the 'Prince' category.

 # Eating

TURMSCHÄNKE German €€
(☏213 533; Karlsplatz 28; mains €19-24, 3-/4-course menu €32/38; ⊙dinner Mon-Sat)
This hushed hideaway in Eisenach's only surviving medieval city gate scores a perfect 10 on the 'romance meter'. Ulrich Rösch's flavour-packed concoctions teeter between trendy and traditional.

ZUCKER + ZIMT Organic €
(Markt 2; dishes €2.90-9.90; ⊙10am-8pm) This upbeat cafe, dressed in mod apple-green, fully embraces the 'bio' trend. Organic and fair-trade ingredients find their destination in light creative mains, bagel sandwiches, stuffed crêpes and homemade cakes.

ⓘ Information

Tourist office (☏792 30; www.eisenach.de; Markt 24; ⊙10am-6pm Mon-Fri, to 5pm Sat & Sun) Staff sell the Classic Card (€19 for 72 hours), which is good for public transport and admission to all the important sights, including the Wartburg.

ⓘ Getting There & Away

If you're driving, Eisenach is right on the A4 and is crossed by the B7, B19 and B84. Direct regional trains run frequently to Erfurt (€11.10, 45 minutes) and Weimar (€14.40, one hour).

Hamburg & the North

Head to Germany's north because you love the water. Mingle with the jet set in posh Sylt or sense the legacy of the Hanseatic League in such historic Baltic towns as Lübeck, Wismar, Stralsund and Greifswald. Beaches abound, and while the temps aren't tropical, the drama of the crisp sea crashing onto the white sand is delightful.

The cities, too, are nothing short of captivating. Hamburg is a metropolis with a love of life that explodes in its fabled clubs and where being close to the water has not only built the city and its harbour but still invigorates it today.

Bremen City, the northern terminus of the fabled Fairy-Tale Road, proves that good things come in small packages, while nearby the exceptional German Emigration Centre awaits in Bremerhaven, the port where the largest number of US-bound emigrants departed from.

Contrary to popular belief, Hanover, meanwhile, is not all buttoned-up business but a lively city with a fresh attitude, stunning gardens and a dedication to public art.

Landungsbrücken, Hamburg (p328)
ATLANTIDE PHOTOTRAVEL/CORBIS ©

Hamburg & the North

Sylt

Westerland

DENMARK

Flensburg

Schleswig-Holstein
Wadden Sea NP

Husum

Kiel

North Sea

Neumünster

A23

A7

Hamburg
Wadden Sea NP

Cuxhaven

Elmshorn

Norderstedt

Lower Saxony
Wadden Sea NP

Lower Saxony
Wadden Sea NP

Hamburg,
Uetersen

Hamburg

Norddeich

Wilhelmshaven

2 Bremerhaven

Emden

A31

A28

A29

Lüneburg

NETHERLANDS

Oldenburg

Delmenhorst

Bremen

Bremen
Airport

A7

Bourtange

A1

A27

A31

Bergen

Coevorden

Celle

Lingen

A7

Nordhorn
Bad
Bentheim

A1

Hanover

A2

Denekamp

Enschede

Rheine

Osnabrück

Minden

A7

Gronau

Hildesheim

A31

A1

A30

Herford

Hamelin

Bielefeld

Goslar

Münster

Detmold

Harz

A2

A33

Harz N

Hamm

Paderborn

Recklinghausen

A44

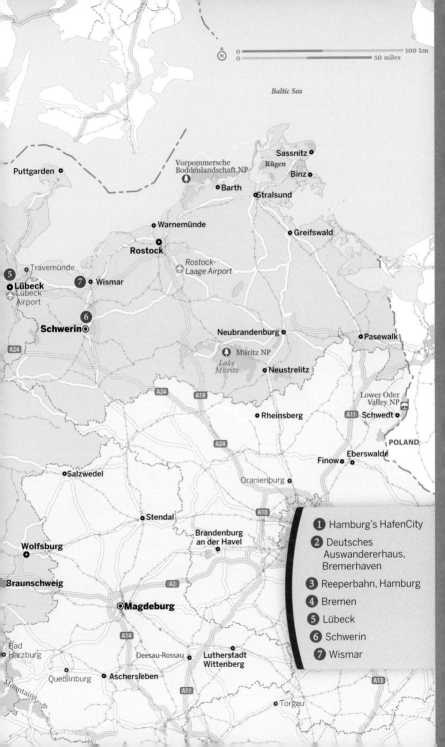

Hamburg & the North's Highlights

1
Hop around Hamburg's HafenCity

It's rare these days that you can witness an entire new neighbourhood being built from scratch. Europe's largest urban construction project, HafenCity is set to be a dynamic quarter where historic and contemporary buildings rub shoulders as sleek cruise ships and mighty container vessels sail out to sea. Above: HafenCity; Top Right: ChilliClub; Bottom Right: Elbphilharmonie

Need to Know

VISIT Whenever the sun is shining! BOOK Elbphilharmonie tour tickets at www.elbphilharmonie.de. SHOP In the boutiques along Überseeboulevard. For further coverage, see p329

Hamburg's HafenCity

BY MARA BURMEISTER, CERTIFIED
HAMBURG TOUR GUIDE

1 HAFENCITY INFOCENTER

A great first stop is the InfoCenter where you can get an overview of the masterplan and the individual construction phases and find out what has already been completed. A huge scale model lets you visualise how the HafenCity fits within the cityscape.

2 ELBPHILHARMONIE

This future concert hall is the most outstanding building in the HafenCity. It was designed by the Swiss architects Herzog & de Meuron and sits right atop a protected red-brick former tea-and-cocoa warehouse. Everything about it is world-class: the ground-breaking design, the shimmering glass facade and the Grand Hall some 50m above the waterline! There's also an ingeniously curved 82m-long escalator (the 'tube') with a stunning lighting concept.

3 ELBPHILHARMONIE TOURS

With a little advance planning, you can take a hard-hat tour of the Elbphilharmonie construction site. It's truly a memorable experience to head up to the 12th floor for close-ups of the unique architectural elements – the 'tube', the concert hall, and so on. The views from the Plaza are extraordinary, too, especially if the *Queen Mary* 2 passes by. Don't forget your camera!

4 INTERNATIONAL MARITIME MUSEUM

This museum (p332) has the world's largest private model ship collection. Look for elaborate ships carved from whale bone and others made out of pure gold or amber. Kids especially love the huge Lego model of the *Queen Mary* 2 and the exhibits about pirates, mutinies and naval accidents.

5 GASTRONOMIC DELIGHTS

One thing's for sure: you won't go hungry! Fuel up on tasty tapas at Coast by East (www.coast-hamburg .de), then head downstairs to the affiliated Sansibar for delicious cocktails. The nearby ChilliClub (www .chilliclub.de) has Asian food and wonderful mojitos. For a quick snack, grab a yummy fish sandwich in the Sandtorhafen (harbour) amid museum ships and fabulous architecture.

Search for Your Roots at the Deutsches Auswandererhaus

At the Deutsches Auswandererhaus (German Emigration Centre, p340) in Bremerhaven you really feel what it was like to leave your home and cross the Atlantic to find a new life. Everyone becomes a part of history as you embark on this personal journey at the site where more than 7 million people set sail between 1830 and 1974.

Deutsches Auswandererhaus Don't Miss List

BY DR SIMONE EICK, DIRECTOR OF THE DEUTSCHES AUSWANDERERHAUS

1 YOUR BOARDING PASS

Everyone gets a boarding card, with the name of a passenger whose story you follow through their voyage. Afterwards, you have the chance to track down your own ancestors – all you need is a name and the approximate year they emigrated. Nearly everyone finds someone – it's an amazing experience.

2 GALLERY OF SEVEN MILLION

The Gallery of Seven Million contains oodles of tiny drawers filled with emigrants' personal items that help explain their reasons for leaving. There are over 2000 biographies here along with photos and goodbye notes and a diary from 1850.

3 SAYING GOODBYE

We have an exact replica of the original wharf where final farewells that were made to loved ones took place. There's menacing dark water and an enormous ship towering over passengers waiting to board. It's extraordinary to stand in this emotional place and to feel the tears, hope and fears.

4 SLEEPING QUARTERS

This seems so real, it makes some people feel a little ill. Every detail of the cramped, overcrowded environment of an 1890 steamship sleeping quarters has been re-created – from the feel of the boat rocking to the dour smell. Passengers spent months sleeping in these dismal conditions.

5 ELLIS ISLAND RECEPTION HALL

Upon arrival you sit on long wooden benches and await the immigration inspector, who asks questions and examines you. It's easy to imagine how nervous the immigrants were – if they answered wrongly or were disabled, they were denied entry to the land of their hopes and dreams and promptly shipped back to Europe.

Reeperbahn, Hamburg's Red-light District

It's tamer than Amsterdam's, but Europe's largest red-light district, the Reeperbahn (p333), is nevertheless a major draw. It comes to life slowly around 4pm but within a few hours thousands stream in to check out its dimly lit bars, peep shows and sex shops. Not your cup o tea? Then just come to visit Beatles-Platz at the corner of Reeperbahn and Grosse Freiheit – the Beatles had their first taste of fame in this neighbourhood.

Town Musicians of Bremen

In the Brothers Grimm fairy tale, the *Bremer Stadtmusikanten* (*Town Musicians of Bremen*) never actually make it to Bremen. But when you arrive you'll find the donkey, dog, cat and rooster who ran away from their owners (intend ing to make their fortune as musicians) standing on each other's backs (p337).

Lübeck's Marzipan

DAVID PEEVERS/GETTY IMAGES ©

Sometimes it's a log, happy to be 'naked'; sometimes it wears a thin chocolate coat. It may be shaped like a piece of fruit, a pig or a potato. When it's feeling fancy, it drapes itself across cakes and sweets, like a luxurious silk blanket. But one thing never changes – classic marzipan is always an almond and sugar concoction, and Lübeck (p341) produces the world's best.

THOMAS WINZ/GETTY IMAGES ©

Marvel at Schwerin's Schloss

With six facades, combining styles from mainly the 16th and 17th centuries, you'll find Gothic and Renaissance turrets, a golden dome and vaguely Ottoman features (among others) at Schwerin's magnificent palace (p345). And it's not just a pretty attraction – it's the official seat of parliament of the state of Mecklenburg–Western Pomerania.

Sample Baltic Flair in Wismar

Wismar's (p340) enticing scenery is no secret, and countless filmmakers have deemed it cinema-worthy – if its Alter Hafen (old harbour) looks familiar, it might be because you saw it in the 1922 Dracula movie *Nosferatu*. Don't be surprised if you stumble across a film crew on your way to its Unesco-listed Altstadt (old town).

Hamburg & the North's Best…

Freebies

○ **HafenCity InfoCenter** (p332) Check out Hamburg's ambitious plans to extend the city limits by 40%

○ **Niederegger** (p344) Learn what marzipan was previously used for (sweet treat is not the correct answer)

○ **Dom St Petri** (p337) Bremen's 1200-year-old cathedral

○ **Holstentor** (p341) Lübeck's much-photographed landmark town gate

Not Just for Kids

○ **Town Musicians of Bremen statue** (p337) Why is the rooster standing on a cat, perched on a dog that is sitting on a donkey?

○ **Die Nanas** (p346) Cute and colourful freeform female sculptures in Hanover

○ **Miniatur-Wunderland** (p332) It's a small world after all…in Hamburg

○ **Fairy-Tale Road** (p351) Following the footsteps of the Brothers Grimm

Harbourside Highlights

○ **International Maritime Museum** (p332) At the edge of Hamburg's gargantuan HafenCity

○ **Ozeaneum** (p340) Stralsund's aquarium journeys through northern seas and oceans

○ **Deutsches Auswandererhaus** (p340) (German Emigration Centre) Set in Bremerhaven, on the very harbour emigrants departed from

○ **Speicherstadt** (p329) The world's largest continuous warehouse complex, in Hamburg

Traditional Taverns

○ **Rattenfängerhaus** (p351) Enjoy 'rats' tails' or play it safe with schnitzel in this Hamelin hotspot

○ **Oberhafenkantine** (p334) Only fresh fish and the 'original' hamburger

○ **Schiffergesellschaft** (p344) Coastal specialities in Lübeck's historic captains' guild quarters

○ **Brauhaus Ernst August** (p348) Raucous Hanover brewpub serves hearty fare

Need to Know

ADVANCE PLANNING

○ **One month before** Reserve a table at one of Hamburg's culinary hotspots.

○ **One day before** Make sure you've packed an umbrella, a raincoat and a sweater, even if the weather forecast is sunny and warm: the weather here is notoriously fickle.

RESOURCES

○ **Hamburg Tourismus** (www.hamburg-tourismus.de) Official Hamburg tourist office site.

○ **Schleswig-Holstein** (www.sh-tourismus.de) Official site of the state tourist office of Schleswig-Holstein.

○ **Mecklenburg–Western Pomerania** (www.mecklenburg-vorpommern.eu) State tourist office site of Mecklenburg–Western Pomerania.

GETTING AROUND

○ **Car** Major autobahns are the north–south A1 and A7 and the east–west A20. If you're only visiting major cities, driving is not recommended because of traffic and expensive parking.

○ **Train** Save money with the **Schleswig-Holstein Ticket** (€26), which is good for travel on regional trains (RE, RB, IRE and S-Bahn) from 9am until 3am the following day (from midnight on weekends) anywhere in Hamburg and state of Schleswig-Holstein. The Mecklenburg-Vorpommern Ticket offers a similar scheme within Hamburg and the state of Mecklenburg–Western Pomerania (eg Schwerin, Wismar, Stralsund).

BE FOREWARNED

○ **Reeperbahn** This area is not for prudes: you will pass strip clubs, peep shows, and insalubrious characters mingling among the throngs of normal folk and tourists.

○ **Women travellers** Don't even consider trying to walk down Herbertstrasse, a fenced-off street block lined with bordellos.

○ **Food** Northern Germany's local specialities look to the sea for inspiration – if you're seeking the epicentre of bratwurst, you're better off sticking to more southern regions.

Hamburg & the North Itineraries

Go cosmopolitan in Hamburg, savour the red-brick splendour of Hanseatic beauties like Lübeck and Wismar and soak up coastal flair while exploring the northern reaches of Germany.

3 DAYS

HANOVER & AROUND
Hanover Beyond Business

This itinerary trains the focus on **(1) Hanover**, one of Germany's most unfairly underrated cities, which is also an excellent base for day trips, easily done on public transport. Start by treating yourself to fine views from the top of the Neues Rathaus, reached by an ingeniously curved lift, then head to the Leine River to meet the whimsical Nana sculptures by Niki de Saint Phalle. Spend the rest of the day in the celebrated Herrenhäuser Gärten, whose splendour is said to rival the gardens at Versailles.

If you've got kids in tow, make a beeline for **(2) Hamelin** the next day. Sitting pretty on the Weser River, Hamelin is a key stop on the Fairy-Tale Road and best known for its *Pied Piper* legend. Car buffs, meanwhile, will feel the pull of **(3) Wolfsburg**, home to the Volkswagen headquarters and its fabulously entertaining Autostadt theme park, a car museum and a science centre.

(4) Celle, meanwhile, beckons architecture fans. The compact town is a virtual symphony of elaborately festooned half-timbered houses but also has a pretty white-and-pink Ducal Palace.

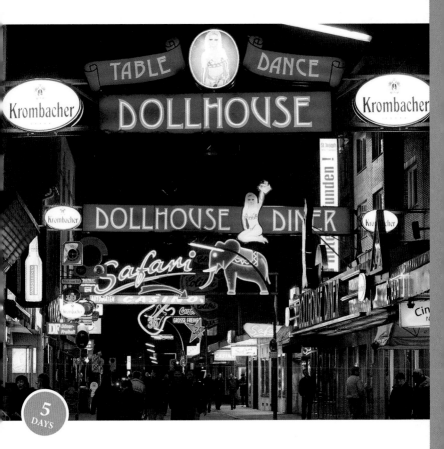

5 DAYS

HAMBURG TO BREMERHAVEN

Hanseatic Delights

This itinerary hopscotches around northern Germany to delightful cities shaped by the sea and a long mercantile tradition rooted in the medieval Hanseatic League. You can drive it or make use of fast and direct train connections. Kick-off is in cosmopolitan **(1) Hamburg**, a city that cradles an elegant centre, an edgy new waterfront quarter, the red-brick Speicherstadt (warehouse district) and a gloriously seedy red-light district under the same self-confident mantle.

Spend a couple of days here before venturing on to **(2) Lübeck**, an enchanting historic town where the landmark Holstentor gate is a shutterbug favourite. Try the delicious local marzipan before heading to pastoral **(3) Schwerin**, a cultural hub and state capital hemmed in by crystalline lakes. Sitting pretty on an island in one of them is the much-photographed golden domed and turreted Schloss Schwerin.

Carry on to **(4) Bremen**, the northern terminus of the 'Fairy-Tale Road'. After greeting the statue of the *Town Musicians of Bremen*, check out expressionist architecture, mummified corpses and Beck's brewery. Wrap up in **(5) Bremerhaven**, which was the port of dreams for millions of souls hoping for a better life in the New World. The Deutsches Auswandererhaus (German Emigration Centre) tells their story.

Discover Hamburg & the North

At a Glance

- **Hamburg** (p328) Cosmopolitan, posh, naughty and historic metropolis
- **Bremen** (p336) Hanse meets high-tech
- **Lübeck** (p341) Hanseatic red-brick beauty and marzipan capital
- **Schwerin** (p345) Charismatic lake-fringed state capital with fabulous palace
- **Hanover & the Fairy-Tale Road** (p346) Glorious gardens, whimsical art and story-book villages

HAMBURG

040 / POP 1.8 MILLION

The 'gateway to the world' might be a bold claim, but Germany's second-largest city and biggest port has never been shy. Hamburg has engaged in business with the world ever since it joined the Hanseatic League trading bloc back in the Middle Ages, and this 'harbourpolis' is now the nation's premier media hub and its wealthiest city.

Hamburg's maritime spirit infuses the entire city; from architecture to menus to the cry of gulls, you always know you're near the water. The city is full of vibrant neighbourhoods awash with multicultural eateries, as well as the gloriously seedy Reeperbahn red-light district.

Sights & Activities

To really see and explore Hamburg, count on spending at least three days prowling its neighbourhoods, waterfront, museums, shops and more.

Altstadt & Neustadt

RATHAUS   Historic Building
(428 312 010; tours adult/child €3/0.50; English-language tours hourly 10.15am-3.15pm Mon-Thu, to 1.15pm Fri, to 5.15pm Sat, to 4.15pm Sun; S Rathausmarkt or Jungfernstieg) Hamburg's baroque Rathaus is one of Europe's most opulent, renowned for the Emperor's Hall and the Great Hall, with its spectacular coffered ceiling.

CHILEHAUS   Historic Building
(cnr Burchardstrasse & Johanniswall; S Mönckebergstrasse/Messberg) The brown-brick Chilehaus is shaped like an ocean liner, with remarkable curved walls meeting in the shape of a ship's bow and staggered

Rathaus, Hamburg
CLARA MONITTO ©

balconies that look like decks. Designed by architect Fritz Höger for a merchant who derived his wealth from trading with Chile, the 1924 building is a leading example of German expressionist architecture.

ST MICHAELISKIRCHE Church
(www.st-michaelis.de; tower adult/child €4/3, crypt €3/2, combo ticket €6/4; ☺10am-7.30pm May-Oct, to 5.30pm Nov-Apr; 🚇Stadthausbrücke) Northeast of the landing piers, the St Michaeliskirche, or 'Der Michel' as it's commonly called, is one of Hamburg's most recognisable landmarks and northern Germany's largest Protestant baroque church. Ascending the **tower** (by steps or lift) rewards with great panoramas across the canals. The **crypt** has an engaging exhibit on the city's history.

HAMBURGER KUNSTHALLE Museum
(☎428 131 200; www.hamburger-kunsthalle.de; Glockengiesserwall; adult/child €10/free; ☺10am-6pm Tue, Wed & Fri-Sun, to 9pm Thu; 🚇Hauptbahnhof) A treasure trove of art from the Renaissance to the present day, the Kunsthalle spans two buildings – one old, one new – linked by an underground passage. The main building houses works ranging from medieval portraiture to 20th-century classics, such as Klee and Kokoschka. Its stark white modern building, the **Galerie der Gegenwart**, showcases contemporary German artists, including Rebecca Horn, Georg Baselitz and Gerhard Richter, alongside international stars, including David Hockney, Jeff Koons and Barbara Kruger.

MAHNMAL ST-NIKOLAI Memorial
(Memorial St Nicholas; www.mahnmal-st-nikolai.de; Willy-Brandt-Strasse 60; adult/child €4/2; ☺10am-5pm; Ⓢ Rödingsmarkt) Nearby St Nikolai, not to be confused with the new Hauptkirche St Nikolai in Harvestehude, was the world's tallest building from 1874 to 1876, and remains Hamburg's second-tallest structure (after the TV tower). Mostly destroyed in WWII, the crypt now houses an unflinching underground exhibit on the horrors of war focusing on three events in World War II: the German bombing of Coventry in 1940, the German destruction of Warsaw and Operation

Hamburg's Fish Market

The Fischmarkt in St Pauli has been a Hamburg institution since 1703. Every Sunday morning, in the wee hours, a fleet of small trucks rumbles onto the cobbled pavement and hardy types turn their vehicles into stores on wheels. They artfully arrange their bananas, cherries, kumquats and whatever else they've picked up that week. Others pile up eels, shellfish, cacti and all manner of goods. It's not yet 5am as the first customers begin to trundle in, often direct from the Reeperbahn action. The undisputed stars of the event – and great, free entertainment – are the boisterous *Marktschreier* (market criers) who hawk their wares. More entertainment takes place in the adjoining **Fischauktionshalle** (Fish Auction Hall), where a live band cranks out ancient German pop songs. Down in the pit, sausage fumes waft and beer flows as if it were evening and not just past dawn.

Gomorrah,and the combined British and American bombing of Hamburg over three days and nights in 1943 that killed 35,000 and incinerated much of the centre. Afterwards, you can take a glass lift up to a 76.3m-high viewing platform inside the surviving spire for views of Hamburg's centre put into context of the wartime destruction.

Speicherstadt & HafenCity

The seven-storey red-brick warehouses lining the Speicherstadt archipelago are a well-recognised Hamburg symbol, stretching to Baumwall in the world's largest continuous warehouse complex.

The Speicherstadt merges into Europe's biggest inner-city urban development, HafenCity. Here, a long-derelict port area of 155 hectares is being redeveloped with restaurants, shops,

329

Hamburg

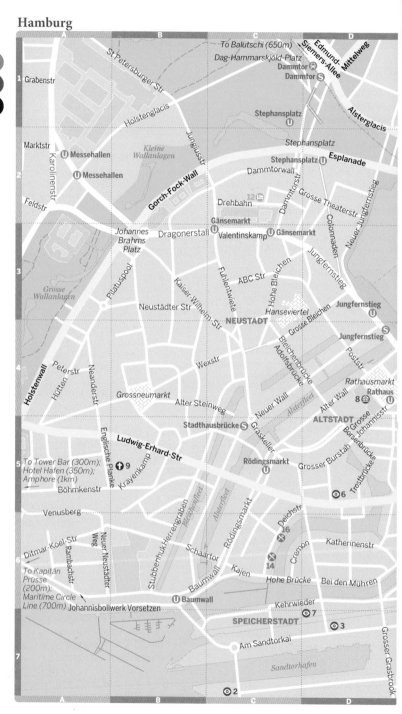

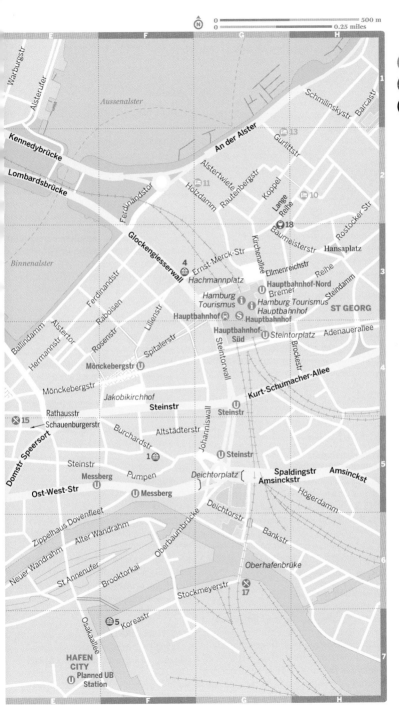

0 — 500 m
0 — 0.25 miles

Warburgstr

Alsteruferr

Aussenalster

Kennedybrücke

Lombardsbrücke

Binnenalster

An der Alster

Schmilinskystr

Barcastr

Gurlittstr

🏛 13

Alstertwiete

Rautenbergstr

🏛 11

Holzdamm

Koppel

Lange
Reihe

🏛 10

Ferdinandstor

Glockengiesserwall

4 🏛

Ernst-Merck-Str

Hachmannplatz

Kirchenallee

Ellmenreichstr

🚇 18

Baumeisterstr

Hansaplatz

Rostocker Str

Reihe

Ferdinandstr

Raboisen

Lilienstr

Hamburg
Tourismus ℹ

Hauptbahnhof-Nord 🚇
Bremer
Hamburg Tourismus ℹ
Hauptbahnhof

Steindamm

ST GEORG

Ballindamm

Alstertor

Hermannstr

Rosenstr

Spitalerstr

Hauptbahnhof 🚇 S Hauptbahnhof

Hauptbahnhof-
Süd

🚇 Steintorplatz

Adenauerallee

Steintorwall

Brockestr

Mönckebergstr 🚇

Mönckebergstr

Jakobikirchhof

Rathausstr

Steinstr

🚇
Steinstr

Kurt-Schumacher-Allee

✕ 15

Schauenburgerstr

Burchardstr

Altstädterstr

Johanniswall

🚇
Steinstr

Domstr Speersort

Steinstr

1 🏛

Pumpen

Deichtorplatz

Spaldingstr

Amsinckst

Messberg
🚇

Ost-West-Str

🚇 Messberg

Amsinckstr

Högerdamm

Zippelhaus Dovenfleet

Alter Wandrahm

Deichtorstr

Bankstr

Neuer Wandrahm

St Annenufer

Brooktorkai

Oberbaumbrücke

Oberhafenbrüke

Stockmeyerstr

✕ 17

🏛 5

Koreastr

Osakaallee

HAFEN
CITY
🚇 Planned UB
Station

Hamburg

apartments and offices, all built to very strict sustainability standards. In the next 20 years, it's anticipated that some 40,000 people will work and 12,000 will live here.

MINIATUR-WUNDERLAND   Exhibition
(☎ 300 6800; www.miniatur-wunderland.de; Kehrwieder 2; adult/child €12/6; ⊗ 9.30am-6pm Mon & Wed-Fri, 9.30am-9pm Tue, 8am-9pm Sat, 8.30am-8pm Sun; ⑤ Messberg) Even the worst cynics are quickly transformed into fans of this vast miniature world that goes on and on. When you see a model A380 swoop out of the sky and land at the fully functional model of Hamburg's airport, you can't help but gasp and say some variation of OMG!

INTERNATIONAL
MARITIME MUSEUM   Museum
(☎ 3009 3300; www.internationales-maritimes-museum.de; Koreastrasse 1; adult/concession €12/8.50; ⊗ 10am-6pm Tue, Wed & Fri-Sun, 10am-8pm Thu; ⑤ Messberg) Hamburg's maritime past – and future – is fully explored in this excellent private museum that sprawls over 10 floors of a rehabbed brick shipping warehouse.

HAFENCITY INFOCENTER   Exhibition
(☎ 3690 1799; www.hafencity.com; Am Sandtorkai 30; ⊗ 10am-6pm Tue-Sun; ⑤ Messberg) You can pick up brochures and check out detailed architectural models and installations that give a sense of the immensity of the project. The centre offers a program of free guided tours through the evolving district.

ELBPHILHARMONIE   Arts Centre
(Elbe Philharmonic Hall; www.elbphilharmonie.de; ⑤ Messberg) A squat brown-brick former warehouse at the far west of HafenCity is the base for the architecturally bold new Elbphilharmonie, which will become a major concert hall.

AUSWANDERERMUSEUM
BALLINSTADT   Museum
(Museum of Emigrants; ☎ 3197 9160; www.ballinstadt.de; Veddeler Bogen 2; adult/child €10/7; ⊗ 10am-6pm Apr-Oct, 10am-4.30pm Nov-Mar) Sort of a bookend for New York's Ellis Island, Hamburg's emigrant museum looks at the conditions that drove millions to leave Germany for the United States in search of better lives from 1850 until the 1930s. The hardships endured are just some of the displays at this excellent museum.

Port Area

Sprawling over 75 sq km (12% of Hamburg's entire surface area), each year some 12,000 ships deliver and take on some 70 million tonnes of goods at Hamburg's huge port. Dozens of port and Elbe River cruises, starting at the St Pauli Harbour Landungsbrücken, put you right in the middle of the action.

MARITIME CIRCLE LINE   Boat Tour
(☎ 2849 3963; www.maritime-circle-line.de; Brücke 10; adult/child €9.50/6; ⊗ 3-5 times daily) Harbour shuttle service connecting Hamburg's maritime cultural attractions, including the Auswanderermuseum

BallinStadt, Hafenmuseum and Miniatur-Wunderland. The entire loop takes around 95 minutes; you can hop on or off at any of its stops.

KAPITÄN PRÜSSE
Boat Tour

(☑ 313 130; www.kapitaen-pruesse.de; Brücke 3; adult/child from €16/8; ☺ year-round) Kapitän Prüsse offers regular Speicherstadt tours as well as various port itineraries.

St Pauli

Even those not interested in lurid late-nights usually pay a quick trip to the St Pauli's **Reeperbahn** to see what the fuss is all about. Long established as a party place, crowds of thousands start to stream in from around 4pm on weekends, cruising the rip-roaring collection of bars, sex clubs, variety acts, pubs and cafes collectively known as the 'Kiez'. Along Davidstrasse, a painted tin wall bars views into Herbertstrasse, a block-long bordello that's off-limits to men under 18 and to women of all ages. It's the notorious sinful heart of the district.

 # Tours

HAMBURG CITY TOUR
Bus Tour

(☑ 3231 8590; www.hamburg-city-tour.de; adult/child €15/free; ☺ half-hourly 9.30am-5pm) Its open-topped double-decker buses pass all the leading sights over 1½ hours; tickets (sold on the bus) allow you to jump on and jump off all day. You can board at stops including the Hauptbahnhof (Kirchenallee exit), Landungsbrücken and the Rathaus.

 # Sleeping

HOTEL WEDINA
Hotel €€

(☑ 280 8900; www.wedina.de; Gurlittstrasse 23; s €70-195, d €120-225; @ 🛜; 🅂 Hauptbahnhof) Margaret Atwood, Jonathan Safran Foer, Jonathan Franzen, Michel Houellebecq, Vladimir Nabokov and JK Rowling are just some of the authors who've stayed and left behind signed books. The hotel's 59 rooms are spread over four buildings, offering a choice of traditional decor in the main red building, which opens to a leafy garden, or modern, urban living in its green, blue and yellow houses.

HOTEL ATLANTIC
Luxury Hotel €€€

(☑ 288 80; www.kempinski.atlantic.de; An der Alster 72-79; s/d from €150/180; 🛜 ☒; 🅂 Hauptbahnhof Nord) Imagine yourself aboard a luxury ocean liner in this grand 252-room hotel, which opens onto Holzdamm. Built in 1909 for luxury liner passengers departing for America, it has ornate stairwells, wide hallways and subtle maritime touches. It has all the services of a five-star hotel and underwent a significant remodelling and restoration in 2010.

HOTEL SIDE
Hotel €€€

(☑ 309 990; www.side-hamburg.de; Drehbahn 49; r €120-300; 🅿 ✳ @ 🛜 ☒; 🅂 Gänsemarkt) A stylish alternative to the city centre's chain hotels, this Matteo Thun–designed stunner is built around a soaring prism-shaped central atrium. Suites feature vividly coloured free-standing bath-tubs. The 8th-floor chill-out lounge, strewn with 1950s-style saucers-from-outer-space sofas, opens to a panoramic sun deck.

HOTEL HAFEN
Hotel €€

(☑ 311 1370; www.hotel-hafen-hamburg.de; Seewartenstrasse 9; r €70-200; @ 🛜; 🅂 Landungsbrücken) Location, location, location. This privately owned behemoth of a hotel (353 rooms, all with highspeed internet) looms over the heart of Hamburg's harbour from a small hill. If you're lucky enough to score a harbour-facing room, the views are extraordinary. In addition to the refurbished, historic main building, a former seafarer's home, there are newer modern wings.

GALERIE-HOTEL PETERSEN
Pension €€

(☑ 0173 200 0746, 249 826; www.ghsp.eu; Lange Reihe 50; s €60-100, d €70-170; ✳ @ 🛜; 🅂 Hauptbahnhof) This delightful *Pension* inside a historic 1790 town house is an extension of its welcoming artist-owner's personality, whose paintings decorate the walls of his 'gallery of dreams'. Furnishings include a mix of contemporary, antique and art-deco styles.

 Eating

CAFÉ PARIS
French €€

(www.cafeparis.net; Rathausstrasse 4; mains €10-20; ⏱ from 9am Mon-Fri, from 10am Sat & Sun; Ⓢ Rathaus) Within a spectacularly tiled 1882 butchers' hall and adjoining art-deco salon, this elegant yet relaxed brasserie serves classical French fare like *croque-monsieur* (toasted ham-and-cheese sandwich), *croque-madame* (the same, but with a fried egg), and *steak tartare* (minced meat, but pan-fried, not raw). Its breakfast for two is a splendid feast.

OBERHAFENKANTINE
German €€

(www.oberhafenkantine-hamburg.de; Stock-meyerstrasse 39; mains €7-16; Ⓡ Steinstrasse) Since 1925, this slightly tilted brick restaurant has served up the very most traditional Hamburg fare using only the best ingredients. Here you can order a 'Hamburger' and you get the real thing: a patty made with various seasonings and onions. Roast beef, pollock, haddock and more round out a wonderful trip back to the days when the surrounding piers echoed to the shouts of seamen and the crash of cargo-laden nets.

ALT HAMBURGER AALSPEICHER
German €€€

(☎ 362 990; www.aalspeicher.de; Deichstrasse 43; mains €12-28; Ⓢ Rödingsmarkt) Despite its tourist-friendly canalside location, the knick-knack–filled dining room and warm service at this restaurant, housed in a 400-year-old building, make you feel like you're dining in your *Oma's* (grandma's) house. Smoked eel from its own smoke-house is a speciality.

DEICHGRAF
German €€€

(☎ 364 208; www.deichgraf-hamburg.de; Deichstrasse 23; mains €18-29; ⏱ lunch Mon-Sat, dinner Sat; Ⓢ Rödingsmarkt) In a prime setting, with the water on one side and long street-side tables on the other, Deichgraf excels in Hamburg specialities cooked to a high standard. The menu changes seasonally and much of the food is sourced from the region.

CAFÉ MIMOSA Cafe €
(www.cafemimosa.de; Clemens-Schultz-Strasse 87; dishes €5-12;
§ St Pauli) A welcome change from the greasy fast-food joints on the nearby Reeperbahn, this gem of a neighbourhood cafe serves delicious pastas, healthy salads, proper coffee and homemade cakes in a theatrical space.

 Drinking

BAR M & V Bar
(www.mvbar.de; Lange Reihe 22; ⊠ Hauptbahnhof) The drinks menu is like a designer catalogue at this grand old St Georg bar that's had a beautiful restoration. Settle into one of the wooden booths, smell the freesias and enjoy.

AMPHORE Cafe
(www.cafe-amphore.de; Hafenstrasse 140; ⊠ Reeperbahn) Beguiling in its trad beauty, Amphore has terrace views out to the Elbe and sidewalk tables for neighbourhood gawking. Inside it's woodsy in a non-fussy way. An excellent St Pauli spot for a drink.

TOWER BAR Lounge
(www.hotel-hafen-hamburg.de; Seewartenstrasse 9; ⏱ 6pm-1am Mon-Thu, 6pm-2.30am Fri-Sun; § Landungsbrücken) For a more elegant, mature evening, repair to this 14th-floor eyrie at the Hotel Hafen for unbeatable harbour views.

ℹ Information

Tourist Information

Hamburg Tourismus (☎ 3005 1200; www.hamburg-tourismus.de) has an excellent range of info in English, including the website. Offices include the following:

Airport (Airport Plaza btwn Terminals 1 & 2; ⏱ 6am-11pm)

Hauptbahnhof (Kirchenallee exit; ⏱ 8am-9pm Mon-Sat, 10am-6pm Sun)

St Pauli Landungsbrücken (btwn piers 4 & 5; ⏱ 8am-6pm Apr-Oct, 10am-6pm Nov-Mar; § Landungsbrücken)

ⓘ Getting There & Away

Air

Hamburg Airport (HAM; www.flughafen-hamburg .de) has frequent flights to domestic and European cities, including on Lufthansa and most other major European carriers; low-cost carriers include Air Berlin and EasyJet. The S1 S-Bahn connects the airport directly with the city centre; the journey takes 24 minutes and costs €2.85.

Train

Hamburg has four mainline train stations. The **Hauptbahnhof** (Central Train Station; Glockengiesserwall; 🚆alt name: centralstation), the most important, and an attraction in itself, is on the city centre's northeastern edge. Three other mainline stations lie west (**Altona**), south (**Harburg**) and north (**Dammtor**) of the centre.

There are direct ICE/IC services to Berlin-Hauptbahnhof (€73, 1¾ hours), Cologne (€83, four hours), Frankfurt (€114, 3½ hours) and Munich (€135, 5¾ hours).

ⓘ Getting Around

Car & Motorcycle

Driving around town is easy: thoroughfares are well signposted, and parking stations plentiful.

Public Transport

HVV (📞194 49; www.hvv.de) operates buses, ferries, U-Bahn and S-Bahn and has several info centres, including at the Jungfernstieg S-/U-Bahn station, and the Hauptbahnhof. The city is divided into zones; **Ring A** covers the city centre, inner suburbs and airport.

Taxi

Try **Taxiruf** (📞441 011; www.autoruf.de), or **Taxi Hamburg** (📞666 666; www.taxihamburg.de).

Bremen City

📞0421 / POP 548,000

Bremen, one of Gemany's city-states, has a highly justified reputation for being among the country's most outward-looking and hospitable places, with a local population that seems to strike a very good balance between style, earthiness and good living.

⊙ Sights & Activities

MARKT   Square

With high, historic buildings rising up from this very compact square, Bremen's Markt is one of the most remarkable in northern Germany. The towers of the 1200-year-old Dom St Petri dominate the northeastern edge, beside the ornate and imposing **Rathaus**, which was erected in 1410. The Weser Renaissance balcony in the middle, crowned by three gables, was added between 1595 and 1618. In front of the Rathaus is one of the hallmarks of Bremen, the city's 13m-high **Knight**

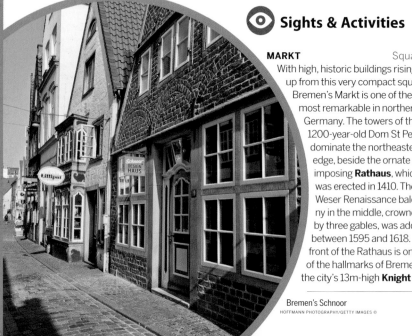

Bremen's Schnoor

Roland statue (1404). As elsewhere, Roland stands for civic freedoms, especially the freedom to trade independently. On the western side of the Rathaus, in front of the **Kirche Unser Lieben Frauen** (Church of our Beloved Lady), is the city's even more-famous symbol: the **Town Musicians of Bremen** (1951) by the sculptor Gerhard Marcks. This depicts a dog, cat and rooster, one on top of the other, on the shoulders of a donkey. The donkey's nose and front legs are incredibly shiny after being touched by visitors for good luck.

The one obviously modern building on the Markt is the **Haus der Bürgerschaft** (State Assembly; 1966), whose geometrical steel-and-concrete structure features artfully moulded pieces of metal attached to its facade, suggesting a Gothic style that blends in with the other architecture of this historic square.

DOM ST PETRI   Church
(St Petri Cathedral; tower €1; ☉10am-4.45pm Mon-Fri, to 1.30pm Sat, 2-4.45pm Sun, tower closed Nov-Easter) Bremen's Dom St Petri is situated on the northeastern side of Markt. Construction of Bremen's cathedral began in 1041 in the style of an early Gothic basilica on the site of Bremen's original wooden cathedral that was located here in the late-8th century. Today's stone incarnation was given ribbed vaulting inside, chapels and its two high towers in the 13th century. For views over Bremen, climb the 265 steps to the top of the southern tower.

BÖTTCHERSTRASSE   Neighbourhood
This charming lane with a golden entrance and staggered red-brick walls is a superb example of expressionism. The 110m-long street was commissioned in 1931 by Ludwig Roselius, a merchant who made his fortune by inventing decaffeinated coffee and founding the company Hag. Most of the street was designed by Bernhard Hoetger (1874–1959), including the **Lichtbringer** (Bringer of Light), the golden relief at the northern entrance, showing a scene from the Apocalypse with the Archangel Michael fighting a dragon.

Hoetger's **Haus Atlantis** (☉free guided tours 10am-noon & 2-4pm Mon), now the Bremen Hilton, features a show-stopping, multicoloured, glass-walled spiral staircase. Hoetger worked around the existing, 16th-century Roselius Haus, and designed the Paula Modersohn-Becker Haus, with its rounded edges and wall reliefs. Today these two adjoining houses are museums comprising the **Kunstsammlungen Böttcherstrasse** (Art Collection Böttcherstrasse; www.pmbm .de; Böttcherstrasse 6-10; combined ticket adult/concession €5/3; ☉11am-6pm Tue-Sun).

SCHNOOR   Neighbourhood
This part of Bremen's centre was once its maritime quarter and then its red-light district. Over the years, however, the district transmogrified into a quaint maze of restaurants, cafes and boutique shops. It's a honey-pot for tourists, but its restaurants are also popular with locals in the evenings. The name 'Schnoor' is north German for 'string', and refers to the way the 15th- and 16th-century cottages – once inhabited by fisherfolk, traders and craftspeople – are 'strung' along the alleyways.

BECK'S BREWERY   Brewery
(☏01805 101 030; www.becks.de/besucher zentrum; Am Deich; tours €10.50; ☉1pm & 3pm Thu & Fri, 11.30pm, 1pm, 3.30pm & 4.30pm Sat Jan-Apr, 10am, 11.30am, 1pm, 3pm, 4.30pm & 6pm Thu-Sat May-Dec) You can see how beer is made during a two-hour tour of the Beck's brewery, run in conjunction with the tourist office. Book online or by telephone and meet at the brewery by taking tram 1 or 8 to Am Brill. *Prost!*

Tours

CITY TOUR   Bus Tour
(adult/child under 12yr €17.90/12; ☉10.30am Tue-Sun) Two-hour tours leaving from platform M outside the Hauptbahnhof are run by the tourist office with English and German commentary. Otherwise, ask the office about its many German-language tours.

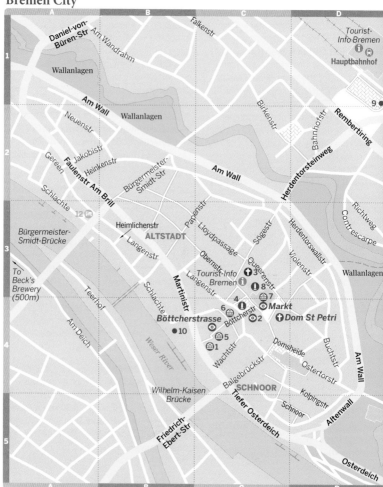

**HAL ÖVER SCHREIBER
REEDEREI**   Tour
(www.hal-oever.de; Schlachte 2, Martinianleger;
harbour & Weser tour adult/child €9.90/5.60;
⊙office 9am-5pm Mon-Fri) Operates a
75-minute **Weser and harbour tour**
three to five times daily from January to
November. Also runs scheduled services
along the river in summer, the ferry
across the river to **Café Sand** (www
.cafe-sand.de; Strandweg 106; Pommes & beer
€5; ⊙from 10am daily May-Sep, from noon Mon-
Sat & from 10am Sun Apr, from noon Fri-Sat &

from 10am Sun Feb-Mar & Oct-Nov, closed Dec &
Jan) and – surely a unique way of getting
to a football game – can even take you by
boat from the Martinianleger to Werder
Bremen's stadium during home matches.

 Sleeping & Eating

HOTEL BÖLTS AM PARK   Hotel €€
(✆346 110; www.hotel-boelts.de; Slevogtstrasse
23; s/d €65/85; [P] 🛜) This cosy family-
run hotel in a leafy neighbourhood has
real character, from the wonderfully

Bremen City

its own sauna and whirlpool – perfect for a honeymoon.

LE GRIL   Steakhouse, International €€
(☑ 3017 4443; www.loui-jules.com; Langen-strasse 72/Schlachte 36; mains €12-36; ☺lunch & dinner Mon-Sat) Located inside Hotel Überfluss, this surf 'n' turf place does excellent wood-coal grills, with steaks starting from €20 but with many cheaper dishes, including an inexpensive burger and midrange seafood.

CASA   Mediterranean €€
(http://casa-bremen.com; Ostertorsteinweg 59; mains €8.40-19.60; ☺from 10am; ☑)
Bremen's long-standing favourite has recently given itself a new name (this used to be known as Casablanca) and a slightly more upmarket splash. It serves lava-grill fish and meat dishes (including its own burger as well as lamb dishes), along with salads and pizza – often with a Mediterranean edge. Breakfast is till noon weekdays, till 3pm weekends.

old-fashioned breakfast hall to its well-proportioned doubles.

**HOTEL
ÜBERFLUSS**   Boutique Hotel €€€
(☑ 322 860; www.hotel-ueberfluss.com; Langen-strasse 72/Schlachte 36; s €120-160, d €131-195, ste from €339; ✳ ☎ ☎) Quite literally 7m above river level, this designer hotel has black bathrooms (some with transparent shower areas) and stunning views from its more expensive rooms. For splashy fun, the magnificently designed suite has

If You Like...
Maritime Towns

If you like to feel the salty breeze in your face, head to these Baltic coastal destinations for a dose of salty spirit.

1 WISMAR
(www.wismar.de) With its gabled facades and cobbled streets, this small, photogenic city looks essentially Hanseatic. But although it joined the Hanseatic trading league in the 13th century, it spent most of the 16th and 17th centuries as part of Sweden. There are numerous reminders of this era all over town. The entire Altstadt was Unesco-listed in 2002.

2 STRALSUND
(www.stralsund.de) Explore Stralsund's Unesco-protected red-brick historic centre and learn about the ecosystems of local waters at the Ozeaneum, the arctic-white wavelike waterfront aquarium. Like Wismar, this town was a Hanseatic League trading centre in the 14th and 15th centuries. It's also the gateway to Rügen.

3 RÜGEN
(www.ruegen.de) A one-time holiday favourite among Nazis and later, East German comrades, Germany's largest island is a mix of towering chalk cliffs, national parkland and a bird refuge. Prora, the former 2km-long workers' retreat built by Hitler, houses a fascinating documentation centre; and the island's main base, Binz, is a quintessential Baltic resort town.

4 GREIFSWALD
(www.greifswald.de) This lovely Hanseatic and university town was largely unscathed by WWII thanks to a courageous German colonel who surrendered to Soviet troops. It has a pretty harbour in the charming district of Wieck and a photogenic skyline dominated by three distinctive churches.

ℹ Information
Tourist office (📞01805-101 030; www.bremen-tourism.de) There is a tourist office in the city centre (www.bremen-tourism.de; Obernstrasse; ⏱10am-6.30pm Mon-Fri, 10am-4pm Sat & Sun) near Markt and another at the main train station (⏱9am-7pm Mon-Fri, 9.30am-6pm Sat & Sun).

ℹ Getting There & Away

Air
Bremen's Airport (BRE; www.airport-bremen.de) is about 3.5km south of the centre and has flights to destinations in Germany and Europe. Tram 6 travels between the Hauptbahnhof and the airport (€2.35, 15 minutes). A taxi from the airport costs about €15.

Car & Motorcycle
The A1 (from Hamburg to Osnabrück) and the A27/A7 (Bremerhaven to Hanover) intersect in Bremen.

Train
Frequent IC trains go to Hamburg (€26, one hour), Hanover (€31, one hour) and Cologne (€63, three hours).

Bremerhaven

'Give me your tired, your poor, your huddled masses', invites the Statue of Liberty in New York harbour. Well, Bremerhaven is one place that most certainly did. Millions of those landing at Ellis Island departed from here, and the **Deutsches Auswandererhaus (German Emigration Centre; www.dah-bremerhaven.de; Columbusstrasse 65; adult/concession €11.20/9.50; ⏱10am-6pm)** now chronicles and commemorates some of their stories.

This is Europe's largest emigration exhibition, and it does a superb job of conjuring up the experience. You re-live the stages of the journey and the emigrants' travelling conditions as you move through the building, clutching the biographical details of one particular traveller.

Bremerhaven is quickly reached via the A27 from Bremen; get off at the Bremerhaven-Mitte exit. Frequent trains connect Bremen and Bremerhaven (€11.30, 45 minutes).

Lübeck

☎ 0451 / POP 210,300

A 12th-century gem boasting more than 1000 historical buildings, Lübeck's picture-book appearance is an enduring reminder of its role as one of the founding cities of the mighty Hanseatic League and its moniker of the 'Queen of the Hanse'. Behind its landmark Holstentor (gate), you'll find streets lined with medieval merchants' homes and spired churches forming Lübeck's 'crown'.

Recognised by Unesco as a World Heritage Site in 1987, today this thriving provincial city retains many enchanting corners to explore.

 Sights

You can easily spend a day wandering amidst Lübeck's steeple-punctuated sights. For respite, head south along An der Obertrave southwest of the Altstadt, you'll pass one of Lübeck's loveliest corners, the **Malerwinkel** (Painters' Quarter). Here you can take a break on garden benches among blooming flowers, gazing out at the houses and white picket fences across the water.

In the Middle Ages, Lübeck was home to numerous craftspeople and artisans. Their presence caused demand for housing to outgrow the available space, so tiny single-storey homes were built in courtyards behind existing rows of houses. These were then made accessible via walkways from the street.

Almost 90 such Gänge (walkways) and Höfe (courtyards) still exist, among them charitable housing estates built for the poor, the Stiftsgängeand Stiftshöfe. The most famous of the latter are the **Füchtingshof**

(Glockengiesserstrasse 25) with its beautiful carvings and the 1612 **Glandorps Gang** (Glockengiesserstrasse 41-51), which you can peer into.

There must be something in the water in Lübeck, or maybe it's all the famous marzipan. The city has connections to two Nobel Prize–winning authors (as well as Nobel Peace Prize–winning former chancellor Willy Brandt).

HOLSTENTOR   Landmark

Built in 1464 and looking so settled-in that it appears to sag, Lübeck's charming red-brick city gate is a national icon. Its twin pointed cylindrical towers, leaning together across the stepped gable that joins them, captivated Andy Warhol – his print is in the **St Annen Museum** (☎122 4137; www.st-annen-museum.de; St-Annen -Strasse 15; adult/child €6/3; ☻10am-5pm Tue-Sun Apr-Dec, 11am-5pm Tue-Sun Jan-Mar) – and have graced postcards, paintings, posters and marzipan souvenirs, as you'll discover inside its **Museum Holstentor** (☎122 4129; adult/child €5/2; ☻10am-6pm Apr-Dec, 11am-5pm Tue-Sun Jan-Mar).

Salzspeicher (p343), Lübeck
JOHN FREEMAN/GETTY IMAGES ©

Lübeck

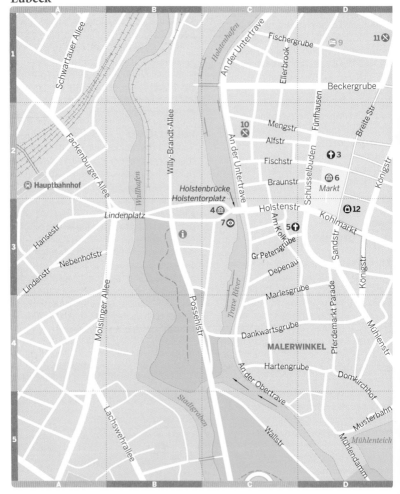

Lübeck

⊙ Sights

1 Füchtingshof	E1
2 Glandorps Gang	E1
Holstentor	(see 4)
3 Marienkirche	D2
4 Museum Holstentor	C3
5 Petrikirche	C3
6 Rathaus	D2
7 Salzspeicher	C3
8 St Annen Museum	E4

🛏 Sleeping

9 Klassik Altstadt Hotel	D1

⊗ Eating

10 Brauberger	C2
Café Niederegger	(see 12)
11 Schiffergesellschaft	D1

🛍 Shopping

12 Niederegger	D3

Sometimes described as a 'fairy tale in stone', Lübeck's 13th- to 15th-century Rathaus is widely regarded as one of the most beautiful in Germany. Unfortunately, the impact of its facade is diminished by ugly modern buildings around the marketplace. Inside, a highlight is the Audienzsaal (audience hall), a light-flooded hall decked out in festive rococo.

MARIENKIRCHE
Church

(Schüsselbuden 13; admission €1; ⏰10am-6pm Apr-Sep, to 5pm Oct, to 4pm Tue-Sun Nov-Mar) Near the Markt rise the 125m twin spires of Germany's third-largest church, the 13th-century Marienkirche. It's most famous for its shattered bells, which have been left where they fell after a 1942 WWII bombing raid. It's a stark and moving display. Outside there's a little devil sculpture with an amusing folk tale (in German and English).

PETRIKIRCHE
Church

(☎397 730; www.st-petri-luebeck.de; Schüsselbuden 13; adult/child €3/2; ⏰9am-9pm Apr-Sep, 10am-7pm Oct-Mar) Panoramic views over the city unfold from the 13th-century Petrikirche, which has a tower lift to a viewing platform 50m high. The interior is starkly whitewashed.

Tours

The Trave River forms a moat around the Altstadt, and cruising it aboard a boat is a fine way to get a feel for the city.

OPEN-AIR CITY TOUR
Bus Tour

(adult/child €7/4.50; ⏰10am-4pm May-Sep) Open-top buses make 45-minute circuits of the historic city. You can join at many points along the circuit.

Sleeping & Eating

KLASSIK ALTSTADT HOTEL
Boutique Hotel €€

(☎702 980; www.klassik-altstadt-hotel.de; Fischergrube 52; s €60-100, d €130-160; 📶) Each room at this elegantly furnished

SALZSPEICHER
Historic Buildings

Just behind the Holstentor (to the east) stand the Salzspeicher: six gabled brick shop-filled buildings once used to store salt transported from Lüneburg. It was then bartered for furs from Scandinavia and used to preserve the herrings that formed a substantial chunk of Lübeck's Hanseatic trade.

RATHAUS
Historic Building

(☎122 1005; Breite Strasse 64; adult/concession €3/1.50; ⏰tours 11am, noon & 3pm Mon-Fri)

DAVID PEEVERS/GETTY IMAGES ©

boutique hotel is dedicated to a different, mostly German, writer or artist, such as Thomas Mann and Johann Sebastian Bach, as well as international luminaries like Denmark's Hans Christian Andersen. Single rooms (some share baths) feature travelogues by famous authors.

SCHIFFERGESELLSCHAFT

German €€€

(📞767 76; www.schiffergesellschaft.com; Breite Strasse 2; mains €12-25) Opened in 1535 as the dining room for the Blue Water Captains' Guild, Lübeck's cutest – if not best – restaurant is a veritable museum. Ships' lanterns, original model ships dating from 1607 and orange Chinese-style lamps with revolving maritime silhouettes adorn the wood-lined rooms, which include an elevated banquet room up the back. As you sit on long benches resembling church pews, staff in long white aprons bring you Frisian specialities (there are many seasonal specials). On balmy nights, head up a flight of steps to the hidden garden out back. Book.

BRAUBERGER

German €€

(📞702 0606; Alfstrasse 36; mains €9-14; ⏱5pm-midnight Mon-Thu, 5pm-late Fri & Sat) The brew-

ing kettles are right in the dining room and the humid air is redolent with hops at this traditional German brewer, which has been serving its own golden amber since 1225. Get a stein of the sweet, cloudy house brew and enjoy one of many excellent schnitzels or other trad fare.

 Shopping

Hüxstraase is one of Germany's best shopping streets. It's lined with an array of creative and interesting boutiques, clothing stores, bookshops, cafes and much more. And there's additional joy on surrounding streets, especially Schlumacherstrasse.

NIEDEREGGER

Food

(📞530 1126; www.niederegger.de; Breite Strasse 89; ⏱9am-7pm Mon-Fri, 9am-6pm Sat, 10am-6pm Sun) Niederegger is Lübeck's mecca for marzipan lovers, the almond confectionery from Arabia, which has been made locally for centuries. Even if you're not buying, the shop's elaborate seasonal displays are a feast for the eyes. In its small museum, **Marzipan-Salon**, you'll learn that in medieval Europe marzipan was considered medicine, not a treat. At the back of the shop there's an elegant cafe.

ⓘ Information

Tourist office (📞01805 882 233; www.luebeck-tourismus.de; Holstentorplatz 1; ⏰9.30am-7pm Mon-Fri, 10am-3pm Sat & 10am-2pm Sun Jun-Sep, 9.30am-6pm Mon-Fri & 10am-3pm Sat Oct-May) City tourist office sells the Happy Day Card (per 1/2/3 days €10/12/15) offering free public transport in Lübeck and Travemünde and museum discounts. Also has a cafe and internet terminals.

ⓘ Getting There & Away

AIR Low-cost carriers **Ryanair** (www.ryanair.com) and **Wizzair** (www.wizzair.com) serve **Lübeck airport** (LBC; www.flughafen-luebeck.de), which they euphemistically call Hamburg-Lübeck. Destinations include Milan and Stockholm. Buses take passengers straight to Hamburg (one-way €10, 55 minutes), while scheduled bus 6 (€2.70) serves Lübeck's Hauptbahnhof and central bus station.

TRAIN Lübeck has connections every hour to Hamburg (€19, 40 minutes), Kiel (€16, 1¼ hours) and Rostock (€24, two hours 20 minutes) with a change in Bad Kleinen.

Schwerin

📞 0385 / POP 95,200

Picturesquely sited around seven lakes (or possibly more depending on how you count them), the centrepiece of this engaging city is its Schloss (palace), built in the 14th century during the city's time as the former seat of the Grand Duchy of Mecklenburg.

Schwerin has shrugged off the 45 years of communist rule that followed WWII. Today there's an upbeat, vibrant energy on its restored streets that befits its role as the reinstated capital of Mecklenburg–Western Pomerania (beating Rostock for the mantle). Cafes and interesting shops make wandering a delight.

ⓞ Sights

SCHLOSS & GARDENS Palace

(📞525 2920; www.schloss-schwerin.de; adult/child €6/4; ⏰10am-6pm mid-Apr–mid-Oct, 10am-5pm Tue-Sun mid-Oct–mid-Apr) Gothic and Renaissance turrets, Slavic onion domes, Ottoman features and terracotta Hanseatic step gables are among the mishmash of architectural styles that make up Schwerin's inimitable Schloss, which is crowned by a gleaming golden dome. Nowadays the Schloss earns its keep as the state's parliament building.

Schwerin derives its name from a Slavic castle known as Zuarin (Animal Pasture) that was formerly on the site, and which was first mentioned in 973 AD. In a niche over the main gate, the **statue of Niklot** depicts a Slavic prince, who was defeated by Heinrich der Löwe in 1160.

Inside the palace's opulently furnished rooms, highlights include a huge collection of Meissen porcelain and richly coloured stained-glass windows in the **Schlosskirche**.

The park immediately surrounding the palace is known as the **Burggarten** and most notably features a wonderful **orangerie** overlooking the water, with a conservatory restaurant and terrace cafe (open May to October). A handful of statues, a grotto and lookout points are also here.

Crossing the causeway south from the Burggarten brings you to the baroque **Schlossgarten** (Palace Garden), intersected by several canals.

STAATLICHES MUSEUM Museum

(📞595 80; www.museum-schwerin.de; Alter Garten 3; adult/concession €8/6; ⏰10am-6pm Tue-Sun Apr-Oct, 10am-5pm Tue-Sun Nov-Mar, to 8pm Thu) In the Alter Garten, the Staatliches Museum has a substantial collection spanning the ages. The 15 statues in the Ernst Barlach room provide a small taste of the sculptor's work. There's also a typically amusing and irreverent Marcel Duchamp collection. Other works include oils by Lucas Cranach the Elder, as well as works by Brueghel, Rembrandt and Rubens.

DOM · Church

(📞565 014; Am Dom 4; adult/child €2/1; 🕑11am-3pm Mon-Fri, 11am-4pm Sat, noon-3pm Sun) Above the Markt, the tall 14th-century Gothic Dom is a superb example of north German red-brick architecture. You can climb up to the viewing platform of its 19th-century cathedral tower (118m), which is a mere 50cm taller than Rostock's Petrikirche. Down to earth, check out the elaborately carved pews.

🛏 Sleeping & Eating

HOTEL
NIEDERLÄNDISCHER HOF · Hotel €€

(📞591 100; www.niederlaendischer-hof.de; Karl-Marx-Strasse 12-13; s €84-124, d €125-170; 🅿🛜) Overlooking the Pfaffenteich, this regal 1901-established hotel has 33 elegant rooms with black marble bathrooms, a library warmed by an open fire, and a lauded restaurant. Room decor ranges from trad luxe to whimsical seaside.

BUSCHÉRIE · Modern European €€€

(📞923 6066; www.buscherie.de; Buschstrasse 9; mains €16-20) Although historic and half-timbered, Buschstrasse isn't stuck in the past, as shown by this sprightly bistro. Foods of the region are prepared with colour and flair. There is a sumptuous seafood spread (€32 per person) but otherwise the meaty mains and small plates are well-priced. There's live jazz some nights; Mondays feature special cocktails and singing.

ℹ Information

ℹ Getting There & Around

TRAIN Links include Hamburg (from €27, one hour), Rostock (from €20, one hour), Stralsund (from €33, two hours) and Wismar (€8, 30 minutes), with less frequent direct connections to/from Berlin (€35, 2¼ hours).

BUSES & TRAMS These cost €1.50/4.60 for a single/day pass. A ferry crosses the Pfaffenteich (€1) from late April to mid-October.

HANOVER & THE FAIRY-TALE ROAD

Hanover
📞0511 / POP 522,700

Lacking the high profile of the Hanse city states of Hamburg and Bremen to its north, Hanover (Hannover in German) is perhaps best known for its CeBit information and communications technology fair, but the city also boasts acres of greenery and its spectacularly baroque Herrenhäuser Gärten (gardens), which is a mini Versailles.

◉ Sights

The city has painted a *Roter Faden* (red line) on pavements around the centre. Follow it with the help of the multilingual *Red Thread Guide* (€2.50), available from the tourist office, for a quick 4.2km, do-it-yourself tour of the city's 36 highlights.

NEUES RATHAUS · Historic Building

(Trammplatz 2; elevator adult/concession €3/2; 🕑9.30am-6.30pm Mon-Fri, 10am-6.30pm Sat & Sun, elevator closed mid-Nov–Mar) An excellent way to get your bearings in Hanover is to visit the Neues Rathaus (built in 1901–13) and travel 98m to the top in the **curved lift** inside its green dome. There are four viewing platforms here. The cabin can take only five people at a time, so queues are inevitable in summer.

In the downstairs lobby are four **city models** showing Hanover from the Middle Ages to today.

DIE NANAS · Sculpture

(Leibnizufer) Hanover's city fathers and mothers were inundated with nearly 20,000 letters of complaint when these three earth-mama sculptures were first installed beside the Leine River in 1974. Now, the voluptuous and fluorescent-coloured 'Sophie', 'Charlotte' and 'Caroline', by French artist Niki de Saint Phalle,

H & D ZIELSKE/GETTY IMAGES ©

Don't Miss Herrenhäuser Gärten

Situated about 5km northwest of the centre, Herrenhäuser Gärten (Herrenhausen Gardens) are a remarkable ensemble of parks and gardens largely modelled on those at Versailles, outside Paris. The jewel in the crown, Grosser Garten is grand both in format and history, having been laid out as a baroque garden in 1714 under the tutelage of the French landscape gardener Martin Charbonnier. The garden contains statues, fountains and coloured tile walls of the **Niki de Saint Phalle Grotto** (creator of the city's much-loved Die Nanas sculptures, and opened after her death in 2002), providing a magical showcase of the artist's work. There's a **maze** near the northern entrance of the Grosser Garten, while the **Grosse Fontäne** (Great Fountain; the tallest in Europe) at the southern end jets water up to 80m high. Popular summer attractions are the **Wasserspiele**, water fountains that are synchronised to do some spectacular spurting, and the **Illuminations**, when the Grosser Garten is lit up for between one and two hours.

To get to the district, take tram/U-Bahn 4 or 5 from Kröpke to Herrenhäuser Gärten.

NEED TO KNOW

📞1684 7576; www.herrenhaeuser-gaerten.de; ⏰9am-sunset

are among the city's most recognisable, and most loved, landmarks. Indeed, *Die Nanas* helped make de Saint Phalle famous.

SPRENGEL MUSEUM   Museum
(www.sprengel-museum.de; Kurt-Schwitters-Platz; adult/concession €7/4, Fri free; ⏰10am-6pm Wed-Sun, to 8pm Tue) The Sprengel

Museum is held in extremely high esteem, both for the design of the building as well as for the art housed inside. At the core of the collection are 300 works by the artist Niki de Saint Phalle, a selection of which is usually on show.

Sleeping

CITY HOTEL AM THIELENPLATZ

Hotel €

(☎ 327 691; www.smartcityhotel.com; Thielenplatz 2; s/d from €59/69; breakfast €9.50; P 🛜) This very central 'budget boutique' beauty has a reception and bar (open until 5am) restyled with leather seating, black-and-white leaf-patterned wallpaper and lots of wood laminate. All rooms have been renovated, mostly in a minimalist style.

🌿 LOCCUMER HOF

Hotel €€

(☎ 126 40; www.loccumerhof.de; Kurt-Schumacher-Strasse 14/16; s €99, d €139-159, ste €169; P @ 🛜) Some of the stylish and well-decorated rooms here are themed by nations ('Australia'), elements ('Air') and feng shui. Others are low-allergy. As well as these walk-in prices, rates are often much less for advance or internet bookings (from €59 for singles).

Eating & Drinking

PIER 51

International €€

(☎ 807 1800; www.pier51.de; Rudolf von Bennigsen Ufer 51; starters €10-13, mains €21-22; 🕙 noon-midnight) One of Hanover's loveliest restaurants, and very romantic at sundown, Pier 51 is walled with glass and juts out over the Maschsee. Expect pasta light dishes and a small selection of fish, poultry and red meats on a changing menu. All dishes can be ordered in half-servings for little over half the price. Book at least a few days ahead if you want a window seat at dinner. Alongside it is boat hire and snack stands with outdoor seating. Take tram/U-Bahn 1, 2 or 8 to Altenbeken Damm and walk 10 minutes to the Maschsee.

MARKTHALLE

Market €

(www.hannover-markthalle.de; Kamarschstrasse 49; dishes €3.50-10; 🕙 7am-8pm Mon-Wed, to 10pm Thu & Fri, to 4pm Sat; 🍴) This huge covered market of food stalls and gourmet delicatessens is fantastic for a quick bite, both carnivorous and vegetarian.

BRAUHAUS ERNST AUGUST

Pub

(www.brauhaus.net; Schmiedestrasse 13; 🕙 8am-3am Mon-Thu, to 5am Fri & Sat, 9am-3pm Sun) A Hanover institution, this sprawling brewpub makes a refreshing unfiltered Pilsner called Hannöversch. A party atmosphere reigns nightly, helped along by a varied roster of live bands and DJs.

❶ Information

Tourist Information

Information and brochures are available from a staffed desk at the Neues Rathaus. The **tourist office** (☎ information 1234 5111, room reservations 123 45555; www.hannover.de; Ernst-August-Platz 8; 🕙 9am-

Hanover's Markthalle
© UNITED ARCHIVES GMBH/ALAMY ©

6pm Mon-Fri, 10am-3pm Sat & Sun) is especially useful during trade fairs.

Getting There & Away

Air

Hanover Airport (HAJ; www.hannover-airport .de) has many connections, including **Lufthansa** (www.lufthansa.com), and the carriers **Air Berlin** (www.airberlin.com) to/from London-Stansted. The S-Bahn (S5) takes 18 minutes from the airport to the Hauptbahnhof (€3).

Car & Motorcycle

Nearby autobahns run to Hamburg, Munich, Frankfurt and Berlin, with good connections to Bremen, Cologne, Amsterdam and Brussels.

Train

Hanover is a major rail hub for European and national services, with frequent ICE trains to/from Hamburg Hauptbahnhof (€43, 1¼ hours), Bremen (€31, one hour), Munich (€125, 4¼ hours), Cologne (€68, 2¾ hours) and Berlin (€65, 1¾ hours), among others.

Around Hanover

Celle

☎ 05141 / POP 70,250

With 400 half-timbered houses and its stately palace dating back to the 13th century, Celle is graced with a picture-book town centre that is among the most attractive in the region. The white-and-pink **Schloss** (Ducal Palace; Schlossplatz; Residenzmuseum €5, combined Residenz-museum, Bomann Museum & Kunstmuseum €8, Fri free, guided tours adult €6; ☉10am-5pm Tue-Sun), Celle's centrepiece set in small gardens, contrasts with the ultramodern **Kunstmuseum** (Art Museum; ☎123 55; www .kunst.celle.de; Schlossplatz 7; adult/concession incl Bomann Museum €5/3, free Fri; ☉10am-5pm Tue-Fri, to 6pm Sat & Sun), which is illuminated at night into a '24-hour' museum and successfully creates an interesting contrast of old and new.

The tourist office (in the Altes Rathaus building) has a good *Walk Through Celle* map in English that takes you from sight to sight.

Sleeping & Eating

HOTEL CELLER HOF　　　　　Hotel €€
(☎911 960; www.cellerhof.de; Stechbahn 11; s €75-80, d €110-115, tr €130-150; P@✿)
The friendly staff, Finnish sauna, tasteful furnishings and central location make this a good all-round option. All rooms have a writing desk, and there's a small lobby bar for relaxing.

**RESTAURANT BIER
AKADEMIE**　　　　　German €€
(www.bier-akademie-celle.de; Weisser Wall 6; mains €11.10-22.50; ☉lunch Mon-Thu, dinner Mon-Sat) This family-run restaurant serves an excellent range of beef, poultry and lamb as well as pork, but its speciality is a local roulade, which you can order as a starter or main course.

Information

Tourist office (☎1212; www.region-celle.com; Markt 14-16; ☉9am-6pm Mon-Fri, 10am-4pm Sat, 11am-2pm Sun) Has a free town map with a walking route and runs guided tours (€5; in German) at 11am Saturday to Thursday, 4.30pm Friday much of the year.

Getting There & Away

Several trains each hour to Hanover take from 20 minutes (IC; €11) to 45 minutes (S-Bahn; €9.10).

Bergen-Belsen

Bergen-Belsen (www.bergenbelsen.de; Lohheide; ☉10am-6pm) began its existence in 1940 as a POW camp, but was partly taken over by the SS from April 1943 to hold Jews as hostages in exchange for German POWs held abroad. In all, 70,000 Jews, Soviet soldiers, political hostages and other prisoners died here. Among them was Anne Frank, whose posthumously published diary became a modern classic. The Documentation-Centre today is one of the best of its kind and deals sensitively but very poignantly with the lives of the people who were imprisoned here – before, during and after incarceration.

Wolfsburg

Arriving in Wolfsburg by train, the first thing you see is an enormous, almost surreal, VW emblem on a building in a scene that could have come from Fritz Lang's classic film *Metropolis*. This is part of the Volkswagen company's nation-sized global headquarters. As well as the hugely successful **Autostadt** (Car City; www.autostadt.de; Stadtbrücke; adult/concession €15/12, car tower discovery adult/concession €8/6; ⊙9am-6pm) theme park, the town boasts a **Phaeno** (www.phaeno.de; Willy Brandt-Platz 1; adult/child/concession/family €12/7.50/9/26.50; ⊙9am-5pm Tue-Fri, 10am-6pm Sat & Sun, last entry 1hr before closing) science centre, a sleek piece of futuristic architecture by celebrity architect Zaha Hadid, and a great collection of rare and unusual vehicles in the **AutoMuseum** (http://automuseum.volkswagen.de; Dieselstrasse 35; adult/concession/family €6/3/15; ⊙10am-6pm Tue-Sun).

From Braunschweig, take the A2 east to the A39 north, which brings you right into town. Frequent ICE train services go to Berlin (€47, one hour). IC trains to Hanover (€17.50, 30 minutes) are cheaper and barely slower than the ICE.

Hamelin

☎ 0441 / POP 57,800

If you have a phobia about rats, you might give this picturesque town on the Weser River a wide berth. According to *The Pied Piper of Hamelin* fairy tale, in the 13th century the Pied Piper (*Der Rattenfänger*) was employed by Hamelin's townsfolk to lure its nibbling rodents into the river. When they refused to pay him, he picked up his flute and led their kids away. Today the rats rule once again – rats that are stuffed, fluffy and cute, wooden rats, and even little rats that adorn the sights around town.

◎ Sights

RATTENFÄNGERHAUS

Historic Building

(Rat Catcher's House; Osterstrasse 28) Among the finest of the houses built in the ornamental Weser Renaissance style – prevalent throughout the Altstadt – is the Rattenfängerhaus, from 1602, with its typically steep and richly decorated gable.

Bergen-Belsen memorial (p349)

HOLGER HOLLEMANN/EPA/CORBIS ©

Fairy-Tale Road

The 600km **Märchenstrasse** (Fairy-Tale Road; www.deutsche-maerchenstrasse.com) is one of Germany's most popular tourist routes. It's made up of cities, towns and hamlets in four states (Hesse, Lower Saxony, North Rhine-Westphalia and Bremen), which can often be reached by using a choice of roads rather than one single route. The towns are associated in one way or another with the works of Wilhelm and Jakob Grimm. Although most towns can be easily visited using public transport, a car is useful for getting a feel for the route.

The Grimm brothers travelled extensively through central Germany in the early 19th century documenting folklore. Their collection of tales, *Kinder- und Hausmärchen,* was first published in 1812 and quickly gained international recognition. It includes such fairy-tale staples as *Hansel and Gretel, Cinderella, The Pied Piper, Rapunzel* and scores of others.

There are over 60 stops on the Fairy-Tale Road. Major ones include (from south to north): **Hanau**, about 15km east of Frankfurt, the birthplace of Jakob (1785–1863) and Wilhelm (1786–1859); **Steinau**, where the Brothers Grimm spent their youth; **Marburg**, in whose university the brothers studied for a short while; **Kassel**, with a museum dedicated to the Grimms; **Göttingen**, at whose university the brothers served as professors before being expelled in 1837 for their liberal views; **Bad Karlshafen**, a meticulously planned white baroque village; **Bodenwerder**, whose rambling Münchhausen Museum is dedicated to the legendary Baron von Münchhausen, (in)famous for telling outrageous tales; **Hamelin** (Hameln), forever associated with the legend of the Pied Piper; and **Bremen**. The Märchenstrasse website has a downloadable map that provides a good overview of the routes and towns.

HOCHZEITSHAUS Historic Building
(Osterstrasse 2) Situated on the corner of Markt and Osterstrasse is the Hochzeitshaus (1610–17), partly used today as city council offices and as a police station. The **Rattenfänger Glockenspiel** at the far end of the building chimes daily at 9.35am and 11.35am, while a carousel of Pied Piper figures twirls at 1.05pm, 3.35pm and 5.35pm.

 Eating

RATTENFÄNGERHAUS German €€
(Osterstrasse 28; mains €10-23; ⊘11am-10pm)
Hamelin's traditional restaurants are unashamedly aimed at tourists, such as this cute half-timbered tavern with a speciality of 'rats' tails' flambéed at your table (fortunately, like most of the theme dishes here, it's based on pork). Schnitzels, herrings, vegie dishes and 'rat killer' herb liquor are also offered.

ⓘ Getting There & Away

CAR By car, take the B217 to/from Hanover.

TRAIN Frequent S-Bahn trains (S5) head to Hamelin from Hanover's Hauptbahnhof (€11.10, 45 minutes).

Germany
In Focus

Karlsplatz, Munich (p51)
JAM WORLD IMAGES/ALAMY ©

Germany Today

> **Some 15 million people living in Germany have an immigrant background**

Berlin market stall

belief systems
(% of population)

68	28	
Christian	Muslim	Other

if Germany were 100 people

92 would be German

2 would be Turkish

6 would be other

population per sq km

GERMANY   UK   USA

 ≈ 7 people

Europe's Economic Engine

Germany seems to have weathered the financial crisis better than most industrial nations, in large part because it now bears the fruit of decade-old key reforms, especially the liberalisation of labour laws. The government also launched a slew of proactive measures, including one that allowed companies to put workers on shorter shifts without loss of pay and another that stimulated the economy by providing incentives for Germans to scrap older cars and buy new ones.

The beginning of the millennium's second decade has seen the importance of Germany's stable economy grow, as the debt-driven crisis in the eurozone has spread from Greece to threaten all of southern Europe. Germany is seen as the key to prop up the euro, the collapse of which could plunge economies across the globe back into recession. So far, so good.

In mid-2012 the European Commission reported that the German economy grew 0.5% in the first quarter while the eurozone

the renewables industry. The country has also reduced its greenhouse gas emissions by 24% since 1990, thus exceeding the requirements of the 2005 Kyoto Protocol (it called for a 21% reduction).

Following the nuclear disaster in Fukushima, Germany became the first industrial nation to completely opt out of nuclear power in 2011, immediately shutting down the eight oldest of its 17 reactors. The same year, the Bundestag passed legislation that would see the remaining nine nuclear plants go off the grid by 2022. Wind farms, solar arrays and other nonpolluting power producers would pick up the slack, generating 35% of Germany's electricity needs.

Land of Immigration

Some 15 million people living in Germany have an immigrant background (meaning they're foreign born or have at least one immigrant parent), accounting for about 18% of the total population. According to the United Nations, only the USA and Russia absorb a greater number of international migrants. The largest group is the Turks, a legacy of the post-WWII economic boom when 'guest workers' were recruited to shore up the war-depleted workforce. Many stayed. After reunification, the foreign population soared again as repatriates from the former USSR and refugees from war-ravaged Yugoslavia arrived by the millions.

Whether immigration enriches or endangers German culture has been the subject of much debate in recent years, but economic reports indicate that newcomers help to keep the economy running. With an ageing population and low birthrate, Germany has the fastest declining population among developed nations. Experts believe that Germany has no choice but to adapt and scale up its outdated laws and policies on controlled immigration.

as a whole stagnated. Manufacturing orders and exports, especially to hungry markets in South America, Asia and eastern Europe were up, helped along by a weak euro. At the same time, the unemployment rate had dropped to 6%, the property market was on the upswing and consumer confidence was high.

Environmental Leadership

As the birthplace of the Green Party, Germany has always played a leading role in environmental and climate protection and is considered a pioneer in the development of renewable energies. In 2000 the Bundestag (parliament) passed the *Erneuerbare-Energien-Gesetz* (Renewable Energies Act), which provides subsidies and incentives to companies engaged in producing renewable energy. In 2011 about 20% of total energy production came from alternative sources. One solar cell in five and every seventh wind turbine hail from Germany, where some 400,000 people are employed in

History

Kaiserthermen (p224), Trier

MICHAEL MUCHA/GETTY IMA

Events in Germany have often dominated the European stage, but the country itself is a relatively recent invention: for most of its history, Germany has been a patchwork of semi-independent principalities and city-states, occupied first by the Roman Empire, then the Holy Roman Empire and finally the Austrian Habsburgs. Perhaps because of this, many Germans retain a strong regional identity despite the momentous national events that have occurred since.

Tribes & the Romans

Early inhabitants on German soil were Celts and, later, the Germanic tribes. The tribes located east of the Rhine and the Romans struggled for control of territory across the river until AD 9, when Roman general Varus lost three legions – about 20,000 men – in the bloody Battle of the Teutoburg Forest, putting paid to Roman plans to extend their rule eastwards. By AD 300, four main groups of tribes had formed: Alemanni, Franks, Saxons and Goths.

800–300 BC
Germanic tribes and Celts inhabit large parts of northern and central Germany.

The Frankish Reich

On the Rhine's western bank, the Frankish Reich became a key political power in medieval Europe. Merovingian king Clovis laid the groundwork in the 5th century but it would be another three centuries before Charlemagne, the Reich's most important ruler, rose to power in 768. From his residence in Aachen, Charlemagne conquered Lombardy, won territory in Bavaria, waged a 30-year war against the Saxons in the north and was eventually crowned Kaiser (emperor) by the pope in 800.

The cards were reshuffled in the 9th century when attacks by Danes, Saracens and Magyars threw the eastern portion of Charlemagne's empire into turmoil and four dominant duchies emerged – Bavaria, Franconia, Swabia and Saxony. The Treaty of Verdun (843) saw a gradual carve-up of the Frankish Reich and when Louis the Child (r 900–11) – a grandson of Charlemagne's brother – died heirless, the East Frankish (ie German) dukes elected a king from their own ranks, thereby creating the first German monarch.

Early Middle Ages

Strong regionalism in Germany today has its roots in the early Middle Ages, when dynasties squabbled and intrigued over territorial spoils, as a toothless, Roman-inspired central state watched on helplessly. The symbolic heart of power was the cathedral in Aachen, which hosted the coronations and burials of dozens of German kings from 936. The first to be crowned was Otto I who, in 962, renewed Charlemagne's pledge to protect the papacy and was rewarded by the pope with the imperial crown the same year.

This created the Holy Roman Empire and made the Kaiser and pope acrimonious bedfellows for the next 800 years until Kaiser Franz II abdicated the throne in 1806. Through the centuries, the empire variously encompassed present-day Netherlands, Belgium, Switzerland, Lorraine and Burgundy (in France), Sicily, Austria and an eastern swath of land that lies in the Czech Republic, Poland and Hungary.

Under Friedrich I Barbarossa (r 1152–90), Aachen assumed the role of Reich capital and was granted liberty in 1165, the year Charlemagne was canonised. Meanwhile,

The Best...
History Museums

1 Deutsches Historisches Museum (p255), Berlin

2 Haus der Geschichte der Bundesrepublik Deutschland (p236), Bonn

3 Zeitgeschichtliches Forum (p304), Leipzig

4 Jüdisches Museum (p263), Berlin

5 Römisch-Germanisches Museum (p225), Cologne

AD 9
The Battle of the Teutoburg Forest halts Roman expansion eastwards.

482
Clovis becomes king of the Franks and lays the foundations for a Frankish Reich.

768–814
The Carolingian Charlemagne is crowned Kaiser and under him the Frankish Reich grows in power and extent.

The Hanseatic League

The origins of the Hanseatic League go back to various guilds and associations established from about the mid-12th century by out-of-town merchants to protect their interests. After Hamburg and Lübeck signed an agreement in 1241 to protect their ships and trading routes, they were joined in their league by Lüneburg, Kiel and a string of Baltic Sea cities east to Greifswald. By 1356 this had grown into the Hanseatic League, encompassing half a dozen other large alliances of cities, with Lübeck playing the lead role. At its zenith, the league had about 200 member cities. By the 15th century however, competition from Dutch and English shipping companies, internal disputes and a shift in the centre of world trade from the North and Baltic Seas to the Atlantic had caused decline.

Heinrich der Löwe (Henry the Lion) extended influence eastwards in campaigns to Germanise and convert the Slavs who populated much of today's eastern Germany. Heinrich was very well-connected and founded not only Braunschweig but Munich and Lübeck, too.

The Reich gained territory to the east and in Italy, but soon fell apart. At this time kings were being elected by *Kurfürsten* (prince-electors) but crowned Kaiser by the pope – a system that made an unwilling lackey out of a kaiser. In 1245 the Reich plunged into an era called the Great Interregnum, or the Terrible Time, when central authority collapsed in a political heap.

Although the central Reich was only a shadow of its former self, expansion eastwards continued unabated.

Ordinary Germans, however, battled with panic lynching, pogroms against Jews and labour shortages – all sparked off by the plague (1348–50) that wiped out 25% of Europe's population. While death gripped the (Ger)man on the street, universities were being established all over the country around this time.

A Question Of Faith

The religious fabric of Germany was cut from a pattern created by the 16th-century Reformation. In 1517 Martin Luther (1483–1546) made public his *Ninety-Five Theses,* which questioned the papal practice of selling indulgences to exonerate sins. Threatened with excommunication, Luther refused to recant, broke from the Catholic Church and was banned by the Reich.

962

Otto I is crowned Holy Roman Emperor by the pope, reaffirming the precedent established by Charlemagne. Emperor Otto I

1273

The House of Habsburg begins its rise to become Europe's most powerful dynasty.

It was not until 1555 that the Catholic and Lutheran churches were ranked as equals, thanks to Karl V (r 1520–58), who signed the Peace of Augsburg (1555), allowing princes to decide the religion of their principality. The more secular northern principalities adopted Lutheran teachings, while the clerical lords in the south, southwest and Austria stuck with Catholicism.

But the religious issue refused to die. It degenerated into the Thirty Years' War (1618–48) that left Europe drenched with the blood of millions. Calm was restored with the Peace of Westphalia (1648), signed in Münster and Osnabrück, but it left the Reich a nominal, impotent state. Switzerland and the Netherlands gained formal independence, France won chunks of Alsace and Lorraine, and Sweden helped itself to the mouths of the Elbe, Oder and Weser rivers.

The Age of Enlightenment

In the 18th century an intellectual movement called the Enlightenment swept through much of Europe. Leading thinkers, such as the philosophers Johann Gottfried von Herder, Immanuel Kant and Voltaire embraced humanist ideals and sought to understand and explain reality through reason and science rather than religion and faith. This went hand in hand with a flourishing of the arts and culture: rulers built stunning palaces and gardens; Goethe and Schiller penned their famous works; and Bach, Haydn, Händel and Mozart composed their immortal music.

One king who embraced the Enlightenment was Friedrich II (r 1740–86) – aka Frederick the Great – of Brandenburg-Prussia. When not waxing philosophical with his friend Voltaire, Frederick was busy on the battlefield, fighting tooth and nail for two decades to wrest Silesia (in today's Poland) from Austria and Saxony, and thus for the first time positioning the Brandenburg-Prussian kingdom as a force to be reckoned with.

Napoléon & Revolutions

In the aftermath of the 1789 French Revolution, a diminutive Frenchman named Napoléon Bonaparte (Napoléon I) took control of Europe and significantly altered its fate through a series of wars. The defeat of Austrian and Russian troops in the Battle of Austerlitz in 1806 led to the collapse of the Holy Roman Empire. That same year, most German kingdoms, duchies and principalities aligned themselves with Napoléon in the Confederation of the Rhine. It was to be a short-lived alliance though, for many of its members switched allegiance again after Napoléon got trounced by Prussian, Russian, Austrian and Swedish troops in the bloody 1813 Battle of Leipzig.

In 1815, at the Congress of Vienna, Germany was reorganised into the Deutscher Bund (German Alliance), a confederation of 39 states with a central legislative assembly, the Reichstag, established in Frankfurt. Austria and Prussia dominated this alliance until a series of bourgeois democratic revolutions swept through German cities in 1848, resulting in Germany's first ever freely elected parliamentary delegation

1455

Johannes Gutenberg of Mainz prints the Gutenberg Bible using a moveable type system, revolutionising book printing.

1555

The Peace of Augsburg allows German rulers to decide their fiefdom's religion.

1618–48

The Thirty Years' War sweeps through Germany and leaves it with a depleted population.

convening in Frankfurt's Paulskirche. Austria, meanwhile, broke away from Germany, came up with its own constitution and promptly relapsed into monarchism. As revolution fizzled in 1850, the confederation resumed again with Prussia and Austria as dominant members.

Bismarck & the Birth of an Empire

The creation of a unified Germany with Prussia at the helm was the glorious ambition of Otto von Bismarck (1815–98), a former member of the Reichstag and Prussian prime minister from 1862. An old-guard militarist, he used intricate diplomacy and a series of wars with neighbouring Denmark and Austria to achieve his aims. By 1871 Berlin stood as the proud capital of the German Reich (empire), a bicameral, constitutional monarchy. On 18 January 1871, Prussian king Wilhelm I was crowned Kaiser at Versailles, with Bismarck as his 'Iron Chancellor'.

When pressed, Bismarck made concessions to the growing and increasingly antagonistic socialist movement, enacting Germany's first modern social reforms, though this was not his true nature. When Wilhelm II (r 1888–1918) came to power, he wanted to extend social reform while Bismarck envisioned stricter antisocialist laws. By March 1890, the Kaiser had had enough and excised his renegade chancellor from the political scene. Bismarck's legacy as a brilliant diplomat unravelled as a wealthy, unified and industrially powerful Germany powered into the new century.

WWI

The assassination of Archduke Franz Ferdinand, the heir to the Austrian throne, on 28 June 1914 triggered a series of diplomatic decisions that led to WWI, the bloodiest European conflict since the Thirty Years' War. Initial euphoria and faith in a quick victory soon gave way to despair as casualties piled up in the battlefield trenches and stomachs grumbled on the home front. When peace came when Germany was defeated in 1918, it also ended domestic stability, ushering in a period of turmoil and violence.

The seeds of acrimony and humiliation that later led to WWII were sown in the peace conditions of WWI. Germany, militarily broken, teetering on the verge of revolution and caught in a no-man's-land between monarchy and modern democracy, signed the Treaty of Versailles (1919), which made it responsible for all losses incurred by its enemies. Its borders were trimmed back and it was forced to pay high reparations.

The Weimar Republic

In July 1919 the federalist constitution of the fledgling republic – Germany's first serious experiment with democracy – was adopted in the town of Weimar, where the constituent assembly had sought refuge from the chaos of Berlin. It gave women the vote and established basic human rights, but it also gave the chancellor the right to rule by decree – a concession that would later prove critical in Hitler's rise to power.

1806

The Holy Roman Empire collapses and Napoléon creates the Confederation of the Rhine.

1815

The Congress of Vienna redraws the map of Europe, creating the Deutscher Bund (German Alliance) with 39 states.

1848

Following the March Revolution, Germany's first parliamentary delegation meets in Frankfurt.

The Weimar Republic (1920–33) was governed by a coalition of left and centre parties, but pleased neither communists nor monarchists. In fact, the 1920s began as anything but 'golden', marked, as they were, by the humiliation of a lost war, social and political instability, hyperinflation, mass unemployment, hunger and disease.

Economic stability gradually returned after a new currency, the *Rentenmark*, was introduced in 1923, and with the Dawes Plan in 1924, which limited the crippling reparation payments imposed on Germany. But the tide turned again when the US stock market crashed in 1929, plunging the world into economic depression. Within weeks, millions were jobless, and riots and demonstrations again ruled Germany's streets.

Hitler's Rise to Power

The volatile, increasingly polarised political climate of the Weimar years provided fertile ground for political extremists. One party waiting in the wings was the Nationalsozialistische Deutsche Arbeiterpartei (National Socialist German Workers' Party, NSDAP, or Nazi Party), led by a failed Austrian artist and WWI corporal named Adolf Hitler. In the 1930 elections, the NSDAP gained 18% of the national vote. By January 1933, Hitler had become chancellor.

Statue of Otto von Bismarck
JONATHAN SMITH/GETTY IMAGES ©

1871
Through diplomacy and war, Bismarck creates a Prussia-led unified Germany.

1914–18
WWI: Germany, Austria-Hungary and Turkey go to war against Britain, France, Italy and Russia.

1933
Hitler becomes chancellor of Germany and creates a dictatorship through the Enabling Law.

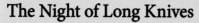

The Night of Long Knives

The brown-shirted SA (Sturmabteilung, or Storm Troopers) was a Nazi organisation charged mainly with policing Nazi party meetings and disrupting those convened by political opponents. Although it played an important role in Hitler's ascent to power, by 1934 it had become quite powerful in its own right, thanks, in large part, to its leader Ernst Röhm. On 30 June that year, feeling threatened, Hitler ordered the black-shirted Schutzstaffel (SS) to round up and kill the SA leadership (including Röhm and at least 75 others) to bring the organisation to heel. On 13 July, Hitler announced to the Reichstag that the SA would, from that time forth, serve under the command of the army. Justice would be executed by Hitler himself and the black-shirted SS under the leadership of former chicken farmer Heinrich Himmler, effectively giving the SS unchallenged power and making it Nazi Germany's most powerful – and feared – force.

Hitler moved quickly to consolidate absolute power and to turn the nation's democracy into a one-party dictatorship. He used the Reichstag fire in March 1933 as a pretext to push through the Enabling Law, allowing him to decree laws and change the constitution without consulting parliament.

The rise of the Nazis had instant, far-reaching consequences. In the 12 short years of what Hitler envisaged as the 'Thousand Year Reich', massive destruction would be inflicted upon German and other European cities; political opponents, intellectuals and artists would be murdered, or forced to go underground or into exile; and a culture of terror and denunciation would permeate almost all of German society.

Jewish Persecution

Jewish people were specifically targeted in what would be a long-term campaign of genocide. In April 1933 Joseph Goebbels, head of the Ministry of Propaganda, announced a boycott of Jewish businesses. Soon after, Jews were expelled from public service and 'non-Aryans' were banned from many professions, trades and industries. The Nuremberg Laws (1935) deprived non-Aryans of German citizenship and many other rights. The targeting of Jews reached a peak on 9 November 1938 with the Kristallnacht (Night of the Broken Glass) when Nazi thugs attacked synagogues, Jewish cemeteries, property and businesses across the country. While Jews had begun to emigrate after 1933, this event set off a stampede.

The fate of those Jews who stayed behind deteriorated after the outbreak of WWII in 1939. In 1942, at Hitler's request, a conference in Berlin's Wannsee came up with the *Endlösung* (Final Solution): the systematic, bureaucratic and meticulously

1935

The Nuremberg Laws are enacted, depriving Jews of their German citizenship.

1939–45

WWII: Hitler invades Poland; France and Britain declare war on Germany. Adolf Hitler

INTERFOTO/ALAMY

documented annihilation of European Jews. Of the roughly 7 million people who were sent to concentration camps, only 500,000 survived.

WWII

WWII began on 1 September 1939 with the Nazi attack on Poland. France and Britain declared war on Germany two days later, but even this could not prevent the quick defeat of Poland, Belgium, the Netherlands and France. Other countries, including Denmark and Norway, were also soon brought into the Nazi fold.

In June 1941 Germany broke its nonaggression pact with Stalin by attacking the Soviet Union. Though successful at first, Operation Barbarossa quickly ran into problems, culminating in the defeat at Stalingrad (today Volgograd) the following winter, forcing the Germans to retreat.

With the Normandy invasion of June 1944, Allied troops arrived in formidable force on the European mainland, supported by unrelenting air raids on Berlin that reduced Germany's cities to rubble and the country's population by 10%. Finally accepting the inevitability of defeat, Hitler killed himself in his bunker along with his wife Eva Braun, whom he'd married just a day earlier, on 30 April 1945. A few days after their deaths, on 8 May, Germany surrendered unconditionally.

The Best...
Third Reich Sites

1 Dokumentation Obersalzberg (p113), Berchestgaden

2 Dachau concentration camp (p90), near Munich

3 Memorium Nuremberg Trials (p134), Nuremberg

4 Topographie des Terrors (p261), Berlin

The Two German States

At conferences in Yalta and Potsdam in February and July 1945 respectively, the Allies (the Soviet Union, the USA, the UK and France) redrew Germany's borders and carved up the country into four occupation zones.

Friction between the Western Allies and the Soviets quickly emerged. While the Western Allies focused on helping Germany get back on its feet by kick-starting the devastated economy, the Soviets insisted on massive reparations and began brutalising and exploiting their own zone of occupation. Tens of thousands of able-bodied men and prisoners of war ended up in labour camps set up deep in the Soviet Union. In the Allied zones meanwhile, democracy was beginning to take root as Germany elected state parliaments (1946–47).

In 1949 the division of Germany was formalised. The western zones evolved into the *Bundesrepublik Deutschland* (BRD, Federal Republic of Germany or FRG) with Bonn, on the Rhine River, as its capital. An economic aid package dubbed the Marshall Plan created the basis for West Germany's *Wirtschaftswunder* (economic miracle), which saw the economy grow at an average 8% per year between 1951 and 1961. A

1939–45

In addition to millions of Jews murdered during the Holocaust, 62 million civilians and soldiers die during WWII.

1948–49

The USSR cuts off West Berlin, so the US and Britain supply the city by air during the Berlin Airlift.

1949

West Germany becomes the Federal Republic of Germany (FRG), East Germany the German Democratic Republic (GDR).

cornerstone of recovery was the arrival of 2.3 million foreign workers, mainly from Turkey, Yugoslavia and Italy, which laid the foundation for today's multicultural society.

The Soviet zone, meanwhile, grew into the *Deutsche Demokratische Republik* (German Democratic Republic or GDR), with East Berlin as its capital. A single party, the *Sozialistische Einheitspartei Deutschlands* (SED, Socialist Unity Party of Germany) dominated economic, judicial and security policy. In order to suppress any opposition, the Ministry for State Security, or Stasi, was established in 1950. Economically, East Germany stagnated, in large part because of the Soviets' continued policy of asset stripping and reparation payments.

The Wall: What Goes Up...

Through the 1950s the economic gulf between East and West Germany widened, prompting 3.6 million East Germans – mostly young and well-educated – to seek a future in the West and thus putting the GDR on the brink of economic and political collapse. Eventually, this sustained brain and brawn drain prompted the East German government – with Soviet consent – to build a wall to keep them in. Construction of the Berlin Wall, the Cold War's most potent symbol, began on the night of 13 August 1961. The intra-German border was fenced off and mines were laid down.

Berlin Wall in 1989 (p246)
PHOTOGRAPHER CREDIT

1961
The GDR government begins building the Berlin Wall.

1971
Social Democrat chancellor Willy Brandt's *Ostpolitik* thaws relations between the two Germanys.

1989
The Berlin Wall comes down; East Germans flood into West Germany.

The Stasi

In East Germany, the walls had ears. Modelled after the Soviet KGB, the GDR's *Ministerium für Staatssicherheit* (MfS, or Ministry of State Security, 'Stasi' for short) was founded in 1950. It was secret police, the central intelligence agency and bureau of criminal investigation all rolled into one. Called the 'shield and sword' of the SED, the sole East German party, it put millions of GDR citizens under surveillance in order to suppress internal opposition.

The Stasi grew steadily in power and size and, by the end, had 91,000 official full-time employees and 189,000 IMs (*Inoffizielle Mitarbeiter*, unofficial informants). The latter were recruited among regular folks to spy on their coworkers, friends, family and neighbours. There were also 3000 IMs based in West Germany.

When the Wall fell, the Stasi fell with it. Thousands of citizens stormed the ministry's headquarters in January 1990, thus preventing the shredding of documents that revealed the full extent of institutionalised surveillance and repression through wire-tapping, videotape observation, opening private mail and other methods.

The appointment of Erich Honecker as government leader in 1971, combined with the *Ostpolitik* (East-friendly policy) of West German chancellor Willy Brandt, allowed an easier political relationship between the East and West. In September that year, all four Allies signed a Four Power Accord that paved the way to the 1972 Transit Agreement that regulated access between West Berlin and West Germany, guaranteed West Berliners the right to visit East Berlin and the GDR, and even granted GDR citizens permission to travel to West Germany in cases of family emergency.

... Must Come Down

Hearts and minds in eastern Europe had long been restless for change, but German reunification caught even the most insightful political observers by surprise. The so-called *Wende* (turning point, ie the fall of communism) was a gradual development that ended in a big bang – the collapse of the Berlin Wall on 9 November 1989.

Prior to the Wall's collapse, East Germans were, once again, leaving their country in droves, this time via Hungary, which had opened its borders with Austria. The SED was helpless to stop the flow of people wanting to leave, some of whom sought refuge in the West German embassy in Prague. Meanwhile, mass demonstrations in Leipzig spread to other cities, including East Berlin.

1990
Berlin becomes the capital of reunified Germany. Helmut Kohl promises economic integration.

2005
Angela Merkel becomes Germany's first woman chancellor.

2008
German banks are propped up by state funds as unemployment and state debt rises.

As the situation escalated, Erich Honecker relinquished leadership to Egon Krenz (b 1937). And on the fateful night of 9 November 1989, party functionary Günter Schabowski informed GDR citizens they could travel directly to the West, effective immediately. The announcement was supposed to be embargoed until the following day. Tens of thousands of East Germans jubilantly rushed through border points in Berlin and elsewhere in the country, bringing to an end the long, chilly phase of German division. The formal Unification Treaty was signed on 31 August 1990.

Since Reunification

In December 1990, Helmut Kohl was elected Germany's postreunification chancellor. Under his leadership East German assets were privatised; state industries were trimmed back, sold or closed; and infrastructure was modernised, all resulting in economic growth of about 10% each year until 1995. The trend slowed dramatically thereafter however, creating an eastern Germany that consisted of unification winners and losers.

Amid allegations of widespread financial corruption, the Kohl government was replaced with a coalition government of SPD (Social Democratic Party) and Alliance 90/The Greens in 1998. This marked the first time an environmentalist party had governed nationally – in Germany or elsewhere in the world.

The rise of the Greens and, more recently, the Left has changed the political landscape of Germany dramatically, making absolute majorities by the 'big two' all the more difficult to achieve. In 2005 the CDU (Christian Democratic Union)/CSU (Christlich-Soziale Union) and SPD formed a grand coalition led by Angela Merkel (b 1954), the first woman, former East German and quantum physicist in the job.

The election of 2009 confirmed the trend towards smaller parties and a five-party political system in Germany. The outcome of Germany's national elections in the autumn of 2013 will reveal whether this fragmentation has become a permanent feature of Germany politics.

2009
The CDU/CSU and FDP achieve a majority in the federal election. Angela Merkel is reelected as chancellor. Angela Merkel

2011–12
Southern Europe looks to Germany as the crisis in the eurozone deepens.

Family Travel

Oberstdorf (p110), Bavaria

CARO/ALAMY ©

Germany is a safe and easy place to travel with children and most places are happy to welcome kids. Keep a light schedule, involve the little ones in trip planning and teach them a few simple words in German. Plus, kids are a great excuse if you secretly yearn to ride roller coasters or go ape in a zoo.

The Low-Down

Practically all hotels can provide cots (cribs), though sometimes for a small fee. Some properties allow small children to stay in their parents' room free of charge if they don't require extra bedding.

As long as they're not running wild, children are generally welcome in German restaurants, especially in informal cafes, bistros, pizzerias or *Gaststätten* (inns). Many places offer a limited *Kindermenü* (children's menu) or *Kinderteller* (children's dishes).

Breastfeeding in public is commonly practised, although most women are discreet about it.

Children under 12 or smaller than 59 inches (1.5m) must ride in the back seat in cars (including taxis) and use a car seat or booster appropriate for their weight. Taxis are not equipped with car seats, so bring your own or reserve one early if hiring a car.

Children under 15 travel free on trains if accompanied by at least one parent or grandparent, as long they're registered on your ticket at the time of purchase. Children under six always travel free and without a ticket.

Kidding Around

Kids might already have seen in picture books many of the things that make the country so special: enchanting palaces and legend-shrouded castles; medieval towns; and half-timbered villages, Viking ships and Roman ruins. This is the birthplace of the Brothers Grimm and their famous fairy tales. If you follow the Fairy-Tale Road, you even get to see Sleeping Beauty's castle and the town of Hamelin of Pied Piper fame.

Outdoor Activities

The great outdoors yield endless variety in Germany. Tourist offices can recommend walking trails suitable for families, including stroller-friendly paths, or can hook you up with a local guide. Also ask about kid-geared activities, such as geocaching, animal-spotting safaris and nature walks.

Germany's beaches and lakes are beautifully clean and usually devoid of big waves and dangerous undercurrents, although water temperatures rarely exceed 21°C (70°F). Many have a *Strandbad* (lido) with change rooms, playgrounds, splash zones, slides, ping-pong tables, restaurants and boat rentals.

All ski resorts have ski schools with English-speaking instructors who initiate kids in the art of the snow plough – in group or private lessons. All resorts, of course, have plenty of off-piste fun as well: snow-shoeing, sledding, walking and ice skating.

The Best... Museums & Theme Parks

1 Chocolate Museum (p228), Cologne

2 Museum für Naturkunde (p258), Berlin

3 Europa-Park (p178), near Freiburg

4 Spielzeugmuseum (p135), Nuremberg

5 Deutsches Technikmuseum (p263), Berlin

Need to Know

○ **Baby food, formulas, milk** Buy in supermarkets and chemists (drugstores).

○ **Changing facilities** Rare;best bring a towel to be safe.

○ **Cots (cribs)** Available upon request in most hotels, especially midrange and top-end ones; best to reserve in advance.

○ **Highchairs & kids' menus** Standard in most restaurants.

○ **Nappies (diapers)** Widely available in supermarkets and chemists.

○ **Strollers** Bring your own.

○ **Transport** Discounts widely available; bring your own car seat or reserve one early if hiring a car.

Arts & Architecture

JOHN BORTHWICK/GETTY IMAGES ©

Germany's creative population has made major contributions to international culture, particularly during the 18th century when the courts at Weimar and Dresden attracted some of the greatest minds in Europe. With such rich traditions to fall back on, inspiration has seldom been in short supply for the new generations of German artists, despite the upheavals of the country's recent history.

Literary Legacies

German literature in the Middle Ages was written in umpteen dialects, based on the oral tradition and typified by lyrical poetry, ballads and secular epics, such as the famous *Nibelungen* saga (from the 12th century). Martin Luther's translation of the Bible from Greek to German in 1521–22 created a common German language and thus paved the way for modern literature. But this didn't hit its stride until the Enlightenment, two centuries later.

The undisputed literary colossus of the period was Johann Wolfgang von Goethe, most famous for his two-part drama *Faust* about the archetypal human quest for meaning and knowledge. Goethe and his friend Friedrich Schiller were key figures in a celebrated period known as *Weimarer Klassik* (Weimar classicism).

In the mid-19th century, realist novels captured the imagination of the newly emerging middle class. Main exponents include Theodor Fontane who's best known for his 1894 society novel *Effi Briest*, and Gerhart Hauptmann whose plays and novels focused on social injustice and the harsh life of the working class.

During the time of the Weimar Republic, Berlin's underworld served as the focus for the novel *Berlin Alexanderplatz* (1929) by Alfred Döblin. Among post-WWII generation writers, Günter Grass became the most celebrated, after bursting into the limelight with *Die Blechtrommel* (Tin Drum; 1959). In East Germany, Christa Wolf won high esteem for her 1963 story *Der geteilte Himmel* (Divided Heaven) about a young woman whose fiancé abandons her for life in the West.

After reunification, literary achievement stagnated at first, as writers from the East and West began a process of self-examination, but it picked up steam in the late 1990s. Thomas Brussig's tongue-in-cheek *Helden wie wir* (Heroes Like Us; 1998) was one of the first post-reunification novels and offers an insightful look at East German society. And Russian-born Wladimir Kaminer's amusing, stranger-than-fiction hit *Russendisko* (Russian Disco; 2000) firmly established the author in Germany's lighthearted literary scene.

Caught on Film

Since the foundation of the Universum Film AG (UFA) studios in Potsdam in 1917, Germany has had an active and successful film industry. Marlene Dietrich (1901–92) became the country's first international superstar, starting out in silent films and later moving to Hollywood. Director Fritz Lang made a name for himself with seminal films *Metropolis* (1927) and *M* (1931).

The best-known director of the Nazi era was Leni Riefenstahl (1902–2003), whose *Triumph of the Will* (1934), depicting the Nuremberg rallies, won great acclaim but later rendered her unemployable.

The 1960s and 1970s saw a great revival of German cinema, spearheaded by energetic, politically aware young directors such as Rainer Werner Fassbinder, Wim Wenders, Volker Schlöndorff and Margarethe von Trotta.

A smash hit after reunification was Tom Tykwer's *Run Lola Run* (1998), which established his reputation as one of Germany's best new directors. Wolfgang Becker's GDR comedy *Good Bye, Lenin!* (2003) was another international hit as was Florian Henckel von Donnersmarck's Academy Award-winning *The Lives of Others* (2006) about the work of the Stasi in the 1980s.

Classical to Electronic Sounds

Forget brass bands and oompah music – few countries can claim the impressive musical heritage of Germany, which generated the greatness of Johann Sebastian Bach, Georg Friedrich Händel, Ludwig van Beethoven, Richard Strauss, Robert Schumann, Johannes Brahms and Richard Wagner, to name a few.

The Best...
Celluloid Classics

1 *The Lives of Others* (2006) Stasi unmasked

2 *Good Bye, Lenin!* (2003) Comedy set around the fall of the Wall

3 *Das Boot* (1981) WWII U-boat warfare

4 *Wings of Desire* (1987) An angel in love with a mortal

5 *The Legend of Paul and Paula* (1973) GDR cult classic

6 *Downfall* (2004) Hitler's demise

7 *Metropolis* (1927) Classic silent flick

8 *Run Lola Run* (1998) High-energy Berlin drama

Germany has also made significant contributions to the contemporary music scene. Internationally renowned artists include punk icon Nina Hagen, '80s red-balloon girl Nena, and rock bands from the Scorpions to Die Toten Hosen to Rammstein.

Kraftwerk pioneered the original electronic sounds, which morphed into techno and became the seminal club music since the 1990s, especially in Berlin and Frankfurt. Today, Germany has the largest electronic music scene in the world, and DJs such as Ellen Allien, Paul Kalkbrenner, Paul van Dyk and Sven Väth have become household names on the global party circuit.

Architecture through the Ages

The first great wave of buildings came with the Romanesque period (800–1200), outstanding examples of which include the cathedrals at Worms, Speyer and Mainz. Gothic architecture brought such traits as ribbed vaults, pointed arches and flying buttresses nicely exemplified in Cologne's cathedral, Trier's Liebfrauenbasilica, Freiburg's Münster and Lübeck's Marienkirche.

For classic baroque, Balthasar Neumann's Residenz in Würzburg, the Passau Cathedral and the many classic buildings in Dresden are must-sees. The neoclassical period of the 19th century was dominated by Karl Friedrich Schinkel, who was especially prolific in Berlin and northern Germany.

No modern movement has had greater influence on design than the Bauhaus, founded in 1919 by Walter Gropius. You can still visit the school and private homes of Gropius and his fellow professors in Dresden-Rosslau. For an overview, drop by the Bauhaus Archive in Berlin. The Nazis shut down the Bauhaus in 1932 and reverted to the pompous and monumental. Berlin's Olympic Stadium and the party rally grounds in Nuremberg are among the few surviving buildings from that dark period.

Frankfurt shows Germany's take on the modern high-rise and for the boldest new architecture head to Berlin where international 'starchitects' including Daniel Libeskind, David Chipperfield and Lord Norman Foster have put their stamp on the city's post-reunification look.

Artistic Achievement

German art's first heyday was during the Renaissance period, which came late to Germany but flourished quickly. The heavyweight of the period is Albrecht Dürer (1471–1528), who was the first to seriously compete with the Italian masters. Dürer influenced court painter Lucas Cranach the Elder (1472–1553) who worked in Wittenberg for more than 45 years.

Two centuries later, the baroque period brought great sculpture, including works by Andreas Schlüter in Berlin. This was followed by neoclassicism in the 19th century, which ushered back interest in the human figure and an emphasis on Roman and Greek

**The Best...
Unesco
World
Heritage Sites**

1 Trier's Roman monuments (p224)

2 Dom (p239), Aachen

3 Speyer's Kaiserdom (p207)

4 Regensburg (p145)

5 Kölner Dom (p229), Cologne

6 Potsdam's parks and palaces (p279)

7 Würzburg's Residenz (p117)

8 Bauhaus sites in Dessau-Rosslau (p307)

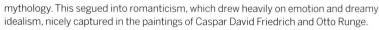

mythology. This segued into romanticism, which drew heavily on emotion and dreamy idealism, nicely captured in the paintings of Caspar David Friedrich and Otto Runge.

In 1905 Ernst Ludwig Kirchner, along with Erich Heckel and Karl Schmidt-Rottluff, founded the artist group *Die Brücke* (The Bridge) in Dresden that turned the art world on its head with groundbreaking visions that paved the way for German expressionism. By the 1920s art had become more radical and political, with artists such as George Grosz, Otto Dix and Max Ernst exploring the new concepts of Dada and surrealism. Käthe Kollwitz is one of the era's few major female artists, known for her social-realist drawings.

After 1945 abstract art became a mainstay of the German scene, with key figures such as Joseph Beuys, Monica Bonvicini and Anselm Kiefer enjoying worldwide reputations. After reunification, the New Leipzig School achieved success at home and abroad with figurative painters such as Neo Rauch generating much acclaim.

Hitting the Stage

Germany's theatre history began during the Enlightenment in the late-18th century, an epoch dominated by humanistic ideals and authors such as Gotthold Ephraim Lessing, Friedrich Schiller and Johann Wolfgang von Goethe.

Starting in the late-19th century, Berlin emerged as the capital of the German theatre scene. At the Deutsches Theater, Max Reinhardt became the most influential expressionist director, collaborating briefly with dramatist Bertolt Brecht whose *Threepenny Opera* premiered in 1928. Like so many others, both men went into exile under the Nazis. Returning in 1949, Brecht founded the Berliner Ensemble and became East Germany's most important director. In the 1950s Heiner Müller – a Marxist critical of GDR-style socialism – became unpalatable in both Germanys.

In West Germany, directors such as Peter Stein earned contemporary German theatre its reputation for producing classic plays in an innovative and provocative manner. Frank Castorf, meanwhile, is arguably Germany's most dynamic contemporary director, heading up Berlin's Volksbühne where he regularly tears down the confines of the proscenium stage with Zeitgeist-critical productions that are somehow populist and elitist all at once.

Outdoors

Bavarian Alps (p106)

No matter what kind of activity gets you off the couch, you'll be able to pursue it in this land of lakes, rivers, mountains and forests. Each season offers its own special delights, be it hiking among spring wildflowers, swimming in a lake warmed by the summer sun, biking among kaleidoscopic autumn foliage or schussing through winter snow. And wherever you go, you'll find local outfitters eager to gear you up.

Hiking & Mountaineering

Wanderlust? Germany coined the word. Ramble through romantic river valleys, hike among fragrant pines, bag alpine peaks or simply go for a walk by the lake or through the dunes. Many of the nicest trails traverse national and nature parks or biosphere reserves. Trails are usually well signposted, sometimes with symbols quaintly painted on tree trunks. To find a route matching your fitness level and time frame, pick the brains of local tourist office staff, who can also supply you with maps and tips.

The Bavarian Alps are Germany's mountaineering heartland, whether for day treks or multiday hut-to-hut clambers. Keep in mind that hiking in the Alps is no walk in the park. You need to be in reasonable condition and come equipped with the right shoes, gear and topographic maps or a GPS. Before heading out, seek local advice and instruction on routes, equipment and weather, as trails can be narrow, steep and have icy patches, even in summer.

The **Deutscher Alpenverein** (DAV; www.alpenverein.de) is a goldmine of information and maintains hundreds of alpine mountain huts, many of them open to the public, where you can spend the night and get a meal. Local DAV chapters also organise various courses (climbing, mountaineering, etc) and guided treks.

For another excellent resource, see www.wanderbares -deutschland.de for information about dozens of walking trails and a handy interactive map. The website is mostly in German, but some routes are also detailed in English.

Cycling

Strap on your helmet! Germany is superb cycling territory, whether you're off on a leisurely spin along the beach, an adrenalin-fuelled downhill ride or a multi-day bike-touring adventure. Practically every town and region has a network of signposted bike routes. Most towns have at least one bike-hire station (often at or near the train station).

Germany is also crisscrossed by more than 200 long-distance trails covering 70,000km, making it ideal for *Radwandern* (bike touring). Routes combine lightly travelled back roads, forestry tracks and paved highways with dedicated bike lanes. Many routes traverse nature reserves, meander along rivers or venture into steep mountain terrain.

For inspiration and route planning, check out www .germany-tourism.de/cycling, which provides (in English) an overview of routes and free downloads of route maps and descriptions.

For on-the-road navigation, the best maps are those published by the national cycling organsation **Allgemeiner Deutscher Fahrrad Club** (ADFC; www.adfc .de). These indicate inclines, track conditions, repair shops and UTM grid coordinates for GPS users. ADFC also offers a useful directory called **Bett & Bike** (www .bettundbike.de), available online or in bookshops, that lists bicycle-friendly hotels, inns and hostels.

Water Sports

Germany's lakes, rivers, canals and coasts offer plenty of water-based action, even if the swimming season is relatively short (June to September) – water temperatures rarely climb above 21°C. Slip into a canoe or kayak to absorb the natural rhythm of the waterways threading through Bavaria's lush Altmühltal Nature Park. Or drift across Lake Constance to Switzerland and Austria with the Alps on the horizon. The season

The Best...
Long-Distance
Cycling Routes

1 Altmühltal Radweg (160km) Easy to moderate; Rothenburg ob der Tauber to Beilngries, following the Altmühl River through the Altmühltal Nature Park.

2 Bodensee–Königssee Radweg (418km) Moderate; Lindau to Berchtesgaden along the foot of the Alps with magnificent views of the mountains, lakes and forests.

3 Donauradweg (434km) Easy to moderate; Neu-Ulm to Passau – a delightful riverside trip along one of Europe's great streams.

4 Romantische Strasse (359km) Easy to moderate; Würzburg to Füssen – one of the nicest ways to explore Germany's most famous holiday route; busy during summer.

runs from around April to October and a one-/two-person canoe or kayak will set you back around €20/30 per day. Stiff breezes and big waves draw sailors, surfers, windsurfers and kite surfers north. Sylt on the North Sea and Rügen on the Baltic have some of the top conditions and schools in the country for water-based activities.

Winter Sports

Modern lifts, primed ski slopes ranging from 'Sesame Street' to 'Death Wish', cross-country trails through untouched nature, cosy mountain huts, steaming mulled wine, hearty dinners by crackling fires: these are all hallmarks of a German skiing holiday.

The Bavarian Alps, only an hour's drive south of Munich, offer the best downhill slopes and most reliable snow conditions. The most famous resort is Garmisch-Partenkirchen, which regularly hosts international competitions and is but a snowball's toss from the Zugspitze, Germany's highest mountain. It has 60km of slopes, mostly geared towards intermediate skiers.

Picture-book pretty Oberstdorf in the Allgäu Alps has 125km of slopes. It's good for boarders with its snow parks and a half-pipe to play on, there's 75km for cross-country skiers to glide along and 55km of skating tracks. For low-key skiing and stunning scenery there is Berchtesgaden, presided over by the jagged Karwendel range.

Can't or won't ski? All resorts offer snowy fun, from tobogganing to ice-skating, and snowshoeing to winter walking.

The Germans

Maypole dancing in traditional costume, Bavaria

There's much fascination with the German state of mind. The nation and its people have seen two 20th-century wars, carry the memory of the Jewish Holocaust, were on the chilling edge of Cold War division, and now live in a juggernaut-like economy that draws half of Europe in its wake and pumps more goods into the world economy than any other.

The National Psyche

It pays to ignore the stereotypes, jingoism and headlines describing Germany in military terms and see the country through its regional nuances. Germany was very slow to become a nation, so look closely to notice the many different local cultures within the one set of borders. You will also find that it's one of Europe's most multicultural countries, with Turkish, Greek, Italian, Russian and Balkan influences.

Germans like to get straight to the point, rather than hint or suggest; they face each other squarely in conversation, give firm handshakes, and a hug or a kiss on the cheek among friends are par for the course.

The Former East

Today around 15 million people live in former East Germany, where, until 1989, travel was restricted, the state was almighty and life was secure (but also strongly regulated) from the cradle to the grave. Not surprisingly, many former East Germans, who lived well in the former socialist state, are still coming to terms with a more competitive, unified Germany.

Green Germany

Germans are the original Greens. While they can't claim to have invented environmentalism, they were there at the outset and coined the word to describe the movement. Concern for the health of the planet and strong opposition to nuclear power are beliefs that strike a chord with the local populace. Germans are vigilant recyclers, often prefer to ride bicycles than drive, and carry their groceries in reusable cloth shopping bags or wicker baskets; these practices are simply second nature in Germany.

Football

Football ignites the passion of Germans everywhere and has contributed much to building the confidence of the nation. The national team has won the World Cup three times – in 1954, 1974 and 1990. Germany has also hosted the World Cup twice, in 1974 and 2006. Domestically, Germany's Bundesliga (national football league) has fallen behind other European leagues, such as England's Premier League, but still throws up some exciting duels. On the European stage, Germany's most successful domestic side is Bayern Munich – it last won the UEFA Champion's League in 2001, but lost the finals twice since then.

Smoking

Germany was one of the last countries in Europe to legislate smoking and most visitors will notice almost immediately how much more secondhand cigarette smoke is in the air. Almost 36% of German men and 28% of women smoke. Smoking bans are different in each state.

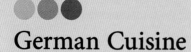
Currywurst (p380)

ARCO IMAGES GMBH/ALAM

Germany might not have the culinary kudos of some of its neighbours, but its robust, fresh flavours have made it a rising star in Europe's kitchen. You'll never forget your first forkful of black forest gateau, the crisp riesling sipped in a Rhineland taverns or the roast pork served with foamy Weizenbier (wheat beer) at a Bavarian beer fest. Bring an appetite, a taste for adventure and get stuck in.

The State of German Cuisine

As in Britain, Germany has redeemed itself gastronomically in the past decade. Of course, if you crave traditional comfort food, you'll certainly find plenty of places to indulge in pork, potatoes and cabbage. These days, though, typical local fare is lighter, healthier, creative and more likely to come from organic eateries, ethnic restaurants and gourmet kitchens. In fact, in 2012 Germany's Michelin skies twinkled brighter than ever before with 208 one-star, 32 two-star and nine three-star restaurants.

Top chefs are putting creative spins on tried-and-trusted specialities in a wave that's referred to as the *Neue Deutsche Küche* (new German cuisine). Many have jumped on the locavore bandwagon, letting the trifecta of seasonal-regional-organic ingredients steer their menus. Many travel to the countryside to source free-range meats, wild-caught fish, farm-fresh fruit and vegetables, handmade cheeses and other delectables, preferably sustainably grown. Menus increasingly champion traditional (and long underrated) ingredients, such as root vegetables, old-fashioned grains, and game and other meats – for example, goat liver or cheeks.

Price Ranges

For one main course:

€	Budget	< €8
€€	Midrange	€8 to €15
€€€	Top end	> €15

Traditional Staples

Bread

As German expats living around the world will tell you, the food they miss the most about their homeland is the bread. Indeed, German bread is a world-beater. Its 300 varieties are tasty and textured, often mixing wheat and rye flour.

'Black' *Schwarzbrot* (rye bread) is actually brown, but a much darker shade than the slightly sour *Bauernbrot* – divine with a slab of butter. Pumpernickel bread is steam-cooked instead of baked, making it extra moist, and it actually is black. *Vollkorn* means wholemeal, and bread coated in sunflower seeds is *Sonnenblumenbrot*. If you insist on *Weissbrot* (white bread), the Germans have that too.

Fresh bread rolls (*Brötchen* in the north, *Semmel* in Bavaria, *Wecken* in the rest of southern Germany) can be covered in poppy seeds (*Mohnbrötchen*), cooked with sweet raisins (*Rosinenbrötchen*), sprinkled with salt (*Salzstangel*) or treated in dozens of other different ways.

Brezeln are traditional pretzels covered in rock salt.

Potatoes

Chipped, boiled, baked, mashed, fried: Germans love their potatoes. The *Kartoffel* is not only vegetable *Nummer Eins* (number one) in any meat-and-three-veg dish, it can also be incorporated into any course of a meal, from *Kartoffelsuppe* (potato soup) as a starter, to *Kartoffelsalat* (potato salad) and *Reibekuchen* (potato pancakes).

In between, you can try *Himmel und Erde* (Heaven and Earth), a dish of mashed potatoes and stewed apples served with black pudding; or potato-based *Klösse* (dumplings). *Pellkartoffeln* or *Ofenkartoffeln* are jacket potatoes, usually topped with a dollop of *Quark* (a yoghurtlike curd cheese).

Cabbage

Finally, the quintessential German side dish that many outside the country find impossible to fathom: *sauerkraut*. Before the 2006 FIFA World Cup, one football magazine suggested: 'It's pickled cabbage; don't try to make it sound interesting.' Okay, we won't. It's shredded cabbage, doused in white-wine vinegar and slowly simmered. But if you haven't at least tried *Rotkohl* (the red-cabbage version), you don't know what you're missing. Braising the cabbage with sliced apples and wine turns it into *Bayrischkraut* or *Weinkraut*.

Sausage

In the Middle Ages German peasants found a way to package and disguise animals' less appetising bits – creating the wurst. Today it's a noble and highly respected element of German cuisine, with strict rules determining the authenticity of wurst

Dining Tips

Restaurants are often formal places with full menus, crisp white linen and high prices. Some restaurants are open for lunch and dinner only but more casual places tend to be open all day. The same goes for cafes, which usually serve both coffee and alcohol, as well as light meals, although ordering food is not obligatory. Many cafes and restaurants offer inexpensive weekday 'business lunches' that usually include a starter, main course and drink for under €10.

English menus are not a given, even in big cities, though the wait staff will almost invariably be able to translate for you. The more rural and remote you travel, the less likely it is that the restaurant will have an English menu, or multilingual staff for that matter. It helps to learn a smattering of German.

Handy speed-feed shops, called Imbiss, serve all sorts of savoury fodder, from sausages-in-buns to doner kebabs and pizza. Many bakeries serve sandwiches alongside pastries.

---

varieties. In some cases, as with the finger-sized Nuremberg sausage, regulations even ensure offal no longer enters the equation.

While there are more than 1500 sausage species, all are commonly served with bread and a *süss* (sweet) or *scharf* (spicy) *Senf* (mustard).

Bratwurst, served countrywide, is made from minced pork, veal and spices, and is cooked in different ways (boiled in beer, baked with apples and cabbage, stewed in a casserole or simply grilled or barbecued.

The availability of other sausages differs regionally. A *Thüringer* is long and spiced, while a *Wiener* is what hot-dog fiends call a frankfurter. Saxony is all about the *Bregenwurst* (brain sausage), Bavaria sells the white, veal-based *Weisswurst*, and Berliners swear by their *Currywurst* (slices of sausage topped with curry powder and ketchup).

Seasonal Specialities

While you shall be forgiven for laughing at the unmistakably phallic shape of the chlorophyll-deprived *weisser Spargel* (white asparagus), between late April and late June Berliners go nuts for the erotic stalks, which are best enjoyed steamed alongside ham, hollandaise sauce or butter, and boiled potatoes. The stalks also show up as asparagus soup, in quiches and salads and even as ice cream.

Spargelzeit (asparagus season) may be a highlight of the culinary calendar that actually kicks off a bit earlier with *Bärlauch* (wild garlic), which starts showing up in salads and as pesto in early spring. Fresh fruit, especially all sorts of berries (strawberries, blueberries, raspberries, gooseberries), red currants and cherries brighten up the market stalls in summer.

In late summer and early autumn, hand-picked mushrooms such as *Steinpilze* (porcini) and earthy *Pfifferlinge* (chanterelles) show up on menus everywhere. A typical winter meal is cooked *Grünkohl* (kale) with smoked sausage, which is often served at Christmas markets. *Gans* (stuffed goose) is a Martinmas (November 11) tradition and also popular at Christmas time.

Fast-food Faves

International fast-food chains are ubiquitous, of course, but there's plenty of home-grown fast food as well. In fact, some of your best German food experiences are likely to be the snack-on-the-hoof kind. Street food is a tasty way to get versed in wurst and chomp your way around the globe, often with change from a €5 note. In the bigger cities, stalls sizzle up Greek, Italian, Mexican, Middle Eastern and Chinese bites.

The Imbiss fast-food stall is a ubiquitous phenomenon, allowing you to eat on the run. Germany's Turkish population invented the modern *Döner* (doner kebab) – adding salad and garlic-yoghurt sauce to spit-roasted lamb, veal or chicken in pita bread. Most kebab joints also do veggie versions. In the briny north, snack on fish (usually herring) sandwiches.

Vegetarians & Vegans

Germany was slow in coming but is now embracing meat-free fare with the fervour of a religious convert. Health-conscious cafes and restaurants have been sprouting faster than alfafa and serve up inspired menus that leave the classic veggie or tofu burger in the dust. With dishes such as sweet potato saltimbocca, tandoori seitan, pearl barley strudel with chanterelles, or parmesan dumplings, chefs strive to push the creative envelope.

Even veganism has made significant inroads: Germany's first all-vegan supermarket opened in Berlin in 2011, followed by the city's first vegan gourmet restaurant the same year. Even many nonvegetarian restaurants now offer more than the token vegetable lasagne. For a comprehensive list of vegan and vegetarian restaurants in Germany, see www.happycow.net/europe/germany.

Kaffee und Kuchen

Anyone who has spent any length of time in Germany knows the reverence bestowed on the 3pm weekend ritual of *Kaffee und Kuchen* (coffee and cake). More than just a chance to devour delectable cakes and tortes, Germans see it as a social event. You'll find *Cafe-Konditoreien* (cafe-cake shops) pretty much everywhere – in castles, in the middle of the forest, even on top of mountains. Track down the best by asking sweet-toothed locals where the cake is *hausgemacht* (homemade).

While coffee in Germany is not as strong as that served in France or Italy, you can expect a decent cup. All the usual varieties are on offer, including cappuccinos and lattes, although you still frequently see French-style bowls of *Milchkaffee* (milky coffee). Order a *Kanne* (pot) or *Tasse* (cup) of *Kaffee* (coffee) and what you will get is filter coffee, usually with a portion of *Kaffeesahne* (condensed milk).

The Best...
Sweet
Temptations

1 Lebkuchen Soft gingerbread made with nuts, fruit peel, honey and spices; popular at Christmas

2 Black forest gateau A multilayered chocolate sponge, cream and kirsch confection, topped with morello cherries and chocolate shavings

3 Aachener Printen Aachen's crunchy spiced cookie, similar to gingerbread

4 Lübecker Marzipan A creamy blend of almonds and sugar – from Lübeck

5 Stollen Christmas-time spiced cake loaded with sultanas, marzipan and candied peel; the best is from Dresden

Beer & Wine

Serving beer, Oktoberfest (p84)

BERNDT FISCHER/GETTY IMAGES

Few things are as deeply ingrained in the German psyche as the love of beer. 'Hopfen und Malz – Gott erhalt's!' (Hops and malt are in God's hands) goes the saying, which is fitting given the almost religious intensity with which beer is brewed, consumed and celebrated – not least at the world's biggest festival, Oktoberfest. Brewing here goes back to Germanic tribes, and later to monks, so it follows in a hallowed tradition.

Beer

The 'secret' of the country's golden nectar dates back to the *Reinheitsgebot* (purity law), demanding breweries use just four ingredients – malt, yeast, hops and water. Passed in Bavaria in 1516, the *Reinheitsgebot* stopped being a legal requirement in 1987, when the EU struck it down as uncompetitive. However, many German brewers still conform to it anyway, seeing it as a good marketing tool against mass-market, chemical-happy competitors.

Beer Varieties

Despite frequently tying their own hands and giving themselves just four ingredients to play with, German brewers turn out 5000 distinctively different beers. They achieve this via subtle variations in the basic production process. At the simplest level, a brewer can choose a particular yeast for top or bottom fermenting (the terms indicating where the yeast lives while working – at the top or bottom of the brewing vessel).

The most popular form of brewing is bottom fermentation, which accounts for about 85% of German beers, notably the *Pils* (pilsner), most Bock beers and the *Helles* (pale lager) type found in Bavaria. Top fermentation is used for the *Weizenbier/Weissbier* (wheat/white beer) popular in Berlin and Bavaria; Cologne's Kölsch; and the very few stouts brewed in the country.

Many beers are regional, meaning that, for example, a Saxon Rechenberger cannot be found in Düsseldorf, where the locally brewed *Altbier* is the taste of choice.

Pils (pilsner) This bottom-fermented full beer, with pronounced hop flavour and creamy head, has an alcohol content of around 4.8%.

Weizenbier/Weissbier (wheat beer) Predominant in the south, especially in Bavaria, this has 5.4% alcohol content. A *Hefeweizen* has a stronger shot of yeast, whereas *Kristallweizen* is clearer with more fizz. These beers are fruity and spicy, often recalling bananas and cloves. Decline offers of lemon, as it ruins the head and – beer purists say – the flavour.

Dunkles (dark lager) Brewed throughout Germany, but especially in Bavaria. With a light use of hops, it's full-bodied with strong malty aromas.

Helles (pale lager) Helles, meaning pale or light, refers to the colour, not the alcohol content, which is still 4.6% to 5%. Brewing strongholds are located in Bavaria, Baden-Württemberg and the Ruhr region. It has strong malt aromas and is slightly sweet.

Altbier A dark, full beer with malted barley from the Düsseldorf area.

Berliner Weisse Berlin's top-fermented beer, which comes *rot* (red) or *grün* (green), with a *Schuss* (dash) of raspberry or woodruff syrup respectively. A cool, fruity summer choice.

Bockbier Strong beers with 7% alcohol. There's a '*Bock*' for every occasion, such as *Maibock* (for May/spring) and *Weihnachtsbock* (brewed for Christmas). *Eisbock* is dark and aromatic.

Kölsch By law, this top-fermented beer can only be brewed in or around Cologne. Its alcohol content is about 4.8%, it has a solid hop flavour and pale colour, and is served in small glasses (0.2L) called *Stangen* (sticks).

Schwarzbier (black beer) Slightly stronger, this dark, full beer has an alcohol content of 4.8% to 5%. It's fermented using roasted malt.

Where to Drink

Up and down this hop-crazy country you will find buzzing microbreweries and brewpubs, cavernous beer halls and chestnut-shaded beer gardens that invite you to linger, quaff a cold one and raise a toast – *Prost!*

Munich offers a taste of Oktoberfest year-round in historic beer halls, where you can hoist a mass litre of Weizen and sway to oompah bands, and leafy beer gardens for imbibing and chomping on warm *Brezeln* (pretzels) and *Weisswurst* (herb-veal-pork sausage). This festive spirit spills into other Bavarian cities, such as Regensburg and Bamberg, and into villages where monks brew potent dark beers, as they have for eons. Breweries offering a peek behind the scenes include Beck's in Bremen.

Wine

For decades the name of German wine was sullied by the cloyingly sweet taste of Liebfraumilch and the naff image of Blue Nun. What a difference a decade can make. Thanks to rebranding campaigns, a new generation of wine growers and an overall rise in quality, German wine is staging a comeback in the 21st century. This triumph was marked at 2012 wine awards including the International Wine and Spirit

Competition (IWSC) held in London, where 71 medals went to German wines, including one Gold Outstanding for a Franconian 2010 riesling from Weingut Horst Sauer.

Even discerning wine critics have been pouring praise on German winemakers of late. According to Master of Wine Tim Atkin (www.timatkin.com), 'Germany makes the best rieslings of all', and, waxing lyrical on the country's Pinot noirs, he muses, 'if only the Germans didn't keep most of them to themselves.'

For a comprehensive rundown of all German wine-growing regions, grape varieties, news of the hottest winemakers, and information on tours or courses, visit www.winesofgermany.co.uk, www.germanwines.de and www.germanwineusa.org.

Grape Varieties

Having produced wines since Roman times, Germany now has more than 1000 sq km of vineyards, mostly on the Rhine and Moselle riverbanks. Despite the common association with riesling grapes (particularly in its best wine regions) the less acidic Müller-Thurgau (Rivaner) grape is more widespread. Meanwhile, the Gewürztraminer grape produces spicy wines with an intense bouquet.

What Germans call *Grauburgunder* is known to the rest of the world as Pinot gris. German reds are light and lesser known. *Spätburgunder* (Pinot noir), is the best of the bunch and goes into some velvety, full-bodied reds with an occasional almond taste.

Wine Regions

There are 13 official wine-growing areas, the best being the Mosel-Saar-Ruwer region. It boasts some of the world's steepest vineyards, where the predominantly riesling grapes are still hand-picked. Slate soil on the hillsides gives the wines a flinty taste. Chalkier riverside soils are planted with the Elbling grape, an ancient Roman variety.

East of the Moselle, the Nahe region produces fragrant, fruity and full-bodied wines using Müller-Thurgau and Silvaner grapes, as well as riesling.

Riesling grapes are also the mainstay in Rheingau and Mittelrhein (Middle Rhine), two other highly respected wine-growing pockets. Rheinhessen, south of Rheingau, is responsible for Liebfraumilch, but also some top rieslings.

Other wine regions include the Pfalz (both Rheinland-Palatinate), Hessische Bergstrasse (Hesse), Baden (Baden-Württemberg), Würzburg (Bavaria) and Elbtal (Saxony).

The Württemberg region around Stuttgart produces some of the country's best reds, while Saxony-Anhalt's Saale-Unstrut region is home to Rotkäppchen (Little Red Riding Hood) sparkling wine, a former GDR brand that's been a big hit in reunited Germany.

The Best... Beer Gardens

1 Biergarten im Schlossgarten (p164), Stuttgart

2 Braunauer Hof (p85), Munich

3 Spitalgarten (p148), Regensburg

4 Prater (p274), Berlin

5 Klosterschenke Weltenburg (p143), near Regensburg

Survival Guide

Christmas market, Rothenburg ob der Tauber (p119)
CUBOIMAGES SRL/ALAMY ©

A-Z

Directory

Accommodation

Germany has all types of places to unpack your suitcase – from hostels, camping grounds and family hotels to chains, business hotels and luxury resorts. Standards are generally very high, and even basic accommodation will likely be clean and comfortable. Reservations are a good idea between June and September, around major holidays, festivals and cultural events and trade shows. In this book, reviews are listed by author preference.

Budget stays will generally have you checking in at hostels, country inns, *Pensionen* (B&Bs or small hotels) or simple family hotels. Facilities may be shared. Midrange properties offer a few extra creature comforts, such as cable TV, wi-fi and private bathrooms,

and overall constitute the best value for money. Top-end places offer luxurious amenities, perhaps a scenic location, special decor or historical ambience. Many also have pools, saunas and business centres.

Note that in Germany, as elsewhere in Europe, 'ground floor' refers to the floor at street level. The 1st floor (what would be called the 2nd floor in the US) is the floor above that. The book follows local usage of the terms.

COSTS

Accommodation costs vary wildly between regions and between cities and rural areas. What will buy you a romantic suite in a countryside inn in the Bavarian Forest may only get you a simple room in Munich. City hotels geared to the suit brigade often lure leisure travellers with lower rates on weekends. Also check hotel websites for discount rates or packages.

RESERVATIONS

○ Many tourist offices and hotel websites let you check for room availability and make advance reservations.

○ If you're already in town, swing by the tourist office, where staff can assist you in finding last-minute lodging. After hours, vacancies may be posted in the window or in a display case.

○ When making a room reservation directly with a property, tell your host what time they can expect you and stick to your plan, or ring again. Many well-meaning visitors have lost rooms by showing up late.

HOTELS

In this book we have aimed to feature well-situated, independent hotels that offer good value, a warm welcome, a modicum of charm and character, as well as a palpable sense of place.

You'll find the gamut of options, from small family-run properties to international chains and luxurious designer abodes. Increasingly popular are budget designer chains (eg Motel One) geared towards lifestyle-savvy travellers.

○ Rates traditionally include breakfast, although this is changing, especially in cities. Unless specified otherwise, prices quoted include breakfast.

○ In older, family-run hotels, individual rooms often vary dramatically in terms of size, decor and amenities. The cheapest may have shared facilities, while others come with a shower cubicle installed but no private toilet; only the pricier ones have their own bathrooms.

○ Many hotels with a high romance factor belong to an association called Romantik Hotels & Restaurants (www .romantikhotels.com).

○ Many properties are now entirely nonsmoking; others set aside rooms or entire floors for smokers.

Book Your Stay Online

For more accommodation reviews by Lonely Planet authors, check out http://hotels.lonely planet.com. You'll find independent reviews, as well as recommendations on the best places to stay. Best of all, you can book online.

Price Ranges

The price indicators in this book refer to the cost of a double room with private bathroom (any combination of toilet, bathtub, shower and washbasin), including breakfast and all taxes.

€   less than €80

€€   from €80 to 150

€€€   more than €150

CHAIN HOTELS

Hotel chains stretch from nondescript establishments to central four-star hotels with character. Most conform to certain standards of decor, service and facilities (air-con, wi-fi, 24-hour check-in), and offer competitive rates and last-minute and/or weekend deals. International chains like Best Western, Holiday Inn, Hilton and Ramada are quite ubiquitous on the German market now, but there are also some home-grown contenders. In this book we generally don't list chain properties, but we do recommend the ones listed below. For locations, see individual websites.

A&O (www.aohostels.com) Combines hostel and two-star hotel accommodation.

Dorint (www.dorint.com) Three- to five-star properties in cities and rural areas.

InterCity (www.intercityhotel .com) Good-value two-star chain usually located at train stations.

Kempinski (www.kempinski .com) Luxury hotel group with a pedigree going back to 1897.

Leonardo (www.leonardo -hotels.com) Three- to four-star city hotels.

Meininger (www.meininger -hotels.com) Well-run hotel-hostel combo for city-breakers on a budget.

Motel One (www.motelone .com) Despite the name, these are budget designer hotels.

Sorat (www.sorat-hotels.com) Four-star boutique hotels.

Steigenberger (www .steigenberger.com) Five-star luxury, often in historic buildings.

PENSIONS, INNS & PRIVATE ROOMS

The German equivalent of a B&B, *Pensionen* are small, informal and an excellent low-cost alternative to hotels with rates starting at €13 per person, including breakfast. *Gasthöfe/Gasthäuser* (inns) are similar but usually have restaurants serving regional and German food to a local clientele. *Privatzimmer* are guest rooms in private homes, though privacy seekers may find these places a bit too intimate.

Expect clean rooms but minimal amenities – maybe a radio, sometimes an old and small TV, almost never a phone. Facilities may be shared. What rooms lack in amenities though, they often make up for in charm and authenticity, often augmented by friendly hosts who take a personal interest in ensuring that you enjoy your stay. Rates always include breakfast.

Tourist offices keep lists of available rooms; you can also look around for *'Zimmer Frei'* (rooms available) signs in house or shop windows. They're usually quite cheap, with per-person rates starting at €13 and usually topping out

My Home is my Castle

If you're the romantic type, consider a fairy-tale getaway in a castle, palace or country manor dripping with character and history. They're typically in the countryside, strategically perched atop a crag, perhaps overlooking a river or rolling hills. And it doesn't take a king's ransom to stay in one. In fact, even wallet-watchers can fancy themselves knight or damsel when staying in a castle converted into a youth hostel (eg Burg Stahleck on the Rhine). More typically, though, properties are luxury affairs, blending mod cons with baronial ambience and old-world trappings such as four-poster beds, antique armoires and heavy drapes. Sometimes your hosts are even descendants of the original castle builders, often a local baron, count or prince. For details, see www. thecastles.de or www.castleandpalacehotels.com.

at €25, including breakfast.

If a landlord is reluctant to rent for a single night, offer to pay a little extra.

For advance reservations, try www.bed-and-breakfast .de, www.bedandbreakfast .de or www.bedandbreakfast .com.

Business Hours

We've listed business hours where they differ from the following standards. Note that, in most cases, where hours vary across the year, we've provided those applicable in high season.

Banks 9am-4pm Mon-Fri, extended hours usually on Tue & Thu, some open Sat

Bars 6pm-1am

Cafes 8am-8pm

Clubs 10 or 11pm-early morning hours

Major stores and supermarkets 9.30am-8pm Mon-Sat (shorter hours in suburbs and rural areas)

Post offices 9am-6pm Mon-Fri, 9am-1pm Sat

Restaurants 11am-11pm (varies widely, food service often stops at 9.30pm)

Customs Regulations

Goods brought in and out of countries within the EU incur no additional taxes, provided duty has been paid somewhere within the EU and the goods are only for personal use or consumption. Duty-free shopping is only available if you're leaving the EU.

Duty-free allowances (for anyone over 17) arriving from non-EU countries are:

o 200 cigarettes *or* 100 cigarillos *or* 50 cigars *or* 250g of loose tobacco

o 1L of strong liquor *or* 2L of less than 22% alcohol by volume *plus* 4L of wine *plus* 16L of beer

o other goods up to the value of €300 if arriving by land or €430 if arriving by sea or air (€175 for under 15yr)

Discount Cards

Discounts are widely available for seniors, children and students. In some cases you may be asked to show ID or prove your age. Tourist offices in many cities sell **Welcome Cards** entitling visitors to discounts on museums, sights and tours, plus unlimited trips

on local public transportation. They can be good value if you plan on taking advantage of most of the benefits and don't qualify for any of the standard discounts.

Electricity

120V/60Hz

Gay & Lesbian Travellers

o Germany is a magnet for *schwule* (gay) and *lesbische* (lesbian) travellers, with the rainbow flag flying especially proudly in Berlin, which is helmed by Germany's first openly gay mayor, Klaus Wowereit. Cologne also has a humming scene and there are also sizeable communities in Hamburg, Frankfurt and Munich.

o Attitudes towards homosexuality tend to be more conservative in the countryside, among older people and in the eastern states.

The 'Curse' of the Kur

Most German resort and spa towns charge their overnight guests a so-called Kurtaxe (resort tax). Fees range from €1 to €4 per person per night and are added to your hotel bill. The money subsidises visitor-oriented events and services, such as concerts, lectures, readings, walking tours, public toilets, beach cleaning and sometimes includes public transport.

o As elsewhere, Germany's lesbian scene is less public than its male counterpart and is centred mainly on women's cafes and bars.

o Gay pride marches are held throughout Germany in springtime, the largest ones in Cologne and Berlin drawing hundreds of thousands of rainbow revelers and friends.

PUBLICATIONS

Blu Print and online magazine with searchable, up-to-the-minute location and event listings.

L-Mag Bimonthly magazine for lesbians.

Spartacus International Gay Guide Annual English-language travel guide for men.

WEBSITES & APPS

Gay Romeo (www.gayromeo .com) Dating site of choice in Germany; iPhone app for €2.99.

Gayscape (www.gayscape .com) Extensive search tool with hundreds of links.

Gay Web (www.gay-web.de) Portal to lesbigay info and events throughout Germany.

Spartacus World (www .spartacusworld.com) Hip hotel, style and event guide; iPhone app for €6.99.

Health

Germany is a healthy place so your main risks are likely to be sunburn, foot blisters, insect bites, mild stomach problems and hangovers.

Practicalities

o **Clothing sizes** For women's clothing sizes, a German size 36 equals size 6 in the US and size 10 in the UK, then increases in increments of two, making size 38 a US 8 and a UK 12.

o **DVD** Keep in mind that Germany is region code 2 if you want to buy DVDs to watch back home.

o **Laundry** Virtually all German towns and cities have at least one *Waschsalon* (self-service launderette). Hostels often have washing machines for guest use, while hotels offer cleaning services as well, although this is quite pricey.

o **Radio** Radio stations are regional, with most featuring a mixed format of news, talk and music.

o **Weights & measures** Germany uses the metric system.

BEFORE YOU GO

No vaccinations are required for travel to Germany but the World Health Organisation (WHO) recommends that all travellers be covered for diphtheria, tetanus, measles, mumps, rubella and polio.

AVAILABILITY & COST OF HEALTHCARE

o Excellent health care is widely available from hospital (*Krankenhaus*) emergency rooms (*Notstation*) and at doctors' offices (*Arzt*).

o For minor illnesses or injuries (headache, bruises, diarrhoea), trained staff in pharmacies can provide valuable advice, sell prescription-free medications and advise if more specialised help is needed.

o Condoms are widely available in drugstores, pharmacies and supermarkets. Birth control pills require a doctor's prescription.

PHARMACIES

o German chemists (drugstores; *Drogerien*) do not sell any kind of medication, not even aspirin. Even over-the-counter (*rezeptfrei*) medications for minor health concerns, such as a cold or upset stomach, are only available at a pharmacy (*Apotheke*).

o For more serious conditions, you will need to produce a prescription (*Rezept*) from a licenced physician. If you take regular medication, be sure to bring a full supply for your entire trip, as the same brand may not be available in Germany.

o The names and addresses of pharmacies open after hours (these rotate) are posted in every pharmacy window, or call 01141.

Insurance

o Comprehensive travel insurance to cover theft, loss and medical problems is highly recommended.

o Some policies specifically exclude dangerous activities, such motorcycling, scuba-diving and even trekking; read the fine print.

European Health Insurance Card

Citizens of the EU, Switzerland, Iceland, Norway and Liechtenstein receive free or reduced-cost state-provided (not private) health-care coverage with the European Health Insurance Card (EHIC) for medical treatment that becomes necessary while in Germany. It does not cover emergency repatriation home. Each family member needs a separate card. UK residents can get applications from post offices or download them from the Department of Health website (www.dh.gov.uk). You will need to pay directly and fill in a treatment form; keep the form to claim any refunds. In general you can claim back around 70% of the standard treatment cost.

Citizens of other countries need to check if there is a reciprocal arrangement for free medical care between their country and Germany.

○ Check that the policy covers ambulances or an emergency flight back home.

○ Before you leave, find out if your insurance plan makes payments directly to providers or reimburses you for health expenditures.

○ Paying for your airline ticket with a credit card sometimes provides limited travel accident insurance – ask your credit-card company what it is prepared to cover.

○ If you have to make a claim, be sure to keep all necessary documents and bills.

○ Worldwide travel insurance is available at www.lonely planet.com/travel_services. You can buy, extend and claim online anytime – even if you're already on the road.

○ Also consider coverage for luggage theft or loss. If you already have a homeowner's or renter's policy, check what it will cover and only get supplemental insurance to protect against the rest.

○ If you have prepaid a large portion of your holiday, trip cancellation insurance is a worthwhile expense.

Internet Access

○ Numerous cafes and bars tout wi-fi hot spots that let laptop owners hook up for free. If necessary, you'll be given a password.

○ Many hotels have an internet corner for their guests, often at no charge. These places are identified in this book with @.

○ A place with wi-fi is indicated with 🛜. Note that in hotels such access is often limited to some rooms and/or public areas, so if you need in-room access be sure to specify this at the time of booking.

○ Wi-fi is available for a fee on select InterCity Express (ICE) train routes, including Frankfurt to Hamburg and Frankfurt to Munich. More than 20 stations, including those in Berlin, Munich, Hamburg and Frankfurt, also offer wi-fi in their Deutsche Bahn (DB) Lounges, free to 1st-class passengers.

○ Locate wi-fi hot spots at www.hotspot-locations.com or www.free-hotspot.com.

Legal Matters

○ By law you must carry some form of photographic identification, such as your passport, national identity card or driving licence.

○ The permissible blood-alcohol limit is 0.05%; drivers caught exceeding this amount are subject to stiff fines, a confiscated licence and even jail time. Drinking in public is not illegal, but please be discreet about it.

○ If arrested, you have the right to make a phone call and are presumed innocent until proven guilty, although you may be held in custody until trial. If you don't know a lawyer, contact your embassy.

Money

Germany's unit of currency is the euro (€). Euros come in seven notes (€5, €10, €20, €50, €100, €200 and €500) and eight coins (€0.01, €0.02, €0.05, €0.10, €0.20, €0.50, €1 and €2). In 2012 the European inflation rate held at 2.4%.

ATMS & DEBIT CARDS

○ The easiest and quickest way to obtain cash is by using your debit (bank) card at an

Geldautomat (ATM) linked to international networks such as Cirrus, Plus, Star and Maestro.

○ ATMs are ubiquitous and accessible 24/7.

○ Many ATM cards double as debit cards and many shops, hotels, restaurants and other businesses accept them for payment. All cards use the 'chip and pin' system: instead of signing, you enter your PIN. If you're from overseas and your card isn't chip-and-pin enabled, you may be able to sign the receipt, although not all places will accept your card, so enquire first.

○ Ticket vending machines used by DB in train stations and local public transport may not accept non-chip-and-pin cards.

CASH

Cash is king in Germany, so always carry some with you and plan to pay in cash almost everywhere. It's also a good idea to set aside a small amount of euros as an emergency stash.

CREDIT CARDS

○ Credit cards are becoming widely accepted, but it's best not to assume that you'll be able to use one – enquire first.

○ A piece of plastic is vital in emergencies and also useful for phone or internet bookings. Visa and MasterCard are more commonly accepted than American Express.

○ Avoid getting cash advances on your credit card via ATMs since fees are steep and you'll be charged interest immediately (in other words, there's no grace period as with purchases).

○ Report lost or stolen cards to your card's provider. Contact details for the more common cards are listed here.

American Express
(☎ 069-9797 1000)

MasterCard
(☎ 0800-819 1040)

Visa (☎ 0800-814 9100)

MONEYCHANGING

○ Commercial banks usually charge a stiff fee (€5 to €10) per foreign-currency transaction, no matter the amount – if they even bother to offer exchange services at all.

○ *Wechselstuben* (currency exchange offices) at airports, train stations and in bigger towns usually charge lower fees. Traveller-geared Reisebank branches are ubiquitous in Germany and usually found at train stations. They keep longer hours than banks and are usually open on weekends.

○ Exchange facilities in rural areas are rare.

TIPPING

Restaurant bills always include a *Bedienung* (service charge) but most people add 5% or 10% unless the service was truly abhorrent. It's considered rude to leave the tip on the table. When paying, tell the server the total amount you want to pay (say, if the bill is €28, you say €30). If you don't want change back, say *'Stimmt so'* (that's fine).

WHERE & WHO	CUSTOMARY TIP
bar	round to nearest euro
room cleaners	€1-2 per day
hotel porter	€1-1.50 per bag
restaurant	5-10%
toilet attendants	€0.20-0.50
tour guide	€1-2 per person
bellboys	€1 per bag
bartenders	5%
taxi drivers	10%

Smoke & Mirrors

Germany was one of the last countries in Europe to legislate smoking. However there is no nationwide law, with regulations left to each of the 16 states, creating a rather confusing patchwork of antismoking laws. Generally, smoking is a no-no in schools, hospitals, airports, train stations and other public facilities. But when it comes to bars, pubs, cafes and restaurants, every state does it just a little differently. Bavaria bans smoking practically everywhere, since 2011 even in Oktoberfest tents. In most states though, lighting up is allowed in designated smoking rooms in restaurants and clubs. One-room establishments smaller than 75 sq metres may allow smoking provided they serve no food and only admit patrons over 18. In any case, enforcement has been sporadic to say the least, despite the threat of fines.

Public Holidays

Germany observes three secular and eight religious public holidays nationwide. Banks, shops, post offices and public services close on these days. States with predominantly Catholic populations, such as Bavaria and Baden-Württemberg, also celebrate Epiphany (6 January), Corpus Christi (10 days after Pentecost), Assumption Day (15 August) and All Saints' Day (1 November). Reformation Day (31 October) is only observed in eastern Germany (but not in Berlin).

The following *Gesetzliche Feiertage* (public holidays) are celebrated in Germany:

Neujahrstag (New Year's Day) 1 January

Ostern (Easter) March/April; Good Friday, Easter Sunday and Easter Monday

Christi Himmelfahrt (Ascension Day) 40 days after Easter

Maifeiertag/Tag der Arbeit (Labour Day) 1 May

Pfingsten (Whitsun/ Pentecost Sunday & Monday) 50 days after Easter

Tag der Deutschen Einheit (Day of German Unity) 3 October

Weihnachtstag (Christmas Day) 25 December

Zweiter Weihnachtstag (Boxing Day) 26 December

Telephone

MOBILE PHONES

- German mobile phone numbers begin with a four-digit prefix such as 0151, 0157, 0170, 0178.

- Mobile (cell) phones are called *Handys* and work on GSM 900/1800. If your home country uses a different standard, you'll need a multiband GSM phone while in Germany.

- To avoid high roaming costs, consider buying a prepaid, rechargeable local SIM card, provided you have an unlocked phone that works in Germany. The cheapest and least complicated of these are sold at discount supermarkets such as Aldi, Netto and Lidl. An inexpensive online provider is www.blau.de. Telecommunications stores (eg T-Online, Vodafone, E-Plus or O$_2$) also sell SIM cards.

- Top-up cards are widely available in kiosks and supermarkets.

- Calls made to a mobile phone are more expensive than those to a landline, but incoming calls are free.

- The use of mobile phones while driving is forbidden unless you're using a headset.

PHONE CODES

German phone numbers consist of an area code, which starts with 0, and the local number. Area codes can be up to six digits long; local numbers up to nine digits. If dialling from a landline within the same city, you don't need to dial the area code. If using a mobile, you must dial it.

Calling Germany from abroad Dial your country's international access code, then 49 (Germany's country code), then the area code (dropping the initial 0) and the local number.

School Holidays

Each state sets its own school holidays but, in general, kids get six weeks off in summer and two weeks each around Christmas, Easter and October. In some states, schools are also closed for a few days in February and around Whitsun/ Pentecost.

Traffic is worst at the beginning of school holidays in population-rich states such as North Rhine-Westphalia and can become a nightmare if several states let out their schools at the same time.

Germans are big fans of mini-holidays built around public holidays, which are especially common in spring when many holidays fall on a Thursday or Monday. On those 'long weekends' you can expect heavy crowds on the roads, in the towns, on boats, in beer gardens and everywhere else. Lodging is at a premium at these times as well.

IMPORTANT NUMBERS

Germany country code	☎ 49
International access code	☎ 00
Ambulance, fire brigade	☎ 112
Police	☎ 110

Calling internationally from Germany Dial 00 (the international access code), then the country code, the area code (without the zero if there is one) and the local number.

Directory inquiries From a landline call 11828 for numbers within Germany (€0.78 per call) or 11834 for numbers outside Germany (€1.99 per minute). Not all operators will speak English. If you want an English-speaking operator, dial 11837 (€1.99 per minute).

Hotel calls Direct-dialled calls made from hotel rooms are also usually charged at a premium.

PHONECARDS

o Most public pay phones are operated by Deutsche Telekom (DT) and only work with *Telefonkarten* (phonecards), available at DT stores, post offices, newsagents and tourist offices.

o For long-distance or international calls, prepaid calling cards issued by other companies tend to offer better rates than DT's phonecards, although they may charge a per-call connection fee. Read the fine print on the card itself. Look for these cards at

newsagents and telephone call shops.

o Phonecards sold at ReiseBank branches found in many trains stations are reliable and offer fairly competitive rates. Landline calls within Germany and to the UK, for instance, are charged at €0.05 per minute, to the US the cost is €0.06. Note that calls made from mobile phones cost an extra €0.23 per minute.

SPECIAL NUMBERS

Customer service numbers in Germany often have prefixes that indicate the rate at which they're charged. The following list details the cost for calls made from landlines. Note that the per-minute charge can be as high as €0.42 for calls made from mobile phones.

NUMBER	COST
0700	€0.063 per minute
0800	free
01801	€0.04 per minute
01802	€0.06 per call
01803	€0.09 per minute
01804	€0.20 per call
01805	€0.14 per minute
0900	up to €2 per minute

Time

Clocks in Germany are set to central European time (GMT/UTC plus one hour). Daylight-savings time kicks in at 2am on the last Sunday in March and ends on the last Sunday in October. The use of the 24-hour clock (eg 6.30pm

is 18.30) is the norm. The approximate (non-daylight-saving) time differences are as follows:

CITY	NOON IN BERLIN
Auckland	11pm
Cape Town	noon
London	11am
New York	6am
San Francisco	3am
Sydney	9pm
Tokyo	8pm

Toilets

o German toilets are sit-down affairs. Men are expected to sit down when peeing except, of course, at urinals.

o Freestanding 24-hour self-cleaning toilet pods have become quite commonplace. The cost is €0.50 and you have 15 minutes to finish your business. Most are wheelchair-accessible.

o Toilets in malls, clubs, beer gardens and the like often have an attendant who expects a tip of between €0.20 and €0.50.

o Toilets in airports are usually free, but in main train stations they are often maintained by private companies such as McClean, which charge as much as €1.50 for the privilege.

o Along autobahns, rest stops with facilities are spaced about 20km or 30km apart.

Tourist Information

o Just about every community in Germany has a walk-in tourist office where you can

Climate

Berlin

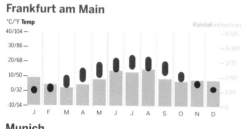

Frankfurt am Main

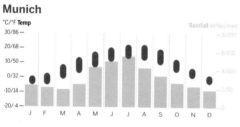

Munich

get advice and pick up maps and pamphlets, sometimes in English. Many also offer a room and ticket reservation service, usually free but sometimes for a small fee.

○ With few exceptions, there's at least one staff member more or less fluent in English and willing to make the effort to help you.

○ A useful pre-trip planning source is the German National Tourist Office (right), where information is available in almost 30 languages.

Travellers With Disabilities

○ Germany is fairly progressive when it comes to barrier-free travel. There are access ramps and/or lifts in many public buildings, including train stations, museums, theatres and cinemas, especially in the cities. In historic towns though, cobblestone streets make getting around quite cumbersome.

○ Trains, trams, underground trains and buses are becoming increasingly accessible.

Some stations have grooved platform borders to assist blind passengers in navigating. Seeing-eye dogs are allowed on all forms of public transport. For the hearing impaired, upcoming station names are often displayed electronically on all forms of public transport.

○ Newer hotels have lifts and rooms with extra-wide doors and spacious bathrooms.

○ Some car-rental agencies offer hand-controlled vehicles and vans with wheelchair lifts at no extra charge, but you must reserve them well in advance. In parking lots and garages, look for designated disabled spots marked with a wheelchair symbol.

○ Many local and regional tourist offices have special brochures for people with disabilities, although usually in German.

○ The following are good general resources for travellers with disabilities:

Deutsche Bahn Mobility Service Centre (www.bahn .com) Train-access information and route-planning assistance. The website has useful information in English (search for 'barrier-free travel').

German National Tourist Office (www.germany.travel) Your first port of call, with inspirational information in English.

Natko (www.natko.de) Central clearing house for inquiries about barrier-free travel in Germany.

Visas

- EU nationals only need their passport or national identity card to enter, stay and work in Germany, even for stays over six months. If you plan to stay longer, you are required to register with the authorities (Bürgeramt, or Citizens' Office) within two weeks of your arrival.

- Citizens of Australia, Canada, Israel, Japan, New Zealand, Poland, Switzerland and the US are among those who need only a valid passport but no visa if entering Germany as tourists for up to three months within a six-month period. Passports must be valid for at least another three months beyond the intended departure date. For stays exceeding 90 days, contact your nearest German embassy or consulate and begin your visa application process well in advance.

- Nationals from other countries need a so-called Schengen Visa, named for the 1995 Schengen Agreement that abolished international border controls between most European countries; as of 2012, there were 25 member states. Applications for a Schengen Visa must be filed with the embassy or consulate of the country that is your primary destination. It is valid for stays up to 90 days. Legal residency in any Schengen country makes a visa unnecessary, regardless of your nationality.

- For details, see www.auswaertiges-amt.de and check with a German consulate in your country.

Transport

Getting There & Away

ENTERING THE COUNTRY

Entering Germany is usually a very straightforward procedure. If you're arriving from any of the 24 other Schengen countries, such as the Netherlands, Poland, Austria or the Czech Republic, you no longer have to show your passport or go through customs in Germany, no matter which nationality you are. If you're coming in from the US or South Africa, full border procedures apply.

PASSPORTS

Passports must be valid for at least three months beyond your intended stay. Citizens of most Western countries can enter Germany without a visa; other nationals may need a Schengen Visa.

AIR

Frankfurt Airport is the main gateway for transcontinental flights, although Düsseldorf and Munich also receive their share of overseas air traffic. At the time of research for this book, Berlin had two smaller international airports, Tegel and Schönefeld, but these will be replaced by the brand new Berlin Brandenburg Airport upon its completion, expected in mid–late 2013. Already new to Berlin are direct flights from such US gateways as New York and Los Angeles. There are also sizeable airports in Hamburg, Cologne/Bonn and Stuttgart, and smaller ones in such cities as Bremen, Dresden, Hanover, Leipzig, Münster-Osnabrück and Nuremberg.

Lufthansa, Germany's national flagship carrier and Star Alliance member, operates a vast network of domestic and international flights and has one of the world's best safety records. Practically every other national carrier from around the world serves Germany, along with budget carriers Air Berlin, easyJet, Flybe, airBaltic, Ryanair and Germanwings.

LAND

BUS

Eurolines The umbrella organisation of 32 European long-haul coach operators connecting 500 destinations across Europe. Its website has links to each national company's site with detailed fare and route information, promotional offers, contact numbers and, in most cases, an online booking system. In Germany, Eurolines is represented by **Deutsche Touring** (☏ 069-790 3501; www.touring.de). Midweek fares from London to Frankfurt can be as low as £35 one-way.

CAR & MOTORCYCLE

When bringing your own vehicle to Germany, you need a valid driving licence, your car registration certificate and proof of insurance. Foreign cars must display a nationality sticker unless they have official European plates. You also need to carry a warning (hazard) triangle and a first-aid kit.

EUROTUNNEL

Coming from the UK, the fastest way to the continent is via the **Eurotunnel** (☏ in Germany 01805-000 248, in the UK 08443 35 35 35; www .eurotunnel.com). The shuttle trains whisk cars, motorbikes, bicycles and coaches from Folkestone in England through the Channel Tunnel to Coquelles (near Calais, in France) in about 35 minutes. From there, you can be in Germany in about three hours.

Shuttles run daily around the clock, with several departures hourly during peak periods. Fares are calculated per vehicle, including up to nine passengers, and depend on such factors as time of day, season and length of stay. Standard one-way tickets start at £60. Eurotunnel's website and travel agents have full details.

TRAIN

Rail services link Germany with virtually every country in Europe. In Germany ticketing is handled by **Deutsche Bahn** (www.bahn.com). Long-distance trains connecting major German cities with those in other countries are called EuroCity (EC) trains. Seat reservations are essential during the peak summer season and around major holidays.

Germany is also linked by overnight train to many European cities; routes include Amsterdam to Munich, Zurich to Berlin and Paris to Hamburg. Deutsche Bahn's overnight service is called **City Night Line** (☏ in Germany 01805-141 514; www .nachtzugreise.de) and offers three levels of comfort:

Schlafwagen (sleeping car; €50-110 supplement) Private air-conditioned compartment for up to four passengers; the deluxe version has a shower and toilet.

Liegewagen (couchette; €27.50-37.50 supplement) Sleeps up to six people; when you book an individual berth, you must share the compartment with others; women may ask for a single-sex couchette at the time of booking, but do book early.

Sitzwagen (seat carriage; €11.50-17.50 supplement) Roomy reclining seat.

Useful websites:

www.raileurope.com Detailed train information and online ticket and train pass sales.

www.railteam.eu Excellent journey planner provided by alliance of seven European railways, including Eurostar, DB and France's SNCF. No booking function yet.

www.seat61.com Comprehensive trip planning information, including ferry details from the UK.

www.railpassenger.info Details on Europe's 200,000km rail network.

Eurostar

The Channel Tunnel makes train travel between the UK and Germany a fast and enjoyable option. High-speed **Eurostar** (☏ in the UK 0844-822 5822; www.eurostar.com) passenger trains hurtle at least 10 times daily between London and Paris (the journey takes 2½ hours) or Brussels (two hours). At either city you can change to regular or other high-speed trains to destinations in Germany.

Eurostar fares depend on such factors as class, time of day, season and destination. Children, rail-pass holders and those aged between 12 and 25 and over 60 qualify for discounts. For the latest fare information, including promotions and special packages, check the website.

Rail Passes

If you want to cover lots of territory in and around Germany within a specific time, a rail pass is a convenient and good-value option. It's valid for unlimited travel during its period of validity on national railways as well as some private lines, ferries and river boat services.

There are two types of passes: the Eurail Pass for people living outside Europe and the InterRail Pass for residents of Europe, including Russia and Turkey.

EURAIL PASS

Eurail Passes are valid for travel in 23 countries and need to be purchased before you leave your home country, via www.eurail.com, through a travel agent or at www .raileurope.com. A variety of passes are available:

Eurail Global Pass Unlimited 1st-class travel, available for 15 or 21 consecutive days or one, two or three month/s. There are also versions that give you 10 or 15 days of travel within a two-month period. The 15-day version costs €549.

Eurail Select Pass Five, six, eight or 10 days of travel within two months but only in three, four or five bordering countries; a five-day pass in three countries, for example, costs €296 in 2nd class, and €348 in 1st class.

Eurail Regional Pass Gets you around two neighbouring countries in five, six, eight or 10 days within two months. The Germany–Czech Republic Pass for five days, for instance, costs €249 in 2nd class and €304 in 1st class.

Groups of two to five travelling together save 15% off the regular adult fares. If you're under 26, prices drop 35%, but you must travel in 2nd class. Children aged between four and 11 years get a 50% discount on the adult fare. Children under four years travel for free.

The Eurail website has all the details, as well as a ticket purchasing function allowing you to pay in several currencies, including euros or US dollars.

INTERRAIL PASS

InterRail Passes (www.interrailnet.com) are valid for unlimited travel in 30 countries. As with the Eurail Pass you can pick from several schemes:

InterRail Global Pass Unlimited travel in 30 countries, available either for 15 days (€267), 22 days (€494) or one month (€638) of continuous travel, for five travel days within a 10-day period (€267) or for 10 travel days within a 22-day period (€381).

InterRail Germany Pass Buys three, four, six or eight days of travel within a one-month period. The cost is €205/226/288/319, respectively. This pass is not available if you are a resident of Germany.

Prices quoted are for one adult travelling in 2nd class. Different prices apply to 1st class tickets and for travellers under 26. Children aged between four and 11 years get a 50% discount on the adult fare. Children under four years travel for free.

 BOAT

Germany's main ferry ports are Kiel and Travemünde (near Lübeck) in Schleswig-Holstein, and Rostock and Sassnitz (on Rügen Island) in Mecklenburg-Western Pomerania. All have services to Scandinavia and the Baltic states. Timetables change from season to season. For fare details and to book tickets, check the ferries' websites or go to www.ferrybooker.com or www.ferrysavers.com.

Getting Around

Germans are whizzes at moving people around, and the public transport network is among the best in Europe. The two best ways of getting around the country are by car and by train. Regional bus services fill the gaps in areas not well served by the rail network.

 AIR

Most large and many smaller German cities have their own airports and numerous carriers operate domestic flights within Germany. Lufthansa, of course, has the most dense route network. Other airlines offering domestic flights include Air Berlin and Germanwings.

Unless you're flying from one end of the country to the other, say Berlin to Munich or Hamburg to Munich, planes

Climate Change & Travel

Every form of transport that relies on carbon-based fuel generates CO_2, the main cause of human-induced climate change. Modern travel is dependent on aeroplanes, which might use less fuel per kilometre per person than most cars but travel much greater distances. The altitude at which aircraft emit gases (including CO_2) and particles also contributes to their climate change impact. Many websites offer 'carbon calculators' that allow people to estimate the carbon emissions generated by their journey and, for those who wish to do so, to offset the impact of the greenhouse gases emitted with contributions to portfolios of climate-friendly initiatives throughout the world. Lonely Planet offsets the carbon footprint of all staff and author travel.

are only marginally quicker than trains if you factor in the time it takes to get to and from the airports.

BICYCLE

Cycling is allowed on all roads and highways but not on the autobahns (motorways). Cyclists must follow the same rules of the road as cars and motorcycles. Helmets are not compulsory (even for kids).

Bicycles may be taken on most trains but require a separate *Fahrradkarte* (ticket). Bikes are not allowed on high-speed ICE trains. For details, enquire at a local station or call ☎ 01805-99 66 33, ext. 'Fahrrad'.

Many regional companies use buses with special bike racks. Bicycles are also allowed on practically all boat and ferry services on Germany's lakes and rivers.

 BOAT

Scheduled boat services operate along sections of the Rhine, the Elbe and the Danube. There are also ferry services in areas with no or only a few bridges, as

well as on major lakes such as the Chiemsee and Lake Starnberg in Bavaria and Lake Constance in Baden-Württemberg.

From April to October, local operators run scenic river or lake cruises lasting from one hour to a full day.

 BUS

LOCAL & REGIONAL

Basically, wherever there is a train, take it. Buses are generally slower, less dependable and more polluting than trains, but in some rural areas they may be your only option for getting around without your own vehicle. Separate bus companies, each with its own tariffs and schedules, operate in the different regions.

The frequency of services varies from 'rarely' to 'constantly'. Commuter-geared routes offer limited or no service in the evenings and at weekends, so keep this in mind or risk finding yourself stuck in a remote place on a Saturday night. Make it a habit to ask about special fare deals, such as daily or weekly

passes or tourist tickets.

In cities, buses generally converge at the *Busbahnhof* or *Zentraler Omnibus Bahnhof* (ZOB; central bus station), which is often near the *Hauptbahnhof* (central train station).

LONG DISTANCE

Deutsche Touring (☎ 069-790 3501; www.touring.de) runs daily overnight services between Hamburg and Mannheim via Hanover, Frankfurt, Göttingen, Kassel and Heidelberg. If you book early, trips between any two cities cost just €9. Fares top out at €49 for the full Hannover–Mannheim route for tickets bought on the bus. Children under 12 pay half the adult fare.

Berlin Linien Bus (www.berlinlinienbus.de) connects major cities (primarily Berlin, but also Munich, Düsseldorf and Frankfurt) with each other, as well as holiday regions such as the Bavarian Alps. One of the most popular

---

By Sea from the UK

There are no direct ferry services between Germany and the UK, but you can just as easily go via the Netherlands, Belgium or France and drive or train it from there. For routes and fares, see the ferries' websites below or go to www.ferrybooker.com.

FERRY COMPANY	ROUTE	WEBSITE
Via Belgium		
P&O Ferries	Hull-Zeebrugge	www.poferries.com
Transeuropa Ferries	Ramsgate-Oostende	www.transeuropaferries.com
Via France		
DFDS Seaways	Dover-Calais	www.dfdsseaways.com
P&O Ferries	Dover-Calais	www.poferries.com
Via the Netherlands		
DFDS Seaways	Newcastle-Amsterdam	www.dfdsseaways.com
P&O Ferries	Hull-Rotterdam	www.poferries.com
Stena Line	Harwich-Hoek van Holland	www.stenaline.com

routes is the express bus from Berlin to Hamburg, which makes the journey to Berlin in 3¼ hours, 12 times daily with one-way fares ranging from €9 to €21.50.

Tickets are available online and from travel agencies. Children under four years travel for free and discounts are available for older children, students, those over 60 and groups of six or more.

CAR & MOTORCYCLE

German roads are excellent and motoring around the country can be a lot of fun. The country's pride and joy is its 11,000km network of autobahns (motorways, freeways). Every 40km to 60km, you'll find elaborate service areas with petrol stations, toilet facilities and restaurants; many are open 24 hours. In between are *Rastplatz* (rest stops), which usually have picnic tables and toilet facilities. Orange emergency call boxes are spaced about 2km apart.

Autobahns are supplemented by an extensive network of *Bundesstrassen* (secondary 'B' roads, highways) and smaller *Landstrassen* (country roads). No tolls are charged on any public roads.

If your car is not equipped with a navigational system, having a good map or road atlas is essential, especially when negotiating the tangle of country roads. Navigating in Germany is not done by the points of the compass – that is to say that you'll find no signs saying 'north' or 'west'. Rather, you'll see signs pointing you in the direction of a city, so you'd best keep hold of that map to stay oriented. Maps cost a few euros and are sold at

International Car Hire Companies

Alamo (☎01805-462 526; www.alamo.com)

Avis (☎01805-217 702; www.avis.com)

Europcar (☎0180-580 00; www.europcar.com)

Hertz (☎01805-333 535; www.hertz.com)

National (☎0800-464 7336; www.nationalcar.com)

Sixt (☎01805-260 250; www.sixt.com)

bookstores, train stations, airports and petrol stations. The best are published by Freytag & Berndt, ADAC, Falk and Euromap.

Driving in the cities can be stressful, thanks to congestion and the expense and scarcity of parking. In city centres, parking is usually limited to parking lots and garages charging between €0.50 and €2 per hour. Note that some parking lots (*Parkplatz*) and garages (*Parkhaus*) close at night and charge an overnight fee. Many have special parking slots for women that are especially well lit and close to exits.

Many cities have electronic parking guidance systems directing you to the nearest garage and indicating the number of available spaces. Street parking usually works on the pay-and-display system and tends to be short-term (one or two hours) only.

AUTOMOBILE ASSOCIATIONS

Germany's main motoring organisation, the **Allgemeiner Deutscher Automobil-Club** (ADAC; ☎roadside assistance 0180-222 2222, from mobile phone 222 222; www.adac.de) has offices in all major cities and many smaller ones. Its roadside assistance program

is also available to members of its affiliates, including the British (AA), American (AAA) and Canadian (CAA) ones.

DRIVING LICENCE

Drivers need a valid driving licence. International Driving Permits (IDP) are not compulsory, but having one may help Germans make sense of your home licence (always carry that one too) and may simplify the car or motorcycle hire process. IDPs are inexpensive, valid for one year and issued by your local automobile association – bring a passport photo and your home licence.

CAR HIRE

As anywhere, rates for car hire vary quite considerably by model, pick-up date and location, but you should be able to get an economy-size vehicle from about €40 to €60 per day, plus insurance and taxes. Expect surcharges for hire cars originating at airports and train stations, additional drivers and one-way hire. Child or infant safety seats may be hired for about €5 per day and should be reserved at the time of booking.

Rental cars with automatic transmission are very rare in Germany and will usually need to be ordered well in advance.

Special Tickets

Deutsche Bahn also offers a trio of fabulous permanent rail deals: the Schönes-Wochenende-Ticket (Nice-Weekend-Ticket) the Quer-durchs-Land-Ticket (Around Germany Ticket) and the Länder-Tickets (Regional Tickets). On any of these schemes, children under 15 travel for free if accompanied by their parents or grandparents. Tickets can be purchased online, from vending machines or, for a €2 surcharge, from station ticket offices.

SCHÖNES-WOCHENENDE-TICKET

○ One day of unlimited 2nd-class travel on regional trains (IRE, RE, RB, S-Bahn), plus local public transport.

○ Available from midnight Saturday or Sunday until 3am the next day.

○ Costs €40 for up to five people travelling together.

QUER-DURCHS-LAND-TICKET

○ Essentially the Quer-durchs-Land-Ticket is a weekday variation of the Schönes-Wochenende-Ticket.

○ One day of unlimited 2nd-class travel on regional trains (IRE, RE, RB, S-Bahn).

○ Available Monday to Friday 9am to 3am the following day.

○ Up to five people may travel together.

○ Costs €42 for the first ticket and €6 each for up to four additional tickets.

LÄNDER-TICKETS

○ One day of unlimited travel on regional trains and local public transport within one of the German states (or, in some cases, also in bordering states).

○ Different tickets available for travel in 2nd class and 1st class.

○ With some variations, tickets are generally valid for travel Monday to Friday from 9am to 3am the following day and on weekends from midnight until 3am the following day.

○ Some passes are priced as a flat rate for up to five people travelling together (eg the Brandenburg–Berlin-Ticket costs €28).

○ Some passes have staggered pricing: the first person buys the main ticket and up to four people may join for a just few euros more per ticket (eg in Bavaria, the first person pays €22, additional tickets cost €4).

○ Some states also offer Nacht-Tickets (night passes) usually valid from 6pm until 6am the following day.

To hire your own wheels, you'll need to be at least 25 years old and possess a valid driving licence and a major credit card. Some companies hire out to drivers between the ages of 21 and 24 for an additional charge (about €12 to €20 per day). Younger people or those without a credit card are usually out of luck. For insurance reasons, driving into an Eastern European country, such as the Czech Republic or Poland, is often a no-no.

All the main international companies maintain branches at airports, major train stations and towns. See the box for contact information.

Pre-booked and prepaid packages arranged in your home country usually work out much cheaper than on-the-spot rentals. The same is true of fly/drive packages. Deals can be found on the internet and through the following companies:

Auto Europe (☎ in the US 888-223-5555; www .autoeurope.com)

Holiday Autos (☎ in the UK 0871-472 5229; www .holidayautos.co.uk)

DriveAway Holidays (☎ in Australia 1300 723 972; www .driveaway.com.au)

INSURANCE

German law requires that all registered vehicles carry third-party liability insurance, including those brought in from abroad. Normally, private cars registered and insured in another European country do not require additional insurance, but do check this with your insurance provider before leaving home. Also keep a record of who to contact in case of a breakdown or accident.

When hiring a vehicle, make sure your contract includes adequate liability insurance at the very minimum. Rental agencies almost never include insurance that covers damage to the vehicle itself, called Collision Damage Waiver (CDW) or Loss Damage Waiver (LDW). It's optional but driving without it is not recommended. Some credit-card companies cover CDW/LDW for a certain period if you charge the entire rental to your card. Always confirm with your card issuer what coverage it provides in Germany. Note that some local agencies may refuse to accept your credit card coverage as proof of insurance.

ROAD RULES

Driving is on the right-hand side of the road and standard international signs are in use. If you're unfamiliar with these, pick up a pamphlet at your local motoring organisation. Obey the road rules and speed limits carefully.

Speed and red-light cameras as well as radar traps are common and notices are sent to the car's registration address wherever that may be. If you're renting a car, the police will obtain your home address from the rental agency. There's a long list of fine-able actions, including using abusive language or gestures and running out of petrol on the autobahn.

The usual speed limits are 50km/h on main city streets and 100km/h on highways, unless they are otherwise marked. Limits drop to 30km/h in residential streets. And yes, it's true, there really are no speed limits on autobahns. In theory. In fact, there are many stretches where slower speeds must be observed (eg near towns, road construction), so be sure to keep an eye out for those signs or risk getting ticketed. And keep in mind: the higher the speed, the higher the fuel consumption and emissions.

Other important driving rules:

o The highest permissible blood-alcohol level for drivers is 0.05%, which for most people equates to one glass of wine or two small beers.

o Seatbelts are mandatory for all passengers, including those in the back seat, and there's a €30 fine if you get caught not wearing one. If you're in an accident, not wearing a seatbelt may invalidate your insurance. Children need a child seat if under four years and a seat cushion if under 12; they may not ride in the front until age 13.

o Motorcyclists must wear a helmet.

o Mobile phones may be used only if they are equipped with a hands-free kit or speakerphone.

o Pedestrians at crossings have absolute right of way over all motor vehicles.

o Always watch out for cyclists when turning right; they have the right of way.

o Right turns at a red light are only legal if there's a green arrow pointing to the right.

LOCAL TRANSPORT

Germany's cities and larger towns have efficient public transport systems. Bigger cities, such as Berlin and Munich, integrate buses, trams, U-Bahn (underground, subway) trains and S-Bahn (suburban) trains into a single network.

Fares are either determined by zones or time travelled, or sometimes by both. A *Streifenkarte* (multi-ticket strip) or a *Tageskarte* (day pass) generally offer better value than a single-ride ticket. Normally, tickets must be stamped upon boarding in order to be valid. Fines are levied if you're caught without a valid ticket.

BICYCLE

From nuns to Tour de France fans, Germans love to cycle, be it for errands, commuting, fitness or pleasure. Many cities have dedicated bicycle lanes, which must be used unless obstructed. There's no helmet law, not even for children, although using one is recommended, for obvious reasons. Bicycles must be equipped with a white light in the front, a red one in the back and yellow reflectors on the wheels and pedals.

BUS & TRAM

Buses are the most ubiquitous form of public transport and practically all towns have their own comprehensive network. Buses run at regular intervals, with restricted services in the evenings and at weekends. Some cities operate night buses along the most popular routes to get night owls safely back home.

Occasionally, buses are supplemented by trams, which are usually faster because they travel on their own tracks, largely independent of other traffic. In city centres, they sometimes go underground. Bus and tram drivers normally sell single tickets and day passes only.

S-BAHN

Metropolitan areas, such as Berlin and Munich, have a system of suburban trains called the S-Bahn. They are faster and cover a wider area than buses or trams but tend to be less frequent. S-Bahn lines are often linked to the national rail network and sometimes connect urban centres. Rail passes are generally valid on these services. Specific

S-Bahn lines are abbreviated with 'S' followed by the number (eg S1, S7).

TAXI

Taxis are expensive and, given the excellent public transport systems, not recommended unless you're in a real hurry. (They can actually be slower than trains or trams if you're stuck in rush-hour traffic.) Cabs are metered and charged at a base rate (flag fall) plus a per-kilometre fee. These charges are fixed but vary from city to city. Some cabbies charge extra for bulky luggage or night-time rides. It's rarely possible to flag down a taxi. More typical is to order one by phone or board at a taxi rank. If you're at a hotel or restaurant, ask staff to call you a cab. Taxis also often wait outside theatres or performance venues.

U-BAHN

Underground (subway) trains are known as U-Bahn in Germany and are generally the fastest form of travel in

big cities. Route maps are posted in all stations and at many you'll be able to pick up a printed copy from the stationmaster or ticket office. The frequency of trains usually fluctuates with demand, meaning there are more trains during commuter rush hours than, say, in the middle of the day. Buy tickets from vending machines and validate them before the start of your journey. Specific U-Bahn lines are abbreviated with 'U' followed by the number (eg U1, U7).

TRAIN

Germany's rail system is operated almost entirely by DB, with a variety of train types serving just about every corner in the country. The DB website has detailed information (in English and other languages), as well as a ticket purchasing function with detailed instructions.

o Tickets may be bought using a credit card up to 10 minutes before departure at no surcharge. However you

A Primer on Train Types

Here's the low-down on the alphabet soup of trains operated by Deutsche Bahn (DB):

City Night Line (CNL) Night trains with sleeper cars and couchettes.

InterCity (IC), EuroCity (EC) Long-distance trains that are fast but slower than the ICE; also run at one- and two-hour intervals and stop in major cities. EC trains go to major cities in neighbouring countries.

InterCity Express (ICE) Long-distance, high-speed trains that stop at major cities only and run at one- or two-hour intervals.

InterRegio-Express (IRE) Regional train connecting cities with few intermediary stops.

Regional Bahn (RB) Local trains, mostly in rural areas, with frequent stops; the slowest in the system.

Regional Express (RE) Local trains with limited stops that link rural areas with metropolitan centres and the S-Bahn.

S-Bahn Local trains operating within a city and its suburban area.

will need to present a print-out of your ticket, as well as the credit card you used to buy it, to the conductor.

○ Tickets are also available from vending machines and agents at the *Reisezentrum* (travel centre) in train stations. The latter charge a service fee but are useful if you need assistance with planning your itinerary (ask for an English-speaking clerk).

○ Smaller stations may only have a few ticket windows and the smallest ones may have only vending machines. English instructions are normally provided.

○ Tickets sold on board incur a surcharge and are not available on regional trains (RE, RB, IRE) and the S-Bahn. Agents, conductors and machines usually accept major credit cards. With few exceptions (station unstaffed, vending machine broken), you will be charged a fine if caught without a ticket.

○ Most train stations have coin-operated lockers ranging in cost from €1 to €4 per 24-hour period. Larger stations have staffed *Gepäckaufbewahrung* (left-luggage offices), which are a bit more expensive than lockers. If you leave your suitcase overnight, you're charged for two full days.

CLASSES

German trains have 1st- and 2nd-class cars, both of them modern and comfortable. Paying extra for 1st class is usually not worth it, except

perhaps on busy travel days (eg Friday, Sunday afternoon and holidays) when 2nd class cars can get very crowded. Seating is either in compartments of up to six people or in open-plan carriages with panoramic windows. On ICE trains you'll enjoy such extras as reclining seats, tables and audio systems in your armrest. Newer generation ICE trains also have individual laptop outlets, unimpeded cell phone reception (in 1st class) and, on some routes, wi-fi access.

Trains and stations are completely nonsmoking. ICE, IC and EC trains are fully air-conditioned and have a restaurant or self-service bistro.

COSTS

Standard, non-discounted train tickets tend to be quite expensive. On specific trains, a limited number of tickets are available at the discounted Sparpreis (saver fare) costing €29 to €99 in 2nd and €49 to €149 in 1st class. You need to book early or be very lucky to snag one of these tickets, though. There's a €5 service charge if tickets are purchased by phone, from a travel agent or at the station's ticket office. Other promotions, discounted tickets and special offers, however, become available all the time. Always check www.bahn.com for the latest deals.

RESERVATIONS

Seat reservation for long-distance travel is highly recommended, especially if you're travelling on a Friday or Sunday afternoon, during

holiday periods or in summer. Choose from window or aisle seats, row or facing seats, or seats with a fixed table. Reservations cost €4 and can be made online and at ticket counters as late as 10 minutes before departure. You need to claim your seat within 15 minutes of boarding the train.

GERMAN RAIL PASS

If your permanent residence is outside Europe, including Turkey and Russia, you qualify for the German Rail Pass. Tickets are sold online (www .bahn.com), through agents in your home country and on www.raileurope.com. The pass offers the following features:

○ Unlimited 1st or 2nd class travel for three to 10 days within a one-month period.

○ Valid on all trains within Germany, Köln-Düsseldorfer boats on Rhine and Moselle, discounts on Europabus 'Romantic Road' line and on Zugspitzbahn.

○ Sample fares: three-day pass €240 in 1st and €183 in 2nd class, seven-day pass €345 in 1st and €254 in 2nd class.

○ Children between six and 11 pay half-fare. Children under six travel free.

○ People between the ages of 12 and 25 qualify for the German Rail Youth Pass, which starts at €146 for three days of travel but only in 2nd class.

○ Two adults travelling together can get the German Rail Twin Pass which costs €270 in 2nd class and €370 in 1st class.

a b c

Language

German pronunciation is very similar to that of English, and if you read our pronunciation guides below as if they were English, you'll be understood just fine. Note that in our guides 'ew' is pronounced like 'ee' with rounded lips, and that 'kh' and 'r' are both throaty sounds. Stressed syllables are in italics.

To enhance your trip with a phrasebook, visit **lonelyplanet.com**. Lonely Planet iPhone phrasebooks are available through the Apple App store.

BASICS

Hello.
Guten Tag.   *goo*·ten taak
How are you?
Wie geht es Ihnen? vee geyt es *ee*·nen
I'm fine, thanks.
Gut, danke.   goot *dang*·ke
Excuse me./Sorry.
Entschuldigung.   ent·*shul*·di·gung
Yes./No.
Ja./Nein.   yaa/nain
Please./You're welcome./That's fine.
Bitte.   *bi*·te
Thank you.
Danke.   *dang*·ke
Goodbye.
Auf Wiedersehen.   owf *vee*·der·zey·en
Do you speak English?
Sprechen Sie Englisch? *shpre*·khen zee *eng*·lish
I don't understand.
Ich verstehe nicht. ikh fer·*shtey*·e nikht
How much is this?
Was kostet das?   vas *kos*·tet das
Can you reduce the price a little?
Können Sie mit dem   *ker*·nen zee mit dem
Preis heruntergehen? prais he·*run*·ter·gey·en

ACCOMMODATION

I'd like to book a room.
Ich möchte bitte ein   ikh *merkh*·te *bi*·te ain
Zimmer reservieren.   *tsi*·mer re·zer·*vee*·ren
How much is it per night?
Wie viel kostet es   vee feel *kos*·tet es
pro Nacht?   praw nakht

EATING & DRINKING

I'd like ..., please.
Ich hätte gern ..., bitte. ikh *he*·te gern ... *bi*·te
That was delicious!
Das hat hervorragend   das hat her·*fawr*·rah·gent
geschmeckt!   ge·*shmekt*
Bring the bill/check, please.
Die Rechnung, bitte.   dee *rekh*·nung *bi*·te
I don't eat ...
Ich esse kein ...   ikh *e*·se kain ...

I'm allergic to ...
Ich bin allergisch   ikh bin a·*lair*·gish
gegen ...   *gey*·gen ...
    fish   *Fisch*   fish
    poultry   *Geflügelfleisch*   ge·*flew*·gel·flaish
    red meat *Rind- und*   rint· unt
                 Lammfleisch   *lam*·flaish

EMERGENCIES

Help!
Hilfe!   *hil*·fe
I'm ill.
Ich bin krank.   ikh bin krangk
Call a doctor!
Rufen Sie einen Arzt!   *roo*·fen zee *ai*·nen artst
Call the police!
Rufen Sie die Polizei!   *roo*·fen zee dee po·li·*tsai*

DIRECTIONS

Where's a/the ...?
Wo ist ...?   vaw ist ...
    ATM
    der Geldautomat   dair *gelt*·ow·to·maat
    bank
    eine Bank   *ai*·ne bangk
    market
    der Markt   dair markt
    museum
    das Museum   das mu·*zey*·um
    restaurant
    ein Restaurant   ain res·to·*rahng*
    toilet
    die Toilette   dee to·a·*le*·te
    tourist office
    das Fremden-   das *frem*·den·
    verkehrsbüro   fer·kairs·bew·raw

Behind the Scenes

Our Readers

Many thanks to the travellers who used the last edition and wrote to us with helpful hints, useful advice and interesting anecdotes:

Wendy Anthony, Sarah Braun, Gisela Dahme

Author Thanks

ANDREA SCHULTE-PEEVERS

Big heartfelt thanks to all these wonderful people who've plied me with tips, insights, information, ideas and encouragement (in no particular order): Henrik Tidefjärd, Miriam Bers, Petra Gümmer, Julia Schwarz, Frank Engster, Myriel Walter, Cookie, Heiner Schuster, Steffi Gretschel, Renate Freiling, Silke Neumann, Kirsten Schmidt, Michael Radder, Christoph Münch, Christoph Lehmann, Patrick Schwarzkopf, Danilo Hommel, Dr Jasper Freiherr von Richthofen, Uve Teschner, Elisabeth Herms-Lübbe, Julia Schröder, Jan Czyszke and, of course, David Peevers. Kudos to the entire Lonely Planet team responsible for producing such a kick-ass book.

Acknowledgments

Climate map data adapted from Peel MC, Finlayson BL & McMahon TA (2007) 'Updated World Map of the Köppen-Geiger Climate Classification', *Hydrology and Earth System Sciences*, 11, 163344.

Cover photographs
Front: Holstentor, Lübeck, Heinz Wohner/ Getty Images
Back: City rooftops and church, Heidelberg, Richard I'Anson/Getty Images

This Book

This 2nd edition of Lonely Planet's *Discover Germany* guidebook was researched and written by Andrea Schulte-Peevers, Kerry Christiani, Marc Di Duca, Anthony Haywood, Daniel Robinson and Ryan Ver Berkmoes. This guidebook was commissioned in Lonely Planet's London office, and produced by the following:

Commissioning Editors Katie O'Connell, Anna Tyler

Coordinating Editor Gina Tsarouhas

Coordinating Cartographer Samantha Tyson

Coordinating Layout Designer Clara Monitto

Managing Editors Annelies Mertens, Martine Power

Managing Cartographers Anita Banh, Adrian Persoglia, Anthony Phelan

Managing Layout Designers Jane Hart, Jessica Rose, Kerrianne Southway

Assisting Editors Samantha Forge, Lorna Goodyer, Bella Li, Anne Mason, Rosie Nicholson, Karyn Noble, Charlotte Orr

Cover Research Naomi Parker

Internal Image Research Aude Vauconsant

Language Content Branislava Vladisavljevic

Thanks to Laura Crawford, Brigitte Ellemor, Ryan Evans, Larissa Frost, Chris Girdler, Bronwyn Hicks, Corey Hutchison, Jouve India, Asha Ioculari, Andi Jones, Anna Lorincz, Trent Paton, Raphael Richards, Jacqui Saunders, Dianne Schallmeiner, Amanda Sierp, Angela Tinson, Sam Trafford, Gerard Walker

Index

INDEX I-M

000 Map pages

How to Use This Book

These symbols will help you find the listings you want:

◉	Sights	◉	Tours	◉	Drinking
🏊	Beaches	◉	Festivals & Events	☆	Entertainment
◉	Activities	🛏	Sleeping	◉	Shopping
◉	Courses	✖	Eating	❶	Information/Transport

These symbols give you the vital information for each listing:

☎	Telephone Numbers	🛜	Wi-Fi Access	🚌	Bus
⊙	Opening Hours	🏊	Swimming Pool	⛴	Ferry
P	Parking	🥗	Vegetarian Selection	M	Metro
◉	Nonsmoking	📖	English-Language Menu	S	U-Bahn
❄	Air-Conditioning	👶	Family-Friendly	🚊	Tram
@	Internet Access	🐾	Pet-Friendly	🚉	S-Bahn

Reviews are organised by author preference.

Map Legend

Sights
- 🏊 Beach
- ● Buddhist
- ● Castle
- ✝ Christian
- 🕉 Hindu
- ☪ Islamic
- ✡ Jewish
- ● Monument
- 🏛 Museum/Gallery
- ● Ruin
- 🍇 Winery/Vineyard
- 🐾 Zoo
- ◉ Other Sight

Activities, Courses & Tours
- 🤿 Diving/Snorkelling
- 🛶 Canoeing/Kayaking
- ⛷ Skiing
- 🏄 Surfing
- 🏊 Swimming/Pool
- 🚶 Walking
- 🏄 Windsurfing
- ● Other Activity/Course/Tour

Sleeping
- 🛏 Sleeping
- ● Camping

Eating
- ✖ Eating

Drinking
- ● Drinking
- ● Cafe

Entertainment
- ☆ Entertainment

Shopping
- ● Shopping

Information
- ● Post Office
- ❶ Tourist Information

Transport
- ✈ Airport
- ⊗ Border Crossing
- 🚌 Bus
- 🚡 Cable Car/Funicular
- 🚴 Cycling
- ⛴ Ferry
- 🚝 Monorail
- P Parking
- S S-Bahn
- 🚕 Taxi
- 🚆 Train/Railway
- 🚊 Tram
- ⊖ Tube Station
- U U-Bahn
- M Underground Train Station
- ● Other Transport

Routes
- Tollway
- Freeway
- Primary
- Secondary
- Tertiary
- Lane
- Unsealed Road
- Plaza/Mall
- Steps
-)=(Tunnel
- Pedestrian Overpass
- Walking Tour
- Walking Tour Detour
- Path

Boundaries
- International
- State/Province
- Disputed
- Regional/Suburb
- Marine Park
- Cliff
- Wall

Population
- ● Capital (National)
- ◉ Capital (State/Province)
- ● City/Large Town
- ● Town/Village

Geographic
- ● Hut/Shelter
- ● Lighthouse
- ● Lookout
- ▲ Mountain/Volcano
- ● Oasis
- ● Park
-)(Pass
- ● Picnic Area
- ● Waterfall

Hydrography
- River/Creek
- Intermittent River
- Swamp/Mangrove
- Reef
- Canal
- Water
- Dry/Salt/Intermittent Lake
- Glacier

Areas
- Beach/Desert
- Cemetery (Christian)
- Cemetery (Other)
- Park/Forest
- Sportsground
- Sight (Building)
- Top Sight (Building)

DANIEL ROBINSON

Frankfurt & the Rhineland (Frankfurt, The Romantic Rhine, The Moselle Valley), Stuttgart & the Black Forest (Heidelberg) In his two decades with Lonely Planet, Daniel has covered both sides of the Franco–German border, sipping as many crisp whites in Alsace as in the Palatinate. When he's not interviewing bouncers at trendy Heidelberg nightclubs or reviewing apple-wine taverns in Frankfurt, he relaxes by 'barge spotting' along the Romantic Rhine and visiting lesser-known sights connected to the Rhineland's long and illustrious Jewish history. Daniel's travel writing on Europe, Asia and the Middle East has been translated into 10 languages.

RYAN VER BERKMOES

Frankfurt & the Rhineland (Cologne & North Rhineland), Hamburg & the North (Hamburg, Luebeck, Schwerin) Ryan once lived in Germany. Three years in Frankfurt, during which time he edited a magazine until he got a chance for a new career...with Lonely Planet. One of his first jobs was working on Lonely Planet's Germany coverage. He loves smoked fish, which serves him well in the north, and he loves beer, which serves him well everywhere in Germany. Follow him at ryanverberkmoes.com. He tweets at @ryanvb.

Read more about Ryan at:
lonelyplanet.com/members/ryanverberkmoes

Our Story

A beat-up old car, a few dollars in the pocket and a sense of adventure. In 1972 that's all Tony and Maureen Wheeler needed for the trip of a lifetime – across Europe and Asia overland to Australia. It took several months, and at the end – broke but inspired – they sat at their kitchen table writing and stapling together their first travel guide, *Across Asia on the Cheap*. Within a week they'd sold 1500 copies. Lonely Planet was born.

Today, Lonely Planet has offices in Melbourne, London, Oakland and Delhi, with more than 600 staff and writers. We share Tony's belief that 'a great guidebook should do three things: inform, educate and amuse'.

Our Writers

ANDREA SCHULTE-PEEVERS

Coordinating Author; Berlin (Berlin, Potsdam, Sachsenhausen Concentration Camp), Dresden & the East (Dresden, Leipzig & Around) Born and raised in Germany and educated in London and at UCLA, Andrea has travelled the distance to the moon and back in her visits to some 65 countries. She's written about her native country for two decades and authored or contributed to some 60 Lonely Planet titles, including the first edition of this guide and all editions of the *Germany* country guide, the *Berlin* city guide and the *Pocket Berlin* guide. After years of living in LA, Andrea couldn't be happier to finally make her home in a classic Berlin flat.

KERRY CHRISTIANI

Stuttgart & the Black Forest (Stuttgart, The Black Forest, Lake Constance, Ulm, Triberg, Tubingen) Having lived for six years in Germany's Black Forest, Kerry jumped at the chance to return to her second home (and family) to write her chapters. Hiking in the hills, cycling around Lake Constance and road-testing black forest gateau (it's a hard life) kept her busy for this edition. Kerry has authored some 20 guidebooks and frequently contributes to print and online magazines, including *Olive*, *Lonely Planet Magazine* and bbc.com/travel. She tweets @kerrychristiani and lists her latest work at www.kerrychristiani.com. Kerry also wrote the Outdoors, German Cuisine and Beer & Wine chapters.

Read more about Kerry at:
lonelyplanet.com/members/kerrychristiani

MARC DI DUCA

Munich, Bavaria A well-established travel-guide author, Marc has explored many corners of Germany over the past 20 years, but it's to the quirky variety and friendliness of Bavaria that he returns most willingly. When not hiking Alpine valleys, eating snowballs in Rothenburg ob der Tauber or brewery hopping in Bamberg, he can be found in Sandwich, Kent, where he lives with his Kievite wife, Tanya, and their two sons. Marc also wrote the History, The Germans and Arts & Architecture chapters.

ANTHONY HAYWOOD

Dresden & the East (Lutherstadt, Wittenberg & Dessau, Weimar, Erfurt, Buchenwald, Eisenach), Hamburg & the North (Bremen, Hanover, Fairytale Road, Wolfsburg) Anthony was born in the port city of Fremantle, Western Australia, and pulled anchor early on to mostly hitchhike through Europe and the USA. Aberystwyth in Wales and Ealing in London were his wintering grounds at the time. He later studied comparative literature in Perth and Russian language in Melbourne. In the 1990s he moved to Germany and has been travelling the country ever since. Today he works as a German-based freelance writer and journalist, and divides his time between Göttingen (Lower Saxony) and Berlin.

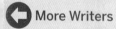 **More Writers**

Published by Lonely Planet Publications Pty Ltd
ABN 36 005 607 983
2nd edition – May 2013
ISBN 978 1 74220 119 1
© Lonely Planet 2013   Photographs © as indicated 2013
10 9 8 7 6 5 4 3 2 1
Printed in China